The State Under Stress

Public Policy and Management

Series Editor: Professor R.A.W. Rhodes, Department of Politics, University of York.

The effectiveness of public policies is a matter of public concern and the efficiency with which policies are put into practice is a continuing problem for governments of all political persuasions. This series contributes to these debates by publishing informed, in-depth and contemporary analyses of public administration, public policy and public management.

The intention is to go beyond the usual textbook approach to the analysis of public policy and management and to encourage authors to move debate about their issue forward. In this sense, each book both describes current thinking and research, and explores future policy directions. Accessibility is a key feature and, as a result, the series will appeal to academics and their students as well as to the informed practitioner.

Current Titles Include:

Whose Utility? The Social Impact of Public Utility Privatization and Regulation in Britain
John Ernst

The State Under Stress: Can the Hollow State be Good Government?
Christopher D. Foster and Francis J. Plowden

Quality in Public Services: Managers' Choices
Lucy Gaster

Transforming Central Government: The Next Steps Initiative
Patricia Greer

Enabling or Disabling Local Government: Choices for the Future
Steve Leach, Howard Davis and Associates

Implementing Thatcherite Policies: Audit of an Era
David Marsh and R.A.W. Rhodes (eds)

British Aid and International Trade
O. Morrissey, B. Smith and E. Horesh

Markets and Managers: New Issues in the Delivery of Welfare
Peter Taylor-Gooby and Robyn Lawson (eds)

Social Care in a Mixed Economy
Gerald Wistow, Martin Knapp, Brian Hardy and Caroline Allen

Social Care Markets: Progress and Prospects
Gerald Wistow, Martin Knapp, Brian Hardy, Julien Forder, Jeremy Kendall and Rob Manning

New Managerialism: Administrative Reform in Whitehall and Canberra
Spencer Zifcak

The State Under Stress

Can the Hollow State be Good Government?

Christopher D. Foster and Francis J. Plowden

Open University Press
Buckingham · Philadelphia

For Kay and Geraldine

Open University Press
Celtic Court
22 Ballmoor
Buckingham
MK18 1XW

and
1900 Frost Road, Suite 101
Bristol, PA 19007, USA

First Published 1996

A catalogue record of this book is available from the British Library.

ISBN   0 335 19713 2 (pbk)   0 335 19714 0 (hbk)

Library of Congress Cataloging-in-Publication Data
Foster, Christopher D.
    The state under stress : can the hollow state be good government? /
by C.D. Foster and F.J. Plowden.
        p.   cm. — (Public policy and management)
    Includes bibliographical references and index.
    ISBN 0-335-19714-0 (hardbound). — ISBN 0-335-19713-2 (pbk.)
    1. Great Britain—Politics and government—1979–   .   2. Government
productivity—Great Britain.   3. Privatization—Great Britain.
4. Decentralization in government—Great Britain.   I. Plowden, F.
J. (Francis J.), 1945–   .   II. Title.   III. Series.
JN318.F76   1996
320.941—dc20   96–21865
                                                         CIP

Typeset by Dorwyn Ltd, Rowlands Castle, Hants
Printed in Great Britain by Biddles Ltd, Guildford and King's Lynn

Contents

Preface

> Ambiguities, and even the discrepancies they cloak, may fortify the political order, so long as no one wants to probe into them . . . By the same token, however, once the customers cease to be taken for granted – once the conventions come under critical scrutiny, once the populace outside the club walls ask what principles they embody and why these principles should be accepted – arrangements of this sort are bound to run into trouble. Regard for the rules of the game will gradually ebb away.
>
> David Marquand[1]

This book is about changes in British government in recent years. It is meant for those in government – MPs, local councillors, civil servants and other officials, those in agencies, quangos and other public bodies – as well as those who watch and comment from outside, in the press and the universities. It argues that some recent changes are good, some bad, some necessary, some not, some reversible, and again some not. They share characteristics with changes in other democratic governments, whose common cause is fiscal crisis (Chapter 1). Three changes in the workings of British government since the end of the 1970s stand out. In the 1970s there was much concern about the increasing power of the executive, with talk of elective dictatorship; since then, and largely unnoticed, within that powerful executive the balance of power has shifted from civil servants towards ministers. At the same time, the long-standing influence exercised on government by corporatist vested interests, such as the Confederation of British Industry and the Trades Union Congress, and their power in negotiation at all levels of government, symbolized by their regular meetings with ministers in the National Economic Development Council, has crumbled and been replaced by an Americanized lobbying process. Last, there has been a decline in the presentation of policy-making as expressed in most white papers and reflected in the quality of bills.

These changes arise from the same cause: the conviction politics of the Thatcher government which believed that a revolution was needed to liberate the economy; which also rightly judged that the civil service as then constituted, and the old networks of vested interests, were powerful obstacles to change; and that it was better to disregard their influence and hurry policies into legislation, however imperfect, and even if early attempts were sometimes botched and one had to try again. One cannot argue against this approach in a democratic country, given the urgency ministers then believed there was to address grave issues and their certainty that they knew how to go about doing so. Therefore ministers, and especially Margaret Thatcher as Prime Minister, gathered into their hands greater powers than their predecessors. She could do so because, not bound by a written constitution, she was able to sweep aside many of the old conventions of government. But after many radical changes had been accomplished, there was no easy way back. Even though it has long since ceased to be necessary, ministers have continued to dominate, tending to treat civil servants as implementers of their policies rather than, as in the old way, partners; and as a result failing to consult widely before legislation; and in so far as they consulted, failing to reflect those consultations in their policy-making. The outcome has been white papers and statutes often of poor quality, having to be revised because of their defects or because of successive changes in policy, often prompted by waves of ideology. Perpetual revolution has tended to turn what was at first a decisive government, knowing its own mind, into a government endlessly seeking and implementing new and hastily thought-up initiatives.

Therefore the challenge might seem to be: how do we return to the old ways? But in politics and history the pendulum never swings back. Neither should it. The *ancien régime* had virtues, but it was far from perfect. It was wasteful of resources in the public sector and as such a principal cause of the fiscal crisis. As shaper of policies, the civil service was often limited in its vision. It was often narrowly selective in the interests it consulted. Its research and analysis were frequently patchy. Moreover, it sometimes upheld policies, especially economic, which served the nation badly. Something called the 'departmental view' often managed to exert a monopoly hold over policy-making to the exclusion of valuable outside opinions.

However, at its best the old system had many strengths: ministers in partnership with civil servants provided an excellent machine for diagnosing problems and testing solutions, for assembling evidence and undertaking con-sultation, even if its focus and its sources were limited. The thoroughness of the machine allowed determined ministers who knew their own minds to achieve considerable innovations, because well tested and commanding much con-sensus. Its processes also helped achieve a degree of consensus and tolerance of opposing views across the nation, which is essential in normal times in a democracy. However, if conviction politics is allowed to go on beyond the emergency which gives rise to it, parliamentary democracy is not sustainable. It requires a high consensus across the nation on many issues, as well as full employment and growth rates which, with hindsight, are now referred to as those of a golden age, although stigmatized as unsatisfactory then. The old regime produced an administrative system of high probity and integrity. On such values as opposing discrimination against sexual and ethnic minorities, and upholding notions of what is fair, the public sector tended to be in advance of the private sector. Moreover, given ministers' overload, their partnership with civil servants enabled them to process a huge amount of business.

But the clock cannot be turned back, both because of changes in external circumstances and because, in many of its parts, it is not the same clock. An incoming government will stumble and quickly lose credibility, support and finally office if it does not appreciate how much has altered. As well as the three leading changes mentioned, there have been countless other tendencies, many of which will be widely recognized piecemeal but perhaps not in their full cumulative effect, which this book explores.

Let us consider the main actors in the drama of government. Ministers have taken power from local government into their own hands or transferred it to quangos appointed by them. They have acquired it from civil servants by taking more policy decisions on their own and within political circles. They have gained more direct power over outlying parts of their departments by turning them into agencies. They have increased their power over the surviving nationalized industries and over many quangos by direction and arm-twisting.

However, they have also lost power, most conspicuously to Brussels, but as seriously by their own leaps to acquire more power. So much power that one cannot wield it can amount to a reduction in power. For at least thirty years there has been a problem of ministerial overload, but it has become worse since the end of the 1970s. The duties that go along with ministers' powers include not only policy-making and the preparation of laws but also innumerable executive decisions, often of the greatest importance to those concerned. The number of such decisions has increased enormously as power has shifted from local to central government and new agencies have been formed. Multitudes of grievances and complaints find their way to ministers from MPs and through other routes. There are negotiations with the Treasury over expenditure, and with Brussels, in which virtually every minister is now involved. There are questions of diplomacy and very occasionally of peace and war for which time has to be found among other preoccupations. There is Cabinet, and its committees. There are ministerial statements, appearances before parliamentary committees and at debates. There are the constituencies.

But it is not even as if these matters are what occupy most ministerial time. In recent times ministers have had to adjust to the demands of, in ascending order of importance, endless speech-making to a wide variety of audiences, receiving innumerable deputations brought by MPs and others and, above all else, the ceaseless demands of the media, none of which in any direct sense bears upon the powers and duties ministers need to exercise. The media have replaced Parliament as the main forum for political public debate.

What has tended to happen to the other actors can be described more simply. Parliament is losing its place to the media as the forum for debate of public issues. The great parliamentary debate is in decline. Parliamentary standing committees are active, but seriously hampered in their scrutiny of legislation by the ill-prepared state in which it reaches them, the very large number of amendments that arrive late and the increasing use of the guillotine; while select committees seem to have concentrated their energies on developing policies alternative to those ministers develop, a competition they cannot win. The media may seem to be the great winners, but by becoming so close to ministers that they seem to conjure up a reaction from them on any topic and at any time they risk public boredom with a recurrent pattern of similar sensationalism in the treatment of political personalities and issues. British journalists may stigmatize much of the American press as dull, but these days the latter has a much better record in explaining issues and challenging policies effectively through a deeper understanding of them, and it still makes money. The civil service has lost from the decline of partnership. Its prestige has fallen. Its careers have become insecure. There are threats of large job cuts and it finds itself acting in a more frantic environment in which it has to make greater efforts not to be politicized.

Underlying these changes is another set even more fundamental. Chapter 1 shows how the growth of government in most advanced nations had become unsustainable by the end of the 1970s, so placing great downward pressure for economies in public expenditure if government activities were to be maintained, let alone improved. That gave impetus to a search for greater efficiency in government. But at the same time as this powerful force for change in government, there were changes within politics which were incentivizing politicians to pursue their own party and personal political interests more actively (Chapter 2). The effect on the structure and behaviour of government of the introduction of these two forces needs the most careful watching. Earlier attempts to achieve greater efficiency in government and to introduce private-sector techniques as a means of doing so had generally foundered on the public sector's prolonged resistance to accepting anything but cosmetic change. But by the late 1980s a new more determined set of initiatives had been developed (Chapter 3) for reinventing government, as it came to be called, and had been applied in New Zealand and in Australia (and attempted in the United States) by left-wing governments and in Britain by a right-wing government. That fact demonstrates that reinventing government is a neutral political position. What was perceived as the success of its principles led to their adoption in a growing number of countries. However, there are real dangers in all these countries that principles are being applied in too crude and simplified a fashion. Chapter 4 sets out the main causes of concern that arise from a crude replacement of the complicated functions of government by attempts at a straight dichotomy between the 'customers' of government in public services and the producer or deliverer of such services.

Yet no government, whatever its complexion, can afford to turn its back on, let alone reverse, the improvement in the efficiency of services that has resulted from denationalization (Chapter 5). That denationalization can take the form of privatization, transition into charitable or other non-profit-making bodies, or the creation of autonomous public bodies. Even the last, to be efficient, must be very different from old-style nationalized industries, which were a failure from any standpoint. A government that would turn the clock back here invites what could be a fatal intensification of the fiscal crisis from which it will in any case suffer. The same applies if it fails to make the quality gains and costs savings that can be achieved through extending the scope of contractorization (Chapter 6). While to attempt contractorization where it cannot be expected to work is not sensible, politicians should reflect how far they need to hang on to levers of absolute power when the price is much greater inefficiency in the provision of public services.

Thought also has to be given to how to preserve public-sector values and probity at the same time as maintaining and improving safeguards against increased opportunities for party and personal political behaviour. If properly done, greater efficiency can be achieved by massive decentralization, but there are many other arguments to back a case for decentralization within government, preferably to elected local authorities (Chapter 7). Properly conducted, a programme based on privatization, contractorization and decentralization, as and where appropriate, can be a powerful source of improvement in the quality and cost of what government does. Such programmes are not themselves political issues of conspicuous public importance, but the savings, and improvements in efficiency and effectiveness, which they can achieve if well done, and the corruption of power if 'politically' done, can have huge, if hidden, effects on the visible parts of the state.

Part of the British experience (Chapter 8) has been the turning of large parts of many government departments into agencies. There are many quality and efficiency advantages in doing so, but there are lessons to be learned from how it has been done. The complicated issues we have examined arise in the relationships between those agencies and the ministers to whom they are responsible (Chapter 9). There is no realistic sense in which ministers can be said to be able to manage agencies, given the experience they mostly have and, beyond that, the sheer weight of their other preoccupations and their priorities. Yet ministers have legitimate interests in many aspects of the behaviour of these agencies. Where the greatest political flexibility is needed, agencies are not a suitable vehicle. The delegation of policy discretion to agencies can, paradoxically, increase ministerial power. There are ways of trying to resolve these issues and they need adopting. Ministers also need to consider how they can reduce their overload and reorder their priorities so that the vital functions of government are better discharged (Chapter 10). Given the transformation of the public sector which cannot be reversed, the roles of Parliament, of structures of government like the Cabinet and Treasury, and of the civil service need to be reconsidered and strengthened (Chapter 11). Otherwise there are risks that democracy and democratic control will be lost. Chapter 12 summarizes our conclusions and recommendation for change. We believe that remedies to meet the severe problems we diagnose are essential for the future of government.

Each of our three national parties may have a different principal objection to these reforms. While many changes the Conservative Party has made to the machinery of government have the potential for greater efficiency and therefore for higher quality and more economic services, it may fail to appreciate that they have been insufficiently well done to realize their full potential and also need other consequential reforms to safeguard good democratic government. The Labour Party may fail to realize how much the workings of government have altered since it was in office and that to accept and build on such changes may be necessary to avoid fiscal crisis. Both the Liberal Democrats and the Labour Party may overrate constitutional change as what is most needed to bring about a well-functioning democracy rather than the mainly administrative and organizational issues discussed in this book. But any government will need to address these issues irrespective of constitutional change.

Note

1 Marquand (1988), p. 198.

Acknowledgements

We have many to thank. Our wives for their forbearance. There are those who have read chapters – some or all of them and several successive drafts: Tam Dalyell MP, the Rt Hon. David Howell MP and Rt Hon. John Morris MP, QC; Sir Geoffrey Chipperfield, Sir Terence Heiser, David Holmes, Sir Geoffrey Wardale, David Worskett as well as a number of serving civil servants in several departments who, following the usual conventions, cannot be named; Professor George Jones and Oliver James (who both attended the seminars we gave at the London School of Economics (LSE) and Helena Tunstall also of the LSE, and lastly Gail Ham, Mark Sutherland, Nicky Parkinson and others, colleagues at Coopers & Lybrand. None of these are responsible for the use we made of their comments and advice, our opinions are our own.

We are grateful to the other civil servants and others with whom we have discussed the ideas underlying the book, who are too many to name, but we would like to mention Sir Peter Lazarus who, before his untimely death, was a source of encouragement and advice. As our sources indicate we have drawn much from other writers.

We are particularly appreciative of those LSE postgraduate students on the course we gave there in 1994/5 on Contested Issues in Public Sector Management who gave us freely of their enthusiastic and penetrating comments, criticism and essays: Cynthia Anderson, Nathalie Ellertson, Anthony Ferrari, Raquel Gallego-Calderon, Stephanie McKennell, Bernardo Ortiz, Christian Theobald, Andrew Miller and Harlie Outhwaite. Lastly our thanks are due to Lee Ewin and Caroline Brown for the vast amount of typing they have done.

1

The causes of fiscal crisis

> Managerial reform in public administration can be seen as a Zeitgeist, a pervasive
> idea whose time has come . . . History may well show that the managerial
> reforms of the late 20th century had as dramatic an impact on public
> administration as the progressive reforms of the late 19th century; and therefore
> on the conduct of government and politics.
>
> Hede[1]

Genesis of the new public management

In several countries since the mid-1980s the processes of government have
changed radically. Starting in a few Anglo-Saxon nations, this transformation is
spreading through countries with other administrative systems. Politicians,
practitioners and students of public administration call it the *new public management* (NPM). But the fundamental changes it is causing are making its symptoms visible to a larger public and promise to have as profound consequences
on government and politics as many more visible, turbulent revolutions have
had. The ideas behind it have two main sources.[2] The first is the economics
literature on public choice, which sees politics as a market with its own
entrepreneurs, rules and conventions. The second source is the latest wave of
business managerialism, mainly brought into the public sector by management
consultants, which emphasizes the decentralization of business management
and outsourcing of as many of its activities as possible.[3] Together they have had
a more distinctive joint effect than could have been expected from either on its
own.[4]

The leading economic ideas have been widely known since the
mid-1960s, while attempts to import private-sector management techniques
into the public sector have been made over many years. That these ideas were
around does not explain why suddenly they became practically influential.
Explanations of extensive influence that rely on fashion or the dictates of public
relations are not persuasive.[5] Neither are those that see its appeal as a quasi-
religious fervour for private-sector management practices or for minimal government.[6] Such partial views cannot explain several NPM features, or why it
took off in the 1980s in many countries at much the same time. They also
underplay its consequences.

Other explanations of its influence are less in the realm of ideas. It is suggested that politicians of all parties, civil servants and various pressure groups, used to be behind the growth of government in a coalition which has been weakened and replaced by more tax-conscious coalitions.[7] This change was provoked by changes in the international economy in the 1970s – by stagflation, national indebtedness, the declining ability of government to realize Keynesian demand-management techniques and a lack of policy resilience following oil-price changes. All led to a declining public confidence in government competence to manage the economy. This decline may have been reinforced by changes in political electioneering, which have made party strategists and their public relations advisers more important than the traditional civil service in devising policies to win elections and therefore in policy-making. For reasons that will be discussed in Chapter 2, these changes have increased the influence of those against tax increases at the expense of those in favour of more public expenditure.[8] A socially more heterogeneous population may also have made it harder to muster vote-winning public expenditure-led programmes.[9] A different explanation is that developments, primarily in telecommunications and information technology, have made new organizational forms possible and reduced the extent of difference between public- and private-sector management styles.

But these factors did not necessitate major changes in the structure and management of government. For an engine powerful enough to explain them, we must look to the impact of the rapid growth in public expenditure from the Second World War to the 1970s; growing appreciation of the rising cost in taxation of that public expenditure; revulsion against that growth from the mid-1970s; and then the flattening of that growth that began at the end of the 1970s. And despite major but spasmodic efforts to reform the management of the apparatus of government, these initiatives have failed either to improve the efficiency of programmes or to reshape the programmes themselves. Only this economic explanation is sufficient to explain the radical moves towards the reduction or 'hollowing out' of the state, which have given NPM its opportunity.[10]

This principal explanation does not deny the influence of changes in ideas, in the technology available to management, or of changes in political behaviour, but practical experience and public-choice theory suggest that political systems are strongly resistant to change, because of the intricacy and strength of the many interests concerned to maintain the *status quo ante*. All other things being equal, organizational and administrative change will tend to remain superficial, unless there is an overwhelming imperative for change from outside the closed system. In our view, fiscal crisis was such an imperative. Other influences shaped the development of the crisis and responses to it, but of themselves were neither necessary nor sufficient to force change.

Growth of public expenditure

Fiscal crisis has arisen in most, and virtually all advanced, economies because public expenditure and therefore taxation have grown faster than income per head over a long period. At the end of the nineteenth century public expenditure was a small proportion of gross domestic product (GDP), even in industrialized countries.[11] Much public expenditure was by local authorities, then largely autonomous in their spending.[12] Central government expenditure concentrated on defence and foreign policy. Larger countries tended to spend proportionately more than smaller countries, mainly because of greater defence expenditure. Small civil services and the judiciary, even prisons – the main objects of central domestic expenditure – did not cost much. Comparative figures are scarce for the early years and incomplete: an indication is given in Table 1.1, showing the growth of central government expenditure from 1900.

Non-military expenditure did not take off until after 1945. But from then until the late 1970s, and in many countries until the mid-1980s, there was an almost inexorable tendency for public expenditure, and therefore taxation, to rise as a proportion of GDP in every developed nation. This period could be seen as a golden economic age when growth in GDP was itself at historically high levels. Detailed comparisons between national figures are difficult, because of the problems of reconciling differences in the ways that the public sector and public expenditure are defined.[13] Nevertheless changes in public expenditure as a proportion of GDP (E/GDP) are the best measure of the relative growth of the public sector. Table 1.2 shows their increase from 1960

Table 1.1   Central government expenditure as a percentage of GDP

	1900	1930	1950	1975
Austria		12.9	12.0	23.5
Belgium		23.1	19.2	33.0
Denmark	4.7	6.3	14.5	35.5
Finland		14.7	18.4	28.1
France	9.9	19.0	26.2	18.7
Germany	4.2	9.8	13.9	15.7
Ireland		14.6	22.4	37.3
Italy	13.6	19.2	21.1	27.9
Netherlands	8.6	11.6	26.4	31.3
Norway	5.7	7.8	16.8	24.2
Sweden	5.5	6.7	14.5	31.1
Switzerland		7.4	8.4	9.7
UK	9.7	15.6	26.9	34.0
Average	7.6	13.0	18.5	26.9

Note: Central Government expenditure is available at more points in time in most countries. Figures in this and subsequent tables refer to West Germany before 1992, all Germany thereafter.
Source: Peacock and Wiseman (1961: 109) OECD annual statistics.

Table 1.2 Public expenditure/GDP ratios on a standardized basis for the OECD member countries 1950–1985, expressed as percentages

	1960	1965	1970	1975	1980	1985	1990	1994
United States	27.8	27.9	31.7	33.5	31.8	33.2	33.3	33.5
Japan	20.7	22.7	19.4	26.8	32.0	31.6	31.7	35.8
West Germany	32.0	36.6	38.6	48.4	47.9	47.0	45.1	49.1
France	34.6	38.4	38.5	43.4	46.1	52.1	49.8	54.8
Italy	30.1	34.3	34.2	41.6	41.9	50.9	53.2	54.1
United Kingdom	32.6	36.1	38.8	44.4	42.9	44.0	39.9	43.2
Canada	28.9	29.1	34.8	38.5	38.7	45.3	46.0	47.1
Australia	22.1	25.6	26.8	31.1	31.5	36.5	34.8	37.4
Austria	32.1	37.8	39.2	45.3	48.1	50.9	48.6	52.2
Spain	13.7	19.6	22.2	24.4	32.0	41.1	42.0	56.1
Sweden	31.1	36.1	43.3	48.4	60.1	62.3	59.1	63.3
Belgium	30.3	32.3	36.5	45.7	51.9	62.2	54.8	59.2
Denmark	24.8	29.9	40.2	48.2	56.2	59.3	58.6	48.0
Finland	26.7	30.8	30.5	35.1	35.5	43.8	45.4	43.5
Greece	17.4	20.6	22.4	30.5	33.7	44.4	46.8	53.1
Ireland	28.0	33.1	39.6	45.7	50.5	52.4	41.2	49.3
Netherlands	33.7	38.7	43.9	51.2	54.8	56.5	54.1	44.0
Norway	29.9	34.2	41.0	45.4	47.5	44.8	53.8	46.1
Portugal	17.0	20.1	21.6	30.2	25.9	43.4	43.0	68.8
Total OECD	28.5	30.6	32.3	36.2	37.3	39.7	39.2	41.4

Notes: The data in this table are measured according to the standard definitions of the OECD-UN systems of accounts. The definition of public expenditure used is 'total outlays of government' which is the sum of lines 23, 28, 29 and 30 less line 26 in Table 9 of OECD (1982a) Vol II. The entry for 'total OECD' is weighted average for those countries for which information is available. 1985, 1990 data refers to General Government Outlays.

Sources: OECD (1992); OECD (1995), Table 28.

when the OECD began to publish good comparative data. By 1980 there was a cluster of countries where E/GDP was in the low 30s per cent: the USA, Japan, Australia, Spain, Portugal and Greece. (However, the last three were catching up from a low base.) There was another cluster in the 50s: Sweden, Belgium, Denmark, Ireland and the Netherlands, most with relatively high E/GDPs in 1960.

The growth of public expenditure has had many components.[14] Upward shifts used to be common during wars. Taxes rose to pay for them, but did not fall back to previous peacetime levels when war-related expenditure declined – the displacement effect.[15] But after the Second World War, politicians were less keen to raise taxes to pay for major wars. The Korean and Vietnamese wars were largely funded by inflation and by its export through international borrowing. Thus, while wars have intermittently increased defence expenditure, the general tendency since the Second World War has been for it to fall – but not in developing countries.[16] For example, in the United States it fell from 14 per cent in 1955 at the end of the Korean War, to 9 per cent in 1983 at the height of the Reagan arms build-up, and to 5 per cent in 1993 after the ending of the cold war.[17] In Britain it declined from 8 per cent in 1962, with temporary increases in 1966 and 1967, and then again between 1980 and 1984, until it fell under 4 per cent in 1990.[18]

The main growth has been in social programmes, comprising *income transfers* (principally pensions and social security benefits) and *public services* (education, health care and housing).[19] (While social expenditure of most kinds grew, education's share generally was stable or fell between 1960 and 1981.)[20] Hence the aptness of the name 'welfare state' to describe most developed industrialized nations towards the end of the twentieth century. In some these programmes started between the last decades of the nineteenth century and the end of the First World War. As other nations became developed, they acquired the same tendency.

Redistribution of income

The greatest growth, accounting for 11 out of the 13 percentage points by which on average E/EDP rose between 1968 and 1988, was in income transfers. Typically these programmes start with small liabilities and costs, then escalate in ways unforeseen at the outset.[21] Politicians have often found easy popularity in starting programmes whose full cost bears on later governments. When Britain introduced pensions for men over 70 in 1908, male life expectancy was 52 and costs were predicted on that basis. When pensions for men over 65 were introduced in the United States in 1937, they were costed on the basis that the average worker lived to 58. In most developed countries now, the majority live well over the age of pension entitlement.[22] From the 1970s growth in unemployment and early retirement over a long period of time also increased the burden on transfer payments, which had become 54 per cent of total government outlays on average by 1988. Both policy and the age structure of the population contributed to this effect. Increases in the growth of transfer payments as a proportion of GDP (T/GDP) between 1968 and 1988 were often by more than ten percentage points (Table 1.3). The exceptions included France and Germany, which already had high ratios in 1968, and the UK, which had a T/GDP just above average in 1968 and below it in 1988. Led by the Netherlands (37.6 per cent), Austria, Belgium, Denmark, France, Ireland, Luxembourg, Norway and Sweden all had T/GDP ratios above or just below 30 per cent. Australia, Japan, Switzerland, the UK and USA had ratios at or below 20 per cent.

Here we have a key difference between the political economies of the continental EU countries and the Anglo-Saxon nations plus Switzerland and Japan. Before the 1980s states which started with high and rapidly growing welfare-state programmes maintained their growth. Countries, including Japan, Australia and New Zealand, which had kept the state out of welfare, and the United States, which had excluded most health expenditures, and even

Table 1.3 Government outlays by economic category (percentages of GDP), 1968 and 1988

	1968			1988		
	Consumption expenditure	Transfer payments T/GDP	Gross capital formation	Consumption expenditure	Transfer payments T/GDP	Gross capital formation
Australia	14.1	6.4	3.6	17.9	15.4	2.6
Austria	14.7	19.1	6.8	18.4	27.4	4.8
Belgium	13.6	19.3	3.4	15.3	33.7	1.7
Canada	16.9	11.5	3.9	18.8	22.9	2.7
Denmark	18.6	12.7	5.0	25.8	31.5	2.9
Finland	15.3	12.6	4.9	20.2	16.7	3.3
France	14.8	20.6	5.0	18.6	28.3	3.4
West Germany	15.5	18.5	5.1	19.5	23.6	3.5
Greece	12.9	10.6	n/a	20.6	25.1	n/a
Iceland	13.1	11.8	8.9	18.6	11.9	6.6
Ireland	13.4	16.1	5.7	17.9	32.1	3.4
Italy	13.6	17.4	3.7	17.2	28.9	4.7
Japan	7.4	6.5	5.3	9.4	17.4	6.1
Luxembourg	12.1	20.7	4.5	16.3	29.9	6.1
Netherlands	14.9	22.9	1.0	15.7	37.6	4.6
Norway	16.6	17.0	4.3	20.6	27.0	3.5
New Zealand	13.0	n/a	n/a	17.1	n/a	n/a
Portugal	13.1	5.5	2.3	15.4	25.0	3.5
Spain	8.8	9.0	3.5	14.0	22.1	5.6
Sweden	20.5	15.4	6.9	26.6	31.2	1.2
Switzerland	10.4	10.3	n/a	12.8	17.6	n/a
Turkey	12.6	2.9	6.4	8.7	n/a	n/a
United Kingdom	17.6	15.9	5.8	20.5	20.7	2.0
United States	18.8	9.5	2.4	18.3	16.5	1.5

Source: Gemmell (1993a: 27).

Britain showed public welfare expenditure, and therefore total public expenditure, as a much lower proportion of GDP than did most European nations.[23]

Thus the main characteristic of the years after the mid-1960s was the concentration of growth on transfer payments. Two points should be stressed. Once a nation has established the structure of its transfer payment policies, its burden of income transfers is largely outside its control, depending on demography, the ageing of its population, unemployment and early retirement. (Britain was rare among nations in effecting a substantial reduction in that burden as a calculated act of policy in the early 1980s by shifting the uprating of entitlement from earnings growth to retail prices.) Moreover, attempts to rein back expenditure almost inevitably involve removing entitlement to benefits from some part of the electorate. Few politicians have had the courage to do so for obvious electoral reasons.

Second, the fact that a nation has a low E/GDP because of low transfers need not materially affect the real burden on the taxpayer of public expenditure at the margin since citizens must still make private arrangements, often enforced by law, to provide for old age and other contingencies. Therefore in these countries perception of fiscal crisis will emerge at a lower E/GDP ratio. Thus the argument that pension and other social security should be privatized because this will reduce the tax burden should be treated with care; as indeed, with any privatization. What make a real difference are any changes in contributions, entitlements or efficiency which may be associated with but are not necessarily the consequence of it. (Indeed, the state may be a more effective agent of such insurance than the private sector; as in health, where the state is better able to deal with experts in whose interest it is to over-provide (see Chapter 4).[24]

Low productivity improvement in the public sector

Table 1.3 shows that final consumption expenditures, that is, largely public goods and services – everything except transfers and investment – generally grew relative to GDP between 1968 and 1988, except in Turkey and the USA where they fell. The growth in the proportion of GDP spent on public goods and services, during a period when rates of increase in GDP were historically high, might have been expected to result in a cornucopia of new public goods and services flowing out upon the public. But it was not so. Most of the increased expenditure on public goods and services went to maintain the existing supply. In a burst of unprecedented and never to be repeated increases in the objects of public spending, the Attlee government initiated 24 new spending programmes.[25] Forty years on, in the mid-1980s, the total impact of these new programmes was to increase public expenditure by £7.5 billion more than it would otherwise have been; but meanwhile expenditure on the 118 programmes the Attlee government had inherited from the wartime Churchill government had tripled to £98 billion. By 1985 only 19 programmes had been terminated since 1945, at a total saving of only 1 per cent of public expenditure.

But the principal reason why there has been such inertia in public spending programmes, at least in that half which is not transfer payments, and why there are so few new and relatively few improved services, has been low productivity growth in the public sector. In addition, strong public-sector unionism increased labour costs more than in the private sector. Labour-intensive public services were long thought to be less capable of productivity improvements than was the private sector, where regular productivity improvements could be expected.[26] If one calculates E/GDP ratios in real terms, allowing for the far lower productivity growth rates in the public sector, what came to be known as the *relative price effect*, the value of what public money

Table 1.4   Increases in public expenditure between 1960 and 1975, as a percentage of GDP, projected to 1995 and 2015

	1995	2015
USA	42	49
Japan	35	43
West Germany	70	92
France	55	69
Italy	57	72
UK	60	76
Canada	51	64
Australia	43	55
Austria	63	80
Spain	47	71
Sweden	71	94
Belgium	66	87
Denmark	79	110
Finland	46	57
Greece	48	65
Ireland	69	93
Netherlands	75	98
Norway	66	87
Portugal	48	65

buys, is seen to decline sharply.[27] Allowing for the relative price effect has a fundamental effect on the interpretation of public expenditure growth since 1950. While its *cost* rose as a proportion of GDP, as the tables have shown, its real *value* as a proportion of GDP, when deflated by appropriate price indices, increased much less. Table 1.4 shows the effect of this in Britain. (Interpretation of the relative price effect is contentious because of the problems in calculating and interpreting appropriate price indices; but it cannot be improbable that half the increase in consumption of public goods and services is to be attributed to increasing relative prices rather than increased quantities.)[28] In Britain the *value* of total public expenditure did not rise in the 1950s, rose modestly in the 1960s and 1970s, and fell from the early 1980s. The value of total current expenditure declined as a proportion of GDP from 1966 until 1978, rose in the early Thatcher years and declined again until 1990.[29]

What this constancy suggests is that the objectives and patterns of public expenditure in Britain were largely set in the late 1940s. Given cost pressures, the British Treasury has been more effective in restraining public expenditure in value terms than has commonly been thought. For long there have been few truly new expenditure initiatives, and what there have been have had to be found by cutting back other expenditure, usually from within the same programmes. Even more important from the standpoint of this book, it shows what an enormous effect the relatively low productivity growth of the public sector, compared with the private sector, has had. If the relative price effect had not been regarded as virtually inevitable and had been overcome, fiscal crises might have even been avoided. As a rough approximation, an increase in public-sector productivity similar to that in the private sector could have prevented stop-go, made the Thatcher revolution unnecessary, and avoided the changes in the organization of government which have made the British political system vulnerable to anti-democratic forces, as will be described later in this book.

There would be comfort if the growth of public expenditure as a proportion of GDP were positively related to economic growth.[30] Indeed, there may be stronger evidence for the reverse proposition, that public expenditure rises less as a proportion of GDP in fast-growing economies such as Japan, if only because a more rapidly rising tax base makes it possible to keep tax rates down.[31] But there have been fast-growing economies with fast-growing public expenditure: for example, Germany, Sweden and Spain.[32] And though Britain had the lowest rate of growth in public expenditure of 17 leading nations between 1950 and 1978, it also had among the lowest rates of economic growth, so that the burden of growing public expenditure on it was among the greatest.[33] In the UK in particular, the openness of the economy, a disappointing growth rate, and the sensitiveness of sterling to balance-of-payments problems, produced crises when governments tried to rein back public expenditure growth. Moreover, in general, until the end of the 1970s, the more open the economy, the faster was the growth of public expenditure, which may suggest a tendency to rather Canute-like behaviour, by which some nations, open to international competition, particularly in Europe, tried to protect parts of their economy through nationalization or other measures likely to increase public expenditure.[34] But there is no general causal relationship between E/GDP and economic growth. A better explanation of the relationship between economic growth and public expenditure would require more analysis of its composition and, in particular, how much it was slanted towards investment in training, education and infrastructure.

Popular support for public expenditure

Nevertheless, most of the widespread growth in public expenditure from the 1940s to the 1970s was deliberately and openly decided and was widely recognized to serve purposes in the public interest – a concept to be more closely defined in the next chapter.[35] In Britain the early history of pensions arose from a growing concern about the poor elderly and hostility to the workhouse. In 1942 the Beveridge Report's recommendations to provide welfare for the poor achieved a wide consensus of support across the political spectrum.[36] Sixteen years later, Galbraith's accusation that modern economic progress was resulting in 'private affluence, public squalor', struck deep.[37] In OECD countries, even Britain, economic growth rates were at historically high levels during the postwar period. As a result, growing economic prosperity and a common belief that even high growth rates should be achievable without too much difficulty, led to widespread confidence during this period that increasing public expenditure was affordable.

Greater affluence, a growing concern about income redistribution, and the growth of collectivist provision and production underpinned the consensus on increasing expenditure. Underlying all three was the apparent fact that many of the goods or services people valued as they grew richer were publicly provided and had a high income elasticity – they were more in demand as people's incomes increased.[38] Many, like education or health, affected everyone's relative lifetime advantages and opportunities.[39] Many benefited the middle classes at least as much as the poorer in society and some, such as educational and environmental expenditure, more. The rise of the middle classes and the extension of those who called themselves middle-class were an impetus to more public expenditure (until, with still greater affluence, more of them began to prefer buying a growing number of services privately, so starting a loss of consensus for public expenditure).

President Kennedy in the United States could proclaim in 1961 in his inaugural speech:

> let every nation know, whether it wishes us well or ill, that we shall pay any price, bear any burden, meet any hardship, support any friend, oppose any foe to assure the survival and success of liberty.[40]

This rhetoric was echoed by President Johnson, when he said that the US government had 'the abundance and the ability to free every man from hopeless want' throughout the world. No wonder that, as he later said:

> I have been guided by the principle that spending by the Federal Government, in and of itself, is neither bad nor good. It can be bad when it involves overstaffing of government agencies, or needless duplication of functions, or poor management, or public services which cost more than they are worth, or the intrusion of government into areas where it does not belong. It can be good when it is put to work efficiently in the interests of our national strength, economic progress and human compassion.[41]

In the 1970s President Ford could base a promise to cut taxes, and President Carter a promise to increase expenditure without increasing taxes, on what turned out to be unrealized expectations of economic growth.[42] Even during the 1980s President Reagan was fortified by the Laffer supply-side doctrine into wrongly believing that tax cuts would stimulate enough growth in the economy to result in an overall increase in tax revenues capable of supporting higher expenditure.[43]

It is no surprise to find that in Britain Anthony Crosland's argument for reconciling capitalism and socialism found so much favour in the 1950s and 1960s, even outside his own party: economic growth should be encouraged, so it might provide more taxes to finance more public services, without reducing anyone's ability to consume and to save.[44] The major streams of public expenditure – on pensions and other transfer payments, and on health and education

– had enormous cross-party support. So did expenditure on improving housing, cities, new towns and the countryside.

Some important assumptions underlay this growth. During this period, politicians tended to argue that public expenditure increases in a democratic state and the taxes need to finance them must be presumed to be willed democratically, simply because elected politicians took the relevant decisions.[45] This apparent consistency between economic and electoral rationality meant that what citizens got, free or subsidized, from the government, could in effect be described as their *social wage*, the presumption being they preferred to have what their elected governments chose for them rather than the equivalent amount in cash. The prevailing outlook of many politicians seemed to suggest that the split between private and public output was rational and efficient: each was only doing what it was best fitted to do. Thus whatever levels of public expenditure and taxation were reached, they could be declared to be 'in the public interest'.

As a consequence, the political opposition to public expenditure growth, which grew in intensity during the 1970s, had to interpret public support for expenditure growth as either electoral myopia or irrationality. Either the majority was prepared to support governments whose policies resulted in such growth without understanding the long-term consequences, especially on taxation, or politicians were moved by considerations other than electoral support in making their public expenditure decisions. But a wedge could be, and was increasingly, said to have opened up between the social wage and what many of its recipients would have preferred, so devaluing it below its equivalent value in cash.

Emergence of fiscal crisis

The growth of public expenditure colliding with electoral, largely middle-class, opposition to higher taxes was the prime reason for the fiscal crises that became more common during the 1970s. Such crises had often been predicted in the past; but despite long-standing arguments that it would be economically disastrous for taxation to rise above some stated percentage, or for public indebtedness to rise above a certain proportion of GDP, nothing drastic had happened.[46] The declining proportion of public expenditure that could be considered investment; the rapidly increasing proportion that was income transfers, between generations as well as between income groups; the low productivity growth of so much public production; the inflexibility of transfer payments and uprating often related to consumer prices in a time of inflation, eventually made public expenditure growth harder to sustain, as did international pressure on the balance of payments in an increasing number of countries.[47] Moreover, in the 1970s inflation caused by the departure from the Bretton Woods system of fixed exchange rates and the oil-price increases of 1973 and 1979, disguised for a time the fact that tax revenues were not rising fast enough to fund public expenditure. A last intensifying cause of fiscal crisis during the start (and again at the end) of the 1980s was the depth of recession which reduced government income from taxes and forced attention on spending in all developed countries, but especially those most exposed to international trade.[48] Together they induced taxpayer resistance to tax increases to pay for more public expenditure.

The definition of fiscal crisis is not straightforward. While it is manifested as a political compulsion to reduce the public deficit, that necessity can arise in different circumstances. In the 1960s and early 1970s public expenditure crises tended to occur as subordinate to economic crises, rather than in their own right. Public expenditure cuts were frequently made to improve the balance of payments or offset devaluation, and were often judged to be temporary until economic growth should allow public expenditure to grow again. In Britain and many other countries public expenditure growth was generally resumed, when the balance-of-payments crisis was over. Such fiscal crises could be regarded as rehearsals for permanent crisis.

During the 1970s prophecies of public expenditure crisis increased. There were also prophecies of political bankruptcy. With foresight Rose and Peters predicted three stages: a first stage, in which nations spent more than they could afford either because citizens demanded more or because economic growth faltered; a second stage, where falling take-home pay would result; and a third stage in which citizens would lose their trust in, and withdraw consent from, governments no longer able to provide them with what they wanted.[49] In 1973 a Marxist writer argued that the growth in public expenditure was caused by the fundamental contradictions of capitalism.[50] By 1976 the view that irreparable fiscal crisis was stalking developed countries was proclaimed not only by Milton Friedman in the United States but also by Roy Jenkins, at the time a Labour cabinet minister, in Britain.[51]

In the same year, Tony Crosland, as Secretary of State for the Environment, told local government that 'the party was over', by which he meant that the long period was finished in which central government had allowed, and even to a large extent colluded in, the rapid growth of local expenditures. A process was started by which central control over local spending increased, and successively more drastic measures were taken to deprive local authorities of their freedom to spend and to tax (to be discussed further in Chapter 7).

By the late 1970s the growth of public expenditure and taxation had become such that it had become easy, by extrapolation of current public expenditure and tax trends, to forecast that there would indeed be disaster if they were not substantially moderated. On such assumptions public expenditure would even exhaust GDP in a few decades.[52] As Table 1.4 shows, if public expenditure increases from 1975 or 1980 had maintained their previous rate of growth, four other countries would have found their public expenditure to be the 70 per cent or more of GDP that Sweden actually reached. While a few countries went on increasing E/GDP, most reduced its growth substantially over 1980–90. Japan, West Germany, the UK, Sweden and Ireland (by as much as nine percentage points) actually reduced E/GDP. But Figure 1.1

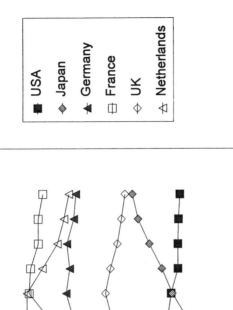

Figure 1.1 General government total outlays as a percentage of nominal GDP

shows what a battle it was even after 1990. The US, Canadian, Australian and Norwegian E/GDP peaked in 1992. The Japanese, German, French, Italian, Austrian, Danish (after earlier successes), Finnish, Greek, Portuguese, Spanish and Swedish (at a high of 72 per cent) peaked in 1993. The UK peaked in 1984, fell to a low in 1989 but then began to rise again. After peaking during the 1980s, only Belgium, Ireland and the Netherlands showed substantial reductions in E/GDP. Yet there can be few of those countries that did not have that intention. Indeed, the last three columns of forecasts are evidence of such an intention to do better, probably similarly repeated and falsified every year since the late 1970s. (Some countries – for example, Japan and Finland – do not as yet seem to have had a fiscal crisis, since their E/GDP ratios have not yet peaked.)

However, Japan, France, Italy, Canada, Spain, Sweden and Greece's actual 1993 proportions were close to the Table 1.4 estimates for 1995, while the Finnish ratio even ended substantially higher at 61 per cent. If the rate of increase in the proportion from 1960 to 1975 were to persist until 2015, most would have exceeded 70 per cent and Denmark 110 per cent. (While public expenditure on goods and services cannot rise to more than 100 per cent of GDP, logically transfer payments can do so since the same income can be transferred more than once.) Among those whose ratios would have grown, and up to 1993 did continue to grow slowly, Japan was remarkable, like many other East Asian economies, in that rapid growth in GDP allowed public expenditure to rise fast even though the proportion stayed low.

Controlling crisis

The catalyst for crisis was not revolutionary thinking inside or outside government, but electoral revolution among the governed, against the tax implications of rising public expenditure. Awareness of tax burdens was heightened at the end of the 1970s and in the 1980s by a fall in real wages in the United States because of a long-term increase in international competition. Between 1948 and 1973 average earnings of 40-year-old full-time male workers almost doubled. Thereafter they fell by 4 per cent in real terms up to 1989.[53] This trend was accentuated in the short term during recessions.[54] Unsurprisingly, then, the revolt happened first in the USA, where local government spenders were financially most directly accountable to the electorate. At local level American government is mostly dependent on the taxes it raises. State and federal government grant is less important than taxes.[55] Expenditure increases impact directly on electors' pockets and the US local electorates are therefore among the most financially conscious in the world. The stimulus for a step-change in US public-sector efficiency-seeking was absolute prohibition on increases in local taxation, of which the first and best known was California's Proposition 13 in 1978, when the state electorate voted directly through a referendum for an absolute ban on state tax increases.[56] Thereafter more governments at state and local levels got into financial difficulty until this type of opposition peaked around 1990.

Table 1.5 General government total outlays as a percentage of GDP

	1978	1979	1980	1981	1982	1983	1984	1985	1986	1987	1988	1989	1990	1991	1992	1993	1994	1995	*Estimates and projections* 1996	1997
United States	30.0	29.9	31.8	32.1	33.9	33.9	32.6	33.2	33.7	33.4	32.5	32.4	33.3	34.0	35.0	34.5	33.5	33.5	33.4	33.2
Japan	30.0	31.1	32.0	32.8	33.0	33.3	32.3	31.6	32.0	32.2	31.6	30.9	31.7	31.4	32.2	34.3	35.8	37.6	39.2	40.0
Germany	47.3	47.3	47.9	48.7	49.0	47.8	47.4	47.0	46.4	46.7	46.3	44.8	45.1	47.9	48.6	49.6	49.1	49.5	48.5	48.2
France	44.6	45.0	46.1	48.6	50.3	51.4	51.9	52.1	51.3	50.9	50.0	49.8	49.8	50.5	52.2	55.0	54.8	53.7	53.7	53.0
Italy	42.4	41.6	41.9	45.9	47.6	48.7	49.3	50.9	50.7	50.2	50.3	51.3	53.2	53.5	53.6	56.9	54.1	52.5	51.1	49.8
United Kingdom	41.4	40.9	43.0	44.2	44.5	44.7	45.1	44.0	42.4	40.7	38.0	37.5	39.9	40.7	43.0	43.9	43.2	42.5	41.6	41.1
Canada	38.7	37.3	38.8	39.8	44.8	45.3	44.9	45.3	44.6	43.5	42.5	43.1	46.0	49.2	50.1	49.4	47.1	46.5	45.8	44.8
Australia	32.7	31.7	31.6	31.6	33.0	35.4	35.7	36.5	37.4	35.4	33.7	33.0	34.8	37.3	37.8	37.6	37.4	37.3	36.0	35.2
Austria	49.0	48.2	48.1	49.5	50.1	50.4	50.0	50.9	51.6	51.9	50.2	49.0	48.6	49.7	50.5	53.2	52.2	52.1	51.9	51.6
Belgium	55.9	57.7	58.6	63.7	63.8	63.8	62.5	62.2	61.5	59.8	57.1	55.0	54.8	56.2	56.3	56.8	56.1	55.4	53.8	53.5
Denmark	50.7	53.2	56.2	59.8	61.2	61.6	60.4	59.3	55.7	57.3	59.4	59.6	58.6	59.2	61.3	63.8	63.3	61.6	61.2	60.5
Finland	39.9	38.4	38.1	39.0	40.8	42.4	42.0	43.8	44.7	45.0	42.0	42.0	45.4	53.9	59.1	60.2	59.2	57.6	54.6	53.5
Greece	28.9	30.7	31.1	35.8	36.7	38.7	41.2	44.4	44.2	44.1	43.6	44.5	46.8	43.7	44.7	46.9	48.0	47.0	46.7	46.0
Ireland	41.5	43.8	47.4	49.0	53.0	53.0	51.3	52.4	53.2	50.6	47.4	40.6	41.2	42.2	42.9	42.8	43.5	42.1	41.6	41.2
Netherlands	51.6	53.3	55.2	57.1	59.1	59.7	58.1	56.5	56.1	57.7	56.3	53.8	54.1	54.6	55.3	55.3	53.1	50.9	49.9	49.2
Norway	50.9	49.5	47.5	47.1	47.5	47.6	45.5	44.8	48.9	50.4	52.4	53.5	53.8	49.9	57.4	50.9	49.3	46.5	45.2	45.1
Portugal	36.4	36.2	25.9	43.9	43.0	47.9	44.4	43.4	44.0	43.5	43.5	41.7	43.0	43.9	43.4	45.0	44.0	44.0	43.5	42.8
Spain	29.0	30.1	32.2	34.9	36.6	37.7	38.1	41.1	40.7	39.6	39.5	40.9	42.0	44.5	44.5	47.6	46.1	44.4	43.7	42.9
Sweden	58.6	60.0	60.1	62.6	64.8	64.5	62.0	63.3	61.6	57.8	58.1	58.3	59.1	61.3	67.2	72.5	68.8	66.7	64.9	62.6
Total of above smaller countries	41.2	41.9	42.5	45.4	46.8	47.9	47.3	48.2	48.1	47.4	46.7	46.1	47.0	48.3	49.6	51.3	50.1	48.8	47.8	47.0
Total of above European countries	43.8	43.9	44.8	47.3	48.3	48.7	48.7	49.0	48.4	47.9	47.0	46.5	47.6	48.8	50.6	51.9	50.9	50.8	49.1	48.4
Total of above OECD countries	35.8	36.0	37.2	38.5	39.9	40.1	39.4	39.7	39.7	39.4	38.5	38.2	39.2	40.1	41.2	42.0	41.4	41.3	41.1	40.8

(a) Current outlays plus net capital outlays.
(b) Excludes deposit insurance outlays.
(c) Includes proceeds of privatization and sales of other assets (BF 32.2 billion in 1994 and BF 13.5 billion in 1995).
Italicized figures represent high points.
Source: OECD Economic Outlook (Dec 94, No 56).

This kind of check was the more effective in reining back spending increases at local and state level because of statutory limitations on those governments' borrowing and on their ability to run a deficit.[57] One cause of the large growth in the US federal deficit in the 1980s was the absence of a similar limit on federal borrowing, combined with a desire to cut taxes and increase expenditure.[58] Yet paradoxically, that very federal deficit had its own effect in keeping public expenditure growth down. Since it was not desired for its own sake, but to keep taxes down, it became difficult for either Republicans or Democrats to justify any new expenditure or sizeable increases.[59] Still as Figure 1.1 and Table 1.5 show, the United States found it difficult to reduce public expenditure as a percentage of GDP. Whatever their resistance to taxes, the US people seemed paradoxically to support the welfare state against right-wing attempts to trim it.[60] Moreover, Congress fought Reagan and Clinton cutbacks, for reasons which will be considered in the next chapter, often while demanding public expenditure reductions in principle and tax increases in practice.[61] While the 1980s saw little fall in public expenditure, especially as defence spending grew, there were substantial tax cuts, leading to huge increases in the federal deficit which remained seemingly out of control until at least the end of the Bush presidency.

Economic pressures in most developed nations were similar to those in the United States. There has been more recession than before. As a result there has been less economic growth to support public expenditure than was predicted, and therefore fiscal crises.[62] While initially there was not the same pressure on take-home pay in most of Europe as in the United States, the poor have generally become poorer in real terms, there has been higher unemployment and income distribution has worsened against the poor. The overall effect of crisis was marked despite the political difficulties caused by attempted remedies. In most nations social welfare programmes were under great pressure, not so much because of their size and the ageing of the population as because of unemployment and early retirement among men aged 50 and over. Even these programmes, which had grown particularly rapidly as a proportion of GDP, levelled off in the 1980s.[63] As a consequence, the rate of growth of E/GDP moderated during the 1980s. In most countries there were years in which the ratio fell, though actual absolute declines in public expenditure were rare, perhaps nonexistent. Tax cuts were also common, though not falls in total tax receipts.

In Britain the Thatcher government found it impossible to avoid increases in public spending in the early 1980s, though because taxes were raised, there was nothing like as big an increase in the UK public-sector borrowing requirement as in the US federal deficit.[64] In so far as the public-sector borrowing requirement was brought down, the main contribution was from privatization proceeds.[65] E/GDP fell from 1983, but rose again from 1989, and with the boom at the end of the 1980s, the factors encouraging public expenditure growth seemed as strong as ever. Thoughts of fiscal crisis were put aside to win elections. Only after the 1992 election was over did attention return to serious cutbacks. Early on the government was more successful in cutting central government employment than public expenditure (as in Australia in the same period). Under the Major administration, the decline in E/GDP was reversed in the run-up to the 1992 election, and then continued to increase until the mid-1990s. The Major government then made ambitious plans for controlling administrative expenditure for 1994/5 to 1996/7 which, if achieved, would have meant significant staff cuts.[66]

Despite the qualified success of the 1980s in most countries in moderating growth in E/GDP, by the early 1990s fiscal crisis still stalked in most developed countries, though the forward projections were not as dramatic as they had been at the end of the 1970s because E/GDP growth had been moderate.[67] Among OECD nations only Belgium and Ireland had substantially reduced E/GDP in the mid-1990s. As a consequence, worries about political bankruptcy remained, while in the Far East democracy was openly resisted partly because of its proven inability to restrain public expenditure and the effect of that on competitiveness.

Attempts to cut public expenditure

From the 1960s onwards governments had attempted to improve their control of public expenditure, initially through controlling the aggregate, but with limited success, as we have seen. As the Plowden Committee (1961) had said:

> the central problem is how to bring the growth of public expenditure under control, and how to contain it . . . Different governments will have different views about the proper size of public expenditure, but all have the same problem of how to keep it within this size.[68]

The committee suggested changes to link expenditure increases to expected resources, improvements in accounting for expenditure, and procedures to ensure all ministers were bound by public expenditure objectives. While durable mechanisms were introduced for planning expenditure and ensuring collective responsibility, resource expectations were invariably over-optimistic and the recommended managerial improvements failed to take hold. Later initiatives in the 1960s and 1970s improved the planning process but, despite them, public expenditure was not controlled.

More persistent fiscal crises came in the 1980s and 1990s and created greater pressures to reduce public expenditure through improved *economy* (reductions or cuts in expenditure itself) and *efficiency* (the ability to get the same or increased output from fewer inputs). *Effectiveness*, the third of the so-called three Es (essentially the improvement in the quality of the output), has been much less in evidence, due in part to finance ministers' concerns that a better case can often be made for increasing expenditure where it can be demonstrated to be achieving its results than where less is known about its effects. Moreover, economies can in practice be achieved by low take-up rates – of social programmes, for example. The drive for public expenditure cuts can thus discourage effective administration of these programmes.

Early reactions to crisis tended to concentrate on achieving economies but real economies were hard to achieve, especially in that half of public expenditure that is transfer payments. The fiscal crises which precipitated economies were likely themselves to be associated with recession, or a balance-of-payments crisis, and hence to increases in unemployment and therefore social security payments (automatically linked in developed nations). Root and branch cuts, such as the elimination of whole activities, have been rare, both in the United States and Britain, because the vested interests in protecting departments and agencies are sufficient to defend them against abolition.[69] The only government departments to have been abolished (rather than combined) in the twentieth century dealt with colonial affairs or religion.[70] Freedom to make real economies was also reduced by the ministerial practice of making commitments which could not be reneged on without huge compensation or because of membership of international organizations. Much defence, agriculture and overseas development expenditure was committed in this way.

Given this background, the likely immediate political effect of fiscal crisis was that initially politicians sought short-term expedients which were apparently, but not really, economizing and which passed the problems on to their successors. Refusals to sanction increased spending meant that either outputs or inputs had to fall. To gain re-election, politicians' objectives were to maintain the most visible form of outputs, that is services, as far as possible, to cope with the desires of voters who wished to keep taxes down while maintaining or improving services.[71] The easiest method immediately available was to extend asset lives and cut down on capital expenditure. Cuts in capital expenditure, deferral of maintenance, and reductions in stocks and out-sourced inputs were the most welcome, because the pain was felt by others, mostly in the private sector.

Earlier in the twentieth century, development of the infrastructure was an important government objective and government capital expenditure had been larger relative to current expenditure.[72] That ratio declined from the mid-1979s (Table 1.3) in most countries, though there were notable exceptions: Japan and a cluster of European nations, Italy, Spain, Portugal, the Netherlands and Luxembourg. In Britain between 1968 and 1988, public capital formation fell to about a third of its 1968 ratio of GDP, a greater percentage reduction than in any other country except Sweden. A consequence of this decline is seen in the massively increased investment programmes of the privatized water industry required to make up for years of neglect under state control. Similar, but more dramatic, effects are observable in most unsuccessful developing countries – especially in Africa. Subsequently capital formation fell further, until to make up the deficiency, British government, in the early 1990s, sought to privatize its capital expenditure through the *private finance initiative*. (While justified by the transfer of cost, and sometimes of demand, risks to the private sector, without privatization it still remains public expenditure in so far as it provides capital goods for public activities. Instead of the full capital outlay being incurred in the years in which the expenditures are often made, they are replaced by annual leasing payments over its life. The immediate effect is a once-and-for-all rephasing of public expenditure, but not necessarily a real reduction.)

So a nation's social infrastructure may be allowed to deteriorate, and provide a few years' respite to take a government through an election. Some of the largest cuts have been in transport investment – especially roads, where an attempt was made to persuade public opinion that not increasing capacity itself restrains traffic growth, a policy which will inevitably result in accelerating congestion. The measures that will restrict traffic growth – investment in public transport, the physical redevelopment of towns and collective services to replace shopping and school car trips – themselves require heavy expenditure which the UK government was not ready to fund.

Politicians also often made arbitrary cuts in both current and capital expenditure in the often justified belief that they could be made without jeopardizing services, but only in the short run.[73] Effort was given to reducing nominal public expenditure and employment through privatization, or through reducing the employment of civil servants (but not necessarily public expenditure) by contracting out activities to the private sector.[74] But where privatization was not practical, the only genuine way outputs could be maintained while public expenditure was reduced was through improvements in efficiency which, sooner or later, would force the job reductions the mass of civil servants and other public employees might be expected to fear.[75]

Governments' overt public expenditure control programmes, with a few exceptions, have been characterized by energy but also incoherence. Initiatives have been launched in rapid but sometimes contradictory sequence and the underpinning ideas expressed well after the event rather than before. Britain has been a good example of this. Mrs Thatcher's 1979 government pushed ahead on a number of fronts simultaneously in an attempt to cut back the size of the state. An almost immediate recruitment freeze was imposed, and over the first few months in office essentially arbitrary targets were developed for reducing the size of the civil service.

When short-term expenditure cuts and palliatives failed, politicians found themselves still needing to win elections. They were tempted to play the electoral game as they had always played it, promising substantial increases in expenditure and reduction in taxes. Often they continued to do so, increasing deficits; or to avoid doing so they tried to renege on their promises after winning the election, as the British Conservatives did after 1992. Another tactic was to replace direct expenditure by regulation. In effect, much regulation was hidden expenditure forced on the private sector to achieve public benefits and as such went largely unremarked: the imposition of employment, safety and environmental and other requirements and regulations bore mostly on firms, whose costs were then passed on to consumers.[76] The 1970s had been a time when these hidden expenditures were increasing rapidly in many developed countries.[77] As the Thatcher government later recognized, there were further increases in regulation during the 1980s despite an intention to intervene less: there was as much legislation as in the previous decade but on average the bills were twice as long. By the 1990s a reaction to deregulation had started: private interests were keen to have regulations repealed, but there were two dangers. One was that regulations would go which could be shown to be in the public interest on a cost–benefit test. The second was that a market could develop in which party funds might benefit from those grateful for either regulation or deregulation. The most interesting development of this tendency was the Labour Party's proposal, announced at its 1995 party conference, for British Telecom to obtain removal of some of its licence restrictions in return for connecting schools to the Internet, an investment which would lead to public expenditure savings. Nothing better showed the jam that government had got into than the opposition feeling the need to consider such an expedient to avoid the accusation of being pledged to expenditure and tax increases.

Thus while in most countries there was a downturn in the growth of public expenditure as a proportion of GDP after 1980, it was never secure and, indeed, in almost every country recurrent fiscal crisis had become a fact of political life and an important influence on politics. Both Reagan and Thatcher had entered office determined not just to reduce the rate of growth of public expenditure but to cut it absolutely by reducing the size of the state. By that measure they failed. The effect of fiscal crisis on conservatives was tremendous. Conservatives became as diverse in their opinions as the Levellers and other sects that marked the Puritan revolution in England or those that contested for the soul of the French revolution. There were Jacobins of the extreme right whose reaction was to demand even more strongly a return to the principles of Hayekian minimalism: redoubled efforts must be made to return to that view of the state which was held not only by Hayek and Milton Friedman but also by Adam Smith and Herbert Spencer.[78] There were also English Montagnards whose reaction was more romantic and moralistic: followers of American conservatives such as Charles Murray who on both moralistic and precautionary grounds did not believe the growing underclass could be left alone, but mostly argued that the task of reducing them should be left to private charities among whose duties would be that of educating the poor in correct family values.[79] There were also Girondins of the centre right whose approach was more pragmatic in accepting that the electorate wanted public services even if they did not want to pay higher taxes for them, therefore seeing attempts at rolling back the state as a perpetual struggle, never to be won but never to be given up. They needed greater efficiency and cost savings as well as more selectivity in determining beneficiaries: income-tax cuts seemed too expensive a way of winning electoral support. Hence a growing emphasis on more targeted, selective tax reductions and expenditure increases. Distinct again were these conservative thinkers who appeared to react against the Thatcherite revolution by becoming more Burkean and laying stress again on the need for One Nation.[80] Such British thinkers had their American counterparts.[81] Indeed, conservative ideas during this period travelled quickly across the Atlantic.[82]

Since the revolt against increased taxation started earliest in state and local government in the United States, its consequences for efficiency have gone furthest there. As a generalization, the revolt has been most effective where there has been the fear, or fact, of defeat at the polls.[83] Politicians who have moved fastest to adopt greater efficiency as an aim have done so to retain power or to make the most of power they have newly won. Although their electorates have rarely been directly interested in efficiency, politicians have come to realize that only through greater efficiency can they produce the public services their electorates want, and meet their tax aspirations. In those circumstances all political parties have had a similar motivation. But, as we will see, not only conservatives needed to react to fiscal crisis by cutting public expenditure.[84]

Thus attention turned more to 'efficiency' and an overwhelming focus on the non-transfer-payment parts of public expenditure. There had frequently been sporadic attempts to diminish the inefficiency of the public sector in order to reduce public-sector spending; but their impact on it had always been limited, because neither elected nor non-elected participants in government were much motivated to achieve it.[85] Even during the most highly publicized attempts to cut public expenditure in the early 1930s and the 1960s in Britain to balance the budget during recession, the motivation was often a felt political need to be concerned about efficiency, rather than determination to achieve it. In general, politicians seeking re-election for themselves and for their parties were not under much pressure to be efficient in their management of government and public-sector activities. It has even been suggested that they cared about organizational efficiency for only symbolic reasons.[86] It was argued by Treasuries that building systems and clarifying objectives to encourage efficiency would end up by encouraging spending. By this logic, since budgeting systems tend to encourage incremental thinking, the less analysis, the better. Moreover, long-standing difficulty in improving the efficiency of government gave support to a view that the public sector was inherently inflexible and arteriosclerotic.[87] It was the source of the view that the expansion of the public sector as a proportion of GDP was largely caused by the inability to improve labour productivity in public services: their outputs were necessarily determined by multiplication of their inputs.[88] But improvement in service productivity in the private sector, which were so much a feature of the 1980s, showed that the relative price effect was not inevitable since similar methods ought to be as capable of application in the public sector. Such methods were cautiously introduced through initiatives such as the Financial Management Initiative but their impact was too slow to satisfy the political imperative of public expenditure reductions. Upward pressures on public expenditure and downward pressures on taxation brought about a realization that the only way of avoiding increasingly difficult annual dilemmas was by attempting to realize productivity improvement on a scale already being achieved in the private sector through more radical structural change. As will be maintained later, results fell short of what was possible because of defects in implementation, but the changes were radical enough to threaten good government in ways to be described. Thus there was a danger that the reforms would realize the worst of both worlds: not enough efficiency to make a real difference but a decline in the quality of government.

Conclusion

What can we learn from governments' reactions to fiscal crisis? Inasmuch as economic policy was uppermost, real economies should have been achieved. The transfer-payment aspects of public expenditure received less attention which was focused on the efficiency of the other – public service – half of public expenditure. Growth was cut back, but it proved much more difficult to reduce the expenditure required for ongoing activities. Whatever the reason, the failure to achieve economies, and the need to maintain (or even grow) outputs, led to searches for solutions to these ever more intractable problems through increasingly radical approaches to improved efficiency. Indeed, only through improvements which make the public sector as efficient and capable of productivity improvement as the private sector and a greater readiness to reassess the underlying principles on which many transfer payments are made, can fiscal crisis be kept at bay. In order to understand how this experience is shaping the development of government one needs to look at the factors which determine political behaviour: they are deeply embedded in political systems and their patterns of representation. The next chapter looks at such reactions to fiscal crisis.

Notes

1 Hede (1991).
2 Hood (1991), pp. 5,6; see also Aucoin (1990); Kooiman and van Vliet (1993), p. 59; Rhodes (1994b).
3 Pollitt (1990), pp. 2–3.
4 Osborne and Gaebler (1992), pp. 20–2.
5 Hood (1991), pp. 6–8.
6 Downs and Larkey (1986).
7 Peacock (1979); Meltzer and Richards (1981).
8 Mills (1986); Hood (1990), p. 206.
9 Hood and Schuppert (1988), pp. 250–2.
10 John Major in Major (1989), p. 1, but see Hood (1991).
11 Peacock and Wiseman (1961).
12 Foster et al. (1980), p. 80.
13 Hood and Dunsire (1981), pp. 11, 247; Heald (1983), pp. 14–18; Flora (1986), vol. 2, pp. 164.
14 See Flora (1986).
15 Peacock and Wiseman (1961).
16 Lim (1993), pp. 41–2.
17 Stiglitz (1988), pp. 309–11, Rowley and Tollison (1994) .
18 Mullard (1993), pp. 25–6.

19 Keman (1993), p. 13.
20 Saunders (1993), pp. 29–32; also in developing countries, Lim (1993), pp. 42–3.
21 Wildavsky (1993), p. 263.
22 Other programmes create legal rights; see Landy (1993), p. 28.
23 Keman (1993), pp. 31–2.
24 Creedy (1993), p. 157.
25 Rose (1989a); Mullard (1993), pp. 10–11.
26 Baumol (1967).
27 Mullard (1993).
28 Gemmell (1993b).
29 Mullard (1993), pp. 22–41.
30 Cameron (1978), p. 1258; see also Maddison (1991); Keman (1993), p. 17; and political implications, Marquand (1988), pp. 93–100.
31 Wildavsky (1975), pp. 232–5; see also Lim (1993), p. 38.
32 Keman (1993), p. 29.
33 Keman (1993); see also Rose and Peters (1978), p. 51.
34 Cameron (1978), p. 1258.
35 Heald (1983), p. 5.
36 Beveridge (1942).
37 Galbraith (1958).
38 See Cameron (1978), p. 1234.
39 Hirsch (1977).
40 Rose and Peters (1978), p. 3.
41 Rose and Peters (1978), p. 52.
42 Rose and Peters (1978), pp. 24–5.
43 Stockman (1986); see also Stiglitz (1988), p. 19.
44 Crosland (1956, 1974); on Keynesian and post-Keynesian views on public expenditure, see Heald (1983), pp. 3–9.
45 On Lindahl equilibrium, see Lindahl (1967) and Mueller and Murrell (1985).
46 Clark (1945).
47 Creedy (1993), p. 157.
48 Keman (1993), p. 19.
49 Rose and Peters (1978), pp. 33–4, 167–70.
50 O'Connor (1973); see also Heald (1983), p. 264.
51 Heald (1983), pp. 12–13.
52 Rose and Peters (1978).
53 Murnane and Levy (1992), p. 185; for the UK, see Rose and Peters (1978), p. 58 and Rivlin (1992), pp. 15, 42–64.
54 Osborne and Gaebler (1992), pp. 33–4; Keman (1993), p. 19.
55 Reeves (1992); Rivlin (1992), pp. 106–9; Zimmerman (1992).
56 Bahl (1984), pp. 184–5.
57 But see Bunch (1991).
58 But see Krugman (1994), pp. 85–99.
59 Rivlin (1992), pp. 100–2.
60 Stockman (1986).
61 Fiorina (1989), p. 133.
62 Keman (1993), p. 19.
63 Keman (1993), p. 20, except in Denmark and Ireland.
64 Dunsire and Hood (1989), p. 13; Mullard (1993), pp. 146–201.
65 But see Foster (1992), pp. 112–14.

66 Hood *et al.* (1988).
67 Rivlin (1992), pp. 14, 110–25.
68 Plowden (1961).
69 Kaufman (1976); Mueller (1988).
70 Rose and Peters (1978), p. 125.
71 Peters (1993), p. 48.
72 Foster *et al.* (1980), pp. 77–9.
73 Sorensen (1993), p. 233.
74 Hood *et al.* (1988).
75 Jorgensen (1993).
76 Daintith (1989), p. 199.
77 Heald (1983), p. 20; Rivlin (1992), pp. 66–7; Willetts (1993), p. 13.
78 See Skidelsky (1989); Duncan and Hobson (1995); Patten (1995).
79 Murray (1990, 1994); see also Duncan and Hobson (1995).
80 See Waldegrave (1994); Willetts (1994).
81 Gray (1994).
82 Finkelstein (1994).
83 Pommerehne and Schneider (1982).
84 Keating and Holmes (1990); Boston *et al.* (1991); Zifcak (1994).
85 Thomas (1989).
86 March and Olsen (1983).
87 Tsarchys (1975); Olson (1982).
88 Baumol (1967); Rose and Peters (1978), p. 158; Heald (1983), pp. 114–18.

2

The politics of fiscal crisis

> There are two parties in Europe. One party considers nations to be the property of their governors, the other holds that governments are established for the good of the many and that is the principle upon which our government was founded in 1688.
>
> Lord Palmerston[1]

Some of the reasons for the rise in public expenditure after the Second World War have been considered as well as the fiscal crises in many nations which produced a reduction in that growth; but what stopped governments going further? Why did governments fail in their aims of cutting public expenditure? In particular, can one understand how governments' reactions to fiscal crises affected and were affected by changes in the nature of politics and in the balance of power within government?

Public expenditure and elections

Elections are the most important political event in a democracy. In developed countries, even in some widely regarded as corrupt, election outcomes have been strongly influenced by an incumbent government's economic success, or lack of it. National election results in the US and UK seem to be most strongly influenced by recent and past experience of inflation, unemployment, and to a less extent, economic growth.[2]

Similar explanations have been confirmed in France, Australia, Denmark, Germany, Japan and New Zealand and, in a broader sense, by many surveys of voters' intentions.[3] It is consistent with the weight political commentators, and many politicians themselves, give to economic factors in determining election results. Nations may differ at any one time, and over time, in the relative weight given to present and past inflation, unemployment and economic growth, without affecting this general proposition.

Most democratic governments towards the end of the 1970s made the reduction of public expenditure a declared aim in the public interest*, in part as

---

* The phrase will in this book be used in broad terms to describe democratic governments following reasonably well-defined policies consistently and openly, until they depart from them, equally openly, to new, well-defined policies. When national security is threatened, it may be in the public interest to follow some secret policy; but even then it must expect to be tested against the public interest at the bar of history. But these qualifications do not concern us over reactions to fiscal crisis.

a response to fiscal crisis. It was among the ambitions of both Ronald Reagan and Margaret Thatcher, an element in their monetarist economic policies. Neither achieved it. Public expenditure *rose* as a proportion of GDP, principally because of the need to pay more out in social security (because of sharply greater unemployment) but also because of various election pledges on defence and law and order.[4]

Even these policy failures tend to show the primacy of the economic public interest in explaining elections. As discussed in Chapter 1, the Reagan administration met the dilemma of rising public expenditure by allowing a huge increase in the federal deficit rather than by raising taxes.[5] This policy was in flagrant contradiction of its own stance on macroeconomic policy and there is evidence enough that public expenditure was allowed to rise substantially for public choice or 'political'[*] reasons. The consequence of deficit financing was a (Keynesian) boom which swept Reagan back into office for a second term.

The Thatcher government was more committed to its economic policies. It set out to honour election pledges, which it mostly kept, but it was hit by unpredicted inflation and recession. Though initially defeated in its aim of cutting public expenditure, it did not allow the deficit to rise, raising taxes instead, so rescuing its overriding aim of achieving fiscal balance and avoiding Keynesian policies. In broad terms the altered policy was consistent with a public interest explanation, given the change in economic circumstances. However, by contrast with the United States, recession persisted longer. That the Thatcher government won the 1983 election was probably in part because of non-economic factors, in particular the Falklands war.[6] From 1983 to 1988 the Thatcher government was able to revert to its original intention of reducing public expenditure, which fell from 45 per cent to 37 per cent of GDP from 1984 to 1989 (but it was not actually reduced in absolute terms). Under John Major, however, the government continued to assert that it had a tight control over public expenditure, while at the same time relaxing that control in the run-up to the 1992 election. Public expenditure rose again as a proportion of GDP until after the election, when it steadied to around 43 per cent before falling once more.[7]

Contrary to earlier experience, when public expenditure was generally allowed to grow, experience since 1980 suggests governments will try to limit public expenditure, if they have been convinced it is necessary to deliver an economic policy in the public interest.[8] Fiscal crisis has altered the position to one where public expenditure control, rather than public expenditure

---

[*] With hesitation 'political' in inverted commas is used throughout this book to signify what the economic and political source literature often call *public choice* political behaviour or explanations of political behaviour: in particular, such behaviour when motivated by personal or party ambitions. Therefore, it can be contrasted with public interest behaviour and explanations of behaviour as defined in the last footnote.

growth, is thought to be needed to deliver vote-winning economic policies. Nevertheless there is substantial evidence that governments in election years try to manipulate events.[9] Two courses of action are particularly common. The first is the use of either increases in expenditure or cuts in tax to woo electors.[10] The second is for an incumbent government to attempt to stimulate the economy in the short term, and at the expense of the future, so as to make economic prospects seem better than they really are. Such stimulation of the economy has adverse consequences which are not felt until after the election. Such endeavours then have to be reversed by the incoming government.

This practice has been named the *political business cycle*, because governments are seen as going through a cycle on attaining or retaining office. First, they must reverse whatever unsustainable actions won them the election, then they have perhaps two or three years of immunity from election to do what they want, and finally they need at least a year or more in which to prepare themselves for the next election.[11] Most investigations of this cycle suggest that, though frequently attempted, it is not easy for governments to contrive a sense of economic well-being. It does not fool the electorate, even in countries where the attempt is made easier by the government's ability to set the election date.[12] The reason for it is not that the electorate is incapable of being fooled, but that politicians do not have rapid enough effective control of macroeconomic levers. Open economies mean that Keynesian stimulation quickly leaks outside the national economy. Financial markets are quick to react to any such behaviour. Politicians may try to manipulate economic policy to achieve a favourable economic outcome before an election as President Bush did, but they normally do not succeed.[13]

Providing the results of elections continue to be significantly influenced by economic performance, there remains some assurance that politicians will strive after the public interest, in so far as economic well-being is regarded not only as their declared aim, irrespective of party, but also in the interest of all citizens. But there are now some signs – in both the United States and the United Kingdom – that voters were prepared neither in mid-term to return even moderate left-wing governments like Clinton's, despite good economic performance, nor to reject a government like Major's, despite poor economic performance. Elections may be becoming less determined by national economic performance. This change may be because national economies are seen to be increasingly at the mercy of international forces beyond governments' control, or because countries' economic identity has become submerged in some larger whole, like the European Union. The consequences of European Union and a single currency for the economic policy of member states have been much in evidence in discussions of the pros and cons of greater European integration, but not the consequences for politics.

Whatever its causes, perceived or real powerlessness over the economy may mean that public interest explanations of election results, based on economic performance, become less relevant. Lower economic growth rates and the relative impoverishment of those with lower incomes may divorce the well-being of some income groups from the general well-being of the economy, especially when economic growth is low. An economic culture of contentment may arise in which a majority feel their own economic well-being is more threatened by the return of the opposition to power than by any possibility that such a change would improve economic performance.[14] As nations lose the ability to control or improve their economies through monetary and exchange-rate policy, altering levels of public expenditure and tax will have a growing importance on the relative economic well-being of individual electors. There will be increasing tension between a macro-economic imperative to reduce both public expenditure and taxation, and a political imperative to increase expenditure, while reducing tax rates. A left-wing government's public expenditure aspirations are likely to be different from and higher than those of an incumbent right-wing government. There-fore, it will be forced to bring down public expenditure even more in some directions to allow it to rise in others, if it is to avoid tax increases or fiscal deficits. Forming electable coalitions of left-wing interests will become in-creasingly difficult. However, there will be similar problems on the right where, as we have seen in Chapter 1, failures to reduce public expenditure as intended have created profound disagreements among conservatives on what to do next.

Why public expenditure grows

These arguments do not satisfactorily explain why public expenditure in all countries has grown as a proportion of GDP over such a long period. Indeed, despite considerable research and the fact that the trends have been similar in most developed countries, no valid general explanations of public expenditure growth have yet been found.[15]

One can instead find some tendencies that run across countries. There is a tendency for overall public expenditure to be less, the more non-federal government is centralized;[16] but also to be more, the more central govern-ment finances local government;[17] for left-wing governments to increase public expenditure by more, early in their terms, and for right-wing govern-ments to reduce it, but for both to converge on macroeconomic policies entailing public expenditure cuts before the next election. Public expendi-ture is likely to be greater, the larger the number of interest groups or political parties;[18] and to be higher in economies where income distribution is more unequal, the greater proportion of the time left-wing parties are in power, and the more frequently there are elections. There is also a tendency to higher public expenditure in countries where high proportions of the population are able to, and do, vote, which is plausible because it usually means that more poor people vote, and they have an obvious interest in redistribution.[19]

Other concurrent political cycles can be observed. In Britain, Labour governments increased current expenditure, which tended to please their supporting interests.[20] Conservative governments tended to try to cut back current spending, and, until the late 1980s, to increase capital programmes instead, which tended to favour some of their backers.

There has also been in most developed nations what Rose and Peters called 'one-eyed Keynesianism' – the tendency for politicians of all parties to generate budget deficits when there was any tendency towards recession, without balancing that by equally Keynesian budget surpluses when the economy overheated.[21] Behaviourial characteristics play a part, as do the incremental tendencies of most budgeting systems. Politicians like starting things. There is little kudos in stopping them or in restraint. In some areas – for example, housing starts – successive governments across the political spectrum fell into the habit of outbidding each other over how many houses they would build. In addition, most budgeting systems examine new proposals for spending while leaving the bulk of inherited expenditure unchallenged. The net effect is an increase – even if many of the new proposals are rejected.

'Political' explanations: bureaucracy

But such explanations seem better at accounting for differences in the rate and pattern of public expenditure growth, but not the remarkable growth itself. As was argued in Chapter 1, in many developed nations most new public expenditure programmes were defensible as in the public interest. Yet public interest explanations of political behaviour have always been concurrent with other, very different, egoistic or 'political' interpretations of behaviour. Some explanations rely on a class identity of interest like those of Marx or of Namier. But where does one look in the twentieth century when class no longer provides enough cement for collective action?

A more promising set of explanations is based on the power actors may gain through operating in the political market-place itself. In these terms the most promising 'class', to explain not only the growth of public expenditure but also the bureaucratic and regulated form it has taken, is the bureaucracy. The view that the bureaucracy is powerful and self-interested is not new. Writing in 1867, Bagehot opined that functionaries were interested in their own aggrandizement.[22] In 1929 Lord Chief Justice Hewart attacked not the British civil service as such, but the 'mischiefs of bureaucracy' which created a 'new despotism' which he saw as:

> a persistent and well-contrived system, intended to produce, and in practice producing, a despotic power which at one and the same time places Government Departments above the Sovereignty of Parliament and beyond the jurisdiction of the Courts. If it appears that this system springs from and depends upon a deep-seated official conviction . . . that this . . . is the best and most scientific way of ruling the country.[23]

Thirty years later, Thomas Balogh, who was to be Harold Wilson's personal adviser after 1964, attacked the civil service more directly as responsible for Britain's decline through its dilettante abuse of its very great power.[24]

These views did not explore the reasons behind the apparent aggrandizement of the bureaucracy, but Downs in the 1960s suggested that as a businessman maximized profits, so bureaucrats maximized their interest at various levels which led them to maximize the size of their bureaucracies.[25] A more rigorous assimilation came from the New Right when Niskanen postulated that bureaucracy used its monopoly power to increase its size persistently, producing a broadly equivalent growth in public expenditure.[26]

There have been many difficulties in attempting to apply either theory with any precision. Variants of these theories try to relate the growth of bureaucracy to the interests of bureaucrats other than those at the top. Other theories allow bureaucrats more diverse objectives, not all related to size, so that how they want to shape their bureaux, for example by concentrating on policy and less on the executive tasks which require large numbers and budgets, is admitted to influence their behaviour.[27] Among other difficulties are differences in institutional arrangements affecting the ability of the bureaucracy to expand. While budgetary and other executive controls may have slowed down the growth of the bureaucracy in Western Europe, Congress in the USA is itself interested in growth for other reasons. Moreover, much recent public expenditure growth originates from the growth of transfer payments resulting from uncontrollable structural changes in the economy rather than any other factor. This growth may have only incidentally increased the size of the bureaucracy to administer the systems.

Even then, the power and interest of the bureaucracy alone seems a slender foundation for a theory of public expenditure growth. It requires politicians to be willing or unwilling puppets of the bureaucracy in a way which hardly seems plausible. Moreover, Niskanen-type explanations could be said to have been undermined by the downsizing of government that took place in the 1980s.[28] Although there were politicians, mostly incoming right-wingers, who saw the civil service as the chief obstacle to cutting back the public sector, the Niskanen and other related hypotheses are not readily consistent with the reductions in the public sector thereafter achieved in most countries.

The reality is probably more complicated in many developed nations. The twentieth century until the mid-1970s was a period of consensus between ministers and the officials from whom ministers were often prepared to take their policies. They questioned them. They altered them, introduced policies of their own or even threw out hints in manifestos which officials then worked up. But while politicians and officials both had their influence on policies, how they were to execute them was largely left to officials who therefore had substantial practical freedom to devise their own means of implementation. With hindsight one can blame officials for accepting the relative price effect, the apparent impossibility of productivity improvements in public services, as a fact, thus making such a significant difference to the cost of public services. Thus while one can claim that politicians and bureaucracy were responsible for the objectives of public expenditure, in so far as its growth also reflected the form it took, the bureaucracy was largely responsible for the extent of that growth by neglecting opportunities to improve its productivity. Before fiscal crisis struck, the nexus of attitudes that let public expenditure grow commanded enough consensus for its own survival.

By the end of the 1970s it had become commonplace to believe that Britain, along with many other nations (especially those others like Australia and New Zealand where new public management was to find its first hold), suffered from an over-mighty executive in which politicians and civil servants worked together to promote their joint power. Left and right criticized both executive power and within it bureaucratic power.[29] Niskanen's views became widely held outside the economic circles in which they originated. As the second head of Margaret Thatcher's personal policy unit said in reflecting on his own time in Downing Street:

> Bureaucrats cannot help becoming 'rent-seekers' in just the same way that entrepreneurs cannot help becoming profit-seekers. It is their occupational deformation to regard the size, financial resources and morale of their department as intimately connected with the public good . . .[30]

With elaborate proofs, economists such as Tullock and Buchanan demonstrated what was perhaps less obvious: that if politicians regained power from bureaucrats, public expenditure growth would decline and might go into reverse because politicians had less direct interest in its growth than bureaucrats had.[31] But few had the foresight of Lord Hailsham in 1978. As much as anyone, he was a determined opponent of what he called 'elective dictatorship':

> We are in fact governed by a bureaucracy of mandarins and their subordinates imposing on a people partisan policies devised by a government of amateurs who have achieved their position by a minority of votes under an unfair voting system, bringing into Parliament candidates elected by local caucuses of activists or outside bodies and having little else to commend them but their party loyalties.[32]

But he went on to question those who in those circumstances sought to weaken the civil service:

> I am not of their number. Given our system of government, I am prepared to go to the stake against any attempt to water down or undermine the quality, the morale, the discipline, or the independence of our administrative civil servants. They do their best to mitigate the system's faults, whereas the various remedies proposed would exaggerate the faults they are supposed to remedy. It is the system itself that I call in question.

Paradoxically, a year later he became a leading member of a Cabinet which began the process of altering the balance of influence within the executive from civil servant to minister. In the early Thatcher years the old ways of working between ministers and civil servants survived through a sense of continued effort to overcome national economic crisis – the legacy of past crises. Then the dominance of Margaret Thatcher in the mid- and late 1980s disguised the fact that a profound change had occurred in the balance of power within the executive, reinforced by organizational change that only gradually became a settled fact in the 1990s.

'Political' explanations: political markets

But if fiscal crises and fulmination against elective dictatorships caused politicians to seek to break the powers of the bureaucracy, why, then, in many countries has there still been a tendency for public expenditure to resume its increase, once policies against that happening were relaxed?

'Political' explanations, applied to princes, have been long-standing. Phrases such as Machiavellianism, *raison d'état* and *realpolitik* may seek to imply that such behaviour is foreign to the Anglo-Saxon tradition of government, but political leaders have often been admired, especially by other political leaders and their historians, for their skills in manipulating events to win or retain power to their own and the national advantage. Admiration has often come easily for those who were ruthless – whether Alexander the Great, Cesare Borgia or Napoleon – since their own self-aggrandizement and that of the state seemed to coincide.

More modern elected presidents and prime ministers have acted in similar style. In Britain such behaviour has until recently been acceptable, if shielded by hypocrisy and kept for crucial occasions. In the United States such Tammany Hall traditions survived in a more open and pervasive manner. Similar exploits by lesser politicians, whose own interest is not so readily interpreted as coinciding with that of their country, or even their party, have been less widely admired; but in the twentieth century there developed in the United States a tripartite system in which public expenditure was often determined by so-called 'iron triangles' of major industrial or other interests, government agencies and committees of the legislature, combining to pursue the growth of sectional budgets.[33] Many other nations developed comparable networks.

'Political' as opposed to public interest explanations of public expenditure decisions are of many different kinds.[34] One explanation sees parties and individuals standing for elections determining their policies rationally, including those on taxes and public expenditure, to maximize support for themselves at the polls: 'Because the government in our model works to maximise its political support, it carries out those acts which gain the most votes by means of those acts of financing which lose the fewest votes'.[35] The best-known inference from this class of theories is the median voter hypothesis, that rational politicians design their policies, legislation and other actions to please voters in the middle of the spectrum, on the grounds that, at least in a two-party state, voters to the left and right of centre will vote for the left and the right party anyway.

While such theories aim to explain the process, others attempt to explain the behaviour of individuals in that they assimilate voters to customers in their preferences:

> Voters and customers are essentially the same people. Mr Smith buys and votes. He is the same man in the supermarket and in the voting booth. There is no reason to believe his behaviour is radically different in the two environments. We assume that, in both, he will choose the produce or candidate he thinks is the best bargain for him.[36]

George Stigler and his followers saw politics, particularly elections, as a market.[37] Wherever firms were able to earn monopoly profits, it was worth their while paying a sum to retain their monopoly up to the value of that profit. Since most monopolies resulted from legal restrictions on the free market, firms had an interest in obtaining laws which would secure the protection of monopoly rights, or such similar advantages as tariffs and quotas.[38] From this hypothesis was constructed a theory of political economy or public choice by which industrial, financial and professional interests used their money to capture legislators and any other politicians and officials having worthwhile favours to dispense.

In Stigler's own Chicago version of the theory, politicians and officials are assumed to be as much profit- or income-maximizers as any firm or gainfully employed person. One intermediate objective on the way to the achievement of their financial goals will be to join the political party most likely to achieve political power (though this aspiration will be more important in countries like Britain where single parties form governments than in the United States, where the influence of parties has become much weaker). Another objective will be to win office. Once elected, they will want to acquire positions as legislators, ministers or committee members which maximize their value to those who have favours to gain from them. They will also want to use their positions to secure lucrative positions after they retire from politics. In economic terms they enter politics to acquire, increase and exploit (monopoly) power, cooperating with others in what is often called log-rolling inasmuch as they have more monopoly power together than if following their interests separately.[39] Chicagoan theory can operate in a non-corrupt world where the prizes are the legitimate financial aspirations of a legislator, a minister and a retired politician but, as the imperative is financial, it also covers occasions of corruption where politicians sell their power to the highest bidder.

A second theory of public choice, the Virginian, differs since it allows politicians other motives than money-making, particularly the gaining of votes to retain or win power. In more complex versions legislators and other politicians are assumed to maximize utility functions, variously weighted in votes, or even ideology, as well as cash.[40] But politics is still a market in which interest groups compete for political favours. It can take a personally financially disinterested form in which the interest of politicians is only to secure their own return to power and, where relevant, the return of their party. The money then needed is to finance elections.

At the height of their influence both theories maintained that their hypotheses explained not only elections, but all legislative and other political behaviour. Their underlying proposition was that politics and politicians were rational. By this Chicagoans meant politicians were income-maximizers. In Virginian theory they maximized votes or some weighted function of money and votes. Whatever claims were once made for the universality of either economic theory of politics, that universality has been falsified by the analysis of past events.[41] Though these theories can be shown not to be necessary explanations of behaviour, and even on occasion to be false, there are many other occasions when explanations based on them are persuasive.[42] More generally, looking back in history, it is as absurd to think that rulers and electors have never been motivated by gaining personal financial or political advantage as it is to think they are their only motives. Though these theories were mostly formulated in the 1960s and flourished in the 1970s, their full influence in representing politics as part of the market-place has had to wait a generation, reaching not only students of economics but also of politics, reinforcing and systematizing a belief in *realpolitik*, which the age has made fashionable and increasingly relevant as professional politicians displace amateurs in most democracies.[43]

How, then, do such theories help explain levels and patterns of public expenditure? Among the most effective ways to induce voters to vote in a particular direction is to tailor public expenditure increases or tax reductions so as to please those sectors of the community whose votes politicians need to attract. However, the more a government aims to broaden its support, the more pledges and therefore the more public expenditure will be needed. Both an incumbent government and an opposition wanting to win an election need to offer more public expenditure bribes to weld different interest groups (or parties) into an election-winning coalition. Politicians are likely be more lavish in their promises than strictly necessary, either because they cannot be exact in their calculations, or because they lack information on just how much they need to promise to get the votes they require. It is rational for them to be myopic: the cost of increased or improved services and programmes will not fall on them directly, and the political cost of losing an election is far greater than that of winning it by a wider margin. They have their careers to make, and many will not be satisfied by the reward of public service alone. There is another possibility: politicians may be ready to make or unmake laws and regulations or to grant licences and other permits in return for cash.[44] While theoretically this process could lead to deregulation, those who want to increase their other exclusive advantages generally have the longer purses, so that a nation whose politicians pursue this route generally ends in more regulation, protectionism and possibly, in the end, economic stagnation.

If politicians (and bureaucrats) have the influence worth paying for, in whose interest is it to pay? Stigler rightly predicted industry, commerce and finance as having the economic interest and resources. Broadly, there are two different possible hypotheses on how they might behave: one is to use their influence to keep public expenditure and the public sector small, to keep tax rates low and thus increase the resources available for private consumption. Such a theory might help explain low increases in the public expenditure/GDP ratio in the USA, Switzerland, Japan and several countries of the Far East. Another hypothesis, which may even coexist with the first, postulates that some parts of the private sector which are interested in government contracts – for example, defence and construction – use their influence and resources to increase the relevant public expenditure.

How can one square these theories with the finding, consistent with the public interest, that national elections are mostly determined by the state of the economy? They can be reconciled by postulating that 'political' behaviour is significant in explaining variations in the pattern of public expenditure. The Stigler view can be rescued by detaching it from presidential and other national elections, and relating it to other 'markets' which could plausibly explain such variations in public expenditure growth. The clue is to recognize the effects of the public interest or of bureaucracy in stimulating public expenditure growth, but to regard these elements as reinforced or overlaid by what was happening in politicians' markets other than national elections. What other political forces are at work must largely depend on the institutional circumstances of the country concerned. In some countries the funding of political parties is a key market. The more parties spend on campaigning, the more likely they are to win elections, especially against incumbents.[45] When companies, particularly the construction and defence industries, contribute to campaign funds, they hope to receive in return substantial benefits in the form of contracts, deregulation, tax loopholes or other favours. In many nations, getting the party into government is sufficient to result in the delivery of the benefits expected. In other countries where contributions to campaign funds are smaller, an impartial and strong civil service acts as protection, limiting the extent to which governments can honour their campaign pledges to particular individuals. It does not prevent industry, industrial sectors and even on occasion particular firms benefiting from such pledges, but only after some due process which limits the possibility of excessive abuse. Another mechanism through which interest groups have influenced public expenditure decisions has been through funding the election of individual politicians in countries where they can have an influence on expenditure decisions.

In many countries parties and individuals are susceptible to such pressures over a long period of time. In some corruption may be endemic, but that is not essential. Parties and politicians may be interested only in the resources they need to win elections. In general, industry, commerce and finance would prefer that because they must be assumed to prefer situations where the cost of advancing their political aims is low. Such a pork–barrel state is cheaper and less problematic for them than a corrupt state. (We reserve the term 'pork barrel' for such non-corrupt influence.) However, in other states pork barrel and log-rolling may make the state work for the benefit of the economy and be consistent with business profitability, though if it turns into blatant corruption, that often leads to economic stagnation. If such 'political' explanations of public expenditure decision-making go with satisfactory rates of economic growth, then they may even be defended by many, inasmuch as they help capitalism to flourish through a system in which influence is weighted by money.

How influence operates varies between countries, as do its effects. To adopt simplified abstractions in each case, there is first what might be called, with deliberate simplification, the *African* model, where most public decisions are up for sale. This generally results in corruption rather than simply pork-barrel politics; but those who are involved in political corruption are often so short-term in their aspirations there is little or no economic growth to provide the profits with which to fuel higher levels of corruption.

There is the *Italian* model, where most public services are subject to pork barrel, if not corruption, at the point of delivery. Payments are used to secure most contracts. Government-side politicians at all levels expect to secure this power and often to increase their wealth directly or indirectly through such payments; but there is strong economic growth and a healthy free-market private sector. It is different from what may be called the *Japanese* model, mainly in one respect. Under the Japanese model a strong bureaucracy – apparently as disinterested as, but also stronger in its power relative to ministers than even the British civil service was in its heyday – allows politicians and parties to exercise influence on behalf of individual firms and to be paid for doing so, while providing a strong interventionist, but impartial, economic policy framework in the economic interest of the country as a whole.

The *American* does not have the impartial strong interventionism of the Japanese model or corruption at point of delivery. Moreover, except in so far as central government agencies may suffer from overload, the disbursement of funds to contractors and other recipients is mostly done fairly and competitively. But in the United States during the twentieth century the unity of purpose of political parties in determining policies has decayed and has been replaced by pork-barrel policy-making. Individual legislators have built their own positions in Congress and on congressional committees which they use to secure their political power and in some cases maximize their own personal political and financial gain. Moreover, running for Congress requires substantial investment. Since most money available comes from individuals and coalitions of industrial and financial interests, these, mediated though lobbyists, become the prime sources of money and influence. Networks of interest groups are built up to work the system.[46] Executive departments and agencies wanting funds to maintain or expand their activities are then drawn into these relationships.

The position of the individual senator and member of Congress has been particularly influential. At the end of the 1970s Morris Fiorina concluded in a

book whose thesis was widely accepted that their main interest was in maximizing local support for their re-election. Almost all their votes in Congress
could be explained as winning or retaining such support from supporters of
their own and the opposition party, a fact which reinforced the strength of the
iron triangle system.[47] A decade later he found it even truer that measures,
including budget appropriations, only passed through Congress if they were in
the personal 'political' interest of enough of its members.[48]

During the 1980s these networks prevented presidents from achieving the
expenditure reductions and tax increases they intended.[49] Occasionally, as with
President Clinton, public concern about an important issue, such as the rising
costs of health care, has allowed a reforming president into office; but thereafter
log-rolling proves more important in Congress than party loyalty, and prevents
the changes happening that the electorate appeared to want. Presidents still find
the greatest difficulty in raising taxes or restraining expenditure of concern to any
substantial number of interested senators or members of Congress.

Depending on the exact constitutional arrangements, ministers and officials in many other countries have a similar influence and pork-barrel interest
in increasing and maintaining expenditure levels, though countries vary greatly
in the extent to which interest groups influence public expenditure growth and
in the routes they use. In states where log-rolling and pork barrel are a major
influence on the pattern of public expenditure, expenditures are not likely to
be substantially redistributive in a public interest sense. Individual politicians, as
distinct from governments, increase public expenditure programmes and taxes
which provide contracts and other opportunities for business enterprise rather
than support anti-poverty, educational or health programmes which do not
have as well resourced private-sector backing.

Countries where individual legislators have had little power to influence
legislation, or other tax and expenditure changes, have been far more immune
from such tendencies. Where political parties retained their cohesiveness and
power to the point that individual legislators toe the party line, it has been a
protection against such systematic lobbying. It is a further protection when
government is formed by the leaders of winning parties, who then necessarily
acquire executive responsibilities and as such hold the main initiative in for-
mulating legislation, and when, as in Britain, it is combined with a strong and
impartial civil service.

The *old British* model, which with minor variations was shared in its
essentials by Commonwealth and many northern European nations, was
largely immune from systematic pork barrel or log-rolling, and was ready to
use public funds to redistribute income and power from the haves to the have-
nots, at least until the advent of fiscal crisis. Here, lobbying through pressure
groups used to take a different form from the American.[50] Until the late 1970s
there was an expectation that groups having an interest in a particular policy
issue would be consulted through civil service channels (with ministers if
necessary) whenever legislation or any other major change was in prospect.
While this process undoubtedly diminished the chances of radical legislation, it

meant that legislation when passed was much more likely to be workable and effective because of the practical criticism it had received.[51]

What has changed to produce what might be called the *new British* situation is not that politicians are greedier than they were. It is probably as wrong to assume that motivation in politics has changed as it is unwise to base reforms on the possibility of such a change. What has happened is that the power of ministers has recently increased relative to that of the civil service, but not that of backbenchers relative to either branch of the executive.

Many politicians were always self-seeking and a few were outrageous in their use of their positions for their own financial advantage. Because most are now in effect professional politicians, they tend to have a much greater interest in policy-making and political influence than their predecessors, who were interested in power and prestige in a more general way.[52] Moreover, rather than combining politics with another job, or retiring into politics, it is usually their career. They start as policy advisers or party officials and secure a seat. They then enter a period when most of them wish to use what influence they can to impress ministers with their suitability for office. The more briefing they receive from outside to supplement their meagre resources, the more impressive they can be in the House and the more talked about in the corridors of power. But such relationships can also be lucrative to a government backbencher who is tempted.

What do backbenchers have to offer in the new British system? At a lowly level their ability to ask parliamentary questions may be worth paying for in that it may lead to government providing, or even researching, useful information which would not otherwise be available. The £1000 per question which was revealed as the going rate in 1994 can add up to a tidy income supplement, even if paid for through a lump-sum consultancy. However, members of Parliament, unlike ministers, have no direct decision-making powers or influence on parliamentary decisions, except when the government has a small or no majority.

There remain various bulwarks against Britain wholly replicating the USA. The relative unimportance of individual MPs in influencing tax and expenditure decisions is a deterrent to pork barrel and log-rolling: hence the importance of the Westminster rules as a protection against corruption. Since the latter half of the nineteenth century the Westminster rules, for which Gladstone is said to be mainly responsible, have governed the procedures the House of Commons has used in considering bills to raise revenue or authorize expenditure.[53] It was developed by the standing orders of the Commons into a position where only government and no individual MP could propose or increase any tax proposal or expenditure item. Neither could more than one such proposal be discussed together, nor any expenditure with the tax to finance it. Moreover, Gladstone kept absolutely separate the discussion of raising revenue – in the Budget – from discussions of expenditure, later collected in the annual statement. By these arrangements, together with other rules, Gladstone and his generation deliberately destroyed most of the opportunities for jobbery and log-rolling which had been such a prominent feature of the eighteenth-century and early nineteenth-century Parliament. The Westminster rules prevented Parliament, and other Commonwealth parliaments which used the Westminster model, from developing like the US Congress, where committees normally consider individual expenditure proposals and related tax proposals together.[54] While it is possible to see the recent unification of the annual Budget and Expenditure statement in the UK as a retrograde move in this sense, making it easier for ministers to consider the political, as well as financial, implications of particular measures, individual members still remain powerless in this significant area.[55]

A second protection is the custom that almost all legislation is introduced by ministers for the government (in contrast to the United States, where all bills are introduced by senators and members of Congress who are not part of the executive). Moreover, when bills are going through committee, British ministers normally resist successfully amendments other than their own. Even when they accept an amendment, they alter it by redrafting. The tradition survives partly because of the strength of the parliamentary party, marshalled by the whips and the government, which leads to the outvoting of backbenchers initiating bills or amendments, but partly of an acceptance of the superiority of civil service drafting.[56] An outcome is a strong protection against backbenchers achieving legislation at the behest of vested interests.

The third way in which MPs might reflect the wishes of vested interests is through influencing ministers' decisions when they use their powers under the law to decide such matters as a planning application, to site and build a new defence establishment or hospital, or award a contract or consultancy. In this connection, MPs have greatly extended their ability to provide access for groups to ministers who have decision-making powers. The old nexus of pressure groups was much reduced in influence, to the point of virtual destruction, by the Thatcher government's deliberate onslaught upon them as symbols of corporatism. But freedom was achieved from corporatism only at a cost: first, some legislation was less practical than it should have been; and second, the same interests, deprived of much of their traditional influence, diverted their attention from formal channels to direct access to MPs, the Conservative Party and, when they could get near them, ministers. As a consequence firms engaged in lobbying have grown enormously in size and influence since the 1970s. Lobbying largely bypasses civil servants, who therefore have less opportunity to apply their critical knowledge and acumen to what is said. The new nexus for lobbying has been given impetus by the development of the new select committee system. The amount of time ministers spend receiving such deputations and other visits through MPs has increased immensely. While this first channel of influence is at present limited in what it can achieve, there must be a danger that lobbyists and backbenchers, having opened up this network and largely supplanted the old civil service dominated interest-group network in doing so, will push so that it acquires the power to establish iron triangles by undermining the Westminster rules.

The second channel through which government may be improperly influenced is the party. Parties are susceptible to vested interests because they need to raise money for their own operations, particularly at elections – the Conservatives mainly from industry and Labour mainly from the trade unions. Individual MPs are protected by strict limits on what they may spend on their elections, and while there are no limits on what parties may spend on elections, the British tradition has been to keep expenditure low. However, the growth in importance of both public relations and advertising has made politics more expensive at and between elections. That may be a sufficient explanation for a greater interest in pork-barrel politics. But this influence has been limited. Ministers, shepherded by civil service procedures, have generally avoided the need to pass laws or make specific decisions in the interests of political contributions. Allegedly more common is reward through appointments and honours in ministers' gift.

Another channel of influence is directly through ministers who have the power to take taxation, expenditure and other decisions as well as to formulate legislation. Many MPs go through a less well-remunerated period as a minister. Nevertheless, they are usually anxious to achieve and retain office both for its own sake – its prestige, reputation and pleasure – and because of the boost it will give to their employment prospects afterwards. So severe is the competition that most know they have only a few years to enjoy office. Therefore, they are under temptation to consider how they may make their money after they stop being ministers. Therefore, one cannot be surprised to find former ministers reasonably hoping to end their careers in, or paid by, the private sector, though they are not helped in this by the growing professionalism of private-sector boards.

Ministers are protected by pressures on their own time which force them to rely on the strength, political impartiality and integrity of a civil service chosen on merit and secured from temptation by lifelong employment. As will appear, the sheer duration of Conservative rule and the end of lifetime employment have weakened the ability of the civil service to provide its safeguards. And in the 1990s, there has been in many departments a growing tendency to detach civil servants from many of their traditional roles and concentrate their attention on implementing policies which ministers decide among themselves or with their internal and external political advisers.

Other nations have other written and unwritten constitutions and relevant conventions; those in the British Commonwealth still share many of the features of the Westminster system. However, in every nation there are likely to be safeguards against 'political' manipulation. It is therefore important to consider changes in the machinery of government from at least two standpoints. The first, discussed in Chapter 1, is the need, through greater economy, efficiency and effectiveness, to keep public expenditure increases at bay either through downsizing the state or by introducing market mechanisms instead. The second is to consider how far changes in the machinery of government may make possible more decisions affecting public expenditure and tax, which have a 'political' rather than a public interest motivation.

It remains important when analysing changes in the management of government to consider how they might serve the public interest and how far there may be hidden 'political' consequences, which could play their part in further transforming Britain into a state more susceptible to vested interests. This theme recurs throughout this book.

The critics of an over-mighty executive have frequently and rightly seen the remedy to that problem as replacing Britain's unwritten constitution by a written one to give greater protection of the individual against the state.[57] But while constitutional safeguards have their place, other safeguards which are only constitutional in the broadest sense of the word may be as important. Long ago Niebuhr wrote that 'liberty depends incomparably more upon administration than on constitution'.[58] That is the broad contention of this book.

It would be too great a simplification to hold that fiscal crisis – itself the product of many forces as argued in the last chapter – was solely responsible for the 'politicization' of Britain, the accompanying shift of power to ministers from officials and therefore the threat to democracy posed by them. Conviction politics and the length of uninterrupted rule by one party have had an independent influence; but fiscal crisis was the most powerful cause of these changes.

Notes

1 Palmerston, quoted in Young (1950), p. 211.
2 Hibbs (1987), pp. 107–92 for the USA, pp. 258–89 for the UK; see also Mueller (1989), pp 277–85.
3 See Butler and Stokes (1969).
4 Mullard (1993).
5 See Stockman (1986).
6 Sander *et al.* (1987).
7 Mullard (1993), pp. 202–24.
8 Wildavsky (1993).
9 Mueller (1989), p. 286; Mullard (1993), p. 50.
10 See Tufte (1975, 1978); Alt and Chrystal (1983).
11 Paldam (1979, 1981); Mueller (1989), pp. 277, 296–306 and the literature therein.
12 Dunleavy (1991), p. 114.
13 Mueller and Murrell (1985); but see also Payne (1991).
14 Galbraith (1992).
15 Mueller (1989), pp. 320–47.
16 Tsarchys (1975).
17 Brosio (1985).
18 Mueller and Murrell (1985).
19 Meltzer and Richards (1978).
20 Foster *et al.* (1980).
21 Rose and Peters (1978), p. 113.
22 Bagehot (1928), p. 173.
23 Quoted in Thomas (1978), p. 203.
24 Balogh (1959).
25 Downs (1967).

26 Niskanen (1971); see also Mueller (1989), pp. 257–66; Keman (1993), p. 21.
27 Dunleavy (1991).
28 Blais and Dion (1991); see also Dunleavy (1991), pp. 154ff.
29 Socialist critics included Crossman, Benn, Meacher, Crowther-Hunt, Alex Lyon and Sedgemore; see also Norton (1982), p. 83.
30 Mount (1992), p. 151; see also Marquand (1988), pp. 95–6.
31 Aucoin (1990), p. 115.
32 Hailsham (1978), pp. 160–1.
33 See Dunleavy (1991), p. 37, who cites Walker (1983).
34 Dunleavy (1991), pp. 3–4.
35 Downs (1957); see also Dunleavy (1991), ch. 4; Mueller (1989), pt. 3.
36 Tullock (1976), p. 4.
37 Stigler (1971); Posner (1971, 1975); Peltzmann (1976); Becker (1983); see also Foster (1992), esp. ch. 11; Mueller (1989), pp. 235–8.
38 Dunleavy (1991), pp. 36–8, 47; Rasmussen and Zapa (1991).
39 Tullock (1970).
40 Crew and Rowley (1989).
41 Mueller (1989), p. 300; Dunleavy (1991), pp. 71–7; Brennan and Lomsky (1994).
42 Foster (1992), ch. 11; McLean and Foster (1992); Foster (1994).
43 Yeatman (1987); Ehrenhalt (1991); Pusey (1991) and Riddell (1993).
44 Frey (1985); Dunleavy (1991), pp. 36–8, 47.
45 Mueller (1989).
46 Lowi (1964); Olson (1982).
47 Fiorina (1977).
48 Fiorina (1989), pp. 130ff.
49 Sundquist (1992), p. 284.
50 Olson (1965); Self (1985); but see also Jennings (1933); Mount (1992).
51 Middlemass (1979); Olson (1982), pp. 77–8.
52 King (1975); Riddell (1993).
53 Reid (1962).
54 Sundquist (1992), pp. 281–94.
55 Letter in *The Times*, 22 November 1994, p. 20.
56 But see Kenneth Clarke's reported intention to use private lawyers to draft tax legislation in *The Independent*, 5 August 1995.
57 They include Radcliffe (1952); Nicholson (1967), p. 419; Johnson (1977), pp. 80–107 and (1980); Hailsham (1978); Sedgemore (1978); Benn (1980); Liberal Democrat Party (1990); Institute for Public Policy Research (1991); Mount (1992); Cornford (1993), pp. 12–13; Hutton (1995).
58 Quoted by Wilson (1887), p. 211.

3

'New public management' examined

We will . . . measure our success by consumer satisfaction.

Vice-President Gore[1]

The prerequisites for efficiency

Those who argue for new public management (NPM) have much on their side: the shortcomings of the old ways of doing things; the failure of the public sector to match improvements in efficiency made by the private sector in recent decades; and the thoroughness of what is proposed. Above all is the impossibility of public expenditure continuing to rise as fast as it once did. Whether it is seen as the price paid to meet demand for public services, or as an engine built to enable political parties to bargain for votes at elections, or some combination of both, public expenditure is unsustainable at the growth rates of the last forty years, unless economic growth can be increased to rates both historically rare and highly unlikely.

In the development of NPM practice preceded precept. From the end of the 1970s, but with greater intensity in the second half of the 1980s, many developed countries produced a number of overlapping administrative doctrines that began to transform ideas on public organization and management.[2] In New Zealand, Britain and Australia governments had adopted what were recognizably such reforms before they were described as such. In the United States they were implemented first at state and local level.[3] While the impetus in Britain came from the New Right, in New Zealand and Australia Labour governments, ostensibly opposed to the New Right, pioneered such changes, while the greatest effort to introduce such changes in US federal government was made by President Clinton.[4]

The first systematic, cogent and economical exposition of the new movement was a document by the New Zealand Treasury (1987).[5] But much of the thinking had been exposed – piecemeal – elsewhere and many of the ideas NPM applied to the public sector had already been canvassed in the private sector.[6] In the early 1990s, several writers produced very similar accounts of NPM, but one book caught the public imagination.[7] David Osborne and Ted Gaebler's *Reinventing Government* (1992) is the most enthusiastic and influential bible of the new movement in public management. One academic, appraising why earlier and deeper books had not had their acclaim, believed it was helped by its anecdotal style, its powerful sponsorship and the unfamiliarity of many public-sector managers with the language of management theory.[8] Indeed, it secured Clinton's personal endorsement. On its cover, the book bore the message: 'National Bestseller: "should be read by every elected official in America, the book gives us the blue-print" – Bill Clinton.' When, in 1992, Clinton gave Vice-President Gore the task of putting their ideas into effect in federal government, Osborne became Gore's adviser and rewrote the Gore Report.[9]

It is a comprehensive exposition of the case for not merely welcoming, but actively pushing revolutionary change in government. Though their background is in economics and management consultancy, they do not believe that the solution to the public sector's woes is to run it as if it were the private sector.[10] They are not against government. They believe in it, are committed to its effectiveness, and think that the system, not those who work in it, are responsible for it being inefficient and ineffective.[11] They believe its failure is one of means, not ends, and hence that it can be transformed if certain principles are applied. They do not rely on right-wing arguments that many public services are not needed, but argue instead they could be more economically and effectively delivered.

Very important is their optimism that improvement can be achieved painlessly. Theirs is the second set of recent ideas to promise something of the sort. Ronald Reagan was encouraged to increase the federal deficit by Laffer supply-side arguments that cutting tax rates would increase tax revenues because of the incentive thereby given to entrepreneurship and economic growth. Similarly, Osborne and Gaebler hold out the promise that, where their principles are followed, governments will be able to cut costs without cutting services: indeed, they should improve.

That Laffer was wrong in his belief does not imply that they must also be wrong; but it suggests caution. To resolve the contradiction at the heart of their argument between the citizen as elector, wishing to keep taxation down, and as consumer, wanting more and better public services, they vigorously promote *entrepreneurial* government as the model they wish to see taking the place of direct public-sector provision.[12] It is defined as that which increases 'productive efficiency' without taking undue risk.[13] 'Productive inefficiency' has an established meaning in economics.[14] It means unit costs can be reduced so that the same outputs can be produced with fewer inputs, or alternatively the same inputs can be used to produce more outputs (or any intermediate possibility). Thus, if government is productively inefficient (or, in ordinary language, wasteful) better government does not require spending more, nor worse government spending less.[15]

Moreover, productive inefficiency is capable of what economists call a 'Pareto improvement': no one need be worse off. Efficiency gains must be large enough to compensate any losers, so as to allow no one to be worse off from the change, and, by implication, others to be better off (though whether in fact the losers are compensated is another question). But in so far as the same or greater outputs can be achieved with fewer inputs, the authors can claim the reforms they advocate can be achieved without making anyone worse off.[16] Indeed, the implication of their book is that so pervasive is waste – they describe it as 'being marbled throughout our bureaucracies'[17] – that citizens can receive all the services they want without having to resort to political conflict or undue pressure. Thus the scarcity problem – the core, defining problem that accounts for the existence of economics – is solved, at least for a time.[18] And fiscal crisis kept at bay.

Such painless, non-controversial change is an attractive prospect. Panaceas and principles aside, it is being argued, what is so appealing about NPM, is its enthusiasm for entrepreneurship: the idea of 'inventing' government attracts those who like

> the can-do spirit, change effected through ingenious new combinations of parts, reform as the product of a single creative event . . . From one end of this book to the other, good ideas just keep on coming.[19]

Moreover, for politicians, it had the appeal that it cast them, central and local, as the real entrepreneurs of change.[20] NPM helps solve another problem: the apparent shortage of government entrepreneurs from other sources. While the Gore Report wanted to reduce the number of civil servants, it did not call for a reduction in the number of politicians. It had in some eyes the further advantage that 'the concept of "reinventing" government was so attractive, yet so broad, that virtually any reform would fit within it.'[21]

As a generalization about NPM this allegation is unfair: all its exponents describe many ways in which services can be preserved, or even improved, with reduced expenditure.[22] Yet those who write about NPM as exponents or analysts see it as derived from underlying principles or precepts. Though there are often differences between such lists, many principles recur. In our judgement there are ten practical recommendations about reform, which summarize the main changes we believe are needed to make government more efficient. But each is often put forward in too crude and blinkered a form. As well as describing each in the rest of this chapter, we also set down the main criticisms which qualify them and which need to be overcome if public expenditure-saving government is to be consistent with good government. The ten principles are as follows:

1 separating purchasing public services from production;
2 serving consumers rather than bureaucratic, political or producer interests;
3 using market pricing rather than taxes;
4 where subsidizing, doing this directly and transparently;
5 extending competition;
6 decentralizing provision;
7 empowering communities to provide services;

8 setting looser objectives, and controlling outputs rather than inputs;
9 bringing about deregulation;
10 prevention of problems, rather than cure, through planning.

These principles summarize the leading ideas of the new movement in public management, as it might be applied in any developed democratic nation. We now discuss each in turn.

Separating provision from production

Recommending the separation of purchasing public services or, as it is often called, their provision from production, 'steering from rowing', is already a well-established tradition.[23] It underlies British government policies in health and education, the policy of creating executive agencies, and the separation of service and productive activities in local government. It is the accepted policy of much cross-party opinion.[24] As developed in the next chapter, it echoes a much older distinction between policy and administration.

One reason for wanting this separation is that governments and public agencies that both 'steer' and 'row' are likely to allow the rowers, or producer elements, to dominate.[25] There are more of them and they absorb management time. The steerers are drawn into altering their objectives in the interests of the rowers (and their unions). Personnel rules are more likely to proliferate. Another reason is that the two types of activity require different types of people – production requires managers; provision requires politicians and civil servants able to determine public policy.

Third, there may be limits to the benefit of deregulation (to be described later in this chapter) achieved in the conventional public sector. If so, rules will be more easily escaped by setting up new bodies outside government, not subject to government-style detailed objectives, or to personnel, financial and other rules.

A fourth reason is that separation facilitates the use of market pricing, the extension of competition, and, ultimately, privatization. However, privatization need not be a panacea, nor is it always best to use private firms as agents. Indeed, one may often prefer the so-called 'third' sector of non-profit-making bodies, a sector which has long been strong in the United States – as Tocqueville noted long ago – and remains stronger there than in Britain.[26] Third-sector bodies' defining characteristic would seem to be they have some other motive than profit, and are thus more likely to help government achieve its mission with altruism and sympathy, while at the same time being flexible enough to be efficient. Thus the Salvation Army is likely to use government money to better advantage among the homeless than would any profit-making company.[27]

Yet what is meant by 'separation' is not unambiguous. What is the relationship between 'provider' and 'producer'? Is it one of customer and supplier, or principal and agent, to mention two very different possibilities?

Does it remain one of command, or become one of purchase? If purchase, is it to be occasional, and impersonal, like many purchases from shops? Or is it to be symbiotic, requiring a long-term contract, and a close and complex working interaction? Are there features these contracts need that ordinary commercial contracts do not have? How is the relationship affected by the absence or extent of competition? If, on the other hand, the relationship remains one of command, can separation achieve much by itself?

Furthermore, who is the 'provider' – minister or civil servant? The quest may be unavailing because it assumes relevant power is concentrated when, in reality, it is diffused. Aside from the difficulty of deciding the roles to be played by ministers and various civil servants within a department, there are other organs within the state which traditionally have roles in government or government-financed activities. What will be the power and duties of the legislature, its committees and national audit office; of the Treasury, the sponsoring minister, the permanent secretary as accounting officer and other officials, and other entities that regulate or interact with any given agency? What powers do they need to control agencies, and will the use of these powers have financial consequences for these agencies? In so far as separation subverts government's traditional powers and sources of informal influence, do they need to be replaced? What place is left for constitutional or judicial checks and balances? One should not neglect the issues prompted by a much older use of 'separation' in government, the reasons for a separation of powers as developed from the ideas of Locke and Montesquieu. Indeed, it has been suggested that reinventors of government, whether they realize it or not, are advocates of a stronger executive – that is, Hamiltonians in American political parlance.[28] If separation is to be real, their functions must change; but the pre-existing government structure will affect the reaction of national institutions to such changes – explaining why Congress in general rejected them while Parliament did not. To simplify a complex network of relationships within and outside the political system into market, or quasi-market, relations between consumers and producers tends to become complicated in practice. It is important to understand the full implications of separation, and for that reason it is discussed in Chapter 4.

Serving consumers

An important aim of the new approach to public management is to give greater weight to the interests of the consumer in service delivery.[29] Otherwise providers may continue with old services designed according to outmoded priorities. Moreover, a prime rationale for government is securing the provision of collective goods such as fire services, police and garbage collection, where the public benefits either outweigh the sum of benefits to individuals or where ordinary market pricing is not feasible. Because they either cannot be or are not priced, and therefore are not directly funded by customers, it is all the more important that services are set up to serve the interests of customers rather than producers.

Moreover, citizens would be better satisfied if outputs were designed with their actual as opposed to their reported interests dominant. In this belief Hayek and the libertarian right, who in the interests of personal liberty would diminish the extent to which the state makes decisions for consumers, join forces with businessmen who know they need to satisfy consumers to make a profit and with economists with their doctrine of consumers' sovereignty.[30] It means more consumer surveys and, given the diverse tastes and needs of people, much greater choice in the services provided if consumers' preferences are followed.[31] Best practice also requires good procedures for handling and responding to customer complaints, customer contact programmes, the use of test marketing, consumer councils, inspectors and ombudsmen. But in practice, outputs have frequently been driven by producers or by intermediate bodies, such as other agencies. Moreover, a multiplicity of agencies often deal with a single customer, especially with welfare cases (the unemployed, the disabled, the homeless). Greater attention to what the customer wants means agencies which attend to the many needs of a single customer. In theory it could be achieved by planned coordination, but, given the failures of economic planning, it is better done through the fragmentation of government into agencies, targeting particular consumer types.[32]

Where a good or service is sold through a market, what consumers buy is held to define what they want, but where there is no market, the proposition that public service delivery should be defined by what consumers, rather than producers, want raises several difficulties. Who is the best interpreter of consumers' public wants? One possible answer is politicians, in touch with some of their constituents individually and with various interest groups inside and outside their constituencies. But politicians are likely to be imperfect registrars of consumers' opinion, beyond the fact that their contacts are probably selective anyway. If the politician were simply an alternative to consumer surveys or other methods of interpreting consumer preferences, then the choice would be one of technical means. But politicians must be expected to seek political advantage in shaping the public services provided, in so far as they are able. Certainly practising politicians often assume that their views on citizens' preferences should dominate, but their interpretation of consumers' wants is unlikely to be neutral. They also seek to promote their view of the general public interest which is distinct from 'consumers' wishes' or 'political preferences'. This difference raises the issue of what distinguishes consumers from clients and both from citizens and taxpayers. Do people have rights in all four roles? In given instances, how does one settle whose right has priority? Is there any operational sense in which one can say there are rights and values shared by a whole community? And, in particular, what is the function of politicians in relation to each one of these roles?

Without some effective method of deciding what consumers want, one cannot simulate consumers' sovereignty as in a competitive market. But whatever the means chosen, consumers or their representatives will need to be kept informed about public services, so they may respond knowledgeably to the propositions put to them. Such information can easily descend into propaganda, and be biased, as indeed may the representatives themselves.[33] The more reliance is put on surveys and other techniques to elicit consumer reactions or reactions from their representatives, the more their independence and truth need to be supervised by an unbiased regulatory body. The problems of consumerism and politics are considered further in Chapters 4, 8 and 10.

Market pricing rather than taxes

Many public activities which currently cost the taxpayer money could instead earn it. Charges can be used to price public facilities, or to pay for many other services which are provided either free or for arbitrary or nominal sums such as garbage collection. Once separated from government, many production activities can price their outputs like any private firm. The arguments for extending the use of charges in the public sector to replace taxes have a long history.[34] Osborne and Gaebler contrast the Los Angeles Olympics, which made money, with other Olympics which have spent local public money and left behind public debt.[35] They instance those who tow away old cars off the streets being ready to pay for the privilege, instead of being paid; or the excess capacity of a prison being sold to jurisdictions other than the one owning it; or a public sports facility being underpriced relative to market demand. Setting up such events or activities as commercial operations can turn cost centres into profit centres.

The same can be attempted for government activities that provide passports, licences, planning permission or other permits. Government can either use them as cash cows or sell them off and use the proceeds. Government can also reduce its need for taxation by renting or selling the surplus land it owns. Even more is to be gained by taking part in development. Governments frequently own underused property and land, where development or alternative use values would be substantial if brought to market. Osborne and Gaebler approvingly cite John Shannon's view that

> the public clearly prefers this approach. All of our public-opinion polls indicate when you confront citizens with their preferences for raising revenue – user fees, property tax, local sales tax, local income tax – user fees wins hands down.[36]

Moreover, the demand for priced services will tend to be less than those for unpriced or underpriced services, so saving on capital expenditure and avoiding the need to ration.

But more than pricing may be needed to create a market. To be sure that such activities are priced fairly, provision needs to be separated from production; and the production units need to be ring-fenced and have their separate accounts. Each unit then can compete on fair terms with private firms. In the absence of competition or economic regulation, an agency may have enough monopoly power to make surpluses. To whom do they belong: the workforce, the management of the agency or the Treasury? Is there a need for regulation?

Surpluses may be disguised by their use internally to finance cross-subsidization: to what extent is this acceptable, especially if the other services are financed out of general taxation so that, in effect, some consumers are paying twice? What is the future of such cross-subsidized services after separation? If an agency adopts some pricing policy other than charging what the market will bear, what should be its pricing principles and objectives? Who is to determine such objectives, and how are they to be reflected in prices and quality of service? Is it government, and if so, where? How much discretion are agencies to be given in such matters?

The British government has introduced charging both directly for its own services and those provided by local government. New or increased charges have been introduced for passports, licences, company information and for 'value-added' services provided by agencies such as the British Library, Ordnance Survey, Land Registry and Meteorological Office. All of these serve to reduce public expenditure to some extent. Although its significance is impossible to assess, it is unlikely to be very significant while it raises major and unresolved issues of principle noted above. Far more important has been the focus on cost savings.

The treatment of subsidy

Embedded in the proposition that politicians should get closer to consumers to find out what they want, is the drawback that consumers will be found to want more than politicians are ready to provide since consumer demand for public services is virtually limitless, if not priced. So either prices will rise, which in practice will be regressive, or politicians will find themselves in increasing difficulty, rationing demand.

The proposition that the business of government is to give the people what they want, even more when coupled with ideas for empowering the community and embedding service delivery in it, tends to support the de-centralization of public service delivery.[37] They can become arguments not only for the fragmentation of government but also for its depoliticization.[38] Proponents of NPM tend to believe that traditional politics, especially if based on a division between right and left wing, at best results in an over-simplification of what consumers need and produces manifestos that do not offer what citizens want. In backing decentralization targeted at client groups, NPM would seem to be supporting a shift from party to issue politics. Achieving optimal efficiency may imply disregarding equal opportunities for all, particularly in ghettos and other pockets of lost opportunity where the costs of achieving equity are especially high. Targeting customer groups makes it less likely to achieve equity, almost regardless of how it is defined. It is cheaper to provide a health service for the elderly, veterans or even the poor, than for all citizens. The more precisely defined, and indeed smaller, the customer group (by identifying characteristic or geographical area), the cheaper the solution. To aim employment-generating policies at small areas is cheaper than funding them for the unemployed throughout the whole state. Within any such customer group, all should pay except those who cannot afford it. They should be subsidized by federal or state programmes or cross-subsidized by others within the group.[39] Under such a regime customers can decide what they want and be empowered to help provide it. Government becomes the smallest safety net needed to provide equity, however defined.[40]

However, in the interests of efficiency and accountability it is preferable – whether the aim is minimum equity or more generally to achieve a programme of income transfers to redistribute income in the public interest – to require that any subsidy, as under the New Zealand State-Owned Enterprises Act 1986, is explicit, transparent and direct:[41] by channelling subsidies directly to persons rather than through agencies, or to earmark cash through agencies to subsidize particular groups of customers. Either limits the ability of such agencies to pursue their own social goals and to redistribute income. Only then can the commercial performance of each service producer be assessed accurately. The value for money of the subsidy provided can also be better scrutinized. Distributional issues are consider further in Chapter 5.

Extending competition

The new approach to public management requires as much competition as possible, and there are many aspects of government production that would benefit from it.[42] This proposition is probably now so widely accepted it needs little supporting argument. Competition and the threat of competition bring down costs dramatically and should raise quality.[43] Nevertheless, government productive units and agencies are often privatized as monopolies, partly because producer interests have sufficient influence on the negotiations to achieve that result; but also because governments often find it hard to imagine competitive sourcing of such activities as social security benefits, welfare agencies, housing management, licensing operations, regulatory agencies, defence and police.

A common result of separating provision from production is to establish bilateral monopoly, where both provider and producer are monopolistic. Unless it can be shown that there are economies of scale or scope, or it is so difficult to define what is wanted that fair competition is precluded, it is economically desirable to create several production units, whether differentiated by type of service, type of client or geography. This conclusion holds whether or not the separated production is market-priced.

But it does not necessarily entail competition, since such units may then amount to local or functional monopolies. Since monopoly suppliers may resist change even when separated, they pose a problem for government, particularly when governments want to change policies.[44] Indeed, while suppliers remain a monopoly, the power of producer interests over government need not be much diminished. To require production to be supplied competitively is a further step towards greater efficiency and lower public expenditure.

There are many possibilities in what is put out to competition. It may be the procurement of particular inputs, or of particular functions produced in-house, or the contracting out of specific services, or of whole activities or departments. Almost invariably it entails the replacement of more informal arrangements by detailed commercial contracts enforceable at law, unless such purchases can be bought from the market at competitive prices. Governments need to use their imagination to devise appropriate competition wherever possible, subjecting more activities to market testing than previously they would ever have supposed possible. They should encourage competition with their own in-house activities from public firms, charities and other public agencies. Experience shows costs can fall substantially. Even without change of ownership there can be benefit from the process, though, as we shall see, there have been many shortcomings in practice.

There are circumstances in which competition is not possible, or if possible, is not desirable. There may be elements of *natural monopoly* which make it inefficient to have more than a single supplier. Even where competition is both possible and desirable, it may not be sensible to leave it simply to the market. It may be necessary to establish a 'level playing field', and to challenge anti-competitive practices. Access may have to be regulated so that competition may be fair. Competition may also have to be constructed – so-called internal market competition – and regulated, where competition is between subsidized entities and where criteria other than the lowest bid determine the winner. Detailed rules may be needed, of the kind that is contrary to the deregulation NPM wants. Moreover, attempts to introduce competition can seem doctrinaire and unconvincing to the practitioner.

Another kind of difficulty arises when there is competition between entities which are not all private firms. Charities which have distinctive features, such as compassion or generosity of feeling, will be driven out by organizations not so motivated. Indeed there is evidence in the USA that charitable aspects of third-sector organizations are becoming more cosmetic.[45] It is therefore essential to determine the role for competition when the form of separation is decided. Neither can one neglect the effect on political power of introducing competition. Competition is discussed further in other chapters, particularly Chapters 5, 6 and 8.

Decentralizing provision

A remote agency is less likely to give customers the public services they want, because it is too far away to know their wishes. Information cannot travel quickly up and down a centralized hierarchy: there is commonly decision overload.[46] Moreover, governments are not usually required by their customers to provide mass standardized services, but instead to fill in niches in the market, varying from one community to another.[47] Local provision enables greater variety in services and hence greater likelihood of meeting local needs. Remote agencies are also more likely to overstate economies of scope, scale and standardization to justify centralization. The nearer agencies are to those that use the services they provide, the more they can rely on personal contact and knowledge in interpreting customer wants.

It is not enough for the agency to be small, sensitive, friendly and close. The agency's policies and actions need to be 'owned' by the community it serves so there is reciprocal commitment. Otherwise it may appear alien and patronizing, however well intentioned. Remote provision also makes flexibility harder, for it is likely to be associated with more rules and regulations, more need for permissions to have to be approved at high levels in a hierarchy. Such organizations are likely to be fewer and therefore less innovative. They are less likely to be able to motivate their workers. Decentralization, by contrast, can result not only in more flexibility but also in greater efficiency and effectiveness and more innovation. Decentralization to charities may not permit the same incentives but what is lost by not relying on the profit motive may be made up by charitable motivations.

Such decentralization can be achieved by relying more either on local government or on decentralization within central government itself or by the use of decentralized third-sector agencies. That there are some 83,000 units of local government in the United States makes these the natural point of delivery for public services. Thus many examples of good practice come from small local authorities.[48] There is a stronger tradition of local government in the United States than in Britain, but in recent decades it, too, has been eroded by increased federal powers.[49] In this context one can stress the alternative possibilities of decentralization of 'steering' within large government.[50] But, as will be argued, these different models of decentralization cannot be regarded as the same either in meeting the citizens' interests or in their implications for politics. Moreover, central politicians often have reasons for avoiding or limiting decentralization, which need examining, particularly in so far as it affects the concentration of political power. Such centralizing influences have been particularly strong in Britain, where they are strikingly inconsistent with the tenets of NPM. In other countries, too, where such reforms have occurred, it is less clear there has been any change in the balance between what is done by central and local government, despite the clear tendencies of NPM on this matter. These issues are further considered in Chapter 7.

Empowering communities

One can go beyond the decentralization of provision to consider how to involve the community benefiting from services directly in production, and to empower citizens in this way, rather than leaving them as passive recipients.[51] Normally government service workers are those whom the labour market naturally provides, and sometimes those employed in public services frequently live far away from those they serve. This is especially true of managers and of those in services catering for the poor. One should instead motivate those living on housing estates to help manage themselves and their neighbours, rather than hire outside housing managers living in the suburbs; or make reformed alcoholics work with alcoholics, ex-convicts with delinquents. Those needing residential care will be happier if their homes are in their old locality: fostering is better than residential homes for most children. Similarly, parents can run schools more efficiently and more cheaply than can bureaucrats. In certain circumstances – dealing with the backward – they can even be better teachers. Their local knowledge will be greater than that of any outsider, and they will want to do a good job.

But to empower some consumers, or others with a personal interest, as producers may cause its own inequity or discrimination in provision by undermining the disinterestedness and fairness expected of public activities as well as limiting the influence of public policies and the policy-maker. An interested producer need not necessarily be the consumer's best friend, as is discussed further in Chapter 7.

Setting objectives

Governments and government agencies are often forced to be inefficient by stringent objectives that others impose on them, sometimes by law, or that they impose on themselves.[52] One result is that they may be required to do things that, if only they were reviewed, would be found to be unnecessary. Or they go on doing them simply from inertia. Until 1970 the Brigade of Guards set a guard each night at the Bank of England. It did not provide security, but was only ended when its daily marches between the Bank and its barracks became too conspicuous a cause of traffic congestion.

But even on the rare occasions when rules are reviewed, even regularly reviewed, there is a tendency to make no change, generally because it is easier to continue as before than take even a small risk; or because vested interests prop them up; or because a change in the law, or something equally difficult and time-consuming, would be needed.[53]

Rather than government departments or agencies being controlled to deliver particular important outputs, it would be far more efficient if they were given objectives of a non-statutory kind which could be changed either by them or by those to whom they report when circumstances alter. If statutory, these objectives should be broad mission statements which can be reinterpreted as needed. Thus the prime aim of deregulation should be to give government and agencies the freedom to shape their own objectives within a loosely defined mission. Osborne and Gaebler quote General Patton to that effect: 'Never tell people how to do things. Tell them what you want them to achieve and they will surprise you with their ingenuity.'[54]

Because producers change their objectives to reflect new needs and challenges, their aim is not deflected by a requirement to adhere to the letter of outdated forms of words. Not only will they be able to discard activities which are the product of old and redundant initiatives, but they will be able to be more flexible and innovative, encouraging new methods and approaches. 'The reason for tight-loose freedom for the supply of public services is that in the private sector to go on producing ever more efficiently what is no longer needed, is a recipe for bankruptcy.'[55] Indeed, there may even be whole agencies which can be shown to be redundant. But government's record in curtailing agencies and activities is poor.[56] It was observed earlier that the only government departments abolished in the twentieth century were connected with either colonies or religion.[57] The review of government agencies by Sir Leo Pliatsky only killed off 30 from a total of more than 1500.[58]

If a new, more efficient, effective and economical relationship between provision and production is to be achieved, government should specify outputs not inputs, control over inputs should be 'loose' but over objectives in some sense should be 'tight'. The usual practice of governments has been to control the amounts agencies can spend in total and also particular budget lines, which usually refer to inputs, such as labour, fuel and stationery. Controlling the cash that may be spent on given inputs means controlling the amounts of those inputs; and, especially with labour, it has become common (and often effective) to supplement budgetary control with physical limits on numbers employed. Thus the producer typically has not been free to choose whatever inputs secure the least cost and most profit.

But there would seem to be an immediate contradiction between the requirement that government and government agencies should have looser, rather than tightly defined, mission statements and the simultaneous requirement that producers' outputs should be specified. Moreover, there is a further complication if traditions of ministerial responsibility and parliamentary accountability are to be preserved across any separation. As it stands, it is all too easy to see it as likely to increase the power of the executive. Resolving these issues raises very difficult questions of parliamentary accountability and ministerial responsibility. The balance between control and flexibility must be explored and settled. Furthermore, output specification is frequently easier said than done and may require great effort, sometimes more than is justified by efficiency. Aspects of these issues are discussed further in Chapters 8 and 9.

Deregulation

As important as flexibility over objectives is the liberalization of rules governing operations. The criticism that bureaucracies are rule-bound is old. It was as much their defining characteristic for Bagehot as it was for Weber. As Bagehot said, harking back to Burke and in words which could be used by many others: 'It is an inevitable defect, that bureaucrats will care more for routine than for results; as Burke puts it, "they think the substance of business not much more important than the forms of it".'[59]

For many, rule-making and working by rule are the defining characteristics of bureaucracy; though it is an unfair criticism of the British civil service which has striven to avoid this aspect of bureaucracy at least in its higher reaches. Nevertheless, in Britain as elsewhere many traditional government operations and agencies have manuals governing what they do, or have detailed sets of regulations governing their activities. The resulting processes are often cumbrous and inefficient, with their origins in times when the number of clerks involved was legion, and their level of education required all processes to be described in immense and unalterable detail. They provided a defence of the higher levels of bureaucracy against failures in the performance of those lower down. To help meet notions of accountability, bureaucracies have often laid more stress on something being written down than on its implementation. When a rule-bound organization makes an error, it is always tempting for it to expand the rule-book rather than to manage the problem away. Because revision quickly becomes too time-consuming and difficult, layers of regulation pile upon each other to the point where no one knows all the regulations; they are often inconsistent and their interpretation an art-form. Deregulation therefore goes alongside a focus on outputs in freeing agencies to be more flexible and innovative.[60]

Yet it is worth remembering why the American, like the German, administrative system laid so much stress on rules and regulations. The Weberian tradition laid the greatest possible stress upon the development of rules as an essential safeguard for the protection of the individual client of the bureaucracy from unfair treatment, for the protection of the politician against the risk that bureaucracy would abuse its discretion under the law and for the protection of the public purse against corruption. Such detailed prescriptions were also a necessary safeguard against inequity of treatment, and against favouritism, nepotism, harassment and corruption.[61] Woodrow Wilson, who had very great influence in this respect, made it clear he saw them as necessary to retain probity in government and avoid corruption.[62] Politicians should pass laws which would be executed by administrators who would lay down in the greatest detail the rules they would follow in using the discretion those laws gave them. If deregulation is in prospect, are the objectives that bureaucratic regulations were intended to achieve – financial probity, the avoidance of fraud, the absence of political patronage and favouritism in hiring, equity as between citizens as recipients of services – worth preserving? If they are, can one assume they will be achieved by the market? Or are other defences, perhaps less bureaucratic regulation, needed? Or the law and legalistic procedures? These issues are discussed further, especially in Chapters 4 and 8.

The case for planning

The final argument is that efficiency can be increased through planning.[63] A precept particular to Osborne and Gaebler, they do not mean the long-range planning beloved of governments in the 1960s and 1970s, though they do see a role for some long-distance anticipation of problems so that preventive or evasive actions may be taken. Their main recommendation is that governments and government agencies should budget and plan several years ahead, to prevent the expenditure of too much money on solving problems that could have been prevented more cheaply if action had been taken in time: fire, health, crime and the environment. The failure to look ahead is a major source of waste. Officials cannot plan ahead without politicians' support. Politicians live from one election to another and respond to problems rather than anticipate them. By the time they are forced to pay attention, massive expenditure is required and the need for action is so pressing that it is rushed. This procrastination both increases expenditure further and makes it likely much of it will be wasteful or otherwise abortive. Furthermore, if producers do not expect more than a low probability of winning a franchise extension, they will not plan beyond the end of their contracts. Enormous savings could be made if planning were better.

But 'hollowing out' the state may exacerbate this short-term focus rather than improve it. Incentives and possibly new initiatives would be needed to overcome political and bureaucratic myopia. If these are not to come from within government, it probably needs special arrangements with external influences, such as think-tanks. However, to acquire the status needed to make taking the long view a politically attractive option, they would have to resist the tendency to be short-term and, as more often in the United States, combine lobbying skills with integrity and foresight. Such external bodies can influence the provision and production of public services through their regular monitoring and audit of performance in the public interest, and through thinking ahead about problems beyond the next election. It is harder to see how one could achieve the same results by any feasible alteration in politics or within government.[64]

There are several ironies here, since planning was once seen by many as the superior alternative to market provision. Because planning is now almost universally considered to have been a failure wherever it was tried, market solutions have been developed instead. One paradox is that the market-place, particularly the political market-place, is not good at looking ahead. But there is a second paradox at the other end of the time spectrum. The recipes of NPM in all its manifestations would assimilate government and public agencies to the model of the firm; but the greater efficiency and profitability of the firm is achieved by management techniques which try as far as possible for certainty in the medium term, usually by setting budgets for a year ahead and managing by them to the greatest possible extent. As will be argued later, there are various developments within NPM which would drive governments in the same direction. The paradox is that society has greatest need for politicians to prepare for the very long term and to be ready to react to emergencies in the very short, to keep the ship afloat in today's crisis. Without being at all clear on how planning can be supplied within their framework, Osborne and Gaebler recognize a defect here; but NPM prescriptions are likely, if anything, to make government less likely to plan ahead. How to resolve these questions is considered in Chapter 10.

New public management – more for less?

This new approach to the management of government is exciting because it relies on releasing the energies of all participants – government, service providers, service producers, and service consumers. The role of government in most services is to be restricted to supplying money where needed, and, as far as possible, markets should take over the production of services. Wherever possible, there should be more than one provider of every service able to compete for the same clients. Governments should specialize in providing only what they can uniquely provide, and in these areas, government interference is to be reduced to the minimum, stripping away the accretion of costly regulations that have stifled initiative and innovation. In deciding what services to produce and the form they should take, the provider should provide what the consumers or clients say they want, not what politicians think they want. Activities should be run by those most interested in doing so, close to the customer, and by people who share their clients' interests and are free to take whatever initiatives they believe will be best to help the clients they serve. Dunleavy and Hood have usefully simplified its essential principles from the ten just discussed to three: *disaggregation* so that public services may be provided by the smallest appropriate units; *incentivization* so that all concerned may strive for public objectives as efficiently as possible; and *competition*.[65] These principles – both the ten and the three – may to be applied to any area of government. Some application of most of them will discover a radically different approach to every political problem. While permitting the release of pent-up energy, taken together, it is argued, they amount to the marketization of public goods and services, necessary to reduce public expenditure and taxation before their increase can be resumed to found new or improve old initiatives, even at the margin.

What makes this stream of ideas so compelling is that no future government, vexed by fiscal crisis, can escape defining its attitude towards them and embracing them in some form if it is to have a chance of being successful. Conservatives and other right-wing parties have the advantage that ideologically they are often inspired by notions of reducing state power, giving them greater zeal for hollowing out. Other Conservatives of a more romantic and historical kind, stressing the 'One Nation' traditions of their party, dislike the reduction of so much of the state to the managerialism and other trappings of the private sector. Right-wing parties are more likely to gain from a state in which there is a stronger private sector both in electoral support and from its greater readiness to provide the type of society business wants. It is not surprising that conservatives, not only from the extreme right but also the centre, look back at the 1980s and 1990s as years of failure in this regard and urge a redoubling of effort to roll back the state.[66]

On the other hand, left-wing parties need the economies that hollowing out can achieve even more than right-wing governments if they are to achieve their traditional objectives of better public services, greater equality and help for those in need. Osborne and Gaebler, in particular, see it is as among government's missions to define and finance anti-poverty programmes.[67] They also stress equality of opportunity as a goal, particularly in education:

> We believe deeply in equity as a goal – in equal opportunity for all Americans. Some of the ideas expressed in [our] book may strike readers as inequitable. When we talk of making public schools compete, for instance, some fear that the result would be an even more inequitable education system than we have today. But we believe there are ways to use choice and competition to increase the equity in our educational system. And we believe passionately that increased equity is not only just and right, but critical to our success as a nation. In today's global market-place America cannot compete effectively if it wastes 25% of its human resources.[68]

Therefore, NPM can suggest that reinventing government is the only option in both conservative and socialist states, and is consistent with the pursuit of redistributive and other political goals. In 1992 the Gore Commission was set up to achieve as much NPM as possible in the shortest possible time. In every government department and agency, policy units were set up to come up with ideas – which they did in abundance. No previous efficiency exercise on US government had ever attracted the same attention and support.[69] Similarly, one can expect a new left-wing government in Britain, if one were to be elected, to take these ideas as seriously.[70] The British adoption of NPM took place more slowly and has been more enduring. In particular, it did not run into the same problems with the legislature that Gore did. The civil servant who was first responsible for leading the UK's government reform initiatives has gone so far as to say that the British government was 'there long before Osborne and Gaebler re-invented government'.[71] It has been argued that the British agenda was more radical than that of any country except New Zealand, which came closest to a coherent NPM manifesto. The British Prime Minister who backed it, John Major, claimed 'when people want to learn something about reinventing governments, they come to Britain to do so.'[72]

If the increase in efficiency were great enough, which presumes the rigorous and extensive hollowing out of the state by NPM, governments would secure a respite from the effects of fiscal crisis on politics. Moreover, the greater attention to what the consumer wants, implicit in NPM, should make higher tax and public expenditure/GDP ratios politically acceptable. Whatever a government's motive in wishing to deploy increases in public services, it could do it while reducing public expenditure and taxes overall. But un-surprisingly, there are practical, political and ethical difficulties in the way of painlessly realizing better government services with lower expenditure and taxes. There are many issues which need to be considered, wherever changes are made according to NPM principles. Yet experience suggests such consider-ation generally does not occur. In fact, very different solutions have been adopted in Britain, as in most countries, for different public activities. While these differences may be right, it would be largely by chance, because there has been no articulated or integrated approach underpinning what has been done.

It is important, therefore, to consider what may be lost, as well as gained – especially if what is lost in 'hollowing out' the state is widely valued in the public interest – and to consider the consequences before it is too late. If the hollow state can contain costs, improve public services, and raise their quality, other unavoidable consequences may be worthwhile. But where these improvements cannot be achieved, we may end up with gravely unattractive political change without the benefit of enough compensation in improved efficiency or value for money. The remainder of this book assesses the consequences of change along NPM lines.

Notes

1 Gore, quoted in Moe (1994), p. 114.
2 See Aucoin (1990); Pollitt (1990); Hood (1991).
3 For example in Minnesota, Barzelay (1992).
4 Kettl and DiIulio (1995).
5 New Zealand Treasury (1987); see also Hood (1990, 1991), p. 6.
6 Influential were Drucker (1968); Peters and Waterman (1982); Kanter (1983); Peters and Austin (1985).
7 Hood (1991); Barzelay (1992); Osborne and Gaebler (1992); Stewart and Walsh (1992).
8 Rhodes (1994a).
9 Moe (1994), p. 111.
10 A position with which Lord Rayner agrees; Metcalfe and Richards (1987), p. 156.
11 Osborne and Gaebler (1992), pp. xvii–xix.
12 Osborne and Gaebler (1992), p. 22; see also Davies (1992), p. 14.
13 Osborne and Gaebler (1992), pp. xix, xx; but see Leibenstein (1966), although Osborne and Gaebler cite J. B. Say.
14 Graaff (1957), ch. 2; Leibenstein (1966).
15 Osborne and Gaebler (1992), p. xviii.
16 Osborne and Gaebler (1992), pp. 19, 37–9, 84, 126–30, 264–5.
17 Osborne and Gaebler (1992), p. 22.
18 Robbins (1932).
19 DiIulio, Garvey and Kettl (1993), pp. 2–3.
20 Moe (1994), p. 16.
21 Kettl and DiIulio (1995), p. 11.
22 But see Moe (1994), p. 112.
23 Derived from the Webbs (see Ostrom et al. (1961); Foster et al. (1980), pp. 569–70; Boston (1987); Osborne and Gaebler (1992), pp. 25–48; Stewart and Walsh (1992), p. 504).
24 For example, of the Social Market Foundation; see Skidelsky (1989).
25 Savas (1987), pp. 288; Osborne and Gaebler (1992), pp. 25–48.
26 Tocqueville (1946), pp. 198–209.
27 For a hostile view, see Bennett and Di Lorenzo (1989); Wagner (1989). For a more favourable view, see Benton et al. (1989); James (1989).
28 Kettl (1995), p. 34.

29 Davies (1992); see also Peters and Waterman (1982); New Zealand Treasury (1987); Cabinet Office (1991); Barzelay (1992), pp. 7–9; Osborne and Gaebler (1992), pp. 166–94; Stewart and Walsh (1992), p. 507; Metcalfe and Richards (1993).
30 Hayek (1944, 1960); Skidelsky (1989).
31 On the long Swedish tradition in this regard, see Lewis (1993), p. 16.
32 Boston (1987), p. 432; Hood (1991), p. 5.
33 Weiss (1993).
34 Seldon (1977); see also Foster *et al.* (1980), pp. 506–41; Rose (1990).
35 Osborne and Gaebler (1992), p. 196.
36 John Shannon, in Osborne and Gaebler (1992), p. 203; see also Davies (1992), p. 14; Rivlin (1992), p. 16.
37 Boston (1987), p. 434; Barzelay (1992), pp. 102–4; Osborne and Gaebler (1992), pp. 250–1; Waldegrave (1994); Willetts (1994).
38 Barzelay (1992), pp. 77–9; Osborne and Gaebler (1992), p. 182.
39 Skidelsky (1989); Osborne and Gaebler (1992), pp. 185–6.
40 Osborne and Gaebler (1992), pp. xix, 101–4, 185–6; see also Godwin (1993), p. 180ff.
41 Boston (1987), p. 433. The recommendation follows that of many would-be public enterprise reformers, Foster (1971), pp. 29–40.
42 New Zealand Treasury (1987); Savas (1987), pp. 250–73; Hood (1991); Barzelay (1992), p. 9; Osborne and Gaebler (1992), pp. 219–49; Stewart and Walsh (1992), pp. 506–7.
43 For example, Stiglitz (1994), pp. 109–38.
44 Osborne and Gaebler (1992), p. 34.
45 Bennett and Di Lorenzo (1989).
46 Oates (1972), pp. 35–8; Hood (1991); Osborne and Gaebler (1992), pp. 131, 183; Stewart and Walsh (1992).
47 Davies (1992); Osborne and Gaebler (1992), pp. 259–65.
48 Barzelay (1992); Osborne and Gaebler (1992), pp. 276–8.
49 Rivlin (1992), pp. 92–102.
50 Boston (1987); Barzelay (1992), pp. 64–5; Osborne and Gaebler (1992), pp. 276–8.
51 Barzelay (1992); Osborne and Gaebler (1992), pp. 49–75.
52 Boston (1987); New Zealand Treasury (1987); Hood (1991); Barzelay (1992); Osborne and Gaebler (1992), pp. 108–14; Stewart and Walsh (1992).
53 See Kaufman (1976); Mueller (1988).
54 In Osborne and Gaebler (1992), p. 108.
55 Barzelay (1992), pp. viii–ix.
56 Kaufman (1976); Mueller (1988).
57 Rose and Peters (1978), p. 125.
58 Pliatsky (1980).
59 Bagehot (1928), p. 171.
60 Boston (1987); Hood (1991); Barzelay (1992); Osborne and Gaebler (1992); Stewart and Walsh (1992).
61 Hood (1994), pp. 126–7.
62 See DiIulio (1994), p. 4.
63 Osborne and Gaebler (1992), pp. 219–49.
64 Fulton (1968), pp. 57–8; though some planning units survive in British government, they have modest influence on policy because generally hidden within the bureaucracy.

65 Dunleavy and Hood (1994), p. 9.
66 Examples of the first are Duncan and Hobson (1995) and of the second, Patten (1995).
67 Osborne and Gaebler (1992), pp. xviii, 277.
68 See also Osborne and Gaebler (1992), p. xix; also pp. 101–4; and Skidelsky (1989), p. 7.
69 Kettl and DiIulio (1995), pp. 3–5.
70 But see Willman (1994), pp. 3–4.
71 Kemp (1993), p. 21; see also Hood (1991), p. 6; Stewart and Walsh (1992), p. 508; Butler (1994), pp. 263–6.
72 Major (1994), p. 2.

4

Separating provision from production

Just as a sailor is a member of an association, so too is a citizen. Sailors differ
from one another in virtue of the different capacities in which they act: one is a
rower, another pilot, another a look-out; and others again will have other
names in the same sort of way . . . it is clear that the most accurate definition of
the excellence of each sailor will be special to the man concerned . . .

Aristotle[1]

The concept of separating provision from production in government has been
widely acclaimed in Britain and has already been put into effect in many ways
through privatization, competitive tendering and the creation of executive
agencies. It has a longer history than might at first be supposed.[2]

The principle was part of the 1968 Fulton Committee's recommendations that 'the principles of accountable management should be applied to the
organisation of the work of the departments. This means the clear allocation of
responsibility and authority to accountable units with defined objectives.'[3] A
further recommendation was to consider the 'desirability of "hiving off" activities to non-departmental organisations' with the subsequent creation of, for
example, the Property Services Agency to manage the government estate.
Separation is claimed to reduce political interference as well as the influence of
producers and their unions on production, to enable the introduction of market pricing, competition, better management and better accountability, and to
be essential to increase efficiency and reduce public expenditure.

Yet what is meant by 'separation' in government is elusive. This chapter
looks at some of the difficulties that make it problematic. We look first at the
ambiguities over the directions in which power may be expected to flow as a
result of separation, at the impact on the consumer and on ministers' roles and
on some of the tensions between them. We then consider the implications for
other overlapping parts and functions of government.

The seat of power

Most countries have constitutions which define where power lies. It is still
common to brush aside the question of where power resides in Britain by

reference to parliamentary sovereignty. Sovereign power is held legally by the Crown, and in practice by the House of Commons. As a result, as Ferdinand Mount says:

> The Constitution, we are told, is parliamentary supremacy and nothing but parliamentary supremacy; it admits no consideration of natural law or human rights, just as it admits no powers for subordinate or external law-making bodies, except insofar as Parliament has defined and granted such powers. And Parliament itself is a thinned-down version of what it once was, the threefold bundle of Kings, Lords and Commons having given way to a single all powerful body impeded only faintly by the encrustations of tradition.[4]

No law passed by Parliament can prevent its annulment by another law passed by a later Parliament (after going through due procedures which are themselves determinable by the House of Commons). The doctrine remains intact however absurd the lengths to which one takes it.[5] Thus Britain has not lost its sovereignty by joining the European Union, because another Parliament can always withdraw from it, whatever any current or future treaty may state on the indissolubility of provisions binding Britain irreversibly. Similarly, since the independence of any former dominion or colony depends on the 1931 Statute of Westminster or a later statute, a British Parliament could in theory withdraw that independence unilaterally by another Act of Parliament. In practice, the actual power of Parliament depends on whether it has the ability to force withdrawal from Europe, or to deprive a former dominion or colony of independence, as in Rhodesia in the 1960s.

As Mount has pointed out, reliance on parliamentary sovereignty as an explanation of the source of political power has often averted attention in Britain from the actual distribution of power within and outside Westminster and Whitehall, as well as from any need to confront the effects of any alterations in that power distribution. Countries with constitutions appear to have more checks on changes in the distribution of power; but in Britain many of the most important changes in the machinery of government do not require constitutional amendment. Separation, and privatization in particular, has altered the distribution of power within Britain and many other countries by reducing the size and scope of the state. While theoretically Parliament could renationalize without compensation, it has not the actual power to do so, because the resulting decline in international trust in Britain's attitude towards business would force a catastrophic balance-of-payments crisis. Even to alter the system of regulating privatized utilities to one where their profits are at the mercy of the government of the day would produce similar consequences.[6]

Most countries are under similar practical restraints on their power. Whatever the constitutional arrangements, separating provision from production will result in a shift in the distribution of political power, and the likely consequences need to be examined. Sometimes the split is said to be between purchaser and provider, or client and supplier, sometimes between provider and producer. We have used the last terminology in this book.[7]* Whatever the terms used, in countries under the influence of NPM it is current policy for governments to be split into two: a providing (purchasing) function clustering around politicians (ministers) at the top, separated from the producing or service delivery activities at the bottom (traditionally a large part of what is done by government departments or agencies).[8] This distinction, between provider and producer, hides within itself all the principal questions of political philosophy, of sovereignty, rights and political obligation and the separation of powers, as well as difficulties raised by doctrines of parliamentary accountability and ministerial responsibility. In the language of the new approach to public management, the politician is a provider of public goods and services, including political decision- and policy-making. Those goods and services are created for the provider by (public) producers. This split is consistent with a variety of relationships of power between provider and producer; and between them and citizens.

At one extreme the provider (or 'steersman') may be seen as having political power over the producers (or 'oarsmen'), so that their relationship is one of masters and servants, or (more neutrally) principal and agent. The consequential issue then is how the principal controls the agent to get what he wants. At another extreme, citizens may see themselves as the principals, and the politician as their agent, reporting back their collective demands. While this relationship is only truly practical in the smallest polity, the rhetoric of the politician as 'servant of the people' implies that in some sense politicians are supposed to give citizens what they want. At a third extreme, the provider may be the customer of the producer, with both engaging voluntarily, and maybe competitively, in a commercial relationship. Such relationships exist within, and are affected by, a variable framework of law. For example, the first case could approach a regime dominated by politicians, even an authoritarian regime; the second could imply a direct democracy of an Aristotelian or New England kind, where every citizen can participate in government; while the third might imply a regime of utmost reliance on the market economy.[9] The first has an affinity to where the British regime may now be heading with its trust in the private-sector analogy of a big business framework; while the second reflects those NPM exemplars who see good government as far as possible as the province of small local government; and the third resembles the tendency in New Zealand, with its emphasis on a polycentric market system.

These possibilities are not merely theoretical. It is vital to ask who gains power from separation. Will citizens gain in political influence as voters, or will they gain in economic power as consumers, because the public goods and services they obtain as individuals are more to their liking? Or do politicians

---

* Many other terms are used; all suffer from ambiguities to be explored in this chapter. To talk of providers as purchasers or being 'engaged in procurement' emphasizes limited aspects of what they do, while 'securing provision' seems clumsy. Production, supply and service delivery can be used almost interchangeably, depending on context.

increase their power at the expense of the old bureaucracy or new decentralized agencies? Or do they gain at the expense of the voters who lose power over politicians because of a decline in the relevant powers of Parliament? Might the bureaucrats and agencies themselves gain power at the expense of politicians or the electorate, or both?

To explore this, let us look at the case where the Benefits Agency, which administers the social benefit system, is separated from its host department. Its sole immediate customer is the social services minister, who is a monopsony purchaser of its services, and to whom it is a monopoly seller. It may be assumed that neither can do without the other. Long-standing economic theorems demonstrate that when a monopsony buyer faces a monopoly seller, the quantity of what is bought and sold, its price, and the monopolist's profits, are indeterminate within a wide range.[10]

That a parliament remains formally sovereign confuses the issue, since the truth that the law can always be changed does not itself affect the relative power of the minister and the agency. The minister will gain if the agency is more submissive than when it was distanced from him by layers of bureaucracy. The adoption of more businesslike methods may also enable politicians to impose their will on government activity to a greater extent than previously. But in not very different circumstances the converse may hold. An agency removed from direct ministerial and official power, with its associated labyrinthine controls and old customs, may develop greater coherence and internal solidarity, as the UK nationalized industries did when they were set up at a distance from day-to-day ministerial control; or US agencies when distanced from congressional and direct presidential control. But equally, the experience with the nationalized industries suggests in time they are as likely to use that greater independence to become more inert and inefficient, serving their own short-term producer interests rather than those of consumers or ministers.[11]

In the course of such a sequence of changes as comprises a process of hollowing out, the likely redistribution of power will depend much upon the attitude taken towards markets and competition. Separation is likely to be much more effective in producing greater efficiency if there is a genuine and realized belief in the benefits of competition. Take, for example, the transport ministry hiving off the licensing agency whose job it is to issue licences upon a basis the ministry determines. Such a relationship is basically one of command or political dominance: of principal and agent. By splitting the same agency into a number of agencies, each of which can issue the same licence in competition with the others, the principal has many agents. He may choose between them according to their efficiency, or any other criteria. The relationship will therefore become more commercial, at least on the principal's side. As a third possibility, if these agencies are also able to perform similar functions for other parts or levels of government so that they have a choice of provider, the relationship between them all becomes more purely commercial.

The less monopoly power with provider and producer, the more the position will approximate to a market. Hence the supreme importance of competition in affecting the distribution of power. Yet central government providers, at least at the highest levels, are commonly wholly monopolistic (and they frequently insist on one producer when there could be several). Therefore, there is a very great difference between the efficiency case for separation if competition is to result from it and where monopoly is to be retained (where greater efficiency will demand regulation and incentivization).[12] The creation of nationalized industries separate from government in the UK did not create efficient entities *per se*, though it gave politicians more power over them than over private industries; but the creation of a bilateral arm's-length relationship, though it reduced the opportunities for efficiency, did reduce ministerial powers over them. Because ministers could not turn to competition for what they wanted, they had to treat with them on the nationalized industries' terms. Competition diminishes that power.

At a more fundamental level, there is an analogy with another separation – the historic, often constitutional separation of powers which cuts across these new ideas of separation. As argued by Locke, Montesquieu and the authors of *The Federalist*, and exemplified in the US Constitution, the main functions of government must be divided to avoid the abuse of power: as it seemed at the time, the legislature, judiciary and executive most needed to be kept apart to avoid despotic power becoming concentrated in any one. Even in the United States that separation has not been and cannot be complete. Moreover, its simplicity is complicated by various other activities. Even in the hollow state the main activities of government are generally separated for similar reasons: deciding what is to be provided; deciding what taxes are to be raised; determining how public expenditure is allocated; contract management and inspection; accounting and performance monitoring; ensuring appropriate standards of behaviour; to which must be added the regulatory functions of the state. All these powers and duties may also, by statute, be undertaken by local government. Related processes are: policy- and plan-making; promoting legislation and secondary legislation; raising taxation and controlling public expenditure; providing public goods and services; producing some public goods and services; monitoring and securing accountability to the law and other requirements. All these processes may relate to the provision of goods and services. For example, policy-making may result in a published plan or document, which may act as a vehicle for persuasion or leadership; it may be a prelude to legislation if the legislature can be persuaded to pass it; or government may go straight to promoting legislation if it does not believe a policy plan or other document is needed. Whatever course is followed, the consequence may be new or changed provision or production of goods and services, which may then require new public finance arrangements, and changes in monitoring or enforcement action. The journey from policy-making to enforcement may take many routes, and at any one time government may be travelling only over part of a given route. To prevent the abuse of power or corruption, a case, similar to the traditional constitutional separation of powers, can be argued for some separation within government of these activities. In practice, in most administrations, formal separation has been less important than have been less formal approaches. However, as NPM progresses the argument strengthens for reinforcing formal and informal separation of powers by more systematic arrangements adapted to the new circumstances.

Thus the meaning to be given to 'separation' depends on how the relationship between provider and producer is defined, and upon the extent of competition. The same, or similar, words can be consistent with very different power relationships. The chapters that follow look at four models. Each can vary in the extent of competition created. The first three, pure privatization, contracting out and the decentralization of provision are put forward as models of separation (though they can overlap). The fourth, the creation of executive agencies, is less predictable in its achievement of separation because less certain in its specification. And in Britain there have been a number of public examples of real difficulty with the relationship.

Underlying these possibilities are two very different principles. The motive for separating provision from production may be a genuine desire to detach an activity from the everyday control of, and interference from, government. The intention is that, in the public interest, the activity can move into a self-reliant context, make itself more efficient, and give citizens and consumers the service they want. Alternatively, the motive may be more 'political', to increase the power of ministers by stripping away the protection from detailed intervention provided by layers of bureaucracy and bureaucratic procedures.

Consumers, clients, taxpayers, electors, citizens and ministers

As the metaphor of steering and rowing was first used the concept of separation was a seemingly straightforward one, between government whose skills were planning and procurement, and the private sector whose skill was its 'uncontested ability to produce and deliver the goods'.[13] Yet this distinction is confused by another between consumer and producer, which is also widely supported by advocates of NPM.

In recent years there have been growing demands that the views of consumers of public services should be better understood and reflected in political decision-making.[14] Therefore, one criterion by which separation is to be judged is by how far it helps the consumer. Indeed, the rhetoric that public services exist to serve the consumer has become almost standard.[15] When such views become public policy, as they have in Britain through the Citizens' Charter movement introduced by John Major, they are welcome.[16] Yet there are problems that arise from the different roles that people may have as consumers, other interested parties, clients, taxpayers, electors, and more generally as citizens; as well as from the functions politicians are to have in relation to these roles.[17] As a consequence, politicians cannot in any simple sense be regarded as the ultimate principals. In this section we consider some of these problems.

Eligibility and rationing

The first set of issues exists because of scarcity. One might suppose that scarcity need not arise in any public service in which receipts at least covered costs since supply could be expanded to meet demand. This does not always hold. Among the principal reasons for the privatization of telecommunications in Britain was that government felt unable to fund the huge sums of capital needed to meet great changes in technology and demand, just as the need to spend vast amounts of capital to meet environmental concerns was a major reason for water privatization.

However, since most public services are not priced to cover costs they generally have to be rationed. Even services which are generally meant to be available on demand, such as unemployment and other social security benefits, are still rationed in the sense that the value of what is provided is less than what the recipients would prefer. There can never be enough public housing or welfare residential accommodation to clear the market at the price at which it is on offer. Neither are public health or police services enough to meet demand. In such cases – and most public services are like them – politicians either set the rules of eligibility and entitlement or they, or their officials, take the rationing decisions. In practice, the greater the willingness to listen to consumers the more likely it is that they will demand better and more readily available services. The need for rationing is likely to increase. Better services will stimulate more demand so increasing further the political need to ration supply. Either consumers' preferences are to some extent overridden or there is a group of consumers who receive service and another group which is queuing. Politicians may exercise their rationing power in the public interest, or 'politically'.

Other interests

Because of externalities – many public services affect others than the direct consumers – it is not always easy to decide who the consumers are who are to be sovereign. Decisions on roads and road improvement affect not only those who run private and commercial motor vehicles, but also pedestrians and cyclists, sufferers from injury, or other environmental impacts. Because all these interests normally cannot be mediated through the price mechanism, those that are not must either be neglected or have their interests taken into account by politicians or officials who override direct consumers' preferences in doing so. Again they may attempt this in the public interest, or be 'political'.

Customers and clients

There are services where it is not obvious that the direct customers' interests are to be preferred. One man's policy is another man's imprisonment. Even within the resources available, prisoners do not determine their own comfort levels; children, or their parents, do not set what is taught in schools. Many kinds of expert determine what the clients of many public services receive. Those who receive such public services may experience them in more or less pleasant surroundings, with greater or less courtesy, but in many cases such factors are tangential to the main purposes of the service. Other activities such as defence, foreign, macroeconomic and trade policy have consumers who in the large are too remote or inexpert to have influence over what is done for them. Again the politician, relying on expert advice, chooses for them.

Taxpayers, electors and citizens

The notion that in general public services should be designed with the consumers' interest in mind is a tenable and an attractive one, but it is not the only possibility. Taxpayers funding such services may be held to have an interest in how 'their' money is spent. In the past the idea that taxpayers had a right over how tax money should be spent led to paupers and pauper children being put into uniforms as a recognition of their status and as an incentive to do better. Whether there should be such taxpayer 'rights' is not a matter of fact, but of opinion which may be reflected in law. However, there remains an understandable argument that simply to give money to the underclass to spend as its members please may increase social problems for many members of that underclass as well as for other members of the community with which that underclass comes into contact. This attitude is found in some quarters of the Moral Right.

Politicians may be asked to act on behalf of the taxpayer in such matters but there may also be a democratic presumption that democratically elected governments have the right to override consumer preferences whenever they decide to do so. There must at least be a risk that wider citizen participation will raise unfulfillable expectations; and the remoter those taking the rationing decisions are from those whom the decisions affect, the less likely these decisions are likely to be acceptable.[18] Asserting that public services are to be run for their consumers is not without its problems.

Nevertheless, what is observable in many governments is a trend towards giving greater weight to the interest of service consumers and less to service producers in designing public services. There are four further strands of thought worth distinguishing. The first three reflect different 'public interest' approaches to the running of government (as discussed in Chapter 2). The fourth reflects the alternative approach, which sees government itself as a market-place and the winning of the 'political' battle as sovereign.

The first strand of thinking sees government as a veil, obscuring the actual wishes of the consumer, arrogating power to itself and then misusing it. Thus the overriding aim is to return choice to the consumer by the privatization of government activity. At a Hayekian extreme, such is the distrust of government that only the barest minimum of public activities are left: defence, law and the policeman.[19] Redistribution is either out altogether, or the minimum needed to look after the poorest or most unfortunate. This point of view is most commonly defended on the ground of the inalienable right of those who have property to keep it (except in so far as they choose to be charitable).[20] It may be further bolstered by a second argument that unless individuals are able to keep their wealth and their incomes, their incentive to maximize both, and thereby create wealth and jobs for others, will be damaged. In this context separation mostly means complete separation from government. Privatization makes customers of us all.

A less extreme view would argue that most public goods and services could be privatized, but that politicians must be expected to retain the right and democratic duty to superimpose other objectives: in particular, to redistribute wealth and income directly or through the provision of subsidized goods and services. Separation in this view means the complete separation from government of activities not needed for redistribution and other political purposes, combined with separation within government, where it seems appropriate, to enable the activities concerned to be pursued more efficiently. We discuss both in the next chapter. The last is also a mainspring of the need for contractorization, to be discussed in Chapter 6. The implications of this second, *rationalizing*, strand include a need to clarify the respects in which people are to be regarded as customers and clients, how other interests are to be reflected and what rights, if any, belong to people as taxpayers, electors and citizens, and how they are to be expressed and mediated.[21]

The third strand is *pragmatic*.[22] It reflects, and does not want to change, the often haphazard mixture of objectives governments tend to have for different services: in part a wish to provide the public goods, services and policies citizens want as consumers; in part paternalistic, expressing what politicians believe citizens ought to want; in part redistributive, helping some citizens at the expense of others; and in part also politically motivated, to help win elections or otherwise secure party or personal political power. The adoption of modern management techniques is seen as enabling these objectives to be achieved more efficiently.

In this context separation is broadly seen as having two consequences. First, it enables producers to adopt modern management techniques because their activities can have better-defined objectives. Second, the hope is that the providers can behave with the discipline shown by the procurement arms of large companies, yet still retain the variety and flexibility of objectives politicians expect. Politicians hope, or assume, that changes in government structure or in the powers of ministers will not go further. But retaining traditional powers to intervene is hard to combine with appreciable changes in efficiency. Furthermore, the objectives governments require from those who supply public goods and services are not as straightforward and unvarying as are the commercial objectives of firms. Thus, this approach tends to run away from the fact that politics and political control will not remain the same after separation. It will be most exemplified in what we have to say about agencies in Chapters 8 and 9.

All these strands of thinking reflect a 'public interest' view of politics, namely that politicians are able to decide what mixture of policies they adopt, and do so to reflect the public interest as they see it. By implication they retain or win power because what they do, or promise to do, is in the public interest. But the fourth attitude, by contrast, regards politicians as determined by, rather than determining, what happens. Thus, it is a 'political' theory (or a number of related theories) about why politicians make decisions, rather than a freely chosen position. As described in Chapter 2, politicians (and officials) are to an extent motivated by party or personal 'political' interest. Members of legislatures, political parties, individual ministers and governments use their power to achieve these ends. Whatever politicians' behaviour, it remains a fundamental question to ask of any existing or proposed separation not just how it will affect the consumer, but also how it will affect politicians' ability to realize their own 'political' interest.

Another fundamental question to ask is how separation may be expected to affect ministers' power and their ability to make changes. In this context, the metaphor of 'steering and rowing' has a double resonance.[23] First there is the difference between exercising power to move the ship of state, and choosing the direction in which it will go. But what the cox of a boat actually does is more complicated than this distinction implies – in a race he exhorts, he shouts, and corrects faults in the rowers, who may themselves through their biases and actions affect the direction of the boat. He may be part trainer as well as steersman. As Plato said in one of the first political uses of the metaphor: a state is well governed when a well-trained captain steers, but there is anarchy when all the seamen try to seize the helm.[24] On the other hand, when practised oarsmen who are used to each other, and not under pressure, row a course they know well, the cox may need to deal only with the unexpected, or become a figurehead entertaining his self-reliant crew.

The state can usefully have a catalytic function, that is to start and steer a new initiative with seedcorn money and then leave it to the 'rowers' to carry on unaided. But there are many state functions – inspection, some aspects of regulation, enforcement, audit, techniques of production improvement and training – which are almost entirely routine, scarcely ever needing political guidance, let alone catalysis. Another difficulty with the metaphor is that it suggests the politician is steering only one boat. A more accurate metaphor may be that of a gang of people leaping from log to log in a fast-moving stream, steering a log past an obstacle here, breaking a log-jam there. There are times when matters need steering and there are times when many can do well without it: fortunately, because politicians, much as some may try, do not have time to steer everything. But whether and when steering is needed is often far from predictable, and not easily defined.

Underlying this is a further difficulty where the metaphor of government as a ship lets us down because it presumes that steersman and rowers have the same destination. This does not hold because the agent may not have the same aim as the principal but may have the power to frustrate the politician partially or even completely. Another difference between their interests is better re-flected by the ship as aircraft carrier. Within wide limits the admiral may not care where the carrier is in the ocean. His interest is to launch various aircraft on missions, some of which may be premeditated while others may occur on the spur of the moment. In practice, what interests politicians is often tangen-tial to the statutory and otherwise main purposes and activities of government or another public body.

Confronted by this complexity, and by so many bodies and aspects of politics for which no parallel can be found in business life, it is perhaps un-surprising that writers about the new approach to public management decide to simplify this tangle of relationships through a more businesslike, if heroic, crystallization of roles into those of 'providers' and 'producers'.

This desire for simplification has led both writers and practitioners to postulate that efficient government depends upon establishing commercial and businesslike relations between politicians, as quasi-customers, and producers. The influence of American specialists in contractual economics, such as Williamson, is particularly marked in the New Zealand reforms but it is latent in all.[25] Another idea is that citizens elect the steersman to do the job: they do not want to do it themselves. The role of politicians is to mediate between producers and citizens: they *provide* packages of public goods and services for the citizens, choosing what groups of citizens would want if they were able to choose for themselves, or what citizens ought to want, in areas where they are relatively inexperienced.

If, however, as *realpolitik* would suggest, the purpose of government is to provide citizens with what they want so that politicians are elected (or re-elected) then attitudes to consumers, and the approach to separation, will differ. Politicians will put first those consumers whose votes are most likely to win or lose elections. Starting with the traditional floating voter, others learn how to use their votes to exert influence, being drawn into lobbies and pressure groups to this end. Some local politicians become more important to national govern-ment because of the existence of marginal constituencies. The provision of public goods and services is increasingly targeted to serve electoral and other political ends. Party and personal ambitions are easily confused. Even safe constituencies and supportive lobby groups cannot be ignored, because such behaviour may then alienate votes. Nor can politicians go too far in neglecting those who will never vote for them, for fear there is some level of selfishness which voters will find intolerable.

From this 'political' standpoint, separation could be in part a way of getting rid of activities in which there is no political interest, or of areas from which the opposition might derive benefit (if returned to power), while keep-ing everything with the reverse characteristics. The purpose of government reform need not be to create more areas in which citizens can make their own choices or to extend the executive's power to act in the public interest, but rather to extend the machinery through which politicians can exert their influence to win elections and advance their careers – mainly through the power of the purse and by patronage. Extending the range of contracts may create more opportunities for corruption. In this context, separation may be a mechanism for increasing rather than reducing 'political' power. Paradoxically, however, privatization (which is complete and absolute separation) is an irrational course of action for those who live by politics at least in the long term, since it reduces their political power and opportunities for patronage. By contrast, contractorization, agencification and, in some of its manifestations, decentralization can provide more opportunities for such influence.

Policy and administration

Misunderstandings can arise because of a false analogy between separation of provision and production, and another use of the term: separation between policy and administration. The modern American treatment of this separation derives from Woodrow Wilson, who, then a professor of political science, noted the failure of the classic doctrine of the separation of powers to protect American public life from jobbery and corruption in the years after the Civil War. In an influential article which helped shape the development of US government administration, Wilson argued for the separation of politics from administration.[26] He was influenced by a forgotten German political philosopher, Karl Bluntschli, who in the course of a panoramic history of the development of government made a point of some subtlety in 1852.[27] He noted the influence of Montesquieu's opinion that separation of legislative, executive and judicial powers was necessary for civil liberty. He then seized on an ambiguity in the common use of the term 'executive':

> It is not true that the government only has to execute in particular cases what the legislature has established in general. As a rule a law is not executed (carried out), but observed and applied . . . The rules which the legislator sanctions, the principles which he expresses, are respected by the government as the legal and constitutional limits of its conduct, but within these limits it decides freely: treats with other states, appoints commissions of inquiry, adopts measures for the maintenance of order, furthers what tends to the public weal, nominates functionaries, controls the army.[27]

Wilson drew on that insight to develop a further separation of powers within the executive between policy and administration. The political part of the executive was to use its discretion within the law to develop policy, which he saw primarily as rules which it was then for the career civil servant to execute as far as possible without discretion.[28] Policy was to be the realm of politicians, who were to be expected to have their 'political' and other interests. The administration and execution of policy were to be left to a career civil service which as far as possible should be immune from corrupt or party influence.[29] If politicians within the executive were limited to rule-making and other policy-making, he believed it would 'dissociate administration from the dysfunctional consequences of the spoils system'.[30] The main point of Woodrow Wilson's position, as it became reflected in US public administration, has been to protect a bureaucracy from what was assumed to be an inherently self-interested, party-interested or even corrupt 'political' level.[31] But one consequence of the process of legislative politics in devising rules to guide administrative discretion is the manufacture of a vast quantity of rules which constitute the very regulation from which deregulation is now sought.

More fundamentally, as countless students of political science and administration have been taught, the distinction between policy and administration cannot be sustained practically or logically.[32] The danger, already recognized by some critics of the Clinton–Gore reforms in the United States, is that it is being transformed into a different doctrine by which politicians become not only the legislators, the policy-makers and the rule-makers, but also the entrepreneurs, leaving implementation, in a much restricted sense, to the civil servants.[33]

Another practical consideration is that, since the time of the Roman republic, well-run states have distinguished between the type of government needed in normal times, which can be reasonably slow and deliberative, and the more autocratic, rapid powers needed in wars or other emergencies. Something which is normally so routine and unpolitical as to escape ministerial attention entirely may, through a scandal or an emergency, shoot so far up the political agenda as to engage cabinet or prime ministerial attention. Hence the force of the aircraft-carrier analogy. But the discretion to vary the way issues are handled may be hard to combine with greater efficiency, and more difficult to achieve after separation has taken place.

The attractions of being able to vary the direction and intensity of ministers' interests are very great in a parliamentary democracy, and there is a lingering belief among ministers that it is possible to achieve both organizational separation and flexibility of ministerial interest. Hence the new executive agencies are expected both to be separated and to stay under ministerial command while ministers retain powers to delegate the activity of provision as and when they please. In practice, this incomplete separation raises many difficulties, as will be discussed in Chapter 9.

The other arms of government

We have spoken thus far as if the minister were the provider, but that may not be the case. The provider may be the legislature – it depends on what the law states. However, in modern states, legislatures rarely have the time, attentiveness to detail or, therefore, inclination to be the provider. Usually the provider is the executive, operating with a framework of law established by the legislature. But the law may give that function to another level of government – regional, or local; and within central government, to an executive president, a cabinet or to particular ministers. In a federal system, the level of government that is the provider is usually well defined, but even in the United States, the use of federal grants and legal powers has increasingly encroached upon state and local freedom to provide. Central governments usually retain real and financial powers even over elected agencies. In Britain, as a unitary state, relations between central and local government are variable, and even fluid, over short periods. Sometimes local authorities have very little administrative discretion over what is provided, sometimes much.

It is still common for politicians to establish some activities at arm's length so that they should not be held responsible for their decisions. Among such activities in Britain are bodies which have traditionally been channels for subsidies to the arts, the national heritage, broadcasting, museums and galleries, and the British Council. More recently these numbers have been increased to include bodies responsible for funding education and for carrying out training at local level. As will appear in Chapter 8, many quangos and other public bodies fall into the category where politicians decide to delegate provision to another person or body or to divide the task of provision, only intervening when they have a special reason for doing so or when a particular decision is embarrassing or outrageous, but retaining accountability for the use of public funds as they must.

There is a real distinction between such bodies designed deliberately to distance ministers from decisions about provision and those, such as executive agencies, which are primarily concerned with production. But the increasing pressure for greater public accountability of quangos and the development of a more systematic approach to management is blurring this distinction. Increasingly, all such 'arm's-length' bodies are being treated as if they were in a contractual relationship with ministers and their departmental officials.

The Woodrow Wilson and Haldane models

There is another fundamental problem with separation. The Wilson model in the United States can be seen as encouraging the notion that there should be separation between politicians and administrators, with the latter concentrating on implementation. Despite the presence of the same doctrine in discussions of ministerial relations with nationalized industries and more recently with executive agencies, it is contrary to the British philosophy of public administration which does not recognize such a separation of politician from civil servant.

The Northcote–Trevelyan report, which effectively established the modern British civil service, defined the role of civil servants in the following terms:

> the Government of the country [cannot] be carried out without the aid of an efficient body of permanent officers, occupying a position duly subordinate to that of the Ministers who are directly responsible to The Crown and to Parliament, yet possessing sufficient independence, character, ability and experience to be able to advise, assist, and to some extent, influence those who are from time to time set over them.[34]

One of the best and most influential discussions of the distinctive British model of ministerial and civil service integration can be found in Haldane's report on the machinery of government in 1918.[35] He argued that, unlike the German or the American systems, the British embodied a system not of rules but of advice. As cabinet ministers constitutionally still acted as advisers to the sovereign, so they in turn were advised by the civil service. As advisers they can advise a minister on anything and there is no need to separate their powers. Among the advice a minister must expect from civil servants is advice on the relevant facts of a case, relevant precedents and relevant law. Thus the civil service is likely to curb the exercise of any arbitrary power by ministers. In theory and largely in practice, civil servants are privy to almost all decisions ministers make, able and encouraged to advise them on every aspect of that discretion, not only in terms of their meeting of their own political objectives but also as a safeguard against illegality and impropriety. Since the Northcote–Trevelyan reforms, this has been the corner-stone of the British administrative tradition, and it could not be more different from the Wilsonian principle. It has also proved more workable. Any separation, by creating agencies or other arm's-length bodies, creates uncertainties for the maintenance of the Haldane principle, an important issue throughout this book.

To try to dissolve the complex relationships of modern government into two – provider and producer – is thus a tremendous over-simplification. Just as it is tempting to rely on parliamentary sovereignty as the source of all political power, so it is tempting to believe that somehow, somewhere, there must be some single authority which has the ultimate power of decision over provision. But government is not like that. There may be a pyramid of providers: legislature over minister over one or more divisions of departments or executive agencies to which the producers actually relate. By setting a framework within which the subsidiary level operates, each layer may give a different discretion to the one below. At each level the controls may be tight and well defined, approximating to a principal and agent relationship, or loose, allowing substantial latitude in interpretation and diversity in provision and production. There may also be other relationships, where the Treasury and other departments or agencies may have powers, for example over appointments and financial authority, differing in nature, and in how they are exercised, from those with which private-sector bodies have to cope in commercial markets.[36] Thus a prerequisite for separation is some clarification of those roles and relationships. They can be distinguished into those that have to do with the efficiency with which public services are provided, given their objectives, and those that concern other matters such as regulation, probity and accountability to Parliament.

Such complication (and at times confusion) of roles cannot make for efficiency, so it is natural to ask what political or other purposes are served by the patchwork of overlapping and conflicting powers that constitute modern government. The explanation is to a large extent historical and accidental, having little to do with achieving efficiency but more to do with the reasons why the bodies concerned were established in the first place. Hence the appearance of confusion and entanglement relative to business, which encourages the adoption of the business analogy among those who argue for reform.

There are some resemblances between the network of relationships in government and what is found within commercial firms and in formal alliances between firms. For example, vertical layering of provision within departments and their subordinate bodies resembles ways in which those who run companies delegate responsibility for procurement or exercise either financial or strategic oversight over divisions and subsidiary companies. Similarly relations between government departments can be seen as akin to those between businesses in the same group, where the overarching board is the Cabinet and the finance function is the Treasury.

From this standpoint, separation can be seen as one aspect of a process which does not readily fit with the needs of politicians who steer and balance, but tries to reflect within government certain maxims of modern commercial life: the need for well-defined objectives and clear responsibility for every activity and at all levels; a clear distinction between executive responsibility and support functions; appropriate management information; and proper incentives for good performance. In such a context separation is a feature of the organization even a monopoly might choose to adopt when introducing more businesslike methods – we look at this incomplete separation in greater depth in Chapter 8. Undoubtedly such changes can greatly increase the efficiency of government operations, but undoubtedly, like all monopolies, protected from competition, they will continue to have the seeds of their own inefficiency within them. One management style may not suit all types of relationships.

However, business organization is an incomplete analogy. The structures and procedures of government have developed over time for very different reasons. In the private sector there are basically two alternatives. One may externalize an activity, in which case the relationship will be one of contract in all except the simplest circumstances. Or one may internalize it when it becomes one of command: however much authority may be delegated, it can always be drawn back to the centre when the centre judges it necessary. What limits abuse of central power is the simplicity of private-sector objectives, which aids transparency within a firm, and the strength of competition. But in government and the public sector, the alternatives need not be so clear-cut.

Administration and the law

It is an important feature of the British system of government that the present patchwork of overlapping powers and functions serves a constitutional purpose in acting as a brake on the exercise of political power. Law performs a different function for government than for ordinary citizens or firms, particularly in states such as Britain where government is traditionally the only initiator of important legal change. Any need to change the law becomes a brake slowing down government's ability to do what it likes. But especially where political parties exchange power frequently or a party remains so long in power that its ability to change the law is almost unchecked, well-established processes of public administration which provide further checks and balances on the exercise of political power are often just as significant brakes on change (if not more so) as the need to get a bill through the legislature. Separation may well affect these relationships, reducing the impact of those checks and balances. While benefiting from the legitimacy and other qualities politicians have to offer, the activities politicians are responsible for may need to be protected from their ignorance, limited competence, lack of deliberation, petulance, self- or party interest. One result of that diffusion of power has been to test ministers' intentions and resolve in pursuing substantial change, as well as its analytical foundations, by submitting it to the questioning of civil servants and of pressure groups outside the government machine. Before the Thatcher years, such a testing of change was further implicit in the workings of the corporatist state, with its multitude of trade, labour, industrial and other associations and lobbies, which had established an expectation of being consulted before any major changes in the law, or in ministerial behaviour.[37] As will become apparent, the new Americanized lobby system, which has replaced it, has disturbed these checks and balances profoundly.

In addition, the many-layered relationships within government have protected executive activities at the bottom of departments from all but the most deliberate and persistent ministerial interference. The very absence of the disciplines, control and incentives which enable the board of a business to effect its will at any time has acted as a protection against ill-considered and conflicting change, though sometimes galling to ministers in a hurry. These safeguards have reinforced constitutional and legal protection against over-rapid change, especially when governments alternate. But they have been eroded by the way some executive agencies have been created and by the thinning down of the civil service role in relation to them.[38]

A result of separation at too high a level is that people who are providers or otherwise policy-makers are to be found on both sides of the line of separation – thus perpetuating the problem discussed earlier of the pyramiding of provision with unclear definition of roles. In theory, separation could come even right at the top, between ministers and permanent secretary, and leave departments intact, though in New Zealand, where such policy contracts exist, ministers have found a need for experts to advise on drawing them up and implementing them.[39] An example of this in Britain was in the establishment of the prison service as an executive agency where the Home Secretary had no policy advice capability outside the agency itself – with damaging consequences, as we shall see in Chapter 9. Whatever and wherever restructuring takes place, ministers (under a centralized system) are seen as the providers but have neither the skills nor the time for the activity of provision, and need support. So some civil servants must be among the providers. The greater the number of agencies sponsored by a department, the less ministers can reserve all significant decisions to themselves, and the more delegation there will be to officials. In practice, therefore, there is frequently fuzzy separation, so that agencies themselves take many of the decisions on what services they provide.

If a contractual regime is to be acceptable to producers or their senior staff, certainly in so far as they are private firms, charities or autonomous bodies, they will expect to be protected to the same extent as private firms normally are in the course of business. Otherwise there will be suspicion that sooner or later they will be used to enhance political power, at their own expense. This suspicion, like other uncertainties, will make producers reluctant to make investments and enter into any contractual arrangements which they see as depending on ministerial whim. To overcome such reluctance, they will require higher profits to reimburse them for risk, so reducing potential public expenditure savings. Genuine separation requires certainty in these matters.

Thus a further set of questions needs to be asked about any separation – where should separation take place? What effect will it have on other relationships with government and with Parliament; is a business analogy the right way to resolve these relationships, or do they serve other public purposes? Is the business analogy appropriate for all types of relationship?

Separation raises more complicated issues than is often recognized if efficiency is to be combined with the safeguards consumers and good government need.

Notes

1 Aristotle, quoted in Barker (1946), p. 101.
2 Foster *et al.* (1980), pp. 569–70 derived it from Ostrom *et al.* (1961), p. 839, whose source was Webb (1963).
3 Fulton (1968), pp. 61–2.
4 Mount (1992), pp. 32–3.
5 Mount (1992), pp. 62–5.
6 Foster (1992), esp. ch. 10.
7 Savas (1987), p. 60.
8 See, for example, Major (1994).
9 Barker (1946), pp. 292–3.
10 Cournot (1838); Edgeworth (1881).
11 On US agencies, Niskanen (1971); on UK nationalized industries, Foster (1992), ch. 3.
12 See Hirschmann (1970).
13 Savas (1987), pp. 287–91.
14 Potter (1988); Barzelay (1992); Davies (1992); Osborne and Gaebler (1992).
15 Barzelay (1992), p. 182.
16 Cabinet Office (1991).
17 See Peters (1993), p. 56.
18 Ranson and Stewart (1994), pp. 122–32.
19 Hayek (1960); see also Gray (1989), pp. 20–30; Skidelsky (1989), p. 14.
20 See, for example, Nozick (1974).
21 See Harden (1992).
22 See, for example, Cabinet Office (1991).
23 Savas (1987), p. 290.
24 Cornford (1941), p. 190.

25 See Williamson (1975).
26 Wilson (1887).
27 Bluntschli (1898), pp. 518–22.
28 Thomas (1978), pp. 10ff.
29 Wilson (1887), pp. 213–14.
30 Thomas (1978), p. 33.
31 See Barzelay (1992), p. 4.
32 Appleby (1946).
33 See Aucoin (1990), pp. 126–7.
34 The Northcote–Trevelyan report was presented to Parliament in 1853 and is reprinted in Fulton (1968), pp. 108–19. This quotation is from p. 108.
35 Haldane (1918); see also Thomas (1978) esp. pp. 33–41.
36 See TCSC (1991), p. xxxi.
37 Middlemass (1979).
38 See Harden (1992).
39 Boston (1992).

5

Complete separation: social objectives and regulation of privatization

Privatisation . . . unfortunately summons forth images from a deep reservoir and causes misunderstanding, premature polarisation and shrill arguments that are beside the point more often than not.

Savas[1]

Privatization and other forms of denationalization can sever the Gordian knot of tangled relationships between provision and production. Most of the criteria discussed in Chapter 3 for reinventing government are met. Privatization produces the greatest possible detachment from politics, as set out in Chapter 4. The consumer is identified unequivocally as the economic consumer. Indeed, even before privatization, but with it in prospect, UK utilities became more customer-oriented.[2] Replacing complicated political by simpler market relationships may solve the efficiency problem. It is often consistent with competition or the creation of competition. If not, some of the same stimulus to efficiency can be achieved through regulation. Privatization results in the reduction of public expenditure and borrowing, and usually in less taxation. It reduces the powers and influence of ministers and of the state. Privatization is a readily defensible ingredient in three of the four attitudes towards government discussed in Chapter 4. It is crucial to the first, or Hayekian, view which would reduce the state to a minimum, and also to the second which would confine public activities to what cannot be better done by the private sector but allow redistribution in the public interest. It has some place in the third, pragmatic view as it has developed in recent years, since politicians of both right- and left-wing parties have now widely recognized privatization as an acceptable policy – although it is frequently and wrongly identified only with right-wing attitudes. On the other hand, it is hard to see the fourth attitude, that is, 'political' interest, as benefiting from privatization except in extreme circumstances because it reduces political power except in the shortest run.

The scope for privatizing provision

Any form of separation that departs from privatization involves greater scope for politics. It results in less efficiency and less consumer satisfaction given the existing distribution of wealth and income.[3] Therefore, to reduce the 'political' aftermath of separation to as small a compass as possible, the logical first step is to decide what can be provided and produced privately and what must be provided publicly. New public management seems strongly influenced by economic theory which has a straightforward analysis of the point: there are privately and publicly provided goods and services.[4] Private goods and services are priced and mostly sold on to reasonably competitive markets. Some firms selling private goods may have substantial monopoly power. If monopoly is likely to persist, it should probably be regulated in the interest of economic efficiency and of consumers. Some other goods and services are provided or produced by third-sector entities such as charities. The remainder are public goods and services.

In strictly economic terms, a small number of goods and services have to be provided publicly. Their defining characteristic is they cannot be priced and therefore no one can be excluded by price from the benefits they provide (though they may be through shortages, queues and rationing) – or indeed the disbenefits, since there are public bads, such as atmospheric pollution and epidemic diseases. A classic textbook example of an *unpriceable public good* is a lighthouse.[5] It cannot be priced efficiently: how can one price the ships far and wide that may be guided by the light? Moreover, whatever its costs are, they are invariant to the sailing past of it of any individual ship: its marginal cost of operation is zero. Therefore, even if one could charge ships for its services, it would be economically inefficient to do so. That ships calling at British ports pay a due, depending on how many ports they call at, but other ships passing do not, makes the point. Some great spending areas of state are such unpriceable public goods – for example, defence, law and order.[6] The direct spending requirements of others are small: examples are foreign policy, economic policy, environmental policy, trade and competition policy, industrial and regional policy. While their cost may vary with population size, one cannot individually charge their beneficiaries: the marginal cost imposed by each citizen is approximately zero.* At local level, street lighting and cleaning, the provision of

---

* The marginal costs of road use rise with volume, especially in congested areas. They used to be impure public goods that could not be priced. However, most roads – like many museums, art galleries and libraries – are no longer unpriceable, as modern technology has made possible electronic road pricing at least on congested motorways and urban areas. One can adopt tolls on many large roads, but it is usually not efficient to do so because it distorts allocation between tolled and untolled roads. Because marginal costs are low it would not be efficient to adopt road pricing on lightly used roads. If priced on market principles, roads or road systems can be candidates for regulated privatization.

unfenced public parks as well as physical planning, traffic and other local policies are public goods.

Privatization has found extraordinarily wide acceptance.[7] In Britain two-thirds of formerly state-owned industries have been transferred to the private sector.[8] Public bodies suitable for privatization divide broadly into two groups. In Britain nationalized industries such as Rolls-Royce, the National Freight Company, British Airways and many more were privatized straight into competitive markets. They traded in national or international markets in competition with private and sometimes with publicly owned competitors. They were not saddled with unprofitable social obligations which their unsaddled rivals would have made unsustainable through price competition. Then there were the monopolies, public utilities such as BT, British Gas, the British Airports Authority, the electricity and water industries. Though in most cases limited competition was introduced from the start, it was not enough to make them efficient. In order to achieve this, and to restrict their ability to maintain monopoly profits, special regulatory bodies (the Civil Aviation Authority, Offer, Ofgas, Oftel and Ofwat) were set up to regulate them and to protect consumers' and other interests: in particular, to replace competition as a spur to efficiency wherever competition could not work because of natural monopoly or the slow growth of competition.[9] An important principle is that whenever bodies are separated from government either competition or regulation must be established to stimulate greater efficiency.

Competition

Competition is high among the forces making for greater efficiency.[10] It forces service differentiation, quality improvements and other innovations that give more consumer satisfaction.[11] It destroys the monopoly of information that causes so much inertia. It undermines outmoded paternalism: the provision by the state of only black telephones and of welfare services designed only by professionals.[12] Some would see it as the only stimulus necessary: firms necessarily select good managers and those managers deliver of their best, because of competition. It is more important than the privatization of ownership.[13] To introduce competition where it did not previously exist is to unleash power which will erode monopoly.[14] Therefore no firms should have a legal monopoly and there should be no restriction on the entry of new firms into a market. But monopolies will not always disappear rapidly. They may have products and product ideas which give them an advantage over new entrants. They may have elements of natural monopoly: there may be such economies of scale and scope in what they do that there is room for only one efficient firm in their market. It would not be efficient to duplicate telecommunications and rail networks, gas and electricity grids, water and sewerage mains or airports. But such firms will be kept efficient if they are 'contestable', meaning that they are constantly under threat from other firms trying to penetrate their markets or take them over.[15] Competition should always be allowed, although it may take time to become effective.[16] New technology – for example, satellite and cable TV in telecommunications – may threaten an old monopoly dependent on obsolete technology. Experience shows that other methods of attempting greater efficiency – state planning, piecemeal state intervention, management education on its own and regulation – are at best less effective in achieving economic growth and prosperity and at worst neutered without competition.

While in some countries most provision has been privatized, in many there remains considerable scope for such privatization (or equivalent de-nationalization); but even in Britain, more provision could be privatized, were governments prepared to allow activities to set prices and otherwise operate commercially.[17] As well as unpriceable public goods there are *policy-determined public goods* or publicly provided private goods that could be priced but are not, or are only partially priced: for example, prescription charges make a partial and highly averaged contribution to the cost of particular medicines. If priced and privatized, large areas of state spending such as education and health could be left to the market. Most social security could be self-funded. Most state spending – central and local – falls under this heading, publicly provided only because of policy decisions to that effect.

These policy-dependent publicly provided goods and services divide into the strictly policy-determined and those that cannot be priced and must be publicly provided in any practical circumstances. If government provides free universal education, that is a free act of policy since schooling could be means-tested. But prisons and hostels for the mentally ill could not be means-tested. Whatever drastic levies or fines may be imposed on inmates and their families, such institutions are unlikely to be viable unless publicly provided. There are other activities (such as opera) for which there would be no market without government financial support because there would not be enough buyers at market prices for the operation to be viable.

Privatization of public production

If provision is privatized, production is usually privatized too. The government disappears from both, leaving consumers buying from the market. But public provision may continue without public production. Less analysis is needed of the case for privatizing or denationalizing public production than of public provision. Taking a robust view, all public production and operation could be privatized or turned over to third-sector or autonomous public producers. This proposition holds virtually by definition: where the public goods and services government provides are publicly produced, both that production activity and any publicly owned inputs into it could be set up on profit-making basis and then de-nationalized. Any internal cross-subsidies could be eliminated. The scope for increases in efficiency by such means throughout the administration of government is great; but one must remember transactions costs. There have been cases where such small activities have been separately privatized for the cost of doing so to exceed the cost saving, as in the case of the UK Property Services Agency.

Thus while some goods and services must be provided publicly if they are to be provided at all, all can be produced privately, or by a denationalized body. Lighthouses could be. Roads could be built, maintained and operated by private undertakings – completely privatized where tolled and where not, provided with public money. Railway privatization is an example of privatization of production where the provision of most passenger services will continue to depend on public funds. Train operating companies, track provision, rolling stock and infrastructure companies can be privatized. However education is financed, schools and establishments of higher education could be denationalized. So could hospitals and clinics. General practitioners have always been self-employed. The production and management of state pensions and social benefits could be privatized even if the principles of funding remained the same. The same holds for law and order. If advocates can be self-employed in Britain, why not judges under contract to the state? Courts as well as prisons could be privately owned and run. The police could also be privatized. Why should the defence forces not be mercenaries as they have been in other countries in the past? In local government the ownership and management of much housing and of social services are being denationalized. Other activities could follow. So one might obtain the efficiency advantages of denationalized production and operation, while retaining public provision. In later chapters we will consider reservations about such thoroughgoing denationalization. For the moment let us accept its possibility.

More numerous are other ancillary activities within government which are inputs to it rather than outputs to the public. All could be privatized or otherwise denationalized. Canteens, publications, reprographic, secretarial and other support services could. Staff could buy or bring their own food rather than use the canteen. Or they could be supplied privately under contract, as they are already in many private and public firms. Many such privatizations have taken place in Britain. Indeed, the same arguments could be valid for policy-advising civil servants who might, as in New Zealand, become self-employed or possibly even set up firms whose services are then supplied on a contractual basis. Thus denationalization could be extensive. The effect on civil service numbers would be greatest if production were privatized, since most civil servants are 'producers' of services rather than 'providers'.

Third-sector production

Does production have to be privatized to be efficient? Privatization is not the only possible future for public production. Public services may also be produced, and even provided, by charities, other voluntary bodies, friendly societies, cooperatives and other third-sector bodies. Some UK public bodies, such as the British Council, have the formal status of charities, but are not charities in the crucial sense that they are autonomous – although government pressure for increased charging for their services is making them more so (as well as bringing them into competition with the private sector). However, governments can rely only to a limited extent on charitable provision. Charities in modern times have a smaller proportion of the funds than the state seems to need for redistributive purposes; and charitable objectives are often not well aligned with the state's own. Thus, charities are more often the state's agents than principals. Moreover, without the profit motive, charities may have no more incentive to be efficient than the public sector they displace.

It is often argued, especially in the United States, that service delivery and other public production are often better done by charities than by firms with a profit motive, because they will reflect objectives other than profit. While still needing to be efficient enough to break even, their objectives are non-commercial.[18] Where a government wants compassionate and altruistic behaviour, it may gain from using them as its agencies.[19] There may be complications in so far as a charitable agency has its own objectives departing in some respects from public- or private-sector objectives.[20] A third-sector charity cannot regard its output purely as whatever the market wants. If it were to, it would lose its character as a charity or other third-sector agency. These objectives may be altruistic or charities may wish, in service negotiations, to impose values or even behaviour of their own. It is possible these objectives are the same as government's, though it is likely they will not be – at least in part. A charity could still be a government's best choice as agent, able to achieve that government's objectives more effectively than others, while the government remains indifferent or positive to the additional objectives such a charity may have.

Unless incentivized by competition to increase their efficiency, charities may not produce cost savings; but then under pressure of competition, they find it hard to maintain their distinctive values. They have to develop commercial skills and employ commercially and financially conscious people, which puts further pressure on their non-commercial behaviour.[21] Charities are to a varying extent run by altruistic members of the general public and by people personally identified with the objectives of the charity – blacks, single mothers, alcoholics, addicts, etc. The more the second type predominates, the greater the benefit from empowerment, both in the sense that the charity is likely to understand the needs of those with whom it works and because as individuals they are motivated to work hard.[22] The more government uses them, the harder it will be to retain their distinctive management skills. To avoid fraud and be efficient they may need a management with objectives and performance incentives not easily distinguished from those of the private sector. Moreover, to be efficient, relations between government as provider and charities need to be as free and equal as between contracting parties in the private sector. Again market dominance is to be avoided.

Altruism sufficient to provide an incentive as strong as the profit motive to efficiency and a high level of consumer satisfaction may be scarce. What there is may escape elsewhere if it finds itself competing with the private sector or used by governments to save money. Disinterested zeal may be a wasting asset in the circumstances described; but even if charities, as they are or might become, are less efficient than the private sector, governments could rationally prefer them because of superior quality in the service they deliver. In 1992/3 fees and grants from central government accounted for more than a fifth of the total income of the 400 leading UK charities. European Union grants accounted for another 7 per cent. Only half of the income of the largest 500 charities is voluntary.[23] Charities are actually important producers of public services, more for local than for central government, and their importance could potentially increase.

Autonomous public producers

Why cannot public enterprise be as efficient as private enterprise? Ownership is not the crucial issue for efficiency (though a change to private ownership will be a protection against subsequent government interference).[24] As well as the failures of state planning and enterprises in Russia, Eastern Europe and elsewhere, there are theoretical arguments why public enterprise directed from the centre cannot be as responsive to market demands.[25] At times – as in the Soviet Union during the mobilization of its colossal war effort in the Second World War and in some countries, mainly in the Far East, where public-sector traditions seem strong enough not to need private-sector incentives – state planning may result in efficiency, but in most nations this does not seem possible. Comparisons of state and private enterprise on occasion show state enterprise performing as well as private enterprise, but such industries – electricity and railways – tend to be where public and private management cultures are similar, regulated and below best private-sector practice. Public ownership could be as efficient as private, but to achieve this requires an assimilation of management cultures, as well as a relaxation of controls over pay and capital expenditure, scarcely, if ever, found in the public sector. Public undertakings would have to be given commercial objectives and allowed to maximize profits, freed from restrictions which prevent them from investing the capital and choosing the size of labour force they need, and subjected to competition. The board, the managers, and perhaps the workers would have to share the risks and the rewards of the enterprise. Above all, the enterprise would have to be financially autonomous to the point that if it failed, it would go bankrupt or at least automatically be placed under new management – if it were to be really motivated to be as efficient. Such circumstances are so far from reality, principally because of the sheer impossibility of effective insulation from the political process, that in default the presumption must be the private sector is always capable of being a more efficient, independent provider and producer than the public sector *as now known*.[26] There is one almost fortuitous fact: preparing an activity for the market so that it may be floated or otherwise sold or transferred to new owners requires very substantial activity by advisers to establish appropriate financial and management accounts and systems of a kind scarcely ever found in the public sector. This activity itself, as well as the improved systems it produces, will result in a great increase in efficiency.[27]

Whatever the shortcomings of traditional public enterprises, they are normally recognizable as firms, while departmental bureaucracies, which are a large part of the state, tend to be very different in their organization and less efficient in their methods of production.[28] Often they need to go through a transitional phase as public enterprises before privatization.

The issues are not as clear-cut for public production in competition with private enterprise as for public provision. There are cases where public production within publicly provided or regulated markets is at least as efficient as private production. It is theoretically possible to imagine publicly owned enterprises being given such freedom from government interference as to be truly autonomous and able to be commercial. Even then it is vital managers and staff have incentives to motivate them to be as efficient as their private counterparts. Moreover, there is a profound difference between those privatizers of the right who wish to shrink government and those who wish for organizational and ownership change to bring about more efficient supply.[29] The latter are far more likely to join with more centralist, left-wing and other viewpoints wishing to retain public suppliers in competition with private and charitable ones.[30] If private production by public producers is fully commercial, another dimension of ambiguity, that of ownership, complicates separation between provider and producer. A further practical difficulty is how to eliminate all cost, cross-subsidy or tax advantages which otherwise give public producers unfair competitive advantage over the private sector. However, even with private or privatized producers, one cannot always assume straightforward independent private ownership. The government may try to retain some share ownership, rights to appoint directors and so-called golden shares which give it rights over some key corporate decisions, such as whether the company in question may be sold at all or be sold to a foreign owner. Moreover, even without such special powers, the relation can easily be one of dependence on government if the supplier sells all or much of its output to one government provider, or even if one in-house producer competes with independent producers. If separation becomes incomplete for any of these reasons, and the relation between government and its providers departs from that of a good working contract between independent parties, the potential efficiency gains will not be fully realized.

More fundamentally, what is one trying to preserve in maintaining public provision or production? As we shall see in the next chapter, confidentiality and long time horizons are reasons for retaining public production in some circumstances. As will be developed further in Chapters 8 and 9, there remain reasons why in some cases, from the Bank of England before it was nationalized to various trusts disbursing subsidies to the arts or running public charitable endeavours, public status seems appropriate. In many countries in the past, and in some still, the idea that the state should to some extent be self-supporting by building up an estate of monopolies whose profits could replace taxes as a source of government revenue has often seemed attractive. (Even now much public investment in Hong Kong is funded from land sales, so keeping taxation down.) The first drawback of such an approach is that it puts a government under strong temptation to increase the share of the economy occupied by public monopoly so as to increase its revenue. A second is that the inertia such monopolies create leads to inefficiency which may lead to a reduction in the revenue base. Nevertheless, government has the choice between privatizing a body or keeping it as a source of revenue which notionally could be of the same value. The greater ability of the private sector to realize efficiency encourages the first alternative.

Another argument for public ownership relies on the view that when confronted by experts whose expertise is hard to challenge, and even more by rival experts in whose interest it must be to increase the price and size of the service in question, it is in the public interest to subject such sectors to public control in the best interests of the consumer.[31] This defence of state intervention to establish public provision (though not necessarily public production) in health and social security is one which even right-wingers have occasionally found convincing.[32] It is given as a reason why the British National Health Service is cheaper than private counterparts for comparable health outcomes. Another reason may be the wish to retain public-sector characteristics that do not easily transfer to the private or even the third sector: management style, the fairer treatment of staff, lack of discrimination, public-sector ethics and social obligations which can more readily be placed on public than on private or privatized firms. But there is a cost to this until public enterprise can be motivated to be as efficient as private enterprise. To design a vehicle that can do this needs to be at the top of the agenda in many states including Britain.

Social obligations of private enterprise

The law can impose requirements on private firms which can, if heavy, damage their ability to compete internationally but not domestically because good legal systems expect a law to apply to all firms equitably. Therefore one might expect state enterprises when privatized to be exempt from any particular social obligations or burdens, but they have not always been. All the UK regulated industries were given some social obligations which they had to sustain out of profits. Because the social obligations required of their predecessor nationalized industries were small, theirs were also small, carried over from that past. Most were required to provide universal service. That, and not to discriminate, are traditional and defensible obligations of monopolies – public or private – since a customer has nowhere else to turn if denied such basic commodities as gas, electricity and water.[33] They were required to keep charges down for certain customers, sometimes below cost, usually in the interests of maintaining or extending universal service. BT inherited more far-reaching patterns of cross-subsidization between rural and urban, large and other consumers, and different parts of the UK. When natural gas made it economical to build a national gas grid in Britain, the offshore gas sources were mainly off the east coast. As the gas price is uniform geographically, users in the west were cross-subsidized by those to the east. Such obligations were written into the licences under which privatization required British Gas to operate.

In some cases more substantial requirements would have been needed: had the Post Office been privatized in the mid-1990s, its licence would have required it to make enough profits to support a nation-wide single letter delivery price which itself would have been price-capped. (By contrast, while there are many (producer) parts of the railways which will be privatized, its provision will not be, as all or virtually all railways will continue to need subsidization with funds directly or indirectly supplied by government.)[34] If monopoly power is great, then the cross-subsidized services could be extensive. In effect, such monopolies are raising their own taxation by charging some customers above cost, so as to cross-subsidize others.[35] However, ministers' ability to alter what uncommercial services these entities provide on such terms is virtually zero until the licence comes to be renewed, usually after a period of 25 years.

In the long run, these non-commercial obligations and prices will not be sustainable if competition erodes the monopoly profits that pay for them. Unless special steps are taken to require competitors to share in the cost of sustaining them, they will last only as long as natural monopoly lasts.[36] Governments therefore have a difficult choice between promoting competition which may eventually make such obligations unsustainable or devising or allowing mechanisms which have the effect of preserving enough monopoly power to sustain those obligations in the longer term.

A move towards commercial pricing implies moving towards reflecting appreciable cost and quality differences in price differences.[37] When faced by market, that is higher, prices, users will use these services more economically. If enough can and do afford these services for them to be viable, then their provision in general can be privatized, though they too may need to be regulated because of their monopoly power. The reduction or elimination of cross-subsidy by introducing market pricing, which will in general increase prices for the poor and disadvantaged and may reduce them for the rich and for business, may therefore be presented as a right-wing policy unless other steps are taken to redress the impact of market pricing.

Redistribution and paternalism

While there are practical limits to the social obligations that can be placed on competitive enterprises, privatization and other forms of denationalization do not necessarily entail the end of social policies, which can be pursued by other means.

All social, that is uncommercial, publicly provided activities are by definition redistributive, paternalistic or both.[38] Redistribution is where government transfers income from some citizens, usually by taxation, to others, either directly (*redistribution in cash*) or through intermediate bodies which can then charge lower prices for their goods and services (*redistribution in kind*). The first is purely redistributive because it allows recipients to spend their extra income as they please. The second is partly paternalistic because the state allows the citizen choice as consumer, but biases that choice by making some goods and services cheaper. Pure paternalism arises when the state prescribes the nature or quality of what is provided so tightly – for example, in education and broad-casting – that citizens cannot buy what they would freely buy, but only what the state wants them to buy. By paternalism one means that politicians provide services other than consumers would choose for themselves. It is unavoidable when services like prisons are provided under duress or where the acutely mentally handicapped are unable to choose for themselves. In a rather different sense, it applies where politicians, as in war and foreign policy, have so much more relevant information than do individual citizens that they are presumed to make better decisions than citizens can, though still on their behalf.

One policy towards redistribution and paternalism is to eliminate it as far as possible, raising only as little taxation as is needed to finance the inescapable minimum of public goods. Where government restricts redistribution in cash or kind, the scope increases for privatization of state activities. The converse also holds. The simpler agency arrangements can be, the more redistribution is in cash not kind. The less paternalistic it is, the less finely its rules need to discriminate between beneficiaries; or alternatively the more discretion an agency is given, the more complicated its controls and monitoring need to be.

Even if a state has major redistributive policies and programmes, the scope for privatization may be increased. One possibility is to detach redistribu-tion from particular agencies or goods and services and to move towards a *unified tax and benefit system* which results overall in the politically required distribution of income. A consequence of such redistribution and paternalism is that policy-determined public goods and services can be converted into com-mercial goods and services and then privatized. At the limit, if such objectives were stripped out of all public services, then the public sector could be dras-tically reduced to the provision of genuine unpriceable public goods (and the provision of law, policy and regulation).

Once economists commonly argued that redistribution was more effec-tive if made through income transfers than through piecemeal redistribution in cash and kind. A more recent argument is that putting cash into the hands of the poor, and making them pay the full cost of the services they then buy, would give them more power, make them more critical consumers and bring down costs, while improving quality.[39] The most effective method is income tax, which would be progressive for taxpayers but extended downwards into a (progressive) negative income tax for those whose income was below a stated threshold, so as to give a guaranteed minimum income.[40] (Other recipients whose needs were not related to their income would receive appropriate tax allowances or cash hand-outs.) The main welfare arguments for a comprehen-sive system are that it would make it easier to ensure that everyone got their deserts; and second, that a system under which individuals chose what they wanted with their cash would give them more satisfaction than if they were given food or vouchers or other services or goods in kind which restricted their choice, or had their choices influenced by explicit or by hidden subsidies affecting relative prices. One further ideological position can greatly complicate such provision: if it is maintained paternalistically that recipients should not have choice but be constrained in their use of the money they receive.[41] The reason may be moralistic: they should not use other taxpayers' to buy drink or drugs. Or prudential: parents should not consume money meant for their children. Such arguments may be supported by the view that taxpayers have some right to choose what recipients do with 'their' money. Such views are commonly associated with parts of the political right and paradoxically imply a larger state apparatus to implement these policies than the right generally desires. It may also encourage the provision of such redistribution by charities who are likely to wish to constrain their clients' choice in meeting their own charitable objectives.

Such a comprehensive system demands high revenue, and therefore high tax rates, because of its comprehensiveness and fairness. It will be high-cost because based on income and not on need: it will inevitably give some more than they need and others less. In general, it will pay more out than a more discretionary or otherwise targeted system. Third, the costs of administering such a system will be large, and it will require its own bureaucracy, as in the UK benefits system. New systems, such as those developed in the banking sector, should economize on administration, but not on the staff needed to prevent cheating. The tracking down and prevention of fraud will be costly and require many people.

Most public goods and services financed from taxation absorb more money than is strictly necessary because they are not means-tested or their qualifying criteria are broadly drawn. Many such services were at first deliberately provided for all citizens at token or no charges – (education, hospitals, roads and many local services) or came to be regarded as a universal entitlement (pensions).[42] The charges made often did not cover costs and may also have been heavily averaged among users. This reflected a more generous approach to public expenditure when the burden of public expenditure was less severe. It also seemed less divisive and even as necessary to win enough political and electoral support for such measures.[43] *Uniform* or *universal* provision, irrespective of class or income, has a cohesive effect on society, promoting ideas of citizenship and of common membership of a community. Because middle-income groups use the National Health Service, they identify with it and wish it to succeed. Universal provision used to be a way of making income redistribution generally more politically palatable when public funds seemed abundant. In some cases all gained equally, although where provision was uniform the poor gained more relative to their income levels. (However, there were cases, particularly in health, education and libraries, where middle-income groups gained more because they used the service more than the poor and knew how to work the system, so that they were absolutely and relatively better off.) But to continue with such universal or otherwise subsidized provision, when there is fiscal crisis, greatly increases public expenditure and complicates separation.[44]

Instead of attempting universal equity, the alternative approach would introduce *means-testing*, changing the system to one where the poor, however defined, had all or part of their bills met, while the rest of the population paid the market price. Similarly, pensions and other elements of social security could be set up on a basis that was self-funding, except for separately identified and means-tested provision for the poor. Proponents of new public management generally favour means-testing as both equitable and as a way of reducing public expenditure and taxes.[45] As the public expenditure savings from doing so will be substantial by comparison with universal provision, not to charge those who can afford to pay strikes many as unreasonable. The logic of Proposition 13 fortified this belief: means-testing not only makes the available taxation go further; but there is evidence that citizens prefer charges to taxes.[46] There is a drawback: as fewer citizens share in the benefits of subsidized provision, the constituency for maintaining and improving a service declines. As Rose and Peters have observed, 'public services provided only to poor people are likely to be poor services because they are confined to a politically inarticulate and disadvantaged minority'.[47] A new conservative thinker of the Old Right has observed with regret the gloom over the prospects of Conservatives retaining power in Britain that the 'dislocations of market competition [were] palliated by the establishment of welfare state in which the middle classes participated fully'.[48]

If general income transfers and redistributive welfare services are eroded or abandoned in favour of piecemeal cash transfers or subsidies, the subsidies can be paid to providers or producers or directly to customers. Whichever subsidy route is chosen, the agencies could be privatized and left to market forces. Since most recipients would now pay for the goods and services they received at market prices, most services could be privatized, with some public-sector agencies concentrating on those who required cash transfers and others on such services as subsidized education, health and discretionary social security. All could be privatized, the agencies being paid to provide services or else the recipients could receive vouchers they could use for this purpose. However, as experience in British education shows, there are considerable practical difficulties in introducing vouchers. The currency in which a voucher is expressed needs definition: science courses cost more to provide than arts ones and the costs of different suppliers can vary widely. And the supply side needs to be capable of responding to the new market just as the buyers need to understand and assess what is available. Much of this is lacking.

If means-testing is done for every public service separately, the result is likely to be confused and confusing and require a bureaucracy to operate.[49] Depending on the prices and quantities of what they choose to buy, people in apparently similar financial circumstances will get different amounts of subsidy, poorly related to their income, wealth or family circumstances. Because the financial consequences of means-testing by different agencies will be difficult to predict, they will have unexpected surpluses or deficits which will complicate the redistributive pattern further, as will subsequent corrective action. It will encourage multiple and false claims and other kinds of fraud or working the system. The total redistributive effect of a complicated set of income transfers will be less easy to establish, when some are in cash but most are in kind, and most are set by piecemeal discretionary decisions throughout the system.

The distribution of support through a network of agencies is likely to cost less than either universal provision or a unified tax and benefits system for a number of reasons. Smaller agencies and local government may find it easier to administer means-testing and prevent fraud more cheaply, especially if their clientele is localized (though this is not necessary). Moreover, because government finances the system, it can afford to be meaner: the consequences of publicity given particular cases will tend to fall more on the agencies which have used their discretion and less on central or local government. Experience also suggests that, in so far as they are used as agents, charities in particular have an objective of weaning their clients from dependence which is likely to reduce their costs.[50]

Such a system more easily allows 'political' and paternalistic considerations to influence who receives what instead of broad-based consideration of equity.[51] Particular groups who have electoral importance, or have the time and capacity to complain – such as the elderly, especially the affluent elderly – are more likely to benefit from redistribution.[52] The poorer, smaller and more vulnerable a group, the more likely it will lose from such a system. (But not necessarily: the political forces working for the education of disabled children have sometimes been strong enough in the USA to pre-empt resources from ordinary children.)[53] Especially through the use of experimental programmes of limited duration and small geographical coverage, one can target groups to have more effect on elections. Before general elections there will be a tendency to target such programmes of one, two or three years' duration, on groups in particular areas where votes may be most influenced. Before by-elections one may find the same targeting at a local level. Such tactics are cheaper and probably more effective than across-the-board tax cuts or expenditure increases.

Their use is likely to lead to interest groups organizing to put pressure on government for such programmes, either separately or in coalition. The poor and the disadvantaged will benefit less from such developments. Such programmes, often first adopted for reasons of economy, have recently become common in US government, but they are less likely to have an overall political bias where there are several layers of government, which may be of different political complexion, than in a highly centralized state, such as the United Kingdom. The effect of adopting such an approach to political redistribution will be to save public expenditure through *targeting*, or piloting, by which an expenditure programme is not made available to all citizens that fall into a particular category – those with incomes of less than a stated minimum, the old, or unmarried mothers, etc. Instead it is targeted at a particular subset of such category, usually those resident in a given area.[54] It will lead to greater fluctuations in the pattern and extent of redistribution when political power changes.

A still more economical policy is to give public funds only to those who win a competition, as in the UK under the Urban Challenge programme or under the arrangements for provision of money by the Millennium Commission or to charities benefiting from the National Lottery. Not only can public funds be rationed to as few recipients as there is available money, but the excitement of preparing and competing may benefit the government's public image. But there will be costs in terms of abortive preparation and the fact that the funds may well not arrive in the amount or at the time needed for investment to be most efficient. Moreover, the danger arises that if the criteria are not utterly explicit, the results may not be judged to be fair and may even be seen as 'political'.

Thus the relationship between the privatization of the provision of public services and subsidy is complicated. Privatization of many public agencies is possible, provided they retain enough customers. However, many agencies may find themselves still entirely, or to a dominant extent, dependent on government for their revenue, however routed. Privatization will then be possible only if continuity of this revenue from government is assured. The critical basis for deciding whether there is genuine privatization turns on business risk. If purchases supported by government subsidy are sufficiently small by comparison with sales to other purchasers for a firm to be able to absorb changes in, or even the elimination of, government purchases within its business risks and remain viable, then genuine privatization is possible. Government, through the customers it subsidizes, becomes a customer like any other. Alternatively, as will be discussed in the next chapter, if the viability of the firm depends on government purchasing, then the contractual relationship cannot be an ordinary market one.

Where government relies on cash transfers or vouchers, only the provision of the cash or vouchers needs to be public: the beneficiaries can purchase as in a private market. But if redistribution is to be in the public interest, the vehicles for it in the machinery of government need to be considered, as does the devising of mechanisms – far more difficult than now – to estimate the overall redistributive impact and progressiveness of taxation and public expenditure taken together. If this is not done, distributive justice by any criterion will neither be done nor be seen to be done.

Thus the possibility of privatizing publicly provided activities depends upon the extent of the political will to eliminate the provision of services on other than market principles or to privatize them and use subsidies in cash or kind to achieve equivalent governmental social objectives. To that end there are a number of policies a state can pursue on subsidies to reduce public expenditure:

(i)   it can eliminate redistributive pricing (and also paternalistic behaviour) and privatize them;

(ii)   it can means-test them and still privatize them;

(iii) it can try to provide an overall equitable system of redistribution through the tax and benefit system, working through cash, kind or vouchers to replace the means-testing of the provision of individual goods and services and then privatize;

(iv) it can, through targeting, produce a redistributive and subsidy system either economical in the public interest or more tuned to winning elections than to equity – the result will be more erratic, short-term subsidies.

By comparison with the present system, all should produce public expenditure savings except possibly (iii), if its effects on tax and public expenditure are taken together. But it will not be easy to achieve effective redistribution. In Labour New Zealand as much as in Conservative Britain, the poorest have become relatively poorer. Overcoming that not only requires determination to help the poorest through tax and expenditure policies, but also training, retraining and employment generation policies outside the scope of this book.

There would seem to be no hard evidence on the extent of the savings produced by the different approaches. In principle, one would expect fiscal crisis to lead to ever greater selectivity; but the replacement of the kind of consensus described in Chapter 1 by which the middle class and poor shared in the benefits of many expenditure programmes may make selectivity harder to sustain politically. These problems are likely to be exacerbated in so far as selectivity is driven more by 'political' than public interest considerations.

Thus the conclusion is reached that the hollowed-out state need not forgo social policy, though it will have to be conducted differently. A hollowed-out state can still be redistributive and paternalistic. That can be achieved through the tax and subsidy system, but also through various combinations of means – comprehensive, means-tested and targeted; in cash and in kind; in the public interest and 'political'.[55] These conclusions apply not only to privatization but also to discussion of contracts, local government and agencies in subsequent chapters.

The regulation of monopolies and public services

While privatization withdraws state control and influence from the bodies privatized, a new relationship with the state is needed where they remain monopolies or in a monopolistic relationship with the state. Private firms, charities or autonomous public bodies may be dominated by the governments for whom they produce services. Frequently they will be in a position where government, as the dominant or exclusive purchaser, could so take advantage of this position as to force prices down to the point that suppliers cannot maintain their productive capacity. In the private sector the need to maintain suppliers long-term is a check on such short-termism; but politicians have much shorter time horizons. These reasons argue strongly for some independent arbiter to protect parties to government procurement contracts from such abuse of monopoly power. For reasons of speed, cost and expertise this is probably better handled by regulatory institutions than through the courts.

How is public monopoly power belonging to government or agencies to be controlled? That monopoly power may be with the provider – indeed, that is almost certain: central government rarely divides itself into competing providers, but local government provision can provide elements of competitive choice. If the producer is also a monopoly, as often happens between government and agencies, there will be a bilateral monopoly. Where enough competition does not exist to make such producers efficient, other means are needed to curb excess profits. There will therefore be a requirement, similar to that for privatized monopolies, for economic regulation to set prices or control profits so as to give an incentive towards greater efficiency. Just as with privatized utilities, it is arguable that a licence will be needed to set down economic and social obligations, especially for bodies with both commercial and non-commercial objectives. There is a particular difficulty where there are substantial non-commercial objectives to meet on which producers must spend money. These objectives are bound to become more transparent in the new arrangements entailed by separation. Therefore non-commercial objectives and their finance must mean that more explicit subsidy will replace previously concealed cross-subsidy. Regulators must watch over the relevant licence conditions in both the providers' and producers' interests. More generally, there is a set of issues over regulation to decide what differences need to be reflected in the regulation of privatized and non-privatized activities, and of charities and other agents. In principle, it is hard to see how any separately produced activities of this kind should escape regulation if one is to ensure there is no abuse of monopoly power.

What has been described will apply also to government contracts: to those between the state and privatized monopolies, which are called licences; to franchises and licences between the state and fixed-period franchisees; and to significant contracts between the state and its quangos or other agencies on the one side, and suppliers of commercial and non-commercial services on the other. Even the clear separation of provider and producer into a relationship which is basically contractual will not avoid all conflict over the interpretation of these contracts. But it would be unwise to leave interpretation to the courts because of the expense of doing so, and because of their reluctance to become engaged in interpreting the intentions of Parliament or ministers, though this last has been declining.[56]

In Anglo-Saxon countries economic regulation is generally thought to exist to police monopoly and anti-competitive behaviour in the private sector rather than in the public sector itself. But natural monopoly regulation applies to some publicly owned firms such as Nuclear Electric, or involves others such as the National Rivers Authority. Railway regulation may apply to public bodies for many years. Furthermore, in logic, the objectives of economic regulation are similar in part to those of administrative law. In countries where administrative law is well developed, it exists to protect privatized and other private, or independent public, interests from government, or government agencies, abusing their powers. Commonly the form of protection requires government and its instruments not only to obey the law but also to go through various procedures which are held to make abuse of power less likely. The safeguards exist because government in certain respects is a monopoly. Procedures need not be enshrined in law or practice. Citizens may rely instead, or in part, on the discretion of those whose job it is to safeguard the citizen.

Finally, a feature of British government has been that the independence of nationalized industries and other separated agencies has been qualified by arrangements to enable ministers in practice to intervene if there appears to them to be a pressing need to do so. Chapter 9 will show it is far from clear that ministers have consciously or actually renounced this habit, and whether ministers mean to give agencies the autonomy they need to manage themselves without political intervention. But even if they do, there must be greater certainty whenever relations are intended to be contractual. That chapter will suggest it is a touch-stone of the difference between a workable and unworkable quasi-contractual relationship. Here there is a fundamental problem: whether ministers manage their departments and their agencies directly or through contracts. As Edmund Burke said: 'One of the first motives to civil society, and which becomes one of the fundamental rules, is that no man shall be judge in his own cause.'[57] While ministers did not manage, and were known not to do so in any real sense, this fiction was acceptable, though sometimes uncomfortable. It would seem there is a choice: either to retreat from managerialism and also from a position where ministers can be held reasonably responsible for the contracts or quasi-contracts, governing their relations with contractors and with agencies and other public bodies, to a position where ministers are thought to have enough detachment to be regulators, or to go the other way. In the latter case, the adjudication of such relationships cannot be left to ministers and their agents, as has often been the reality in the past. The former seems inconsistent with all the tendencies of modern government and new public management. It is particularly so, if the relationships between minister and others are truly commercial and there is a real risk that intervention will mean substantial loss of profit, or loss of opportunity to bid for a new contract. In such circumstances the parties will insist on forms of mediation and regulation they regard as independent and not political. But there is a worse alternative: that a position develops where vested interests prefer to go to ministers because they know that they can secure the decisions they want in return for 'political' considerations. An example in recent years is that ministers have altered competition policy so as to allow the emergence of dominant or more dominant firms in several industries. The development can be justified as reflecting the importance of Britain developing large firms which can be global players. But there is a thin line between this and a position where firms achieve that extra power through the 'political' market.

It is ironic, therefore, that at the same time as the state is being hollowed out by the removal of activities through privatization and contractorization, it does not seem likely to revert to a condition in which ministers will be acceptable as regulators of the relationships created. Perhaps there could be a return to the regulatory state only if privatization and contractorization were accompanied by a decline in redistribution and paternalism. To turn to law, administrative law and independent regulation instead is not an unmixed blessing. Whatever constitutionalists and protagonists of a bill of rights may say, ministers (advised by civil servants) are capable of being more dexterous, sensitive, publicly acceptable defenders of those rights not capable of precise legal expression, than the courts can ever be. But to achieve this ministers have to be regarded as impartial in their decisions, taking advice on the basis of submissions put to them by civil servants in the spirit of partnership implied by the integrated or Haldane model of ministerial and civil service relations.

Privatization, politics and ethics

Nationalized industries and other public bodies have provided numerous opportunities for patronage. Privatization amounts to a withdrawal from politics. When public enterprises are privatized without subsidy, patronage is destroyed. Though politicians create the boards that will carry the entity through privatization, thereafter directors are appointed as in private companies, except in so far as the government may retain the right of appointment of some directors, reflecting any (minority) shareholding it keeps. Privatized companies have been criticized for appointing to their boards the ministers that privatized them; but such gratitude can hardly be expected to persist. Moreover, whatever formal power they may retain, ministers would be unwise to use their power or influence to appoint, or have appointed, their nominees to boards they subsidize after they have been privatized, since that would give them, in the eyes of the public, responsibility without power. In any case the obligation of the director of a private company as such is to put the interests of that company first. In this case and that of any improper regulatory influence over the firms he regulates or vice versa, it might still be sensible to impose restrictions on taking up appointments with such boards greater than the post-Nolan restrictions on all ministers leaving office.

Privatization results in a reduction in the powers ministers can use to influence the behaviour of boards. While the formal powers ministers had in their relations with nationalized industries were small, their informal powers were much greater, especially where the enterprise was substantially subsidized or needed to borrow.[58] Bodies without subsidy or otherwise substantially not dependent on government contract will be much more immune from such influences after privatization. Except when contracts are renewed, bodies that were part of government departments or directly under ministerial control will gain greater freedom, even if they are in receipt of subsidy since that will be received under contract (see Chapter 6).

As ministers found when they wished to close fewer coalmines in Britain than market forces would have done, by requiring the power generators to buy more coal than they believed in their market interest, ministers often have found it difficult to accept that privatization has reduced their powers between licence renewals, generally to those they have under the law over other private companies. At a technical level, if they were to try to change the law to increase their powers, the bills would be hybrid, that is affecting the rights of particular companies, which would greatly complicate the passing of such legislation. Compensation might often be payable in many countries under domestic or European law. Even if not, a subsequent reduction in the value of a company would deter inward investment and might even lead to a flight of capital, were it thought such a government was ready to resort to confiscation.

The greatest uproar in Britain has been over profits and directors' remuneration. High profits subsequently show in part that the companies were sold too cheaply.[59] It seems difficult to avoid this outcome when a company being privatized has more information than the government selling it, and a more powerful, because less diffuse, incentive to drive a good bargain. If driving a good bargain had not been subordinated to the policy objective of wider share ownership, the state would have realized more money in Britain from the proceeds of privatization, and the regulators would have much less subsequent difficulty in curbing excess profits, which also reflect the inefficiency of those bodies before privatization. The difficulty of any retrospective reduction in profits is that it will deter further efficiency-seeking, if it is expected to set a precedent. The form of price control used in Britain is to allow a period during which a privatized company can make as much money as it can: thereafter the more it has made, the harsher its price controls will be in future.

Finally, one must expect public-sector ethics, management style and industrial relations styles to converge towards their private-sector equivalents. One cannot expect privatized industries to retain any special standards over discrimination or to be an unusually good employer, especially if subject to competition with others subject to less stringent standards. Rather, they will do no more than obey the law on such matters.

Conclusion

Where the objectives of the state are, or can comparatively easily be, aligned with those of the private sector, denationalization of provision and production as a way of achieving efficiency gains and shrinking public expenditure requirements should not be spurned by left, right or centre. Such denationalization of production may be privatization, third-sectorization or giving greater autonomy to public producers. Moreover, it can be as consistent with a redistributive state as a Hayekian minimalist state; redistribution can in varying proportions be in cash or through the provision of services; and such a state can be paternalistic if it chooses to be, but it will also require new extensions of independent regulation.

Notes

1 Savas (1987), p. 227.
2 Richardson (1993), pp. 133–5.

3   Stiglitz (1988), ch. 4.
4   Stiglitz (1988), ch. 5.
5   See, for example, Mill (1852).
6   See, for example, Gray (1989), pp. 20–36.
7   Savas (1987), pp. xi, 291.
8   *Financial Times*, 3 November 1994, p. 6.
9   Oftel, Ofgas, the Civil Aviation Authority, Offer and Ofwat.
10 Stiglitz (1994), pp. 114–18. For competition in public sector see Common *et al.* (1992).
11 Davies (1992), p. 19.
12 Ingram and Schneider (1993).
13 See, for example, Bocherding *et al.* (1982).
14 See Hood and Jackson (1991), pp. 80–1.
15 Baumol *et al.* (1982).
16 See, for example, Scott *et al.* (1990), p. 146.
17 Tullock (1959); Olson (1965).
18 James (1989); Skidelsky (1989), p. 15; Clotfelter (1992); Mont (1993).
19 Smith and Lipsky (1993); Kanter and Summers (1994).
20 Wagner (1989).
21 Bennett and Di Lorenzo (1989); Benton *et al.* (1989), p. 9.
22 Shubik, cited by Hood and Jackson (1991), p. 51.
23 *Charity Trends 1993*, cited in Duncan and Hobson (1995), p. 337.
24 Foster (1992), ch. 10.
25 See Stiglitz (1994).
26 Osborne and Gaebler (1992), pp. 76–107.
27 Foster (1992), pp. 126–8.
28 See, for example, Niskanen (1971).
29 Moe (1994), p. 119.
30 Moe (1994), p. 113.
31 Le Grand and Bartlett (1993).
32 Duncan and Hobson (1995).
33 Foster (1992), ch. 9.
34 Foster (1994).
35 See Posner (1971).
36 For example, British Telecommunications' licence, sections 11 and 19.
37 Implied by prohibitions of price discrimination under Article 8 of the Treaty of Rome.
38 Following Musgrave (1959), pp. 5–14.
39 Godwin (1993), pp. 107–8.
40 Green (1967); Foster *et al.* (1980), pp. 515–19.
41 See Hochman and Rodgers (1969).
42 Beveridge (1942).
43 Abel-Smith (1973), p. 272; see also Rose and Peters (1978), p. 82.
44 Ranson and Stewart (1994), pp. 89–91.
45 Osborne and Gaebler (1992), pp. 185–6, 204–5.
46 Osborne and Gaebler (1992), p. 204.
47 Rose and Peters (1978), p. 83.
48 Gray (1994), p. 16.
49 Heidenheimer *et al.* (1973), p. 65.

50 Wagner (1989).
51 Benton *et al.* (1989), pp. 6–7 on Skidelsky (1989); see also Field (1989), p. 14.
52 Ingram and Schneider (1993).
53 Landy (1993), pp. 28–9.
54 See Mueller (1989), pp. 333–7.
55 For example, Bendick (1989).
56 See Jowell and Oliver (1988).
57 Burke (1845), p. 80.
58 See Foster (1971), pp. 83–120; Foster (1992), ch. 3.
59 Foster (1992), ch. 4.

6

Impermanent separation: contractorization

This separation of the roles of the purchaser and provider offers the opportunity not only to pursue economy, efficiency and effectiveness, but also to enhance individual rights and the accountability of government for policy decisions. However, the contractual approach cannot bring about these results by itself. It can only do so as part of a broader legal constitutional framework for public services which, at present, does not exist.

Harden[1]

The previous chapter concentrated on government activities of provision and production with wholly or mainly commercial objectives, which could as such be privatized. But where privatization of provision is impossible, or has not happened, there are other circumstances in which there can be commercial, or contractual, relations between the government as 'provider' and the 'producers' of the goods and services the government needs. This chapter considers the second model of separation: contractorization. It explores what is implied generally by contractorization in the public sector, and then explores some of the common problems involved. The nature of these problems sets practical limits to what can be contractorized. Finally, the implications of widespread reliance on contractorization are considered for both politics and the civil service.

The scope for contractorization

Subcontracting or out-sourcing has become a significant part of the value added in certain subsectors in the private sector, especially electronics and consumer products, such as fashion goods, with a short product life. This is nothing new: outwork has existed in manufacturing since the nineteenth century. What is new is its scale and its migration across borders, made possible by modern communications and computing. For example, the US toy manufacturer Lewis Galoob, a multimillion dollar company in the mid-1980s, was

> hardly a company at all. A mere 115 employees run the entire operation. Independent inventors dream up most products while outside specialists

do most of the design and engineering. Galoob farms out manufacturing to contractors in Hong Kong and China.[2]

Organizations such as Nike, in athletic footwear, Amstrad in computing and Nintendo in computer games do not own any manufacturing capacity and subcontract many of their other traditionally core functions. This development has led some to christen those organizations the 'hollow' companies.

One of the most important areas in which out-sourcing has grown is computing; in the UK it has been estimated that the value of this business is likely to grow between 1994 and 1997 from £1 billion per year to over £2 billion per year. Many of the largest contracts have been with central government: the Inland Revenue spends some £100 million per year and the Driver and Vehicle Licensing Agency £25 million per year. As another example, a 'virtual company' has been created to take the statutory responsibility for car parking in London on behalf of all 33 local boroughs with a tiny staff managing one contract with a computer facilities management organization.

Wherever production is denationalized and handed over to private, third-sector or autonomous public bodies, contracts between government and such entities are powerful instruments for ensuring the required outcomes and improving efficiency. But it must be well done: poor contracts can be much worse than useless.[3]

Good contractorization may be regarded as a variation on the theme of principal and agent: it is driven by the principal's need to find the most effective agency within a framework of law, regulation and administrative procedure. He will want to strike a balance between achieving the certainty most likely to result in securing the services he specifies and leaving his own discretion as unfettered as possible so as to be able to change his mind over exactly what services he wants. For there to be substantially greater efficiency, relationships between provider and producer must be simpler and more predictable than is typical of command relationships between politicians and those who supply services to them.

A contract establishes separation. Public contracts broadly fall into two categories: those that provide inputs into government of virtually no political interest – from car pools to most office equipment – where some part of government is the consumer, and public services where government acts for the consumer or client.[4] As will become apparent in this chapter, a contract specification of either kind will be more effective if it is precise in defining what the provider wants, but is loose in allowing the contractor as much freedom as possible to be efficient and innovative. That implies the rules and regulations surrounding contractorization be kept to a minimum.

The conditions for successful public-sector contracting are for the most part as in the private sector.[5] Contracts work best when both principal and contractor know what is wanted; when the contractor is expected to take a profit, provided this is consistent with the specification; when what is supplied is least specific to the contract, being in supply elsewhere; when there are enough contractors for there to be workable competition; and when there are enough principals in the market for contractors not to be dominated by any one of them. These problems may appear individually or together.[6]

The potential for contractorization

The potential for contractorization is enormous. Government may buy from the market like any other buyer, if its purchases are indistinguishable from those made by others. Government's sheer size as a buyer should, but does not always, allow it to buy at substantial discounts. Centralized buying can in practice be slower and more expensive than decentralizing the responsibility as some of the efficiency reviews of the 1980s demonstrated. Nevertheless, there will be a vast number of such competitive, more or less standard contracts that are straightforward to specify.

There is scope for standardization, which may still be loose enough to allow discretion in production and therefore contractorization in the provision of public services. Among the contracts which are or can relatively easily be made standard are public services: not only refuse collection, street lighting and cleaning but also many welfare and health services which are predominantly straightforward, immediately measurable in output, if not outcome, and suitable for monitoring.[7] Many other instruments of government policy could probably be contractorized and still serve the policy objectives required, including the management of most government activities.

More difficult issues arise when purchases are not of standard goods and services or cannot be supplied from competitive markets. For example, the ever-increasing technological content of defence equipment may make standard purchases impossible. The specification may be complicated or innovative; there may be only one or a few purchasers, or producers (or both); delivery may be required over a long time, creating difficulties if requirements change; or the contract may serve other than commercial objectives. But even in such circumstances government's relationships with its suppliers may be capable of contractual expression.

Good contracts become still more important when purchases are not only special but one-off. The problems of one-off procurement are not unique to the public sector. Good procurement of building in all sectors implies that a clear, and as far as possible final, specification is produced before tenders are invited. Increasingly the private sector finds it best in these circumstances to work with a few contractors in partnership for repeat business, which helps achieve high quality and lower prices. Competition remains inasmuch as a firm has a big enough order book to work regularly with more than one contractor or, failing that, is ready to test the market by occasionally requiring its preferred contractors to compete with others. Experience has shown that a market-tested partnership is more efficient and costs less in the long run than frequent changes of, and many different, contractors, however low an initial bid. Good contracting needs clear specifications, not lightly departed from, an efficient tendering service, adequate management and financial controls, and incentives to efficiency on both sides, as well as effective procedures to resolve disputes and avoid litigation as far as possible. Lack of specificity over objectives, poor specifications when tendering and then changing those specifications after tendering have led to the waste of many millions.[8]

Good contracting and its skills remain important where there is no case for competition, often associated in practice with assets which are costly, long-lived and specific. It is inefficient to have more than a single supplier where there is natural monopoly. Monopoly exists where there are sufficient economies of scale and scope that unit costs are lower if there is a single supplier than if there is more than one.[9] The best-known examples are grids and networks such as gas, electricity, telecommunications, railways, water and sewerage systems which cost so much that it is not profitable or feasible to duplicate them. As observed in Chapter 5, it is inefficient to privatize them without regulation because of the absence of competition.

In these arrangements regulation takes the place of competition because of natural monopoly and longevity of investment. If ownership were to change at the next bidding round, the business of valuing the assets might be so problematic as to be impracticable. The risk of such revaluation would be a serious deterrent to a potential franchisee making the optimal investment. Where long-lived capital is less pervasive or absent, however, franchises are an attractive method of contracting for public services.

Chapter 9 argues that more of the activities of many agencies could be franchised or contracted out on a shorter-term basis if ministers had the will. In many circumstances it would be efficient if it became normal to have competition for a fixed-term franchise, instead of the current 'prior options' of privatization or agency status. This argument was first advanced by the Victorian reformer, Sir Edwin Chadwick.[10] As he put it, where competition *on* the ground is impossible, try competition *for* the ground. Let firms compete by bidding for the service to be provided. The lowest bid for running operations (for example, prisons) to a required specification and quality will minimize the public contribution or subsidy, as will bidders paying most for the right to build and operate tollways, television stations or passenger rail services. The presumption thereafter is that the winner will maximize profits by cost savings as long as the specification continues to be met.

Time-limited contracts and franchises are preferable because the knowledge that they will be competing to retain their franchises later stops incumbents using their monopoly power to go slack. It allows new firms to enter with new ideas. When there is new competition it allows the provider to change the specification to meet new needs – customer and political –and in some cases new, probably increased, levels of competition.

Most public services contracts can be short-lived. Contracts to run residential homes or benefit offices could be short. The contracts must specify in necessary detail what is to be provided. So railway franchises will set down the services that must be run, in particular the frequency, reliability and standard of comfort required – the *minimum service requirement.* In television franchising, however, the Independent Television Commission reserved powers to itself to assess quality, largely reflecting the possibility that in the mind of the franchisee or contractor non-commercial objectives might decrease in importance after the franchise was awarded. This uncertainty on standards added to the risk and reduced the financial value of the bids made. It follows that the clearer the specification before such a franchise or other contract is awarded, the more likely it is that the public purchaser will get the service it wants. The longer the franchise, the greater the incentive on the incumbent to increase profit through greater efficiency, especially if substantial capital investment is required. But long franchises have drawbacks. They do not give as frequent opportunities for the provider or purchaser to realize the benefits of competition. More especially with public services, there are other difficulties. They tie the hands of politicians more than they may wish, especially if there is a change of government during the life of the contract. The sheer scale of profitability may become politically difficult. A particular issue here is that the more successful the contractor in managing the contract the greater the potential for public criticism. The successful establishment of the National Lottery in the UK and the apparently high profits of the operator attracted demands from opposition parties for lower profits and for a not-for-profit operator. And there may build a groundswell of dissatisfaction among the consumers of a service which from time to time it is sensible for the politician or his deputy as provider to address by altering the contract.

The ability of government to alter contracts during their life must be limited, except on payment of compensation. If the specification is poorly drawn, government often pays heavily for all the variations in the contract imposed during the subsequent process of clarification. Contractors, experienced in the vacillations of incompetent or inexperienced purchasers in both private and public sectors, often count on making profits through variations. Indeed, the effectiveness of any contract or franchise competition can be destroyed if a contractor comes in with a low bid on which he knows he cannot make a profit, but relies thereafter on contract variations to make up his profit, confident that the client will not stick to the original specification. The innumerable occasions on which contract costs increase by a factor of 100 per cent or more are commonly of this kind.

Problems with contractorization

Contracting out and competition are not new. They have been practised by government for many years and on a large scale. Under the influence of Bentham, they were both common in nineteenth-century local government.[11] Until the Second World War governments were largely able to buy armaments, ships and aircraft off the shelf since any one government's technical defence requirements were similar to any other's: hence the growth of international armaments manufacturers, whose activities were often attacked as creating wars to provide markets for their goods. With the Second World War, however, as technical requirements became more complicated governments tended to move to cost-plus contracts. But public–private partnership was still the vehicle, and, as one US analyst has commented:

> The irony is rich – despite the enthusiasm for entrepreneurial govern-
> ment and privatisation, the most egregious tales of waste, fraud and other
> abuse in government programmes have often involved greedy, corrupt
> and often criminal activity by the government's private partners and
> weak government management to detect and correct these problems.
> Why . . . ? The answer in brief is that the competitive prescription is not
> a magic bullet . . . Government's relationships require . . . aggressive
> management by a strong competent government. The competition pre-
> scription in fact does not so much reduce government as fundamentally
> change its role.[12]

Problems may be seen in the experience of both the USA and UK.

Technical innovation

The private and public sectors are least likely to use contracts of the type described when what is being supplied is innovative for technological or other reasons. Firms in the electronics industry may subcontract their manufacturing to lower-cost suppliers but retain in-house their research and development. Nike, the athletic footwear company already mentioned, subcontracts all its manufacturing to countries with low labour costs. But the research and product development function is retained in its headquarters in Oregon. In govern-ment, where innovation is required it would be better for them to supply in-house or, if they go to contractors, as is often sensible, to use a cost-plus contract.[13] For that to be as efficient as possible requires that both sides should be equal in power (with other clients or contractors available), but also that they should be as open as possible in the exchange of information with open books where the clients use inspectors to help ensure efficiency; where the contractor knows in advance what achievements and improvements would be helpful; and where it is agreed in advance how any additional costs and savings are to be shared, as well as rewards for quality improvements, to achieve workable incentives for both parties. The public sector is equally wise if it relies on command or cost-plus in such circumstances.

Political innovation

Politicians, more than businessmen, are often not clear and definite in their needs. They wish to be able to react to public opinion and other changes of circumstance. When ministers or governments change, they dislike their freedom being restricted by contracts they cannot alter without difficulty or compensation. However, there remain many services and other purchases which are sufficiently unlikely to be the focus of political attention that contracts would be wholly beneficial. In the past the civil service used to be good at maintaining flexibility so as to be able to act if some aspect of a service became a matter of sudden public concern. As ministers have increased in relative power, there is less certainty in service delivery. Yet if contractual or quasi-contractual certainty is not there, efficiency savings and public expenditure gains will not be delivered. Chapter 9 returns to this dilemma. There are many important and mundane government objectives which can be secured contractually without unreasonably limiting ministers' freedom.

Transaction costs and efficiency gains

Even if specifications are capable of careful definition and there is the competence to manage contracts, contracting out need not be the best policy. Setting up, monitoring and managing contracts cost money. Contracting out is worthwhile only if the projected savings promise to exceed these transaction costs. If the transaction costs are greater than the gains from contracting out, then contracting out is best avoided. Cities often spend 20 per cent of the cost of a service on contract management.[14] If so, benefits need to be at least 20 per cent for the change to be worthwhile. But transaction costs are bound to be greater for public than for private providers because of bureaucratic procedures to prevent abuse and to respond to the genuinely different issues concerning the use of public money.

In the USA persistent efforts were made from 1967 onwards to establish contracting out in the federal government. Despite limited progress in the 1970s, Office of Management and Budget reported 45,000 jobs lost in 1981–7, and an average of 30 per cent cost savings: 20 per cent when government teams won, and 35 per cent when external contractors won. Government won 45 per cent of the time, outsiders 55 per cent. But implementation was clumsy and the results uncertain. Those involved went through a process of establishing goals and working methods, which was time-consuming and disruptive. To write the work statements took 18 months for many programmes.

Many programmes ran into difficulties because contract costs often turned out to be higher than the original bid. Incentive payments were often easily won. There were complaints: it was said that to save money libraries hired inexperienced workers so that information became virtually inaccessible. The cost savings claimed were challenged. In particular, the large costs of the review process itself were normally left out. Congress complained that whatever savings were claimed, they never seemed to be returned to the Treasury.

While one observer concluded that on balance the programme had the right objectives and was worthwhile, it remained difficult to defend contracts which did not produce net savings except as part of a very slow learning process.[15] Another concluded that deregulation of federal procurement was needed.[16] A 744-page manual governed procurement, both reflecting and reinforcing government's difficulty in specifying tenders accurately, and therefore its inability to focus on the lowest tender for a given specification.

Nevertheless, even the strongest critics of contracting out in the United States believe that the system of putting government activities out to competition could be saved and extended to other activities, if only government could become a better buyer. But an important lesson from the US experience is that bureaucracy delays when threatened; and if a bureaucratic system finds it necessary to rely on regulation to ensure probity, rather than on a partnership between politicians and civil servants of the British Haldane kind, transactions costs can easily mount to an unacceptable level.

The UK government experience has a longer recent history in local government than in central government where it quickly followed the establishment of executive agencies, frequently covering the same services. The main vehicle for its introduction was the 'market testing' programme which, following an equivalent policy in local government, was introduced in 1991. Compulsory competitive tendering in local government had required authorities to follow a rolling programme of exposing designated services to outside competition. Market testing, recognizing the more heterogeneous nature of departments, required them to identify their own programmes of competitive tendering, which were approved, or not, by the Prime Minister's Efficiency Unit. As in compulsory competitive tendering, under the market-testing policy the current in-house service provider can compete with external bidders. The first two rounds of market testing in central government exposed £2.3 billion worth of services, accounting for 79,000 employees, to competition.[17] Savings of over 20 per cent were identified from completed reviews. Posts were reduced by 16,000, of which more than 10,000 were transferred to the private sector and the balance made up of natural wastage or redundancies and early retirement. Over £1 billion worth of work was contracted to the private sector, while in-house teams were awarded nearly £500 million worth of work – 73 per cent of that where they competed.[18] Much of the reduction in posts came from transfers to the private sector where no in-house bid had been allowed – so-called *strategic out-sourcing*.

Market testing was obligatory in all 'core' departments, executive agencies and other non-departmental public bodies. The requirement to offer a satisfactory programme and the size of some of these bodies meant that the initial tranche of activities to be tested tended to focus on support services. They are straightforward, relatively uncontentious and, in large measure, were already out-sourced in the private sector. There has been some tendency to the trivial. In one instance, at least six firms of consultants were invited to bid for an assignment to help a six-person reprographic unit in a public body prepare itself for the market test.

But whatever the efficiency gains – and, as with all government initiatives of this type, the claims are in advance rather than demonstrated in practice – the discipline of preparing a specification against which contractors were invited to bid was itself constructive. As in local government, managers were required, sometimes for the first time, to think through what levels of service they provide and what they wanted in future. This discipline was itself useful; while it may not have had any permanent effect on efficiency, it carried forward thinking about outcome specification.

In the second wave of market testing, especially in some departments, and rather depending on the personality of the minister responsible, there was a focus on major areas of executive activity such as information technology and, in some instances, a refusal to allow the in-house service provider to bid – so-called *strategic contractorization*, that is to say, a decision was taken in principle to transfer production from government. This thrust has been given added impetus by so-called prior options reviews. These subject the activity to a number of test questions, such as whether it is needed at all or could be abolished; whether it has to be provided by government or could be privatized; and whether it could be provided by other means, as through contractorization, partnership with the private sector or by being market-tested.

There has been little systematic evaluation of the costs and benefits achieved in practice. Much of the available information is derived from those parts of government responsible for promoting the policy which, inevitably, take a rosy view. Evaluation in local government indicated that contracting out of refuse collection initially cut costs by 20 per cent for equivalent service levels, although this trend was reversed after about four years, suggesting initial underbidding to win or retain the work.[19] The Audit Commission found that the cost of refuse collection had fallen substantially since 1980 but that much of the gain was before contracting out, and found it hard to attribute savings between changes in specification or service standards or from actual efficiency gains.[20] Central government claimed that average annual savings of 20 per cent were achieved through the market-testing programme from 1993 to 1995 while improving quality of service, a claim which has reinforced the view that the civil service could be radically downsized without reducing outputs.[21] But it may be too early to say if these gains can be retained.

Too few producers

If there are too few actual or potential competitors in the market, an efficient outcome is unlikely. Simple instances are common. While the progressive reforms in local authority refuse collection produced between 1984 and 1992 an average cost reduction of 20 per cent,[22] some see the service as bedevilled by a shortage of competitors – some councils receiving no outside bids; many local authorities rigging the competition in favour of their own workforces; the same members and officials running the inside teams, issuing the tender documents and assessing the tendering process; as well as a shortage of publicly available information on costs and standards.[23] In this as in other services there has been a tendency for such competitors as there are to merge and reduce competition.

This example illustrates that when government contractorizes it often creates an incompletely competitive market. To stimulate supply, it should sell the production unit to an outside firm, or allow it to establish itself as an independent producer through a management buy-out. Because legislation makes this course difficult, or simply because of a disinclination to follow such a course, the incumbent is allowed to compete against outside competitors. Frequently the inside operator is allowed to keep the activity, but at a reduced cost. But unless enough contracts are then won by external bids to create a competitive industry, competition becomes less credible at each successive round, and the incumbents may learn that they do not have to strive so hard to stay put. The reluctance of external competitors to bid will be increased if they believe, rightly or wrongly, that the bidding was unfair and that therefore the in-house team won unfairly.

Even where steps have been taken to ensure that outside bidders have as much information as inside bidders, and that the insiders' full costs are included in their bid, the insiders are still likely to bid lower because they know, consciously or not, that if they make a loss, local or central government must come to the rescue. This knowledge is reflected in the not uncommon finding that, when franchises are tendered, the costs are underestimated by all bidders and that, whoever wins, government pays later, either by paying more or receiving a worse service.

For competition to be effective when producers are scarce, it must be fair and be seen to be fair. In general, fairness entails clear, even contractual, separation of the inside team from its parent and the awarding body, so that the bidding team is seen to bear fully the risks of the franchise. It also means there should be a strong independent element in the awarding of the franchise and its regulatory oversight thereafter. For the awarder of a franchise to be its regulator (as happens in TV) is to make it a judge in a situation where it may be tempted to favour its own interest.

In many parts of government little specialized knowledge is needed to compete so that, provided competition is fair, there should be no difficulty in finding potential sources of supply. But there are other areas where the specialized knowledge required is so great that the number of bidders available is small. When the US government put out its internal telephone system to tender – the largest system in the world – it had the greatest difficulty in finding competitors to AT&T, since AT&T had run the service from the outset.[24] Government had to build rival consortia itself. The technical complexities of what was required were formidable, but with difficulty three consortia were finally cajoled into bidding. Because of its size, interest and knowledge, however, AT&T submitted by far the cheapest bid. To retain the possibility of competition in the long run, the market was divided between AT&T and another consortium, and some government departments were forced to pay more for their calls than others.

This need to build up competitors even where they do not win at first, has not been recognized in Britain, and indeed is not easily consistent with the European directive on procurement which requires tenders to be awarded to those who offer best value for money. The problem is common in defence, computing and most high-technology franchises, but it seems endemic in many of the more skilled caring services. In the United States it is often difficult to find two charities which are equally credible competitors for a welfare service franchise.

Too few providers

Under this heading it is useful to distinguish two issues. The first arises because central governments are commonly able to dominate the producers with which they have contracts. They cannot benefit from observing how other buyers gain from similar contracts to help them decide what efficiency gains are possible. This fact is a strong argument for decentralization of provision to local government wherever possible so there may be competition among both providers and producers.

The second issue is where there may be too few people trained in contract design and management. One manifestation is that, as providers, ministers are a scarce resource. They have many other claims on their time and do not have the training. Moreover, the period they spend in any one office is short. Neither do their most senior civil servants have the relevant training at present.

By contrast, ensuring that goods and services are produced to the right specification and at the right cost is the essence of what firms' senior managements do. Paradoxically, because they have fewer distractions than ministers, and because management is what they do, they can rely more on non-formalized command relationships and still be efficient. Rather than formal contracts, they often expect the heads of their subsidiaries and divisions to make 'promises' about the sales and profits they will deliver: promises that will be tested rigorously before they are accepted and turned into closely monitored budgets for the following year. Considerable attention will be given to important external contracts with suppliers, especially to acquisitions, disposals and other major deals.

Ministers and senior civil servants do not have the time or competence to be good contractors, but neither do they have the time or experience to be reassured that the contracting has been done by others. And since they are not able to be providers in a real sense – except possibly in a very limited number of cases – a basic rule of good management is broken and provision itself may be delegated within a government department or to an outside arm's-length body.[25] It raises the issue of what relations should exist between ministers and those to whom they have delegated their powers of provision (see Chapter 8).

The Environmental Protection Agency: a cautionary tale

The scarcity of provision skills in a more general sense is well illustrated in the story of the mission of the Environmental Protection Agency (EPA) to rid the United States of toxic waste.[26] In the late 1970s there was alarm at the discovery that there were a number of toxic waste dumps around the United States. In principle the remedy seemed simple – the polluter must pay: find the polluter responsible for each dump and have him clear it up.

This proved difficult in practice, and in 1980 the Carter administration passed a law requiring an already existing agency, the EPA, to enumerate dumps and set standards for clean-up. It was given a small budget to clean where polluters could not be found.

When Congress passed the law there were thought to be 1000 priority sites. But by 1989 another 800 had been found, with a further 2100 expected by 2000. There were thousands of others besides that would need treatment eventually: 25,000 sites were expected by the EPA to be eligible for funds, though the General Accounting Office predicted 378,000. Despite downward pressure on public expenditure during the 1980s, the federal cost of cleaning up rose from $1.6 billion for the first five years to $8.5 billion for the next five, while private costs of pollution abatement rose from $30 billion in 1970 to $60 billion by the end of the 1980s.

The EPA in effect determined the size of the market for cleaning up, first by finding sites (or having sites forced on it), second by finding more noxious substances, and third by setting the regulations for each substance. Given the shortage of firms with relevant experience and the strident political clamour for immediate action at every dump, the EPA had an acute problem of prioritization. As a regulatory agency, its instinctive priority was to set regulations. It saw its next task as the selection of a priority list of target sites from the many hundreds forced on its attention. Consequently, most of its budget went on these studies, and on administration, and by the end of the 1980s it had finished cleaning up only 41 priority sites and had started only another 200. It was adding priority sites to its list faster than it was cleaning them up.

Even to make so little progress it had to employ an army of contractors and consultants. Moreover, rapid R&D was needed before starting to clean up in many cases. The opportunities were glaring. Private firms entered the market in droves, in every kind of capacity, not only implementation. The relevant technical skills were scarce inside and outside the agency, and the staff the EPA had recruited were quickly tempted into the client private sector by higher salaries. Staff turnover reached 30 per cent per year in some regions. EPA training courses proved to be of greater advantage to contractors than to the agency itself. In effect the contractors took over provision:

> Contractors helped EPA respond to compensations, inquiries, analyse legislation and draft regulations and standards. Contractors even drafted records of decisions . . . They drafted memos, international agreements and congressional testimony for top EPA officials. Contractors trained staff and wrote statements of work for other contractors, and then evaluated their performance.[27]

The results were innumerable conflicts of interest. Six large firms won 70 per cent of the clean-up work. Vertical integration took place throughout what was almost a new industry. At the same time, billions of dollars were spent with little record of what had been achieved.

Most of the agency staff had been recruited as postgraduate scientists. Half – and a much higher proportion of the more junior staff – found themselves managing contracts for which they had not been trained and had little inclination. Moreover, they had no inducement to manage contracts well, because escape from that function, and their promotion, still rested on their scientific ability. In the meantime ill-informed senior officials believed the contracting process beneath them was working well, while at the top were political appointees whose job was to placate politicians in Congress and the executive. The first manager of the programme was fired in 1985 for planning and postponing clean-ups to help Republicans and hinder Democrats running for political office, as well as for shredding evidence and keeping a hit-list of EPA employees who disagreed with Reagan. More than 20 EPA officials were sacked, following the discovery of these scandals.

It would be wrong to believe that this kind of story could happen only in the USA. The combination of lack of relevant skills, inappropriate use of contractors and ignorance by politicians may be unusual, but it is not unique. It is too early to evaluate the major out-sourcing contracts in the UK such as the out-sourcing of the Inland Revenue's information technology function to Electronic Data Systems. But such an evaluation is required, preferably by a body without a vested interest in demonstrating the success of the policy.

The skills needed in the core: procurement
To avoid inefficiency and lack of probity a hollow state, which obtains many of its services and administrative inputs through contracting out, must develop a formidable procurement capability. Three types of skill in particular seem to be pre-eminently required by the hollow state: expertise in procurement, financial control and management. They need to be developed both in quality and in quantity beyond what already exists, if efficiency gains and public expenditure savings are to be realized. In each case we need to consider what is needed from officials and expected from ministers.

If the full potential for hollowing out the state were realized, we might ask whether procurement is the only skill central government would require.[28] We argue in Chapters 9, 10 and 11 that the answer is 'no'; but the more privatization and contractorization occur, the stronger government will have to be in procurement skills if it is to reap the efficiency gains possible. The previous section showed how shortage of expertise in the US EPA created a situation in which negotiations with contractors were often biased in their favour, and sometimes even conducted by other contractors or by consultants. Similar situations arose in hard-pressed and expanding UK development corporations in the 1980s boom. Nor is it unknown in the private sector, when firms having no sustained experience of commissioning new buildings out-source their project management but cannot then exert sufficient control themselves. Such clients must expect to be taken for a ride. If they cannot develop the competence, they should avoid contracting.

Traditionally, the responsibility for public procurement has often been left to staff with no great specialism or other quality, chosen because they were ready to do what was seen as boring work and relied on set bureaucratic procedures to obtain the cheapest price. If what is in-sourced is fairly standard, a special procurement arm, separate from line management, may be workable. However, procurement is particularly susceptible to attempts at fraud. Isolation of procurement from central management may leave a company or government department exposed to fraud, inefficiency and poor contracts. Thus in recent years private companies have paid increasing attention to securing efficiency, loyalty and probity by improving the quality and salaries of contract and procurement staff, their financial controls over them and the monitoring and management of contracts.[29]

However, there is also a need to retain understanding across the separation of provision and procurement from production. In an ordinary market buyers do not generally need to have any technical or other specialized knowledge about the production of what they buy. They can learn from mistakes, change suppliers or buy a different quality at a different price until satisfied. For the most part, however, government in buying a service is more like a private individual buying a home, or a firm involved in deeply technical discussions with key suppliers. If procurement experts are to be effective, they must have considerable knowledge of the techniques suppliers use. The obvious way of acquiring such knowledge is for staff to move between supplier and purchaser, acquiring the technical and practical knowledge that will help the supply chain become more transparent. This movement is much easier with multiple sourcing. But even in the private sector it raises difficult questions of loyalty, especially when there are few places in which relevant experience can be gained.

A first requirement of the hollow state, therefore, is that it should have an ample supply of procurement experts with the best possible experience. But as good ones tend to be scarce even in the private sector, selection and training will be a major undertaking – even training the trainers may be a substantial task. This problem is often treated as if it is enough to recruit more and better people to perform the same role as for standard products. It is a mistake. The commercial, and even more the non-commercial, contracts and franchises that governments draw up tend to be towards the more difficult end of the spectrum. For sponsors of projects and services to obtain what they want, procurement staff have to be expert in teasing out requirements and pinning them down. They need to have enough understanding of the costs of varying the *specification* to identify at the design stage trade-offs between quality and cost, so that what is specified is based on a rational estimate of the options available, given the budget. In the *tendering* stage the selection of a short-list and the drawing up of tender documents require expertise, as does the choice of contractor. To secure output as planned requires expert *project* or *programme management* as well as systematic storage of information to learn from experience.

Treating procurement as a separate activity is defensible in the public sector as long as it is for the supply of standard goods and services: from stationery and photocopying to canteens. But if procurement is remote from central attention, there will be greater danger of inefficiency and fraud.

When what is supplied is not simple, for example defence and other complex technological equipment, and arguably in regard to all matters likely to interest ministers, a separate procurement arm is in an impossible position. More often than not its members have had nothing to do with the design or specification of what is bought, nor with the management of the subsequent project or contract, and no responsibility for reviewing the value for money obtained. Thus, unless the politician is a knowledgeable client, or has access to expert advice he trusts, he may well end up obtaining something he does not want, with shortcomings he had not appreciated, and paying more for it than he should (or, more likely, his successor will).

If procurement is a key activity in securing the efficient economical and effective provision of public services, then procurement experts must be integrated into the process of ministerial and senior civil service policy-making and decision-making. When the task is to manage a huge procurement programme, whether in the hollow company or a hollow department, the distinction between procurement expertise and line management ought to be meaningless. In essence procurement *is* management. Standard purchases aside, the task of the procurement adviser will be made extremely difficult by the sheer number and variety of contracts to be negotiated, as well as the unpredictability of the political timetable and mind. It is a peculiarly difficult task in government to achieve the certainty which efficient specification requires, and still ensure that it reflects the political will.

An apparent way out, which has become common in Britain, is to allow so-called *non-compliant* bids. A sensible justification for this is the thought that bidders should not be prevented from suggesting a better way of achieving a given outcome than that laid down in tender documents (although such documents should not prescribe in any way the inputs by which a specified outcome is to be achieved; indeed, only outcomes should be specified). The means should be left to the ingenuity and resourcefulness of the contractor, which by definition excludes the possibility of non-compliant bids which relate to input. Set aside that type of non-compliant bid, and such a bid necessarily becomes one where the contractor alters the specified outcome. In practice, it becomes a means by which the specification becomes fluid after the tendering stage. Therefore, it may subvert competition and in doing so must be expected to stimulate less efficiency. In search circumstances compliant bidders can have a justifiable grievance and may claim compensation directly, or try to recoup their losses indirectly in subsequent bills for other contracts, so gradually inflating contract costs. European law rightly allows that lowest cost need not be the sole criterion for procurement and also allows value for money. In such circumstances value for money easily shades into political and even 'political' factors determining the selection of the contractors.

At one level the requirement to test out what is wanted, ensure ministers understand and alert them to the cost and other consequences of change, may seem to be just a further development of what civil servants have always done; that is, to challenge the ambiguities and arguments in party manifestos and ministerial statements to produce clearer policies for action or legislation. But the specificity and detail required for drawing up a successful contract is of a different order, and getting ministers to take exact specification seriously will be next to impossible. Occasionally there are legendary figures such as Duncan Sandys or John Stanley with a relentless nose for detail, but they are rare and may in some cases have corresponding shortcomings.

In a theoretical hollow state what, then, is the ministerial role? Does the minister become, in effect, the salesman and marketing intelligence, acting as interface between the political 'market' and the service production process? Conversely, a model of bureaucratic domination would suggest that officials fashion what is produced, with ministers as salesmen whatever the constitutional formalities.

For many civil service purchases – from canteens and photocopying services to passports and the activities of Companies House – there is little or no need for ministers to define the product or to be salesmen. This indeed is the implication of the Citizen's Charter approach to the provision of public goods and services. Where the customer is obvious and requirements straightforward, his needs are better defined by market research than by a minister. Nor is it essential for ministers to be involved in new contracts. What matters for effectiveness is that the consumers of services receive the services they require, given the constraints of the budget available. Ministers are often brought in when decisions become contentious or otherwise difficult, as in defence procurement, though generally they are not the best people to decide on inter-service rivalries or technical disagreements. What would be preferable is more systematic, quantifiable analysis of key procurement issues and trade-offs, a quintessential civil service activity. Ministers would then only come in because there was, in effect, a random element, for which they could take responsibility. Many procurement decisions have no real political content at all, and involving politicians makes them more political than they are and can lead to their being 'political' as well.

Some important procurement decisions have political content. Resources may be scarce, so there is a genuine rationing problem; or defining the consumer may be problematic, and a balance may have to be struck between competing needs.[30] What balance should be struck between consumers of food, farmers and tourists in agricultural, countryside or forestry policy, or between the various interests in granting planning permission; or between the economy and public health in environmental policy? Prisons should not be run for prisoners, though their interests must be taken into account, nor for prison officers, but to meet public expectations. In these more complex cases the job of the procurement arm becomes particularly difficult in the absence of clear political guidance.

If ministers and civil servants are to become closely involved in efficient procurement, not only will it be necessary for them to find the time and resources for it, but also they will require considerable training supported by appropriate systems. The qualities required for procurement – painstaking thoroughness, a drive for unambiguous expression and the avoidance of needless variation – are not those normally required of ministers or their senior officials. Indeed, ministers in particular need to acquire much greater clarity of purpose and a determination not to change their minds once made up. It is inconceivable that ministers would have either the time or the inclination to become procurement experts themselves, unlike chairmen and chief executives in private companies for which out-sourcing is equally important. Efficient relations require trust between ministers and civil servants and an approach which integrates ministers and civil servants. More often than not ministers move on before implementation. As a result, there are likely to be problems with cost, time and quality if specifications have to be negotiated with ministers. Furthermore, the integrated model is essential if contracts are not to be subject to 'political' manipulation which could easily broaden out into corruption.

Civil servants can be given the time and the training. This is an argument for creating a larger and more robust specialism within the civil service by training and recruitment, with a mixture of lifetime specialists and others who are cross-posted. They can be expected to manage those contracts from start to finish that are entirely or mainly commercial or where the political and social objectives can be fixed with relative ease or without substantial demands on ministerial time. Ministers must recognize that once they have made up their minds, or agreed, they cannot change specifications except at considerable cost, for which – if the system is to be efficient – they must be accountable. Yet there are corresponding advantages that ought to make such painstaking thoroughness sometimes worth ministers' while. The first is that as a result, public service and other contracts become what they want them to be, tempered by considerations of practicality and cost, rather than the results of civil servants' best endeavours at interpreting of what ministers are thought to have wanted. The second is that public expenditure requirements will be reduced.

Public ethics

While contractorization can be efficient, there are difficulties with retaining and improving public service values. Unlike privatization itself, contracting necessarily provides many 'political' opportunities for political parties and individual politicians, as the experience of many countries has shown.

Politics may endanger both efficiency and contractual certainty. There is a clear choice here, either to go for contractual certainty of a commercial kind within a framework of law and economic regulation, or to remain in a quasi-contractual world in which ministers retain powers to vary or abort their quasi-contracts. Such a choice is an important factor in deciding which of the two results of separation is the more likely: greater efficiency or greater political power. If contracts are to have real effect, then powers of ministerial intervention reflecting the doctrine of ministerial responsibility cannot be as arbitrary, or parliamentary accountability be as ill defined, as they now are. Moreover, the circumstances within which variation is possible must be set to limit providers' and producers' potential risk.

Such changes ought to require changes in law. In general, privatization has required legislation. However, new laws have not been needed for public contracts. Therefore, there have been no formal attempts to establish new laws about the multiplication of these relationships.[31] An alternative is the further development of administrative law, as in France where special laws and courts to administer them control the behaviour of government. A further consideration is that central and local government's roles may extend from that of provider to that of inspector or regulator, or the giving of policy advice, or some combination of roles, the legal basis for which may be itself unclear. These roles are not always separated clearly from each other. Therefore, there may well be a formal or informal regulatory and monitoring framework to consider, as well as the legal framework. Separation will alter the effect of any existing checks and balances.

In Britain, where there is no tradition of administrative law, the most likely issue will be how far informal relationships should be replaced by more formal, legal ones. These not only give separation a contractual form but also allow informal arrangements to be replaced by such formalized protection for consumers as citizen's charters, safety and environmental safeguards, and competition law as well as other limitations on ministers' discretion, all to create contractual certainty.

The framework of public-sector values is also important. What is likely to be the impact of separation on standards of behaviour in public service? The effect of contractorization on politics and on values is not clear-cut. A contract culture may provide opportunities for corruption. Public service values and attitudes may be replaced by private-sector ones, as under privatization.[32] Potentially there is a great difficulty here. While public bodies in most countries are subject to laws, regulations are passed with the same effect which will then require inspection and arbitration. The greater the regulation, the greater the inhibition to many forms of efficiency saving.[33] Moreover, relying on the law in ethical matters is less effective than relying on the culture. In the United States concerns about this problem within government departments and agencies and in their relations, contractual and otherwise, with others have led to the setting up of ethics offices in them.[34]

Discrimination

While the prevention of fraud can be regarded as consistent with profit maximization, and while regulation can be consistent with increased economic efficiency, attempts to ban discrimination can plausibly be seen as at the expense of profits. The Chicago economist, G. S. Becker, has argued that firms discriminate only because it is profitable to do so.[35] If it were as profitable for them to hire women, members of minority ethnic groups, or disabled people, they would do so. Often the factors that persuade businessmen to discriminate are roundabout and not easily substantiated. If a satisfactory labour force becomes restless and disruptive, or if customers go elsewhere when minority groups are hired, it can be argued that it is not in the company's commercial interest to do so.

Public-sector bodies have been expected to be less discriminatory than private-sector bodies, and in general have been. Instead of recruitment and promotion being done by the manager of the workforce concerned, it is done through appointment boards, or other bodies working to non-discriminatory rules and procedures. There may be quotas for positive discrimination (though they are illegal in Britain) to try to move recruitment towards the proportion a group has in the population. Certain jobs may be reserved for the disabled. Where, despite these actions, the promotion of enough women or members of minority ethnic groups poses difficulties, steps are taken positively to try to remedy them. Such policies may add substantially not only to administration costs but also, where special provision is required, to production costs. The public sector has been able to absorb such extra costs because of its monopoly position and being financed by the taxpayer. When public provision and production are separated, or even when managers are given much greater freedom in hiring, it is possible the bodies in question will discriminate more.

There are other forms of discrimination in the private sector which are harder to identify and tackle. Much has been said about loyalty as a way of reducing fraud. A firm may achieve greater loyalty from existing employees, as well as better recruits, if it hires their sons and daughters in preference to others. It may secure a better-trained and more highly motivated workforce if it does not recruit from known disadvantaged areas, or if it avoids those who have been unemployed for a long time. More insidious is preferential treatment in terms of jobs to children of major suppliers or customers, though this policy may well be in the commercial interest of the employer.

Similar issues arise with the ideas of *empowerment* described in Chapter 3. It is considered to be an advantage of contracting with community organizations for welfare and other services on the assumption that it will result in jobs being created for disadvantaged groups. But the freedom given to charities and others to do these things can be used or abused by those who run them, placing those they favour in the jobs they have to offer, so substituting one form of discrimination for another. Handing over the management of public and charitable housing to tenants often leads them to wish to discriminate in favour of tenants of whom they approve, who may not be those in greatest need and may even be their own friends and relations. Where resources are scarce, freedom to employ, or to allocate scarce underpriced resources, can become a source of financial corruption.

The procedures the public sector has devised to prevent labour-market or other discrimination often make the tasks of management harder. To hire and fire quickly and to promote successes on the job are an important prerogative of management. Avoiding discrimination slows operations down, and may lead to problems in the labour force or to the under-utilization of assets. Yet it is deep in the tradition of a liberal state that government should use its power to offset discrimination elsewhere by ensuring equal opportunities and to avoid giving preference to those who have pull because of their parents, schooling and connections. The larger the private sector (where discrimination is more likely) the harder the public sector needs to work if it is to provide anything approaching equal opportunities for all.

Even if legal powers against discrimination are strengthened, there is a high probability that there will be more discrimination if government and public-sector bodies, which have the practice of non-discrimination bred into their culture, are released from the practices and procedures built to prevent such discrimination. They will have little direct incentive to continue to promote equality of opportunity, and cumulatively there will be less influence on private-sector bodies to improve their practices. It is important to recognize these consequences as significant potential disbenefits of changes necessary to realize public expenditure savings.

Fraud

The prevention of fraud is consistent with efficiency. A public, or publicly financed, body against which fraud is practised is likely to have excessive costs (or deficient revenues) which will damage its efficiency. It may be led to inefficient decisions by the false signals it is given, confusing actual with potential profitability. Traditionally governments have used various methods to protect themselves against fraud. Most civil servants have been appointed by an independent public service commission, and have been trained and promoted within the civil service without political or external influence. Their appointments have been for life to encourage their loyalty to the system. If they have transgressed, their disgrace is final: they stand to lose their jobs and their pensions as well as their reputation. Fraud is made difficult for them by job rotation. This and lifetime employment mean that their characters and, to some extent, their home lifestyles become well known to many colleagues.

The checks upon individuals' ability to carve out a position where it was easy for them to commit fraud meant the civil service and ministers were largely immune from the effects of fraud. There were occasional major frauds, usually in work such as procurement which has tended to have less rotation because of its lack of interest to policy-minded civil servants. But on the whole fraud was and still is rare. The system worked without the multiplication of bureaucratic safeguards characteristic of more Teutonically inspired regimes.

The private sector, too, relied on a tradition of appointing mostly long-term staff employees as its principal method of checking fraud. But that habit has almost disappeared. Most able employees feel the need to have business experience in several companies if they are to rise to the top. Mergers, acquisitions, the growth of some companies, the decline of others, mean that most companies, voluntarily or involuntarily, have a high proportion of transient employees whose loyalty to the firm inevitably is less than to themselves. Many of the 'golden handshakes' and 'handcuffs', as well as basic salaries whose seemingly excessive size infuriates the general public, are attempts to establish a greater loyalty among employees and to provide a greater incentive against their misbehaving.

The take-up of references when recruiting used to be some check on character. But in recent years the referencing system has almost collapsed, because of fears of being sued, and because some firms are so anxious to shed staff that honesty has often been driven out of both written and even telephone references. Thus it has become probable that a proportion of new recruits will have misled their recruiters, and that increasing numbers will subsequently have to be asked to leave for various reasons.

Readiness to commit fraud is difficult to detect. But as public-sector employment becomes more like that in the private sector, more rigorous methods to prevent and detect fraud will have to be adopted. One option entails the development of complex systems involving personal accountability and corroborating signatures for every important receipt, purchase and other disbursement as well as random checks to ensure that the system works. They result in more regulation not deregulation. Moreover, the public sector would be wise to adopt the common private-sector policy of paying high wages to those in procurement positions, which are especially open to abuse, to encourage their loyalty and reduce the incentive for fraud. But the major defence against fraud is cultural; the common attitudes and values of those who work in an organization. If these are weakened by some of the factors described above, other steps need to be taken, by means of training and development programmes, to reinforce them. Explicit codes of conduct are a start, but insufficient on their own.

But if the costs of fraud prevention are not to be very high, the public sector must follow the private sector in accepting that some level of fraud is inevitable and not cost-effective to reduce. This will be unattractive to the House of Commons Public Accounts Committee, and to similar institutions in other countries, which have argued that only an absence of fraud is tolerable. In one instance the unwillingness of the Committee to accept the inevitability of some fraud in the Property Services Agency led to the dismissal of its chief executive when he was unwise enough to state this in front of the Committee.

But whatever measures are adopted, separation must be expected to result in more fraud. If it happens without necessary safeguards, in some areas at least the costs of separation could outweigh the benefits.

Conclusion

In contracting out, specific skills are needed to write and manage a contract. But, where these and other difficulties can be overcome, contractorization is a powerful instrument for efficiency in appropriate circumstances. Through privatization and contractorization the direct activities of the state can be much diminished with benefit to the consumer. Privatization of provision reduces public outputs, replacing them by private outputs produced and sold through the market. Privatization and contractorization of production are complementary. The more a public provider can contractorize his commercial relations with private (or third-sector) producers, the more private-sector techniques and management can be used to reduce the costs of publicly provided outputs, and improve their quality.

Notes

1 Harden (1992).
2 *Business Week*, 3 March 1986, p. 61.
3 See, for example, Lane (1993).
4 See Harden (1992).
5 See Williamson (1975).
6 Williamson (1990).
7 Bendick (1989).
8 See Barker (1992).
9 Sharkey (1982); Berg and Tschirhart (1988); Foster (1992).
10 Chadwick (1859); see also Demsetz (1968).
11 Hood and Jackson (1991), pp. 83–4.
12 Kettl (1993), p. 5.
13 Kettl (1994), p. 26.
14 Osborne and Gaebler (1992), pp. 87–8.
15 Kettl (1993), pp. 199–202.
16 Kelman (1994), pp. 102–28.
17 As minister responsible at the time, David Hunt claimed savings of £400 million, about 20 per cent of the value of government services reviewed (*Financial Times*, 10 January 1995).
18 Market Testing Bulletin Special Report, 9 January 1995, Cabinet Office (1995).
19 Szymanski and Wilkin (1992).
20 Audit Commission (1995).
21 Cabinet Office (1995).
22 Davies (1992), pp. 22–4.
23 Painter (1991); Walsh (1991).
24 Kettl (1993), pp. 67–8.
25 Kettl (1993), p. 194; Milward and Provan (1993), p. 225.
26 Kettl (1993), pp. 99–129.
27 Kettl (1993), pp. 112, 194.
28 Dorrell (1994).
29 Hood and Jackson (1991), pp. 57–8.
30 Kettl (1995), p. 56.
31 See Harden (1992).
32 Sullivan (1987).
33 Dunleavy and Hood (1994).
34 Burke (1994).
35 Becker (1957).

7

Decentralization: empowering local communities

> It is true that government offices are sufficiently intelligent to distrust their own capacity to administer the whole of England in detail, and honest enough to wish to do what they know they will do badly. But unsought powers may be thrust upon them by politicians who despair of moving local councils in what they believe to be the proper direction either by their arguments or their votes.
>
> Edwin Cannan[1]

During the course of the twentieth century local government in Britain has steadily lost functions to central government or to nationalized industries.[2] Central government and agency intervention in services provided by local government has increased, as it has in local medical services and community care. So extensive has this intervention become in the 1980s and 1990s that elected local authorities are now regarded as little more than the tied agents of central government.[3] A shift so relentless might seem irreversible. However, other countries have retained or even strengthened local government, and most rational arguments support decentralization of provision to elected local authorities. This paradox needs explanation.

The functions of central and local government

One of the earliest attempts at answering the question what central and local government should do was by John Stuart Mill writing in 1861.[4] He noted that many public activities needed to be shared between central and local government to be efficient, because there were too many services for a single tier of government. He argued, in addition, that local government was needed as a nursery for central politicians[5]; this point is still valid, as local government remains an important route to Parliament.* When Mill was writing, many MPs

---

* In 1895, 19 per cent of MPs had previously been local councillors, a figure which remained constant over the next decade, before rising to 37 per cent in 1931 and 59 per cent in 1945; it then fell to 26 per cent in 1964 and 22 per cent in 1979, before rising again to 34 per cent in 1992.

either were or had previously been Justices of the Peace, with many local administrative functions.

Mill divided activities into three categories. The first consisted of purely local business of no greater interest to the centre than the private business of its citizens. Central government merely provides a framework of law within which local government takes its own decisions. Paving, lighting, cleaning and domestic waste removal are still such matters. The second group consisted of activities nationally administered while localized in their operation – for example, central government may decide that schools or policing cannot fall below a certain standard in any area because of the effect on other parts of the country. The third group took in other services where the importance of detailed local knowledge outweighed the possibility of local shortcomings in management and the desirability of uniformity. Such services, including sanitation and the poor law, required policy guidance and perhaps the setting of minimum or other standards from the centre, with local authorities engaged in operational management but retaining some discretion in provision. In practice, Mill's analysis allowed the division of functions to turn on what central government decided was the extent of its policy interest.

Over the years, the tendency has been for the second and third group to increase at the expense of the first, mainly because central government has progressively taken a policy interest in more local services, which has generally turned into a controlling interest helped because the distinction between policy and management is ill defined in practice.[6] Central government has always held that ministers may intervene in local authorities when they feel the need, and that laws should be drafted to allow such intervention. Once ministers and their officials intervene in the running of a service, they are unlikely to withdraw again completely. In one service after another central interest has grown through occasional intervention into regular, routine control.

Something sounder than Mill's imprecise analysis is needed as a basis for strong, local government while providing defensible and effective roles for central government. It can be developed from the discussion of public goods in Chapter 5.[7] Other than in a few cases, there is no necessity for central provision. Only a few *pure unpriceable public goods* such as defence and foreign policy are national in extent, in that all citizens derive benefit and are their 'customers'. A central, or federal, element is needed in any decentralized form of government, to handle such issues as international trade and macroeconomic policy and to decide and control environmental policy, where the necessary decisions cover all local authority jurisdictions (for example, emissions into the higher atmosphere) or subsets of adjacent authorities (for example, whenever pollution from one area affects neighbouring areas). On similar grounds economic and other regulations which affect a large number of jurisdictions are a proper area for central government.[8] It must also be the prime mover in policy against poverty. But most unpriceable *services* are local. They include refuse collection, street lighting and cleaning, the improvement and maintenance of minor roads, environmental health monitoring and the provision of local parks.

The question to be asked of all such unpriceable or unpriced public goods is what is the extent of their 'market'. Most public services will satisfy consumers better the more localized their design and delivery, since what consumers want varies locally.

Policy-determined public goods are more important. They include the largest local services such as education and local welfare services, as well as others such as development control and recreational activities. Such services could be provided by any size or level of local authority, or by central government. One may need a minimum size of region to provide a catchment area for schools of different types or for certain kinds of health or recreational facilities, but great flexibility remains none the less possible. As a result, discussion of the optimal division of labour between central and local government may seem to depend only on how much policy-making and therefore provision central government is ready to delegate.

There is an argument which helps determine this question further. Taken as a whole, local authorities can be seen as a market in which each local authority sets out what it provides for current and potential citizens. Assuming that information about services is available, where people do not get services suitable to their needs, they, at least those who are mobile, will tend to migrate to places where they can. Charles Tiebout, who first formalized this view of local government, saw it as a frictionless market in which, by making costless moves between a very large number of differentiated local authorities, people could receive exactly the local services they wanted, as much as if they were able to buy them across shop counters.[9] But many have since shown that such an equilibrium is impossible.[10] The assumptions required are too demanding – moves are not costless; there are many other factors that draw people to particular locations; there are not enough local authorities to provide enough choice; and the housing stock in any one place, especially if it has a history, will probably be too differentiated to shelter a homogeneous population. Moreover, in the real world the rich and the mobile have more choice than the poor and the immobile.

Nevertheless there is something to the Tiebout hypothesis. To use only British examples, the wandering of the vagabond poor in Tudor times after the dissolution of the monasteries was in a large part a response to the differences in poor relief available between parishes.[11] The same differences were a main reason for the rationalization of local poor relief under the 1834 Poor Law, as they were for the nationalization of that poor relief in 1934 into what has now become the Benefits Agency, a Department of Social Security executive agency. Several recognized Tiebout tendencies before Tiebout.[12] Similarly, the prisons were nationalized in 1865 (they are now run by an executive agency of the Home Office), because some prisons were much softer than others, which was alleged to affect the distribution of crime.[13] Even in a country as densely populated as Britain, with its restrictive planning laws, there is some evidence that house prices as a measure of attractiveness are higher where local services, especially schools, are better.[14] Recent events in Wandsworth and Westminster provide an extreme example of the Tiebout hypothesis at work. Both councils took the view that if they paid other local authorities already housing poorer families to house their poorer families, and then replaced these families with others who would appear as purchasers of the properties the poor had left, no one would be worse off and everyone would be better off. Because their electorates would become more homogeneous and affluent, they would re-quire fewer or less costly local services. Provided the tenants moved volun-tarily, they too should be no worse off. (The principal allegation made to this practice was that this was gerrymandering, in that it increased the numbers of Conservative voters in the two boroughs.)

In some countries local governments are expected or even encouraged to pursue local redistribution policies, generally in favour of the poor. But if they go far in this direction they will set up Tiebout tendencies. Even a moderate belief in such tendencies leads to the conclusion that redistribution is best determined centrally, particularly if consistency in redistribution policy across the nation is an objective.

Arguments for decentralization

The argument for local authorities as associations of consumers is an old one. Touched on by Mill, it received extensive treatment and powerful backing from Sidney and Beatrice Webb.[15] Local provision is able to put to use local goodwill, enthusiasm and knowledge. Services can be more easily tailored to the requirements of local people, which can vary greatly from one place to another. Local diversity allows more easily for experimentation and innova-tion. More cautious authorities may be readier to adopt good ideas if others adopt and succeed with them first.

But there are other more recent arguments. Local services are better delivered if the local communities served are involved in the provision and production process through *empowerment*. Community policemen are more effective in maintaining local law and order, because they are able to involve more members of the community. Residential homes and fostering in the community are cheaper and more effective if local people are involved in and committed to them. Many services will be more effective, and probably more economical in the use of taxpayers' money, if devolved to local producers of all kinds (and whether or not they are part of a national network). Finally, em-powerment may revitalize democracy by motivating more people to care enough about their local community to vote or even stand for election.[16]

This view of local government is reinforced by another that it is a better vehicle for *citizenship*. Disenchanted by adversarial government at national level, one US commentator argued that

> making the state 'citizen friendly' requires a reconsideration of the funda-mental responsibilities of senior bureaucrats. They must come to see themselves primarily as civic educators. Because they comprise that

segment of the expert realm that is most insulated from the adversarial process, they are best situated to take the lead in framing the questions so that public debate can be made intelligible. They have the prime responsibility for teasing out the essential social and ethical issues at stake from the welter of scientific data and legal formalism in which those issues are enveloped.[17]

While that debate could be national, the failure of Washington comes from

the inability of participatory politics to cope successfully with the vagaries and complexities of a political world dominated by administration . . . the degree to which the very nature of administration renders it a poor venue for democratic life.[18]

The conclusion reached is that the 'centralisation of policy direction at the national level is inimical to citizenship because it deprives local civic forums of weighty matters to deliberate about'.[19] Politics and considerations of efficiency dominate national policy and law-making. Efficiency, and therefore the cost and quality the consumer wants, should equally dominate the provision of such local services as waste disposal:

but not in how children are schooled . . . It is precisely because a public school system limits 'shopping' that it encourages parents to think like citizens. Since they are situated in a particular school district, they have very strong incentives to exercise their political skills to make it better.[20]

As noted, John Stuart Mill in 1861 had stressed the importance of local government as a nursery for political education, a belief echoed in British political thinkers from him through T. H. Green to Oakeshott.[21] Despite difficulties in motivating parents and others to become involved in local decision-making, it is worth persevering because involvement encourages citizenship and that encourages neighbourly and community altruism.[22]

The difficulties of improving *ethical* standards in government are more easily addressed and solved at the local level. In Britain, local government has been more susceptible to charges of corruption than has central government, but one should not rely on individuals suing to maintain standards, or on the multiplication of bureaucratic and legalistic codes of conduct.[23] Recourse to the law and reliance on regulation are inimical both to efficiency and to ethical government.[24] They can be avoided by the use of informal procedures, easier to achieve in Minnesota than in Washington. If there is a problem concerning how to interpret and enforce a ban on discrimination or another issue of public-sector values, rule-books can be inhibiting, inefficient and never exhaustive. A US writer has suggested that instead a task force should be set up for every agency, consisting of a politician from the legislature, another from the governor's office, a representative of the agency chief and others of management and staff down the line to thrash out what is needed and how it is best implemented.[25] Such a flexible, participatory and problem-solving approach to the enforcement of public-sector values can only be realized in small, cohesive local government (and one where power periodically changes hands).

Thus empowerment, and more scope for citizenship and ethics, requires the power to shape and manage service delivery to clients in each community, and the delivering organizations themselves to have decentralized structures. This vision of empowerment, citizenship and ethics can be genuinely realized only if provision is local.

The proposition that as far as possible service provision and delivery are best decentralized is powerful. It underlines the extent to which the British among other governments have for too long ignored local government's potential, whether because political considerations have been more important than the interests of consumers or because of central government's perception that it is a better controller of expenditure or its wrongly perceived greater efficiency, or the equally wrong belief that central government's redistributive and paternalistic concerns are best served by tight service specifications from the centre.

The optimal size of government

How to give substance to the sensible, if empty, principle of subsidiarity, requiring everything to be done at the lowest tier of government able to do it?[26] Once the most influential arguments were analogous to those over the optimal size of a private firm, being a matter of economies and diseconomies of scale: for example, how large a local authority should be to produce pure public goods such as public parks, libraries, museums and physical plans at lowest cost, or local natural monopolies such as water and sewerage systems, trunk or local roads and lighting?[27] As with firms, the optimal size will vary depending on the good or service. But local authorities run many unrelated services whose optimal sizes are different on efficiency grounds. Unless one is prepared to enter an even more complicated discussion of the pros and cons of distinct authorities for different services, given that in Britain there are at most two (and often only one) statutory local authorities in any geographical area, compromises must be made, whatever may theoretically be best for each service taken separately. Almost always the economies of scale are overstated, and the diseconomies of loss of control understated, while agreement on optimal size is seldom reached.

In practice, two other arguments ought to be more important than size. The first is the strong probability that the costs of changing the *status quo* in any direction are greater than the efficiency gains from doing so, and they are in any case less easily quantified. Neither has stopped local government reorganization in the past: however, the transactions-costs argument against change has become more powerful, partly because of pressure on public expenditure and partly because experience does not demonstrate net savings from local government reorganizations.[28] The second is that the economies-of-scale argument used to be distorted by the historic preference of central government for fewer, and therefore larger, local authorities, for counties rather than districts.

However, the vexed issue of optimal size in service delivery can be disregarded altogether if local authority provision is separated from production. No longer confined within given territorial boundaries, production can take on the size most appropriate to every service market. Producers can acquire or be acquired by other firms or by charities or autonomous public bodies. Producers of services such as waste disposal or residential homes for the elderly may become national or even international in scope. Other services may be suitable for a large number of small service deliverers, others again may work well if different-sized firms, third-sector and autonomous public bodies compete. What matters, and is emerging in Britain, is that there should always be free entry; the competition authorities should be able to ensure through regulation that there is fair competition; that no service market is dominated by a small number of firms; and that central government should state with clarity what standards of supply or other central constraints on local discretion are to obtain; and what procedures are to exist to resolve conflicts between central and local government and between local authorities.[29] Provided those conditions hold, service efficiency will improve because subject to competition or regulation. Even officials whose activities are regulatory (for example, environmental health officers) are more easily denationalized in a local than in a national context. Local authorities could franchise the activity knowing that in the event of failure they can turn to other firms – as, for example, with school inspectors. However, for reasons to be discussed in the next chapter, there are functions – of which the police is the most obvious – where there are strong arguments against trying to create a competitive market.

Some argue that authorities could be too small to do provision well, but many US local authorities have small populations and yet organize themselves none the less satisfactorily as buyers of services and arrangers of competitions, buying procurement expertise from consultants. As Gordon Tullock has put it: 'If the voter must elect officials on the basis of their dealing with 1000 problems, he will exert less influence on the average problem than he would if there were only 100.'[30]

The case for elected local government

John Stuart Mill advanced the most relevant criterion for local authority size. At that time it was common to have distinct local authorities for different activities: administering the poor law, paving, sanitation, water, and later for schools.[31] While Mill agreed with separating all these and other services into separate executives – largely continued until this day – he believed there should be 'but one elected body for all local business', instead of many, mostly elected on a great variety of franchises.[32] He made what we now would recognize as a distinction between production and provision. He saw the activity of control as better done by a single body which has 'for its proper business to consider the interest of the locality as a whole, composed of parts all of which must be adapted to each other'.[33] He then went on to say that the best unit was whatever place had sufficient sense of identity to act together, whether town or county, which was, in more modern terms, a community. A strong inference from this and other arguments advanced in this chapter, is that there is no obvious case for regional government. If there was one, it would be to reduce overload in central government (see Chapter 11).

In this context *locally elected* authorities are more likely to reflect local preferences than are the localized agencies of central government.[34] Not many agencies have local boards, but those that do are appointed, and usually non-executive. Their powers vary from supervisory to purely advisory. No clear philosophy of management underlies these variations. The more boards are supervisory, the more independence they are supposed to have, but this independence is generally qualified by the fact such boards generally depend on central government for all or most of their money. Moreover, the multiplication of such jobs has meant an increase in patronage which in recent years has resulted in the majority of these posts going to Conservatives or Conservative sympathizers. This trend may lead to reflection of central government's 'political' priorities rather than local 'political', let alone actual consumer priorities. It is not efficient in terms of the consumers' interest.[35] What are these appointments for, if not to make localized boards responsive to ministers as agents? Are they to be chosen because they know local conditions or wants, or for some other reason? If the latter, is it managerial or in some other identifiable respect in the public interest, or is it 'political'?

Contrast this position with that of locally elected authorities. Election is a necessary but not sufficient condition for independence. Rules, regulations and other forms of central control can so restrict the freedom of locally elected councillors that they have no real independence. But where they have discretion and are able to select and influence their own executives, greater diversity in policy and provision between areas should result. It is the crucial argument for local election that those elected must be presumed to be better interpreters of local consumer needs because they are less subject to direction and influence from the centre, and because it is in their interest to get to know as many different types among their constituents as possible and to act for them where they can. For the same reasons, where services require experts as purchasers, their supervision and surveillance are better done by local councils than in remote Whitehall.

In many locations, and in Britain more than elsewhere in Europe, the sense of local coherence Mill sought has declined over the last century. A local sense of identity, drawing upon local sources of enthusiasm and knowledge, may need to be encouraged. No local services are so sophisticated that they need large local authorities to provide enough technically expert staff, because such experts can be hired short-term when needed. Economic development is more likely to gain energetic backing if it is local, but be more likely to capture international attention if national or regional. However, local government can cooperate over that and both strategic and transport planning, though central government needs the authority to intervene if there is significant noncooperation. Though there will be difficulties however boundaries are drawn and many issues will be of intense local interest, its necessary scope need not be 'national' in the UK. Inter-governmental externalities might retain enough importance in transport and some other aspects of planning to make larger associations of local government useful, but rarely are they sufficient to justify regional government.

We believe that regional government is too large to be best for the efficient provision of public goods and services. It would not be needed in the great areas of policy, which seem rightly national, but may be in secondary legislation where a regional capability might speed up action and where there might be scope for acceptable variations (as currently in Scotland, Northern Ireland and Wales). However, this development would be at odds with the role of Parliament unless carefully distinguished. The strongest administrative case for regional government is to reduce overload at the centre, but it is not one we will make in Chapters 11 and 12. Nevertheless, the cry for stronger regions is an understandable protest against a process of centralization which has imposed the values of the South of England and, for a long period, of the Conservative Party on the rest of the UK, and has threatened the minimum necessary consensus upon which the identity of any nation depends. The right answer is to restore diversity at the most local level rather than create a regional diversity still remote from the individual citizen.

Where services are sufficiently important to those who use them and are likely to command enough local publicity and interest, there is a case for extending local government by establishing special-purpose authorities with their own elections. Because of the probable ease with which such interest could be created in education and health, there is a case for creating them in the consumer's and the citizen's interest. An elected health or education authority could develop a strong local voice to act as an expert purchaser or overseer of expert purchasers (see the discussion of internal markets below). However, US and nineteenth-century UK experience suggest that if too many elected special-purpose authorities are created, electors tire of voting.[36] Moreover, such authorities develop tunnel vision: they cannot decide on community priorities. A balance needs to be struck between activities where it ought to be possible to galvanize local communities into sufficient interest to sustain special-purpose authorities and the rest which should stay with general-purpose authorities.[37]

Thus emphasis on consumerism makes it hard to resist the conclusion that local provision should be decided as close to the consumer as possible. Where it cannot be done through the market, the best proxy would seem to be the smallest elected authorities that reflect a local sense of community. Moreover, one can follow the market in positively welcoming the fact that services will be better where populations are more affluent: better services for areas that want and can afford them if people are prepared to pay. If a community wants two refuse collections a week and another wants one, why should the first not pay more? Local diversity entails such differences.[38] Indeed, as a result, the argument for decentralization has been called one for effectiveness.[39]

Despite the recent and growing use of consumer surveys, it remains harder for national than for local government to monitor in detail who uses the services it provides, and harder still to use such information to devise or manage the services most suitable for each and every local community.[40] The more defined the rules and standards governing service performance can be, the easier it is to set its priorities from a distance, and the less need for local discretion. But relying on uniform rules, determined at a distance, can be very demotivating for those delivering the services and can also result in great inhumanity. Conversely, the more discretion there is, the harder it is to manage centrally. Where clients are least able to look after their own needs, a provider close at hand is likely to result in a higher standard of services; but perversely, central politicians are frequently more interested in services where there is a large element of discretion than in those which are rule-bound. The worst situations arise when there is a pretence that a service – such as the prison service – can be managed through a mixture of central rules and delegated powers; while in practice central ministers believe they need to intervene frequently from afar and without detailed knowledge of local circumstances. The greater selectivity implied by current thinking on social welfare programmes and by greater reliance on targeted expenditures because of fiscal crisis will make it harder to manage such programmes centrally.

Protection for minorities

If local authorities first look after the interests of those who give them their majority, there will then be minorities whose interests will also need protection.[41] The further proposition that as far as possible those who stand to gain from the provision of services should be involved in their management and delivery raises the possibility that their own interests may be given undue weight, which will raise problems for minorities. Sometimes substantial cost savings and physical quality improvements flow from empowerment, but it may also mean that the benefits going to a dominant (ethnic) group will increase. However, central government can protect minority interests without taking services over. It can make universal service a statutory requirement or discriminatory taxes or charges illegal. It can ensure that services are provided for specified minorities on specified terms. But it cannot require local authorities to use their discretion in particular ways, since it would be self-contradictory. Consequently, there may be services which central government wishes to keep from local government because such a conflict of interest is endemic. There was a major clash between central government and some local authorities in the 1920s over what was called 'Poplarism'. It started when the Poplar local authority decided to pay its workers more than market rates and its citizens on poor relief more than standard rates.[42] This led to litigation, which central government won because the courts decided that it was unreasonable in law to pay more than market wages or standard rates of poor relief. But it was a factor leading to poor relief's eventually being taken away from local authorities in 1936. However, it should be possible to reverse such centralization in many instances, replacing it by a framework of rules, compliance audit and systems of inspection which protect designated minorities.

Minorities may also need to be protected from central government. The diversity local government provides means that some minorities at least are more likely to find some authorities to their liking in a country where local authorities have discretion. And central government may not wish to protect all minorities – indeed, central powers may even be used to discriminate against minorities which would have otherwise been over-favoured locally (opted-out schools with Moslem governors are an example). This again justifies the case for independent systems of audit and inspection so that the relevant facts may be known.

The practice of redistribution

Therefore when central government wishes to pursue redistributive or paternalistic policies through local government services, central government does not have to provide, let alone produce, such services. Efficiency arguments tend the other way. Instead, it can use a well-designed system of grants to achieve its redistributive and paternalistic objectives, while leaving provision and service delivery local. Even where standard services are desirable, which we would argue matters only where exact equality of opportunity or access matters, as in education, neither the transfer of services to central government nor central government interference in the provision of local services has, in practice, resulted in standardized services across the nation.

It has been normal policy in the UK to ensure that different authorities are able to provide a minimum level of service, irrespective of their relative affluence. For many years relations between central and local government were eased by a succession of block grant regimes which used central grants and funds to enable all local authorities to provide some notional minimum standard of service in most of their activities, at the same cost per head to ratepayers.[43] It has been done through various forms of equalization grant, which make up the difference between local taxes levied per head and the standard cost of providing these services in a bench-mark authority. Over the years standard costs have often been replaced by estimated needs, so that authorities, for example with a particularly high proportion of non-English-speaking children, will have this need reflected in higher grants from central government. Minimal standards were rarely stated. The great advantage of this was that it was left to local authorities to determine their own standards. The principle was that authorities were able to provide more than the minimum if they could persuade a majority of their ratepayers to go on electing them to do so. While local authorities are not forced to spend additional money on the services in question, inspection can ensure that at least minimum-standard facilities are provided to meet need. In such ways minority interests may also be safeguarded.

Therefore, it is possible for provision to be local for most services, including many currently provided by central government or by agencies and quangos, while allowing central government to intervene redistributively or paternalistically to require local authorities to follow redistributive policies; to pursue such policies of its own, to that extent using local authorities as its agents; to protect minorities; and to give local authorities grants with which to subsidize some or all of their activities. As argued in Chapter 3, there is an additional argument that local preferences will be better satisfied the looser the redistributive and paternalistic specifications given local authorities so they have more freedom to specify and manage in the local interest.

The flawed case for centralization

In the UK between 1979 and 1990 more time was spent in legislation, Cabinet and Cabinet committee on local government than on any other topic.[44] Yet the outcome was almost entirely to diminish local government.[45] Between 1979 and 1995 over 150 acts altered, mostly reduced, local authority powers. There seem to have been four main arguments why.[46]

The first concerned the superiority of central provision. The Thatcher government asserted that most services were more efficiently provided centrally because local government was incompetent and wasteful and there were a few local authorities strongly resistant to any improvement in their efficiency.[47] This argument is no longer tenable. Whatever may have been true in the 1970s and early 1980s, the efficiency of local government has greatly improved since, in part because of a more thorough and earlier adoption of techniques such as contracting out than in central government. Moreover, the Audit Commission and the various inspectorates have had a greater effect in stimulating innovation, efficiency and better quality there and in the National Health Service than the National Audit Office has achieved in central government.

A second reason for distrusting local government at the beginning of the 1980s was its alleged lesser legitimacy because of electoral turn-outs which were lower than in general elections and lower than in most other nations' local elections (those of the United States are an exception, despite that country's reputation as a home of active local government), coupled with the argument that British local elections are most often determined by national issues.[48] However, these arguments can be turned around: local election turn-outs had stayed around 40 per cent since the early 1970s. Around a third of local electors could name a councillor. More than three-quarters were satisfied with local services. While in many countries central issues are more important than local ones in local elections, there is still evidence that local performance and issues make a difference.[49] Local turn-out increased during the period of the poll tax, which indeed was one of the hopes central government had had in adopting it. Giving more importance to local government and increasing what it does is likely to increase turn-out and raise the impact of local issues on local elections.

A third argument was that during the 1970s most local authorities altered from being 'officer'- to 'member'-led, so reducing their efficiency and increasing the opportunities for 'political' behaviour. This accusation is ironical on two counts. A great many initiatives were taken in the 1980s which reversed this, increasing the powers of officers relative to members, and thus restoring the Haldane position in local government.[50] The second irony was that this shift which the Thatcher government stigmatized, but reversed, in local government is the mirror-image of the change of power within central government from official to politician, to which central government has no objection.

The fourth and final argument is concerned with overspending. Central governments commonly contend that local governments will overspend if given the chance. With central government encouragement, local spending grew rapidly from the end of the 1950s. Fiscal crisis from the mid-1970s prompted the view that local authorities should also contribute to the necessary reduction in overall public expenditure. Committed to a reduction in public expenditure which they found hard to achieve (see Chapter 1), the Thatcher governments were incensed by increases in local government spending, despite ministers' efforts to restrain it.[51] This macroeconomic consideration was the most powerful factor driving central government to restrict local government's taxing and spending powers. But it worked. Almost all local authorities restrained their expenditure as central government wanted, often with greater success than central government had in restraining its own. (Much of the increase in local expenditure could also be attributed to central government either from extra requirements imposed by it or dealing with the consequences of central policies such as the poll tax.)

By the mid-1980s, however, high spending in a very few authorities was sustained by an electoral majority who did not pay rates because they were exempt as too poor, but who benefited from the expansion of services for which they did not pay, though in many cases their spouses or those from whom they let rooms may have paid for them.[52] It was another reason which led central government to cap local authority spending, thereby removing discretion to provide additional services of higher quality (or the same services inefficiently). As the struggle to contain local expenditure grew, more local authorities found their rates and later their council taxes capped. It would have been better if central government had recognized there was no sound macroeconomic reason for limiting local government expenditure provided it was funded 100 per cent at the margin by the local taxpayer.[53] Instead central government determined both the minimum and maximum levels of services.

Some commentators have tried to relate the growth of public expenditure itself to the extent of decentralization. It has been argued that the greater the extent of Tiebout competition the lower will be tax and expenditures as local governments compete with each other. It is also argued that electors will vote for and receive more public services, and hence pay more taxes, if local authorities are relatively more powerful, because local governments are better able to provide what citizens want.[54] On the other hand, it is argued that, as a centralized system approaches a monopoly, it will give more force to Niskanen-style pressures (see Chapter 2) to increase the size of the public sector. The difficulty in practice is that empirical investigations give no clear idea on the broad direction of the relationship between public expenditure growth and the extent of decentralization.[55]

However, the cost to local government of providing services is less than their full cost because of government grant and also because of what is in effect a grant from businesses, the non-domestic rate. From an economic standpoint, grants create excess demand: greater dependence on central government grant is positively related to the growth of local expenditure. This problem may be mitigated by limiting central government sources of finance to where there are specific contracts with local government as a producer or provider or by giving them as a lump sum a block grant which is unalterable within the year. Otherwise local government has to finance its own expenditure from taxes paid by its electors (and by borrowing on its own credit). Central government grant should be cash-limited, or 'close-ended', so that any additional expenditure above that funded by grant falls entirely on the local taxpayer, who also benefits exclusively from any underspending of grant.[56] A resolute course of action would be for a central government to freeze its grant in real terms or even allow it to decline to reflect a predetermined expectation of local productivity improvement (provided any new services or improved services statutorily required of local government are clearly specified and funded by appropriate additions to grant).

The transfer of more services from central to local government, even of large services such as the National Health Service and social security, could be financed by increasing grant pro rata. Such dependence on grant money which it had no discretion to alter would make no concessions to long-standing arguments that free local authorities need a tax base of their own which they can vary at will.[57] In practice, local authorities could find some of the resources they need to improve their services or introduce new ones through their own greater efficiency, if they were able to keep and use a reasonable, predetermined proportion of those efficiency gains. Certainly it would be both unwise and unnecessary to delay further decentralization of public services to local authorities until after a fundamental reform of local government finance.*

Even in these circumstances there may be a problem in a very few local authorities because of a mismatch between taxpayers and electors. For example, business ratepayers in Britain no longer have the local votes they once had. More materially, rate, and more recently council tax, rebates of up to 100 per

---

* The issue is constitutional and legal rather than practical. Is local government a partner in a federal or quasi-federal system? If so, that may be held to imply that it needs its own source of finance. If not, its practical freedom depends on its being able to spend its own efficiency savings. However, the belief that he who pays the piper calls the tune has a long history. A strand in NPM is the need to get away from that belief in the interests of efficiency and consumer choice.

cent to poorer citizens meant that in many local authorities there was an electoral majority with no financial interest in restraining its spending. But the mismatch could have been dealt with specifically as there were few such authorities. The poll tax produced a device by which even the poorest paid some local taxation: those on income support paid 20 per cent of the normal entitlement but were compensated by extra social security up to the average value of that 20 per cent. They therefore had to pay 20 per cent of any increase in taxes beyond that average value or norm. Since the possibility of this type of expedient was ended by the débâcle of the poll tax and affected very few local authorities, consideration could have been given to special arrangements – indeed rate-capping – for such authorities.

Frequently a distrust of local power, and therefore a tendency by central government to prefer centralization, reflects a central party in power unable to tolerate local diversity, especially if it means accepting what other political parties want to provide. Such centralization will naturally appeal to a party that hopes to stay in power for a long time, or believes it can keep its opponents out by limiting their chances to shape and gain experience locally. In this case the argument for centralization is circular, in that the 'political' interests of central government may determine what localized services it provides (or does not want to provide, such as gypsy sites) – and it may be a stronger reason for centralization than any arguments from efficiency or consumer choice.[58]

Thus it can be maintained that the arguments for centralization could be countered reasonably by the establishment of appropriate measures which would allow much provision of public services to be given to local authorities.

Internal markets

Provision may be best left to local authorities in most circumstances, but there are others where expert purchasers may be preferable. The redistributive framework is generally best left to central government which may wish to reflect its own, or need to reflect EU, paternalistic requirements. Beyond that, there are inspection and audit roles best played by independent bodies which could include local authorities where they are not providers. There is also the important requirement that there should be effective grievance-handling pro-cedures. A way of deciding how these different roles should be performed is through the creation of internal markets, where competitors inside the system compete only with each other. Competition is restricted because free competi-tion would lead to 'cream-skimming' the most profitable services. In a free market some hospitals might offer to take only those cases which were rela-tively easy to treat – as broadly determined by some simple parameters such as age, previous health record and presence of complications – because it would yield most profit. Similarly, free competition in schooling could mean that schools targeted pupils more likely to achieve certain standards or whose par-ents were willing to top up public money with fees or donations. Restricting competition in such cases is designed to protect certain principles of equity such as equality of opportunity or access. It is consistent with competition between private and voluntary or other third-sector and autonomous public bodies, as both health and education in the UK illustrate.

Housing

Public policy in recent years has been to reduce local authorities' role in the provision of housing. Almost all new housing is now produced by housing associations which are third-sector bodies. Tenants pay them full economic rents. Those who cannot pay market rents have the difference made up by rent allowances. There is also a policy of encouraging of transfer the ownership and management of existing public housing to housing associations or trusts. This can be done more easily where estates have been well maintained and there are no undue problems with tenants, though even then the sheer size of many such estates can alter the balance in housing associations from their being developers of housing into managers. But on bad estates where there are many manage-ment problems and policy is difficult, housing associations may be reluctant to take this management on.

The general assumption is that the enthusiasm of empowered manage-ment groups will produce higher quality and lower costs than if all the labour were professional and paid as such, because of the greater dedication and higher motivation of those who are paid. But such a policy will not always be cheaper; nor is there a guarantee of superior productivity or ability. If tenants in a block or neighbours in a street were to determine who gets vacant properties, experi-ence, largely American, suggests they would then adopt their own priorities. There would be a danger that what can be justified in efficiency grounds can also be criticized as gerrymandering. The interests of the managers might prevail and they would often be different from those of the majority of tenants. Since they would be likely to be appointed rather than elected, their biases would not be justifiable democratically, and there could be conflicts between their objectives and other political goals. Finally, there would be the possibility of corruption.

However, local authorities retain one important power in public hous-ing. They decide who receives new or vacant accommodation according to their priorities. Otherwise would-be tenants would have to rely solely on the policies of different housing associations operating in their area. Private or third-sector bodies could not be equipped to take on the comprehensive duty of providing for the statutorily homeless, even though collectively they pro-duce most of the accommodation. However much new housing is privatized, or management responsibility handed over to housing associations, some func-tions remain to be provided publicly. The problems arise because markets are not allowed to work – there is a shortage of supply in many locations that creates a need for rationing, while the homeless have a right to housing, irrespective of their means. In these circumstances there is a strong argument that the determination of provision should be given to elected representatives, as they have a mandate to decide what priorities should prevail and to trade off one policy against another. Such rationing cannot be done efficiently or fairly by central government. Another role for local authorities could be, armed with inspectors' reports, to step in when public or housing association management fails to the point where existing management needs strengthening or replacing.

Thus an internal market could be set up where the overall policy and financial framework is determined from centre, where there are independent systems of regulation, inspection and audit, where provision becomes the task of local government; and yet most production and housing management is the responsibility of private, third-sector and autonomous public bodies.

Welfare services

In the same way, welfare services can be produced privately or by third-sector bodies, but these organizations cannot ensure that there is a place for everyone who needs it, either in a crisis or in the long term, even if there were always sufficient money through social security to pay for the accommodation and other needs of the various welfare groups. To rely solely on individuals armed with state money and family support for help would result in very uneven provision; moreover, there is a need for expert inspection of standards of care and audit of the use of state funds. The problem of rationing supply, and the need to ensure that what is provided does not fall below a standard the community regards as the minimum tolerable, make a case for elected local government being involved as provider and remover or reformer of poor management, with independent regulation, inspection and audit. Additionally, there is no reason why local government should not provide better services than the minimum central government lays down and finances, if it so chooses.

Education

Parental choice and grant-maintained status might at first suggest that there is no need for local education authorities. But the internal market solution presumes a spare capacity in the system, which exists in some places but not in others. As parents flock to the best schools, these become full and have to turn pupils away. Though successful schools could expand their accommodation, public expenditure constraints make it difficult through continued central control of capital spending. Moreover, schools may not wish to expand for fear of losing their excellence. The theory is that schools losing numbers will be galvanized into becoming better. Though there is a cash inducement for them to tempt more pupils, there is no discipline equivalent to bankruptcy to replace old by new management to make better use of old assets. The more likely outcome is that schools will become highly differentiated – some will become 'sink' schools for already disadvantaged children, while the better schools will have fewer problems, more affluent parents and will spend more on pupils. Not only will it be socially divisive but it will be unfair on late developers: many pupils from poor homes will end up in the wrong schools. While there is some justification for service differentiation inasmuch as a different education is needed for different vocations, a society which prizes equality of opportunity must not let any school fall too far below a standard level of competence. Moreover, not all parents are knowledgeable and responsible. Local education authorities – whether special or general – ought to be in a good position, because of the expertise they can acquire and their closeness to parents, children, teachers and local employers, to help parents and teachers discharge their responsibilities as governors, while stepping in if a school becomes too bad – within a financial framework provided by central government and independent inspection and audit. There are many decisions currently taken by ministers, for example on school closure and sixth-form provision, which could be transferred to local education authorities. However, the internal market for education needs measures to equalize opportunity, including positive discrimination.[59] It is hard to see this equalization as achievable except with funds and within a framework laid down by central government, though there may still be a role for local authorities to ensure local equity is achieved and as producers alongside private, charitable and opted-out (autonomous public) schools.

Health

The development of the internal market in health may be expected to lead to area health authorities being cut out as providers and producers. Self-managed hospitals, health centres and practitioner units might gain from being independent of health authorities whose role is becoming more problematic as new arrangements take over. In the health system expert opinion is a probably more important characteristic of a purchaser than general local knowledge and the sanction of election. But it remains to be seen how well and how universally general practitioners manage to combine their purchasing and medical roles as there are dangers in leaving provision entirely to experts. Whitehall is too remote to be credible in being involved in as much health management as it is.

As a minimum there would seem to be a case for locally identifiable and elected authorities to oversee and inspect local health care to develop a view on whether citizens are receiving a good deal, and to form a view on behalf of the electorate on the adequacy of the criteria doctors use in determining priorities and rationing the budget accordingly. There would still be a need for purchaser authorities to act on behalf of the hospitals and general practices. As in education, there will be a tendency for more affluent areas to give better provision, topped up by additional resources, while 'sink' hospitals provide for the less fortunate. But there were great disparities before there was an internal market and only inspection and audit intervention would be able to help local authorities avoid this differentiation. Moreover, a health service in which expenditure is to be controlled requires both managed competition and limits on total spending.[60]

Extensions of the internal market

As these examples show, the case for local public provision rests upon the extent to which it involves a local community interest. On this basis many executive agencies, from the prisons to social security and employment offices, many of which originated in local government, could be returned to it. If services have to be rationed, the case for a local political resolution is at its strongest, since only elected politicians have the legitimacy and knowledge to decide priorities on behalf of the local community – except possibly where decisions require expert opinion on the likely success of different procedures or institutions. Moreover, the more local the elected politicians in relation to the client group, the more likely it is that they will know and understand local needs and feelings. However, against the undoubted advantages of closeness to the client group must be set the probability that politicians and officials may be less experienced and in the limit more susceptible to influence, patronage and corruption. Accountability via audit, inspection and good grievance procedures are therefore key. It is sometimes argued against small authorities that there are not enough good members to go round, but this may be a chicken-and-egg problem: give them more responsibility and their members will rise to the occasion. The answer to 'bad' authorities is to give them publicity through inspection and audit, and in the limit for continuously poor services to be taken over for a limited time.

Conclusion

Both theory and practice suggest that the belief that central government must be more efficient than local government has little to recommend it – rather the reverse. Some local authorities will always be more efficient than others. But localized agencies are unlikely to be as capable as elected local authorities of reflecting local interest. Moreover, they must be more susceptible to the risks of ministerial and national party patronage. Our discussion shows that, if the political wish is to give as much rein as possible to actual consumer wishes in providing public goods and services, there is a powerful argument in favour of decentralization. It provides more scope for competition, eliminates layers of bureaucracy, and avoids the imposition of policies designed with only national political objectives in mind. Minorities may be protected by relying on rules and other procedures to secure minimum standards, which nevertheless leave considerable discretion to local politicians to reflect the needs and wishes of their communities. The more central government devolves provision in this way, the more its role is restricted to policy-making, that is, the initiation of legislation, rule-setting and regulation. Government in Britain at least has missed an important trick in not relying more on decentralization, especially elected decentralization, to hollow out government and reduce overload at the centre.

Notes

1 Cannan (1927), p. viii.
2 Robson (1948), pp. 16–55; see also Foster *et al.* (1980), pp. 56–63; Loughlin *et al.* (1985).
3 Duncan and Hobson (1995), pp. 358–62; Jenkins (1995); Marr (1995), pp. 342–6.
4 Mill (1910).
5 Mill (1910), p. 348.
6 Griffith (1966).
7 Based on Foster *et al.* (1980), pp. 39–76.
8 Foster *et al.* (1980), pp. 538–40, 574–6.
9 Tiebout (1956); see also Brennan and Buchanan (1980).
10 See, for example, Bewley (1981); Stiglitz (1983); Thoni (1992).
11 Harrison (1876), ch. 10, 24.
12 For example, in the 1890s, Marshall (1926), pp. 342–53; Cannan (1927), ch. 8.
13 Foster *et al.* (1980), pp. 50–1.
14 Foster *et al.* (1980), pp. 326–37; Dowding *et al.* (1994).
15 Webb and Webb (1963), pp. 130–1.
16 Osborne and Gaebler (1992), pp. 49–75.
17 Landy (1993), p. 25.
18 Milkis, cited by Landy (1993), p. 25.
19 Landy (1993), p. 40.
20 Landy (1993), p. 38.
21 Green (1889); Mill (1910), p. 348; Oakeshott (1962).
22 Murray (1990, 1994).
23 Widdicombe (1986).
24 Barzelay (1992), pp. 90–5.
25 Barzelay (1992), pp. 37–57.
26 Based on Foster *et al.* (1980), pp. 559–83; see also Oates (1972); King (1984).
27 See, for example, Redcliffe-Maud (1969).
28 See, for example, Leach (1990).
29 Painter (1991); Walsh (1991).
30 Tullock (1965), pp. 221–2.
31 See Webb and Webb (1922).
32 Mill (1910), p. 351.
33 Mill (1910), p. 351.
34 Ranson and Stewart (1994), p. 102.
35 Aucoin (1990), p. 129.
36 Webb and Webb (1922).
37 See Foster *et al.* (1980), pp. 584–94.
38 But see Oakland (1983).
39 Jones (1991), p. 12.
40 Bramley *et al.* (1992).
41 See, for example, Downs (1967).
42 Branson (1974).
43 See, for example, Foster *et al.* (1980), pp. 242–83.
44 Jones (1991), p. 5.
45 Jenkins (1995).

46 See Butler *et al.* (1994), p. 265.
47 Baker (1993), see also Clarke in Balen (1992), p. 70; Thatcher and Ridley in Butler *et al.* (1994), p. 89 and pp. 98–9 respectively; Waldegrave (1994), p. 6.
48 Widdicombe (1986), pp. 27–41.
49 Butler *et al.* (1994), p. 283.
50 Following the Widdicombe report (1986).
51 Lawson (1992), ch. 43; Butler *et al.* (1994).
52 Widdicombe (1986), p. 40.
53 Foster and Jackman (1982).
54 Oates (1972).
55 Gemmell (1993c).
56 Foster and Jackman (1982).
57 Foster *et al.* (1980), pp. 30–4.
58 But see Metcalfe and Richards (1987), pp. 76–94.
59 Fallon (1993).
60 Aaron (1992), p. 56.

8

The agency: incomplete separation

> As a general rule, every executive function, whether superior or subordinate,
> should be the appointed duty of some given individual. It should be apparent
> to all the world who did everything and through whose default anything was
> left undone. Responsibility is null when no one knows who is responsible.
> Not, even when it is real, can it be divided, without being weakened.
>
> J.S. Mill[1]

What other than privatization, contractorization and the creation of internal
markets can improve the quality of public services while making substantial
public expenditure savings? This chapter compares a third model of separation –
the creation of arm's-length bodies within government, and in particular Next
Steps agencies – against the principles and models described in earlier chapters.

Departments, agencies and other public bodies

Most governmental systems have agencies under some name, that is government units not headed by a minister. In the USA, because the president
appoints both cabinet officers and federal agency heads, and because both are
under his executive control, there is little real administrative difference between government departments and large federal agencies. Indeed, the most
recent departments have been created largely by combining existing agencies;
while many remaining agencies remain comparable to departments in their
political and budgetary importance. The Clinton–Gore reforms in 1992 to
achieve greater efficiency in government were directed towards both.[2]

In countries where there is no similar tradition of unified executive
power, there may be greater differences between ministerial departments and
other public bodies. In Britain, the doctrine of ministerial responsibility means
that public bodies, including long-established bodies and the post-1988 executive agencies, have almost always been in some sense the responsibility of
departmental ministers (except in a few cases where responsibility is to Parliament). The degree of that responsibility varies from bodies which have a
statutory independence defined by legislation to those which have no formal

legal existence. At both extremes their reliance on central finance affects the actual degree of independence.

Public bodies have been of every kind and description. There were persistent attempts in the nineteenth century to abolish or prevent autonomous statutory public bodies not accountable to Parliament.[3] However, they were invariably found to be a convenient method of doing business. There was a spate of appointed commissioners during the 1830s and 1840s.[4] The most famous were the Poor Law Commissioners, who had to dismantle the old Speenhamland system of poor relief, and replace it by a harsher regime.[5] They were established to overcome local resistance to the new regime and secure uniformity of application. But the independent power they arrogated to themselves became resented and they were abolished. Nevertheless, as the state grew in the twentieth century, the constitutional principle of ministerial responsibility for all executive action, other than that of bodies whose powers and duties were defined by statute, became increasingly difficult to uphold in its entirety.[6] Parliament created public bodies by statute in ever-increasing numbers. There were public trusts, boards, nationalized industries and other public corporations, even public bodies with the status of charities. There were standing statutory commissions, councils and committees. As well as statutory bodies there were many parts of government departments given their own labels and at times substantial practical independence. The ancient tax-collecting departments of the Inland Revenue and Customs and Excise had the status of non-ministerial government departments, a status also acquired much later by the independent regulators of privatized utilities.

There thus developed a profusion of public bodies for which no typology was ever satisfactory.[7] Quangos – 'quasi non-governmental organisations' – as they were somewhat loosely and inaccurately called (since they are definitely governmental), are not constituent parts of government proper, central or local.

Quangos and 'quangocracy', meaning rule by these bodies rather than by ministers responsible to Parliament, were themselves the symptoms of rapid public expenditure growth as ministers sought to increase the span of government without increasing their workload. They were a target of the incoming Thatcher government in 1979, and significant effort was put into reducing their numbers, without great success.[8] Some, such as royal commissions, were put in abeyance. Others, mostly nationalized industries, were privatized. But many survived (though reviled as a class). However, by 1988 the government appeared to have turned full circle, creating separate bodies partly to replace functions previously carried out by local government and, in the case of executive agencies specifically, in the interests of better management in central government itself. Between 1988 and 1994, 97 new 'executive agencies' were created as part of the Next Steps programme, embracing around two-thirds of the central civil service – around 340,000 people.[9]

Quangos and other similar bodies had varying degrees of practical independence depending as much on convention as on statutory powers. Their boards or their heads were ministerial appointments, but once appointed they could not be dismissed easily during their term of office. However, most quangos rely on public money for their funds, and the chief executive is usually accountable for funds to Parliament. British practice is for the civil service to operate to ensure that ministers' wishes are reflected in the actions of quangos, unless there is a special reason – as with the BBC – for distancing a quango from ministers. Therefore, in a general sense, all quangos and executive agencies are agencies. And, indeed, comparable functions may be carried out by quangos and agencies. For example, Historic Scotland is an agency while English Heritage is a quango; both are concerned with historic buildings. From the viewpoint of improving efficiency, quangos and executive agencies raise similar issues, and therefore will be considered together in the remainder of this chapter.

The administrative case for change

In many respects the British departmental system has worked well but the administrative forms which were current even at the end of the 1980s had been created in essence before the Second World War, and the administrative structures and attitudes in government departments were permeated by private-sector management theories of the interwar period. Span-of-control ideas determined the number of grades in a hierarchy. As government departments and the agencies grew larger, the number of levels in the hierarchy multiplied. In the United States the number of layers grew to the extent that there were 32 senior levels and 52 levels altogether in the federal hierarchy by 1992.[10] Smaller countries such as Britain, with small bureaucracies may have had fewer levels, but the same tendency was there.

Given the strong managerial arguments for change, it would have been logical if each reforming government had thought through what was needed from first principles. In Britain one might have expected that the lessons of the nearly completed privatization programme had been digested. Conclusions might have been drawn on what provision and production within government might have been privatized, what transferred to third-sector or autonomous public status, what contractorized, what provision assigned to central and local government, what internal markets formed and what was not suitable for such changes. Given the Conservative governments' reluctance since 1979 to have independent inquiries on such matters, it is not surprising it did not happen, and given the speed and sequence with which changes took place, it is as surprising how well much of it has worked, although not without significant wasted effort. The Gore–Clinton reforms, though not without their successes, had more problems.[11]

The scope for agency status

Let us consider what those first principles might have been before going on to see what happened. To recapitulate: efficient privatization requires that a body's output can be priced and that it has (or can be given) commercial objectives. Non-commercial constraints on its behaviour can be written into its licence, if it has sufficient monopoly power to sustain their net cost, or these costs are separately funded by government. Since the number of public goods and services technically incapable of being priced is small, it follows that what provision may be privatized depends largely on political willingness to stop pursuing non-commercial objectives.

Where provision cannot be privatized, it is still generally possible to privatize delivery through contractorization (or devolve it to third-sector or autonomous public bodies). However, if a clear specification is not possible, a contract will not be efficient. The project or service may be technically too complex or innovative, there may be too many objectives to be met, or there may be too many possible variations and contingencies.

Similar difficulties arise where contracts have to be changed frequently. Volatile and unpredictable demands require changed investment, short contract periods, and hence limited scope for efficiency gains. In such circumstances the case for using private or other contractors is generally, as in defence, that there are international markets in which they can realize economies of scale. Scaled down, a similar argument may justify their use by local governments. Otherwise it ought to be possible to achieve as great or greater efficiency by internalizing production within government departments or other public bodies and without the complications of formal contractual arrangements.

Similarly, if ministers' intentions change rapidly and unpredictably, there will be difficulties in achieving efficiency gains. Predicting what changes ministers will wish to make, and what constraints on their freedom they will be prepared to accept if activities are privatized or contractorized, is difficult even within the lifetime of a single government, especially so as ministers become more political. In all these circumstances command relationships within government may be more appropriate.

There are other arguments for command relations in certain circumstances. In some defence and police services it could be too dangerous to contemplate the possibility that the terms of privatization or of contract could be broken without the state being able to enforce obedience and maintain security. A government would be reluctant to hand over the civil or military security of the state to mercenaries, because of the implication that their loyalty could be bought by someone else. Moreover, they would possess secret information which could be valuable to other countries or to criminals. For similar reasons there may be a reluctance to privatize senior civil servants who have access to secret information, or bodies that possess information of importance to the state – for example, the security services, or even the passport office or other licensing, taxing or regulatory authorities.

The issue is not one of confidentiality of information as such.[12] Many private concerns hold confidential information that could be damaging to their customers – including government – if divulged. Nor is it because there are economies of scale in a monopoly in information. Even if in private ownership, they could be regulated to ensure they do not abuse their monopoly power. (Too much can be taken on trust: government learned only through the press that temporary staff taken on by the Inland Revenue, presumably for economy reasons, could through lax management have access to secret Whitehall and other security telephone numbers).[13] A single national licensing system for vehicles or drivers could be regulated to prevent abuse and allow the police and security services to have access to it where the public interest requires. Concern about improper disclosure to others is matched in data collected in the private sector by banks and other institutions where there are also data protection safeguards. That the management of information should have to be a monopoly does not prevent competition among those who issue vehicle or other licences. As a natural monopoly it is identical in principle to grids and networks which require regulation to ensure fair access. But confidential information should not be subject to competitive tender if there were likely to be an acute conflict between the incumbent's source of financial gain and the public interest. A tendering process with a finite franchise period, after which the incumbent may be displaced, will accelerate such conflicts of interest. In such cases the public interest, so defined, may be a good enough reason for continuing public production.

The damage that could be done if sensitive information is divulged to enemies of the state makes it dangerous for the state to forgo ownership and a command relationship. Despite the New Zealand experience on contracting out policy advice, it would be surprising if ministers were content for all their confidential advisers to be, in effect, mercenaries, willing and able to transfer their allegiance and by implication, ready to tell what they know. Countries such as the United States who rely on temporary advisers at senior levels often find that, when disappointed or dissatisfied, they are willing to reveal, embroider or invent confidential advice they have given.

Disquiet over privatization and contracting out may arise where a body exercises regulatory or other quasi-judicial discretion, for example, benefit offices and immigration officials. If the rules for granting licences, payments and benefits are easily written down so that discretion is limited, privatization or third-sectorization is easier, except that some kind of complaints and appeals system is necessary to replace the process of redress obtainable from ministers through parliamentary questions and other channels of complaint. When an administration of this kind is quasi-judicial, it becomes more difficult to imagine it non-public. This view readily connects with an observation by the political scientist, Aaron Wildavsky, that where (as is normal with public services) objectives are unclear, conformity to procedures replaces financial or other quantitative assessments as a test of appropriateness.[14] It is particularly difficult to insist on, and monitor, such procedures in non-public bodies, unless they themselves are recognizably quasi-judicial. But, as Kettl puts it:

> the harder it is for government to define and monitor its goals, the more it retreats to procedural safeguards. The more it formulates its procedures

the further it seems from focusing on results and the more distant it can seem from citizens and their concerns.[15]

Legal and administrative procedures protect the public interest in so far as they require decision-makers to review evidence, open themselves up to representations and give reasons for their decisions. They increase the probability that a decision-maker bent on reaching a given conclusion against the evidence will not be devious enough to reach that conclusion without patent lies or inconsistencies. The reinforcement of such procedures by an evaluative one (see below) makes it harder still to reach a conclusion against the evidence, but generally not impossible. The same holds for all the regulatory activities of the state.

Another problem area is any activity where the interests of the present generation of users and managers differ from those of future generations. An extreme example is nuclear energy which will find its balance sheet dominated by huge liabilities representing an obligation to decommission plants and dispose of waste into the distant future. Notionally the obligation to meet such liabilities can be the contractual obligation of a private firm; but no government is likely to feel sure that such massive obligations are safe from bankruptcy, given the nature of private interests involved. In the end such assets have to be the responsibility of the state, since the possibility that someone else might have the responsibility and then default on it is too great a danger to the state.

An analogous argument is that in some research government is more likely than the private sector to secure the interests of future generations. Research on long-term environmental issues or on preventive medicine may involve genuine pure public goods where benefits are not easily aligned with any commercial enterprise. No one other than government is likely to fund a long-run research programme on the likelihood of global warming and what to do about it.

Even if activities can be privatized, there may be difficulties in introducing competition. A data base may be a natural monopoly, for example the information gathered by the Ordnance Survey, the Public Record Office, or Companies House. When a franchise is coming to an end, the knowledge that an incumbent could misuse the data it holds could severely inhibit change, while restricting the number of bidders to those known to be secure may limit the effectiveness of the competitive process. In such cases there may be a choice between retaining them within government and setting up a separate regulatory apparatus.

Similar considerations arise where disloyalty could do great damage. The most obvious examples are defence and policing, but the argument can be extended to broadcasting, to avoid the possibility that the government might be excluded from the airwaves in a national emergency. Security interests affect other sectors: a highly fragmented telecommunications system might pose severe difficulties for control of telephone tapping.

Similarly, while private police forces with territorial contracts awarded under franchises are theoretically possible, the conflicts of interest created when such a police force lost or was expected to lose a contract, could be acute. The temptation to misuse knowledge would be great. Such strains have been visible in Russia and Eastern Europe, as well as in many less developed countries. The same holds for troops who are likely to be tempted abroad, if they lose a contract in one country. As Machiavelli said:

> Mercenary contractors are either skilled in warfare or they are not: if they are, you cannot trust them because they are anxious to advance their own greatness, either by coercing you, their employer, or coercing others against your wishes.[16]

There are scientific and technological secrets which it is hard to imagine belonging to anyone other than the state: knowledge of how to make a nuclear bomb, of biological and chemical warfare, and of how to make and decommission weapons using this technology. In certain circumstances the extent of the danger arising from loss of secrecy is a strong argument for avoiding any separation or competition.

A last argument for retaining at least part of the activity within government arises, as in health and some aspects of social security, when there is reason to believe that commercial interests on their own will increase the cost and quality of provision, and no person or body other than the state can be expert enough buyer to restrain them. In health care, expenditure per capita in the UK ranks towards the bottom among major industrial countries, but its results in terms of health outcomes place it near the top. The evidence seems to indicate that expenditure is correlated with the extent of public-sector involvement in its provision: 'in average terms a one percent increase in the ratio of public to total health spending results in an almost equivalent fall in total health expenditure per head'.[17] Thus there are circumstances in which activities may be efficiently retained within the public sector under a command relationship. If contracted out their experience suggests that cost-plus may be the most efficient contract available, provided it is combined with rigorous inspection and periodic evaluation. In effect, cost-plus remains a command, rather than a real contractual, relationship. Thus Kettl sees this as an example of where, 'instead of privatising the [public sector], the federal government's strategies have tended to governmentalise the private sector',[18] because the dependent private firms become more like government firms in their organization and staffing. So that one should not be tempted to let all these arguments justify an indefinite retention of activities in the government and other public sector, the necessity of better organization and management to achieve public expenditure savings must be set against them.

The Next Steps initiative

The British efficiency initiatives of the 1960s, while useful, had failed to bring about real efficiency gains, and the reforms of the early 1980s were perceived to be slow in achieving results. Structural change was recommended on the basis that the uniform design of departments was not necessarily appropriate for all government activities. The main recommendation was that 'agencies should be established to carry out the executive functions of government within a policy and resources framework set by a department'.[19] Thus what was proposed was the establishment, at arm's length, of the executive operations of government in an attempt to give them more managerial autonomy within a quasi-contractual framework.

Substantial effort was put into the creation of executive agencies. This included the creation of a special unit in the Cabinet Office headed by a permanent secretary to facilitate the change. Units were created in a number of departments to push through the creation of agencies. Significant delegated authority for people, pay and money was given to the new agencies. A significant proportion of their new chief executives were appointed from outside the public sector.

As much as anything, the creation of executive agencies recognized that civil service activities were diverse in nature and that the structure of a 'traditional' department was not necessarily – if at all – the most appropriate organizational model. Diverse agencies have been created. One is Her Majesty's Stationery Office,* which to all intents and purposes operated as if it were in the private sector with a private-sector financial regime, in competitive markets, with no obligation on other departments to buy from HMSO. Another very different type is the Chemical and Biological Defence Establishment (now to be part of the larger Defence Research Agency), a research establishment with some production capability and with a policy remit to make an expert input to chemical and biological weapon arms limitations talks. Executive agencies also include organizations as diverse as the Queen Elizabeth II Conference Centre in Parliament Square, the Fire Service College, the Coastguard Service, the Chessington Computer Centre.

The purpose of dissolving complex departments was, as the Prime Minister put it in accepting the report:

> to give much clearer roles for the units which become agencies, clearer roles both towards their departments and their customers, clearer and more demanding performance targets and accountabilities for the agencies, their executives and managers and all their staff – and crucially – a greater sense of corporate identity.[20]

But, notwithstanding the focus on what we have called the economic customer, subsidy was not ruled out. Agencies were to provide, in Major's words, 'public services of the quality citizens deserve at a price the taxpayer can afford'. This stress on quality was not Thatcherite. Neither did this revolution

---

* HMSO existed as a trading fund, and thus effectively a separate entity, before the Next Steps initiative. The major change for HMSO was greater delegated authority to fix its own pay arrangements. In 1996 it was being privatized.

rely on increased charging to raise revenue.[21] Rather, old subsidy patterns were carried forward even under privatization.[22]

The new initiative recognized the view that not all state functions could be privatized. Even so:

> Just because the state remains responsible for ensuring that a public service is provided, it does not mean that it shall be deprived of the energies of private enterprise, the stimulus of the free market or the clarity of independent regulation which have transformed privatised companies.[23]

Nevertheless, at the beginning ministers seem to have been persuaded of the virtues of reinforcing the Next Steps initiative with privatization and competition where possible. The new agencies were to remain within government, but their eventual privatization was not ruled out.[24] The emphasis on privatization increased when there was a change in influence within the Cabinet Office.[25] In 1991 it was said, however, that if an agency were to be privatized, this would normally be declared early on, to avoid the uncertainty that otherwise accompanied the granting of agency status.[26] But the agencies that were privatized in their entirety were few in number, and while the 1994 White Paper reaffirmed the intention to privatize, it too held out only limited examples.[27] It was left to a Treasury minister to reaffirm a stronger commitment, and even then the words suggested a voluntary approach, rather than a concerted government initiative: as agencies flexed their wings, they might well wish to escape into the private sector.[28]

Competition

As described in Chapter 6, the main vehicle for introducing competition was the Government's market-testing programme which cut across the Next Steps initiative. Establishing agencies required a significant and costly investment in new accounting and information systems, in structures of authority, and in new senior management brought in from outside. It is hard to see the logic of doing so if, in a relatively short time, significant parts of the organization are to be transferred, under the market-testing programme, to new managers or owners who will not need the paraphernalia of delegated authorities and may well not want the existing accounting and other systems. Indeed, the opportunities for synergies and economies of scale should make those systems more efficient than public-sector ones. This is equally true where the operation may be transferred partially (under market testing) or wholesale (under a prior options review) to the private sector.

The Driver and Vehicle Licensing Agency was first created out of the Ministry of Transport. Subsequently DVLA information technology was carved out of it, market-tested and privatized. What was left behind was largely the regulatory function, which arguably need never have been separated from the department. Companies House and the Passport Office are activities which could have been divided into a regulatory component to be kept in-house and various process activities which could have been privatized or contractorized. If efficiency were the objective, the provider should have been separated from the producer, and production divided into whatever units – product or geographical – were most likely to suit the market, thereby maximizing the possibilities of competition. Such entities could stand on their own feet, or be sold to others, depending on what was most likely to secure their survival. Thus the failure in so many circumstances to solve the aggregation problem was fundamental.

Conversely, establishing agencies paved the way (after the decent interval provided by the 1992 general election) for consideration of their subsequent privatization. But the ability to do so may have been inhibited by market testing, at least where the process has resulted in transfers of activities to the private sector. Where the activities market-tested, and transferred, were support services, this failure is of little consequence, but the closer market testing moves to the core functions of the agency, the more likely is it that a wholesale privatization may be adversely affected. It happens because the synergies which could have been obtained by the transfer to one private-sector producer are no longer available or because what remains is simply too small to be worth bothering about. The same result may have been achieved whichever route – market testing or privatization – the activity went down. But to undertake both routes consecutively is wasteful in terms of the costs of implementation and destructive of the morale of those working in the organization. While it is difficult in government to reach a concerted view of what should be done before acting, the failure to decide the right units of aggregation and disaggregation for market testing, as for privatization, made the endeavour less successful in realizing efficiencies than it could have been.

If competition is such a powerful stimulus to efficiency, the question arises whether it can be used to improve efficiency in government, even where provision or production remains public.[29] For example, HMSO, which currently remains in the public sector, publishes many books and pamphlets which could equally well be produced by commercial publishers, but also has facilities for producing some documents at speed and under conditions of great confidentiality. HMSO could compete with other publishers to produce books and pamphlets, provided government met the full cost of confidential and rapid publications where HMSO has a monopoly. More freedom to compete might enable HMSO to use this subsidy to undercut commercial competition unfairly. Thus, economic regulation is required to ensure there is no cross-subsidy.

From this argument some far-reaching conclusions may be reached about promoting competition under public ownership. The first is that competition threatens the ability of public bodies to practise cross-subsidization, unless special arrangements are made to avoid distorting competition.[30] Creating obstacles to competition through barriers to entry so as to raise profits is often the preferred method of financing such cross-subsidization, since it means consumers finance it through higher prices rather than having to rely on funding from taxes. It also gives private and public producers the appearance of independence from government intervention.[31]

Government has been ambivalent about allowing greater competition. A continued squeeze on running costs, coupled with exhortation for more commercial behaviour, led many public-sector bodies to increase the level and range of charges to supplement their parliamentary funding. These range from Ministry of Defence training for aircrew of other nationalities to the British Council charging the Overseas Development Administration – a quango charging a 'core' department – for project managing and executing aid programmes in developing countries. In practice, many anomalies and inconsistencies have arisen.

Universities which, although not public bodies in the strict sense, receive almost all their funding from the state, provide free the enabling infrastructure for academic staff to act as consultants in competition with the private sector. The British Council, in the example given above, is in competition with the private sector. In August 1995 it was revealed, as a consequence of concerns about the drought that summer, that the Meteorological Office – an executive agency – was providing long-range weather forecasts for the private sector for a fee while keeping the information secret from the wider public. As the *Financial Times* put it, 'the Met Office has sacrificed public service to its commercial interests'.[32] Equivalent difficult issues about what should be funded by general taxation and what by specific charges on 'customers' apply in many government-owned information providers, from the supply of maps by Ordnance Survey to the British Library. But while Companies House was not allowed to engage in value-added searches in competition with private-sector agencies,[33] the British Library was actively looking at ways to increase its revenue from value-added services.

There is long-standing parliamentary reluctance to allow public bodies to compete with private firms, because they might use public money to undercut private competitors.[34] The knowledge that government would have to meet any deficits might encourage them to charge lower, predatory, prices which a more risk-averse private sector could not follow. The public sector often takes great risks because in the end they can be absorbed (by the taxpayer). Giving agencies the power to compete outside the civil service for customers again raised the prospect of unfair competition. For competition to be workable, public bodies must compete on equal terms with private ones. They must neither be burdened with extra costly obligations, nor be able to use public money, or a public guarantee of their risks, to compete unfairly. The difficulty of establishing these requirements in practice is itself a powerful argument for privatization.[35]

Can these problems be resolved? Cross-subsidization can be policed and prevented by ring-fencing of productive activities with adequate accounting arrangements in place. But it presumes an effective structure for management and competition.[36] Such structures frequently do not exist.[37] Public bodies often have odd bundles of activities inherited from the past. Their composition is administratively convenient, not driven by any business logic. Take a naval dockyard such as Plymouth or Portsmouth. Despite an apparent overall coherence, each is a historical collection of small, individual businesses. No successful private firm, whether diversifying its risks or building from strength, would now keep them together. They do not easily slip into competitive markets and are hard to franchise as they stand.

In the Next Steps initiative there was no sustained drive to provide accounting information for a prospectus, as there was for privatization. And because the accounting information previously available to departments was so poor, it was felt that an agency had to be created before there could be information which could be used to decide what could be privatized or contractorized. The more sensible course would have been to create the information and then make organizational decisions. But this course might have meant delay and inaction.

At worst, the creation of an agency without restructuring can be a way of preserving the *status quo* as a monopoly. In our view, many agencies have been maintained unnecessarily as monopolies. Competition would have been possible for driver and vehicle licensing. While licence fees and terms and conditions have to be set centrally, the cost of issuing and maintaining licences could have been reflected in a separate, variable management fee, instead of being negotiated en bloc each year. Different licensing offices could then have competed directly on price and quality of service, or the centre could have developed an internal market, allocating market shares between competing offices or contractors on the basis of price and quality.

Similarly, there need not be a single agency for the licensing of drivers and vehicles. Different offices could compete for public business through differences in their quality of service and management fees, and customers could choose the prices and level of service they wanted. There could be internal competition: if some offices were able to undercut others in the prices for which they could process licenses, government could award them a larger market share, the losers having to take a decision whether to run down their operations as a result.

More difficult is the effect on competition through the Treasury being regarded as the ultimate guarantor of the deficit of any public body, so increasing the risks a public body might be ready to take in competition with a private one. One route out of this dilemma was to let public bodies go bankrupt. But when the government in the early 1970s allowed the Mersey Docks and Harbour Board to go bankrupt by relying on the obscurity of the wording of its 1858 founding statute, it still felt it had to secure its succession, and ended by finding a solution which was more difficult than if it had kept the board solvent.[38] Another route was to allow bankruptcy, but to incentivize management to prevent it: a route foreshadowed by the provisions of the 1933 Act that brought the London Passenger Transport Boards into public ownership.[39] Neither route was popular with the Treasury.

Effects of Next Steps

While one can argue that the effects of Next Steps would have been greater if the aggregation problem had been faced and solved, the Prime Minister's statement in February 1988, accepting the Efficiency Unit's recommendation that autonomous executive agencies should be established, was momentous.[40] By and large it was to take existing parts of government departments and other existing bodies, as they were, and give them a considerable measure of autonomy.

To understand its significance, let us sketch a picture of the typical executive departmental division or outlying body before Next Steps. Despite enormous differences in detail and appearance, there were strong family resemblances. Their civil service heads were responsible to ministers through a civil service hierarchy, and as a result the heads had generally low grading and low pay, in turn compressing and lowering the pay of those below. Such posts were not sought after, because speedy promotion within the civil service has always depended more on policy advice and policy management, and because executive operations were often far from London, making return difficult. Even when the heads of large agencies received higher grading and pay during the 1980s, they often felt the ignominy in practice of having to report and justify themselves to those who were their juniors in the civil service. Consequently, such posts tended to be filled by those whose civil service career was flagging, or by those with a scientific or professional background. Occasional high fliers were prevailed on to do such a stint on the clear understanding it would not last long.

The outcome was a hierarchy which the private sector would not recognize as a management structure.[41] Usually perched towards the bottom, the job of an executive head was to look both up and down, but satisfying ministers and officials above was more important for his tranquillity.[42] If heads were lucky they might escape close attention for years, since ministers were rarely interested in executive activities and they were not often encouraged to be otherwise by politically orientated civil servants. This sense that ministers often had of peering down from the top of a vast hierarchy, whose bottom steps were lost in a vast distance from them, had the advantage of deterring some kinds of interference, but it was inconsistent with efficient organization.

Downward, agency heads generally relied on those who did the work to get on with it. Rigid pay and grading structures with limited chances for promotion gave them few instruments with which to do more. Moreover, any efficiency gains would be pocketed by the Treasury which controlled the creation of virtually every post and every request for additional expenditure. There were many facets of the time-honoured technique called 'candle-ends', but at its heart was a correspondence up and down the departmental hierarchy and across to the Treasury so lengthy and laborious as to discourage all but the determined.[43]

A paradox of the system was that it combined managerial remoteness of ministers with a high degree of interest in detail of importance to them that could make administration time-consuming and costly.[44] Among the victims of the process there was a belief that formalized budgetary control and bureaucratic processes were indeed the main reasons why efficiency in the public lagged behind that in the private sector.[45] Freed from its chains, could not the public sector do as well? Indeed, this very attitude contributed to the disregard for structural concerns, and therefore for the insufficient attention given to the achievement of workable competition.

The positive aspects of change have been felt in four main ways.

Redefining the consumer

The new emphasis on the consumer was signalled from the start, but, while Mrs Thatcher was prime minister, competition was thought enough to lead to the satisfaction of the consumer.[46] It was then swept up and reinforced by the Citizen's Charter movement.[47] Often what was accomplished was a series of small things: the Driving Standards Agency in 1993 reported the following improvements in service: allowing tests to be paid for by credit card; to be bookable over the phone; to take place in the evening; and their outcomes to be better explained to those tested.[48] For the first time most agencies began to conduct consumer surveys and other market research to help them improve their performance.[49] Many of the key performance indicators came to reflect such citizens' concerns.

Yet even here there were problems. Many public bodies had a wide spread of types of customer with different needs. In the National Health Service were some 10,000 different recognized diagnoses, and hence kinds of customer: customers needing to be considered not only clinically, but also for the effects on their families and working lives, and their own comfort and morale.[50] In welfare services, attempts to single out particular aspects of quality of service for targeting could lead to the damaging treatment of some vulnerable clients who needed to be looked at in the round for their own special problems.[51] Sometimes there were problems because the client could not be regarded as sovereign: children could not always be the best judges of their own interests. Nevertheless, on balance this development has greatly increased the effectiveness of government services and the quality of their delivery.

Deregulation

A further beneficial consequence of agency status has been that it has given agencies more freedom from bureaucratic constraints, sometimes of a very simple kind. One executive officer, when asked what agency status meant for her, replied that she could now buy her own envelopes.[52] Deregulation has principally affected personnel and financial management.

Personnel rules constrain hiring and firing, qualifications, the nature of competitive entry and the selection procedures used, but have the advantage of transparency and being capable of application by non-specialists. They constrain pay and pay bands, make it difficult to relate pay to performance, and may inhibit the promotion of the best. Their effect is to reduce the flexibility and economy with which government and agencies can react to changing events; and they add to cost.[53]

Such rules need to be replaced by incentives to perform well, if the potential for improved efficiency is to be realized.[54] The first aspect of pay deregulation was over salaries for agency chief executives.[55] It was reinforced by attempts (from almost nothing in 1985) at introducing performance pay throughout the civil service, to provide some flexibility in agencies.[56]

Although traditional budgets and accounting systems were already in the process of change, Next Steps reinforced and accelerated more specific accounting for activities and decentralization of responsibility. Resource management was shifted away from central managers of people and cash to operational line managers. But dividing a small number of central budgets into a larger number of smaller budgets complicated the traditional year-end management of actual spend to the budgeted amount.

An important constraint is what in Britain is called the 'annuality' rule. Because money unspent before the year's end has to be returned to the Treasury, budget holders rush to spend any surplus before the year's end as underspending is often taken as an indication that less money should be allocated the following year. Such last-minute expenditure may be wasteful. By and large the rules are not dissimilar, and have similar effects, in the United States and many other bureaucracies. As one might expect, there are reasons for it: the imperative to control the total of public expenditure as a macroeconomic policy assurance to the markets. Escaping this constraint means finding disciplines the market will accept instead.

If savings are made, there is a need to decide who will benefit, and in what proportions: the manager who made the savings, the agency to whom he belongs, the programme that finances it, the sponsoring department, or the taxpayer. The importance of management incentives suggests budget holders should in general be allowed to keep at least a part of any savings they make.

However, the scope for deregulation is not limitless. Even Osborne and Gaebler allow that some personnel and financial rules are necessary, though they rely again on a nautical metaphor rather than on detailed discussion to suggest where the line should be drawn:

> Government needs some rules, of course. The ship of state needs a coat or two of paint; if one takes it down to base metal it will rust. The problem is, most governments have acquired several dozen coats of paint and layer upon layer of barnacles.[57]

Targets and indicators

A theme intertwined with the other aspects of government public-sector reform has been an emphasis on defining outputs and standards that are necessary for greater accountability. The Citizen's Charter required that standards of service for the whole public sector are published, that performance against them is published and that, in some instances, compensation is paid to consumers where failure to meet the standards results in loss to the consumer.

In the early years agencies were set targets and performance indicators which were easy to achieve, as an integral part of acquiring a separate identity.[58] Agency status led particularly to an interest in unit costs and to targets defined by aggregate cost efficiency.[59] But there were difficulties. It is always tempting to gain the credit for setting impossibly demanding targets, especially if those setting them are likely to move on before performance is audited, and some ministers may not have been immune from that temptation.[60]

Targets need to be realistic and appropriate. The Employment Service initially missed almost all its targets because they were set as absolute cost and staff savings at a time of an unpredicted rise in unemployment over which it had no control.[61] An early problem was the sheer number of targets most agencies were set. Sometimes it was justified, since an agency comprising many services might have a target or indicators for each. But the multiplication of targets went much further. Even commercial agencies were often set a battery of measures. HMSO had separate targets for sales; for prices relative to private-sector prices and input prices; and an array of service quality indicators.[62] Other commercial agencies have complicated key performance indicators.[63] Partly it was because of the absence of competition, which precluded the choice of a profit target (which is an unreliable indicator of efficiency when there is monopoly power). Another reason for the multiplication of performance indicators was it seemed natural to establish what consumers wanted from surveys and derive targets from them. A third reason was the emergence of formal and informal stakeholders – in Parliament and elsewhere – with an interest in some aspect of an agency's performance: it often seemed an easy concession to them to establish more indicators.[64] Government and Parliament seemed slow to recognize that the existence of a large number of objectives makes it difficult for an agency to balance one against another, where resource constraints prevent the achievement of all; and that this begged the question of whether such decision-making was to be left to the agencies or reserved to ministers.

Targets about outcomes are in general to be preferred to targets for inputs or for outputs.[65] Targeting outputs may restrict effectiveness: governments may fund patients rather than prevention or cures, arrests rather prevention or convictions, numbers of convictions irrespective of their seriousness, numbers of schoolchildren in schools, rather than their successful education. Hospitals and welfare homes that are paid per patient will have an incentive to keep as many in-patients for as long as possible, rather than cure them or give them out-patient treatment.

Outcomes focus on the achievement of predetermined standards in restored health, educational achievement or standards of care. Training establishments are better incentivized by how many they place in jobs than by numbers under training. Inevitably outcomes are much easier to define in some instances than in others – and in some cases, for example diplomacy, may be next to impossible – but without the effort, perverse incentives are likely.[66]

Poor tests of performance can have a distorting effect on behaviour, but the right reaction is to refine performance measures, not drop them. A constant process of refinement should be expected as mistakes are revealed and consumers' needs change, as demonstrated by the experience of educational 'league tables'. After initial hostility to the concept, there is the beginning of a debate about what the indicators should be, not just on whether any indicators are possible or not.[67] If targets are closely defined and measurement is accurate they can illuminate differences in performance, for example between different branches within the same government activity, enough to be surrogate for competition. But such measurements are never as effective as competition and severe data problems make them fraught in practice.

Insufficient attention was given to the problems of setting up well-defined objectives weighted on a rational basis, with explicit trade-offs between them. In the review of the prison service following breakouts from maximum security prisons, the difficulty of reconciling two apparently conflicting objectives – those of custody and care – and expressing these in terms that were operationally useful was a major theme in the criticisms of the state of service which led to the dismissal of the chief executive.[68]

The importance of a single commensurate objective equivalent to profit is underrated in the public sector. It makes the measurement of performance, and therefore good management, more workable. Let us call this activity social benefit maximization, or the maximization of some objective other than profit, which reasonably describes the objective of government as provider of a given good or service. Other objectives must also be met as constraints, but in principle this is no different for a commercial firm which must ensure that an over-zealous pursuit of profit does not alienate the customer. Such an ideal, however, does not always suit politicians who like to juggle and balance. In the case of prisons the apparent irreconcilability of care and custody is, at least in part, due to repeated and confusing changes in emphasis by ministers and an unwillingness to be specific.

Such non-profit objectives remain easiest to handle where there is a single objective: for example, to maximize the number of licences or passports issued per staff member, subject to an overall constraint of cost, or of cost per item. A rather more complex single objective advocated for railways, used by London Transport in the 1970s and of wide applicability for subsidized transport, is the number of passenger miles carried per pound of subsidy. A great advantage of such measures is that current performance can be appraised on an identical basis as in normal financial annual, quarterly and monthly reports, and also investments and other changes can be evaluated in the same terms.

The UK government already uses indices which reflect improvements in safety on a uniform and similar basis. They imply using money not as a measuring tool to make benefits and costs commensurate. In ranking road safety schemes, costs may be mainly or wholly financial, and are mostly incurred by the parties involved in an accident, but the benefits of reductions in fatal and non-fatal accidents and in damage to vehicles and other property, as well as savings to the NHS and police. Some are immediately capable of financial expression, while conventions have been developed in putting money values on fatal and non-fatal accidents. In the NHS a measure of output has been developed called the 'Qaly' (quality adjusted life), which is closely related to the measures used for safety programmes, since the main benefits of NHS activity are the cure, containment and prevention of disease and the avoidance of death. With all its difficulties, it is better than any output measure of what is wanted from the NHS and therefore of comparative evaluation of the performance of hospitals and doctors. Regular monitoring against 'Qaly' targets should improve both the efficiency of NHS activities and its ability to respond rapidly to changes in circumstances, though there will always be rationing problems.

Some enthusiasts write as if outputs could nearly always be specified – even if refinement is required over time.[69] While difficulties can be exaggerated, certain problems must be recognized.[70] In some services, needs change too rapidly for outputs to be specified; examples are defence, police and emergency services, and social welfare services in so far as they have to meet volume changes in the numbers of clients. The problems are not insuperable but various compromises must be made with the ideal of output specification. However, there are some activities of government, particularly policy development, or where multiple objectives change frequently, where it is next to impossible, or perhaps just not sensible, to specify outputs. Such activities best remain the responsibilities of ministers and their advisers.

Other areas of complexity require a difficult balance of professional, cultural and management judgements, but cannot expect to command much ministerial attention. In such circumstances there are far worse possibilities than falling back on the notion of a public trust. Indeed, many 'quangos', especially those set up before 1945, were constituted on such a basis. If ministers do not have the time, motivation or expertise to determine how best to run an art gallery, a funding council or a research establishment, or if there is a need for political impartiality and independence, then there is a case for appointing trustees able to respond to the needs of users and other interested parties. But in this instance ministers and departmental officials should stand back and allow the trustees to take their decisions subject only to the requirements of propriety and evidence of good and systematic management.

Internal restructuring

It has already been said that a failing of Next Steps was that restructuring and reaggregation were not done first so as to make the agencies more readily suitable for competition. A further consideration of Conservative policy for reform of central government in 1994 contained few new initiatives and appeared to be an attempt, not wholly convincing, to rationalize the sometimes conflicting, or at least overlapping, impact of previous initiatives.[71] This white paper recommended that departments adopt current management techniques from the private sector: delayering, process re-engineering and priority-based budgeting as well as resource accounting and budgeting. More importantly, it implicitly recognized that the various initiatives launched from the centre of government were, in some instances, contradictory, and that the centre had been over-prescriptive. The white paper effectively delegated the responsibility for deciding which technique to use to departments themselves within a framework of tight expenditure controls and a requirement on departments to produce an annual 'efficiency plan'.

The two elements in the 1994 white paper on transferring best private-sector practice to the public sector were made possible and easier by access to the better information made available by low-cost computing power. They are flattening hierarchies and process review. The arguments for flatter hierarchies (delayering) are that the best decisions are taken closer to the client interface, and that reference upwards for review adds costs and time and is demotivating to those nearer the action. Delegation and clearer accountabilities empower people and release otherwise wasted energy. Better information allows monitoring by those remaining at the centre to coach, guide and mentor but not to direct. There is something in this, but a limitation in government is that much government activity is not 'entrepreneurial', in the way that in the private sector greater discretion can lead to better deals for commercial advantage. Entrepreneurialism is or should be constrained by requirements of fairness, equity and access.

The second theme is process review, which has become widely practised in the private sector. Traditionally, most organizations are structured vertically with functional demarcation lines. However, whatever is produced by an organization, whether a service or product, and whether an internal product or something ultimately destined for the external customer, tends to pass through several functional boundaries before completion. Thus a purchase transaction can involve the original purchasers, an ordering or procurement department, the physical receipt of the purchase, an invoice and an associated accounting transaction. A direct service or product passes through a multiplicity of internal functions before reaching the ultimate customers. Traditionally when organizations are looking for efficiency improvements they regard each function separately and see what can be squeezed out of it. Current management theory ('business process re-engineering') claims that this approach does not sufficiently take into account the links between different parts of the organization and the consequences (and thus cost implications) of the activities carried out in the various functions. Re-engineering the whole process and, for example, increasing effort and thus costs in one function may lead to greater efficiency improvements overall than will a review of any of the functions separately.

However, where individual functions have been market-tested and this has resulted in their being out-sourced, they require interfaces which may themselves be costly. More important, this separation may, at the very least, inhibit advantage being taken of efficiency opportunities identified through a comprehensive look at the process as a whole. A more strategic view of the reform process as a whole should have identified this drawback in advance.

Has separation worked in practice? Evidence from published reports and consultancy work by one of the authors indicates that executive agencies have begun to transform the operations they are responsible for. There is evidence of greater clarity of purpose, commitment to the organization and real changes in management systems (for example, accounting and cost information). There have also been efficiency improvements, although these do not appear to have been any greater than the efficiency gains achieved in the same period in 'traditional' departments. There are claims for improvements in quality of service which, while difficult to substantiate, are probably true – but from a low base. The *Market Testing Bulletin* of January 1995 gives somewhat mundane examples where quality has improved but at lower cost: for example, as a result of contracting out Customs and Excise's fleet management to Avis; or improved office services at the Chessington Computer Centre.[72] But such changes in quality are unsurprising, given the almost total neglect of vast areas of the civil service in earlier years and the step-change in attention they have been given since 1979. While some of these changes would not have happened without the creation of separate agencies, perhaps the original thrust of the Financial Management Initiative was at least as instrumental in bringing about change as the subsequent creation of agencies. There are two views. One is that the Financial Management Initiative flowed into Next Steps, the first being an essential prerequisite of the second. The other is the first had gone as far as it could and something radically different was needed. The second would be more convincing if the management units, the agencies, created had been better structured to reflect activities, had themselves in many cases been decentralized first and in various ways prepared so that competition could have been more effective.

Furthermore, the very public review of the Prisons Service Agency concluded that its management arrangements were not greatly different from what we described as those typical of an outlying part of a department before agencies were established.

> The Director General needs minimum political involvement in the day to day operation of the service . . . The Prison Service is a politically sensitive area and ministerial involvement is bound to be relatively high. Such a level of upward-focused activity needs to be carefully managed if it is not to interfere with the Headquarter's proper downwards supervision and control of the organisation.[73]

In other words, the Chief Executive was facing both ways at once, to the detriment of management of the operation.

Moreover, there was fundamental disagreement between the Home Secretary and his Chief Executive as to their respective responsibilities, with the former claiming to have responsibility for policy only while the Chief

Executive was responsible for operations. It is hard to understand what this can mean in practice, since the management of prisons is an essentially operational activity and, at the time, the Home Secretary had no policy advisory capacity outside the prison service. As the Chief Inspector of Prisons said: 'if you are dividing policy and operations it means the Home Secretary is not responsible for anything at all'.[74] Or, as the sacked chief executive put it more bitterly: 'you . . . invented a new definition of the word "operational" which meant "difficult" '.

Nevertheless, the UK experience indicates that, though agency status may not have been strictly necessary for the introduction of many of the measures associated with the new approach to public management, it has in practice facilitated greater efficiency. Whether as many efficiency gains as possible have been realized is harder to establish. First, there have been almost no before and after studies; and second, policy changes have come too thick and fast to assess the improvements from each management change. As in the previously nationalized industries, substantial improvements may be expected in the early years after such radical changes. The improvements made could be an institutional version of the Hawthorne effect, where greater labour productivity was achieved as a consequence of the greater attention paid to the workforce through the management experiment process rather than as a result of the nature of the experiments themselves. Ensuring that efficiency savings continue to be realized, on a scale materially affecting aggregate public expenditure, requires effective relationships to be established in the long term between ministers and agencies – issues which the next chapter considers.

Notes

1 Mill (1910), p. 332.
2 Kettl and DiIulio (1995), p. 10.
3 Webb and Webb (1922); Bagehot (1928), pp. 164–8.
4 Lubenow (1971), pp. 30–68.
5 Gregg (1973), pp. 186–92; Checkland and Checkland (1974), pp. 42–7.
6 Dicey (1885), pp. 329, 364, 374–5, 382–3. For a modern analysis see Turpin (1989).
7 See Lewis (1989).
8 Pliatsky (1992).
9 Major (1994), p. 13.
10 Light (1995), pp. 7–13.
11 Kettl and DiIulio (1995); Foreman (1995); see also Garvey (1995).
12 Cabinet Office (1994), pp. 16–17.
13 *The Independent*, 15 November 1994.
14 Wildavsky (1993), p. 227.
15 Kettl (1994), p. 189.
16 Machiavelli (1961), p. 78.
17 Benezal *et al.* (1988).
18 Kettl (1993), p. 74.
19 Ibbs (1988), p. 9.

20 Major (1994), p. 5.
21 Cabinet Office (1994), p. 1; but see also Rose (1989b, 1990); Heald (1990).
22 Foster (1992), ch. 9.
23 Major (1994), p. 6.
24 Cabinet Office (1989), p. 7.
25 From the civil servant, Sir Peter Kemp, to the banker, Sir Peter Levene.
26 Rt. Hon. T. Renton MP in TCSC (1991), p. 41.
27 Major (1994), p. 14–15.
28 Dorrell (1994).
29 Osborne and Gaebler (1992), pp. 76–107.
30 Hughes (1994).
31 Rasmussen and Zappa (1991).
32 *Financial Times*, 25 August 1995.
33 TCSC (1991), p. 22.
34 See Chester (1975).
35 See Foster (1992), ch. 10.
36 Department of Trade and Industry (1990), p. 72.
37 Lewis (1989).
38 Foster (1971), pp. 157–8.
39 Foster (1992), ch. 10.
40 Thatcher (1988).
41 Light (1993), p. 16; Kettl (1995), p. 28.
42 See Dunleavy (1991), pp. 181ff.
43 Foster (1971), pp. 171–88.
44 Foster (1971), pp. 83–118.
45 See, for example, Chubb and Moe (1990); see also TCSC (1991), pp. 15–16, 23.
46 The same could also be said of the USA, see Moe (1994), p. 114.
47 Cabinet Office (1991).
48 Driving Standards Agency (1993).
49 See, for example, TCSC (1991), p. 17 (HMSO); p. 28, Benefit Office.
50 Aaron (1992), p. 54.
51 Diane Abbott MP in TCSC (1991), p. 54.
52 Richards (1989).
53 Osborne and Gaebler (1992), pp. 124–30.
54 Osborne and Gaebler (1992), p. 23.
55 Butler (1988).
56 Beadle (1993), esp. p. 45.
57 Osborne and Gaebler (1992), p. 115.
58 Renton in TCSC (1991), pp. 42–3; see also Flynn (1988); TCSC (1988).
59 TCSC (1991), pp. 11–12, 24.
60 TCSC (1991), pp. 42–3.
61 TCSC (1991), pp. 6–7.
62 TCSC (1991), p. 11.
63 TSCS (1991), pp. xxi, 16, 17.
64 Diane Abbott MP, in TCSC (1991), p. 54.
65 For example, for the police, Davies (1992), p. 29.
66 Osborne and Gaebler (1992), pp. 38, 141; see also Carter (1991).
67 Epstein (1992).
68 Learmont (1995).

69 For example, Osborne and Gaebler (1992).
70 Mayston (1985).
71 Major (1994).
72 Cabinet Office (1995).
73 Learmont (1995).
74 BBC interview quoted in the *Financial Times*, 19 October 1995.

9

Ministers and agencies: separation as metaphor?

> When a bedpan is dropped on a hospital floor, its noise should resound in the Palace of Westminster.
>
> Aneurin Bevan[1]

This chapter considers the nature of the relationships between ministers and public bodies, and, in particular, whether 'separation' in this context is real or merely a metaphor. The devolution of production to executive agencies has not so far established the certainty necessary to achieve efficient public provision and production, delivering real savings in public expenditure. The looser, quasi-contractual arrangements are hard to analyse because they reflect the ambiguous political and legal environment in which contracts (or quasi-contracts) are awarded, and therefore uncertainty over how far particular rules will apply throughout the contract's life.[2] Indeed, the defining characteristic of a framework document is that the agencies are *not* private, third-sector or autonomous public producers, and therefore cannot enter or forgo these contracts voluntarily. In addition, the introduction of the contractual concept for executive agencies has led to attempts to apply it in other circumstances where other forms of relationship may be more appropriate.

Previous chapters have argued that there are many more instances where 'quasi-contracts' could be replaced by real contracts through contractorization. However, whatever may be possible in theory, ministers in practice seem to prefer the limited certainty which framework documents provide. Indeed, much of what is interesting in the way the new approach to public management has been applied in the UK, in particular most instances of separation, has been achieved within the framework of the agency initiative. Thus, services which could be readily contractorized, as well as some which could not, have been separated into agencies. There would seem to be no limit to what could be separated into agencies. The scope of agencies has not been limited to those activities without the contractual complications which, it was argued in Chapter 6, should be a deterrent to contractorization. More ambitious separations could be planned, leaving hollowed-out departments as cores controlling quasi-contracts with agencies and other public bodies: private firms, third-sector and autonomous public bodies.[3] So one might reach the appearance, but not the reality, of a hollow state.

However, where producing bodies remain public – as quangos and executive agencies are – and have the same ownership as the providers, it is difficult to conceive the relationship as other than one of dependency or command in which both goals and means are capable at any time of being altered by ministerial decision. Is the relationship any different than that between ministers and integral parts of their departments? If it is, what makes separation real? Real separation can only be achieved through a contract (or equivalent document) which defines the rights of both the provider and producer. These characteristics distinguish a real binding contract from a quasi-contract which might be better renamed a pseudo-contract for the binding force it has.

As it happens, however, government has made clear that it sees its relationships with agencies as one of command, notwithstanding any inconsistency with what it has also said about their being 'quasi-contractual'. Britain is not helped here by the absence of a constitution or administrative law which might clarify this difficulty.[4] However:

> In constitutional theory the minister continues to take precedence before the ministry. In law it is the minister who is usually responsible for the actions of the ministry . . . the minister has unlimited liability for political mistakes made by his ministry. A minister's position at the top of a hierarchy is an ambiguous eminence. The minister is responsible for everything that happens within the ministry (and often outside it), yet is remote from what is done by officials at the base.[5]

The principle of ministerial responsibility for agencies was reaffirmed by the Prime Minister, John Major, as being the same as that for departments.[6] Thus, notwithstanding the rhetoric to the contrary, the relationship between minister and agency may be described as one of command and it is misleading to consider a framework document as contractual.

The result of so much uncertainty is a number of tensions, which, though present in the past, agency status has accentuated.

Contractual certainty and ministerial responsibilities

The first difficulty is over accountability. The prime accountability of agencies and quangos is to Parliament, through ministers.[7] Framework documents give an agency its instructions and define its independence.[8] They set down agencies' objectives and targets, in most cases for three to four years, and every agency publishes an annual report in which it comments on how far it met its targets.[9] Typically targets are specific, numerous and detailed, suggesting that ministers prefer this approach to the idea that agency mission statements should be flexible to maximize opportunities for efficiency. The chief executive is usually the accounting officer and as such is accountable, together with the departmental accounting officer (usually the permanent secretary), for ensuring that expenditure has been incurred for the purposes which were voted for by Parliament. In addition, various secondary accountabilities have developed, of which some of the more important in practice are informal. In many agencies professional accountability is of great practical importance.[10] It often has a formal, quasi-judicial aspect in that professionals may be summoned before a tribunal and punished; but in practice professionals may feel as powerfully constrained in what they do by their wish to retain peer-group respect.[11] The Citizen's Charter initiative and consumer committees, where they exist, provide another channel of accountability: direct to an agency's consumers. An activity may be accountable to more than one government. For example, while the Intervention Board for Agricultural Produce is an agency of the Ministry of Agriculture as an agent of the Common Agricultural Policy, it is also accountable to the European Commission. An agency may have accountability to a local authority, a health authority or some other part of government, including another agency, in so far as it has a contract or quasi-contract with it; or, by contract, to a private firm or third-sector body. There is also accountability to the National Audit Office and to the Public Accounts Committee as distinct from accountability to Parliament through ministers. Many of these have a place, it will shortly be argued, in the network of relationships that constitutes the existing state, let alone one which is more hollowed out.

Parliamentary questions are one of the main ways in which ministers are held accountable for those under their command; but understandably they are unwilling to be drawn into all questions of detail about their agencies, as they must about their departments. They have thus fallen back on the Woodrow Wilson distinction between 'policy' and administration or 'operations' which had its British origins in ministers' relations with the nationalized industries, by which ministers were to answer questions on policy matters, and boards on operational matters.[12] We have seen already in Chapter 4 how hopeless a logical distinction this principle was in fudging the issue of discretion, though in practice it settled down so as to be workable for ministers' relations with nationalized industries.

There are more problems in relying on this distinction for ministers' relations with agencies and other public bodies. First, the basis for the independence of nationalized industries was statutory, whereas that for executive agencies is not.[13] Second, nationalized industries raised most of their revenue from their consumers, which gave them greater practical independence from ministerial intervention. Third, while it is reasonably clear what nationalized industries did, and what ministers' roles were, it was much less clear what distinguishes agencies' and ministers' roles.[14] Such distinctions were not made in framework documents.[15] In practice ministers often seemed to dive down and assume responsibility for some operational matters, but it was also said that agencies were encouraged to influence ministerial decisions on policy.[16]

In the case of the Prison Service Agency, both these aspects appeared to obtain. Given the absence of a policy capability in the Home Office (and the size of prisons headquarters), there was bound to be policy-making in the Agency. The circumstances which led to the sacking of the Agency's chief executive in 1995 indicated personal involvement by the Home Secretary in detailed administrative matters and much detailed involvement from the Home Office. The Learmont Inquiry found that the prison service submitted over 1000 documents to ministers in 83 working days, of which 'one hundred and thirty seven were "full submissions", containing substantive advice about policy or operational matters'.[17] Conversely, in the case of the Child Support Agency, a campaign against the government's policy administered by the Agency led to the increasing public involvement of the chief executive in defending the policy – a posture that proved untenable and led to her resignation.

It is reasonable to argue that, to some extent, as with the nationalized industries, this uncertainty of roles may be clarified in time. For many years a satisfactory division of responsibility on this basis was made between the Treasury and its agents, the two non-ministerial government departments of the Inland Revenue and Customs and Excise. Much policy work was done within them on their own or in response to ministerial initiatives; but they well understood when they needed to go to the Treasury and its ministers. A constraint on their doing otherwise was that most of their policy changes needed to be expressed either in the annual Finance Act or other legislation. Ironically there have only recently been signs that the old relationships here may be creaking. Recommendations made by the Greenbury Committee on the taxing of share options were accepted and announced by ministers as policy without realizing their full and politically embarrassing implications. This resulted in the extraordinary spectacle of Ministers blaming a group of volunteers (not appointed by them) for not doing the spadework in examining the proposition which should have been undertaken by their own officials.

The Treasury and Civil Service Committee was sufficiently dissatisfied with the pursuit of agency accountability through parliamentary questions for some of its members to raise the issue of whether a more appropriate system of administrative law or regulation were not needed as in Sweden.[18] If that had been the only issue, the TCSC might have concluded in favour of greater certainty about responsibilities being laid down in a framework document which determined what questions MPs should address to ministers and what to the agencies. But the doctrine of ministerial responsibility is reflected in a further concern expressed by the TCSC about framework documents. There were complaints about the meaninglessness of many targets and 'key performance indicators' (KPIs), about the difficulties in finding the criteria underlying them, and about changes in KPIs which were not reported to Parliament.[19] The TCSC demanded that all policy changes should be reflected explicitly in framework documents and reported to Parliament.[20] They also objected to changes which made impossible year-to-year comparisons. That there should be as much year-to-year comparability as possible is sensible in any organization, as any private firm will recognize.[21] And yet their most abiding concern was exactly contrary to any real contractual spirit: it was that ministers should not regard themselves as contractually bound by targets set in the framework document, so upholding the notion that a framework document was a one-sided contract: in politics there can never be contracts since politics requires a flexibility inconsistent with them.

Typically framework documents contain many objectives, often overlapping and sometimes inconsistent.[22] Both the TCSC and ministers believe ministers have the power to alter objectives, even though the TCSC would have preferred a more formal procedure; while ministers believed they should be able to change these objectives whenever they feel the need, with only retrospective reporting. Indeed, they expect the same freedom as they have in their departments.

Consumer satisfaction and political objectives

A source of difficulty may develop when an agency's objectives and those of ministers are not aligned. From one standpoint, an agency exists to serve its clients or consumers, a view accentuated by the Citizen's Charter, but ministers often have multiple and shifting objectives, frequently tangential to agency concerns. They may be altered by particular complaints, by newspaper campaigns, by pressure groups, MPs and party members. Ministers want credit from new initiatives, to deploy patronage and seek electoral advantage. Departments, too, may have their own agenda, whether it is implementing some government-wide agenda (of little direct interest to ministers) or sometimes pursuing long-term objectives (or prejudices) independent of ministers. As a result, many agencies will feel they are serving three masters. They may have difficulty in deciding what weight to give to each. This tension may be reflected not only informally at all times, but also, when quasi-contracts are negotiated, in a clutch of not easily reconcilable targets and other objectives. An agency management team does not know what combination of successes and failures will be judged failure overall. In practice, ministers often seem to be most embarrassed and distressed by incidents that often have no formal reflection in targets (for example, escapes from high-security jails) or that are trivial, objectively speaking, but politically important. For example, the cones hotline was set up to inform road users about roadworks, but public mockery provoked ministerial intervention with the Highways Agency. Lack of clarity about the definition of 'success' or 'failure' can result in great unpredictability over the criteria by which an agency will be judged. Delegation of discretion to resolve this tension will sometimes be complete and at other times tightly constrained.

Departmental ministers and other parts of government

Another difficulty with the private-sector analogy is confusion over who has responsibility, notwithstanding the formal doctrine of ministerial responsibility. First, the creation of agencies has not put an end to multiple responsibilities for provision decisions. Government permits some subordinate providers or producers to define what they do in detail and then determine their own objectives, even when providing them with money. Quangos are often given such a role. Many non-departmental bodies were established specifically to distance ministers from the decision-making process either because of the subject matter (the BBC) or because of lack of time (museums and galleries). What, then, is the nature of ministerial responsibility?

Another example is the deliberate discretion given to benefit offices and other disbursing offices to award discretionary payments. But other tools of government may be used to constrain or even effectively to eliminate discretion, so again undermining separation. The Cabinet, other ministers and the Treasury continue to have roles which blur single-point responsibility for the initiation of contracts but also their variation thereafter.[23] Again, government has a tendency to want to have it both ways: to be able to bind an agency by contractually enforceable powers, but also to vary such a contract at will.

Ministers and management

Chapter 6 argued that departments, from ministers to officials, must learn to manage procurement and finance if contracts are to be efficient. In so far as relations with agencies may be better described as command relationships, they too need to be managed. Subordinate areas may be allowed to continue without significant new commands, even for long periods; but the nature of the relationship implies that there is always ministerial responsibility for those activities, that ministerial power can be asserted, and that new commands can be issued.

The idea that the doctrine of ministerial responsibility implies that ministers in some sense command their department is long-standing, but more stress has been given to the minister as manager in recent years in line with the greater emphasis on the importance of management throughout society. This may in part reflect the background of ministers; around 40 per cent of those appointed after the elections in 1979 and 1992 had some kind of business experience. By contrast, most senior civil servants had no business experience and only limited experience of management because of the traditional career paths to the top through policy branches and ministerial private offices.

Michael Heseltine (who had management experience) and Margaret Thatcher (who greatly valued it) pleaded with the Cabinet at length to take seriously the concept of ministers as managers.[24] Heseltine wrote: 'Efficient management is a key to the [national] revival . . . And the management ethos might run right through our national life – private and public companies, civil service, nationalised industries, local government, the National Health Service.'[25] But a very different appreciation has echoed down the years. Sir George Lewis, the legendary permanent secretary who became Chancellor of the Exchequer under Palmerston, said: 'It is not the business of a cabinet minister to work his department. His business is to see it properly worked. If he is doing much, he is probably doing harm.'[26]

As Heseltine and Thatcher were exhorting ministers to management, one permanent secretary, Sir Peter Carey, said that:

> Ministers are amateurs at management: it is not their skill nor frequently, inclination . . . Extremely few have had experience in genuinely managing a large organisation over a prolonged period. And in the isolated cases where they have, they haven't been notably successful as politicians – which is essentially what they need to be.[27]

Lord Hunt, former cabinet secretary, made a similar point:

> I'm all for ministers managing but it is not their primary role . . . In many cases it would be better if the Civil Service was left to get on with the management job. What ministers need to do is to take more time and have better advice on the political directions in which they want to go and have a coherent strategy which lumps together and will stick.[28]

Sir Frank Cooper, former permanent secretary at Defence, reportedly one of the best civil service managers, said:

> Personally, I regard the minister as manager as nonsense. It's not part of the ministerial stock-in trade . . . It's not what they went into politics for. They went into politics because they are interested in politics and the use of political power and political authority.[29]

The report that was the trigger for Next Steps and for creating separate agencies observed that ministers 'said that in practice they were so overloaded that they looked to their permanent secretaries to do the management. A few said candidly that they did not have the skills to manage their departments.'[30]

Against these views must be set those of Lord Rayner, a businessman with extensive experience of Whitehall:

> Sir Frank Cooper's views, I'm afraid, are quite different to my own. The view that you can develop politics – politics, policies – and . . . have the vision and qualities of leadership that presumably politicians have; without managing the resources that are needed to bring those changes about, is ridiculous . . .'[31]

Lord Rayner's view reflects genuine incredulity from an industrialist that ministers are not really interested in resource management or results, since a private-sector manager who was not would not last. He misjudged the concerns of a minister. The results that ministers want are not similar to the profitability that is the concern of business management. As we have seen, they are interested in electoral success. In the short term their own advancement and the standing of the government depend little on efficiency and good management. They depend for political success principally on the avoidance of failure of or embarrassment to the services and agencies for which they are responsible. Together with the reception of new initiatives they have proposed, or legislation they have introduced, these results matter to them: a concern even more short-term than this year's profits. They are certain to have been moved to another job or left the government before the achievement of results from any new management or other efficiency initiative, most of which take years to show results. Thus only about a third of all cabinet ministers in the reforming governments of 1945 and 1979 were in the same post after two years.

Furthermore, what Rayner and the civil service mean by efficient management is unlikely to be the same. The management skills which the civil service has traditionally needed have been more to do with the avoidance of failure, and the management of resources, than with actions required to achieve a determinate goal. Traditionally civil servants had high among their management objectives the maintenance of orderly processes which ranged from the systematic testing of ministerial intentions already described, to systematic keeping of their files as a record of the discussion which eventually would be available to the public after 30 years or so. (Such procedures were undermined by the size and pace of the Thatcher revolution, so much so that in many departments historians working in the next century will often not find the materials to which contemporary historians have become used.)[32] They also aimed to avoid the overload on their departments which would result from ministers taking too many, perhaps even contradictory, simultaneous initiatives.

The diversity of the skills needed in managing the process of government is compounded by the diversity and fuzziness of the relationships that exist within government, as discussed earlier. Nevertheless, if efficiency is to be raised and public expenditure cut, then the civil service is a more hopeful instrument of such changes than politicians can ever be. They are in a better position to retain and restore old notions of good administration and civil service management, at the same time as learning to manage contracts and agencies as efficiently as the best private-sector management, because they have a long-term interest in government.

But the price of achieving such levels of efficiency is that the role of the minister must be limited. In practice, even the ministers with the greatest managerial experience, a Michael Heseltine or Lord Young, have not acted as more than hands-off non-executive chairmen. They do not have the time for more, even if they had the inclination. The reforms in New Zealand did not expect ministers to be managers, despite an overt commitment to applying private-sector techniques to government.[33] Neither did the Gore Report:

> The president should craft performance agreements with cabinet secretaries and agency heads to firm in on the administration's strategy and policy objectives. These agreements should not micro-manage the work of the agency heads. They do not row the boat. They should set the course.[34]

This is similar to what the UK Efficiency Unit had already said: 'Ministers and civil servants must stand back from operational details . . . leaving managers to manage.'[35] The issue that remains is what ministers are, if not managers, and what the relation is to be between political control and departmental management.

Tensions within the civil service

The creation of the new arrangements threatens to divide the civil service into three groups: those who work in agencies; those who occupy the control functions within departments and in central departments; and those who advise ministers. There has been repeated insistence that the unity of the civil service is to be maintained across these divisions, especially in the more senior posts.[36] Such unity is necessary to secure the understanding across these divisions which is as essential for good policy-making and management as it was argued in Chapter 6 to be for good procurement. But the practicality of such exchange of experience depends on what is done by civil servants in departmental cores and in agencies.[37]

The creation of agencies has led to fears that central staffs might rise as posts are duplicated on both sides of the separation.[38] It has happened where departments have retained the capacity to advise ministers on the Haldane model at the same time as agencies have felt the need to build up policy divisions of their own. In addition to the volume of ministerial briefing referred to earlier, the director-general of the prison service deals with 4000 letters from MPs a year and the responses to 600 parliamentary questions.[39] In this way they are following the model of most of the old nationalized industries. The drawback is not only that there are no direct staff savings, possibly the reverse, but the bunching of staff around the top of an agency interferes with line management below and hampers its ability to achieve economies.

But in practice the opposite danger has arisen, where ministers have been left with too few advisers of their own within the core. The Home Secretary had no advice below permanent secretary level when the Prisons Service Agency was formed; similarly, the Chancellor of the Exchequer had less advice on tax matters except either from the head of the Treasury or the revenue departments themselves. Three consequences are likely. One is that ministers will come to rely on the agencies for policy advice, which is likely to lack both objectivity and the blend of policy and operational experience which was said to be a feature of the postwar civil service. The second is that ministers will turn to their own and other political advisers, internal and external, which raises many public interest issues, as will be discussed in the next chapter. The third is that civil servants in the centre will concentrate solely on management or the implementation of ministerial wishes. Delayering in department cores, when the activity required for better management and procurement from the civil service is increasing, will make it impossible to maintain a knowledgeable civil service, able to advise ministers with an understanding of the agencies and of all the other parties with which an agency has dealings.

Therefore, there are two dangers. One is that, detached from their civil service advisers, ministers will be able to exercise more arbitrary power given their discretion within the law. The establishment of agencies will not have been an instrument for improving parliamentary accountability, but an opportunity for ministers to exploit the doctrine of ministerial responsibility for their own benefit, delegating responsibility for everything in which they have no interest, while retaining the prerogative of intervention where they wish to use it; and that will invite more attempts to bind them by rules and codes of conduct as indicated by the Nolan Report.[40] Standing behind that would be an extension of judicial review. The second danger is that the executive agencies, most of which are monopolies, will learn to devise mechanisms to protect themselves from what they regard as excessive interference, as nationalized industries did. Ministers and agencies would develop an agreed but often shifting split between policy and operations which means that agencies accommodate ministers on the small things that concern ministers while running their internal affairs mostly as they determine given their budgets.

This is not a model that gives one confidence that efficiency savings will be realized which will reduce public expenditure requirements.[41] Therefore, it is not surprising that, as late as 1994, the new arrangements had achieved no further reduction in the size of the central civil service,[42] despite the fact that in 1991 it had been suggested the new arrangements ought to lead to a reduction of as much as 25 per cent in central staffs.[43] The civil servant responsible for the Next Steps initiative in its first years has suggested that the central civil service could return to the 50,000 figure it was in 1900, some 6 per cent of current levels;[44] but it is hard to see how this is possible unless government stops making new policies and the agencies and other bodies proceed unmonitored. While delayering may be able to reduce management and staff in the agencies without reduction in efficiency, it is arguable that it can only happen in the core by effectively abandoning the Haldane model, with all the dangers for rational policy-making, decision-making and probity that would follow.[45]

One possible outcome is a further increase in ministers' power, as one retired permanent secretary has said: 'Ministers have discovered that the system can be used for shedding personal responsibility, rewarding friends, etc.'[46] It is at least arguable that the heads that should have rolled in the prison service and Child Support Agency were those of the ministers, not those of the chief executives. The corollary is that: 'the practice of contemporary governance may make civil servants into "mere managers" and to attempt to assign all significant policy decisions to political leaders.'[47] One permanent secretary has commented that ministers were often dissatisfied with agency status because most 'policy' questions causing ministerial embarrassment were specific operational matters rather than in any sense matters that were strategic, policy-making or related to the overall performance of the agency.

Possible improvements

Several kinds of improvement would seem possible.

Consumers and clients

There would seem to be a strong case for: clarifying who are the designated consumers of each agency; establishing regular consumer surveys and perhaps other mechanisms, such as focus groups, to monitor consumer opinion; setting up consumer committees; and establishing complaints and other grievance procedures which lead upwards to ministers.

Clarification of client relationships could be achieved by more direct relations with consumers or clients.[48] In so far as most agencies are monopolies, consumer satisfaction cannot be tested by the market, and other arrangements are required. The usual approach is for customers to complain to their MPs, who then seek satisfaction from the minister responsible. But this can be slow and ineffective. Furthermore, there may be a conflict of interest between the minister's role in command of the agency, and his role as consumer watchdog. Here, the old nationalized industry model of consumer councils has advantages. If there is a regulator, these councils will derive greater strength if they have consumer protection as part of their task. Complaining through MPs could then be seen as a route of appeal providing a check on the effectiveness of ordinary channels of complaint.

However, many public bodies are too small, specialized or remote from the public consumer for such arrangements to be appropriate. In such circumstances reasonable protection of the consumer remains necessary and may be achieved through appointing suitable representatives of the consumer interest on an external board or advisory committee of some kind. Such arrangements are even more usefully underpinned by requirements for regular consumer surveys and other research.

Charging

Differences in their sources of funds have an impact on the independence of public bodies. Since the seventeenth century the sole right of the House of Commons to levy taxes has meant that public funds are subject to scrutiny by Parliament, now discharged through the Public Accounts Committee and the National Audit Office. As a corollary, there has long been a convention that public bodies in deficit have been especially subject to scrutiny and the only public bodies practically able to free themselves from financial scrutiny have been those able to meet their expenditure from charges. Many agencies – the Passport Office, Companies House, the Driver and Vehicle Licensing Agency – could or do cover their expenditure with fees. However, framework documents do not often distinguish between quasi-contractual payments for specified services and unplanned deficits.

True public accountability in this regard requires that every activity is separately accounted for and that the extent of any subsidy each activity is to receive (and how it is to impact on different classes of consumer) should be predetermined. Any activity incurring a deficit should be identified separately, rather than an overall subvention agreed after difficult discussions with the Treasury or requiring a further transfer from another part of the departmental budget. (New Zealand sets an excellent example in that any agency required to supply an uncommercial good or service has to be reimbursed by government on a commercial basis.)[49] The existence of revenue flows and annual budgeting has made ministerial and departmental arm-twisting easier. There is a great danger that ministers will fall too easily into the temptation of playing about with budgets, even at short notice, or otherwise withholding or commandeering funds for particular purposes unless the ring-fencing and reporting of accounts makes this impossible. To increase both independence and efficiency, agencies should be free to charge reasonable prices to consumers. In so far as subsidies are needed for redistributive or paternalistic purposes, they should be ring-fenced and their purposes clearly specified.

Two streams of accountability

An important improvement would be to make a clearer distinction between ministerial responsibility and public accountability. There is already in current practice the basis for such a distinction. Ministers make policy and promote bills. They are responsible to Parliament for the exercise of their powers and duties under statutes, with the possibility of review by the courts. The other chain of accountability flows to the House of Commons because of its tax-raising prerogative. Whoever is ultimately responsible for a public activity, whether directly or indirectly, is required to be ready to give an account of it to Parliament, usually through ministers but also by appearing before a select committee.

Moreover, as government is hollowed out and becomes more subject to new public management ideas, the need for parliamentary scrutiny of government activities will increase. The importance of management to avoid fiscal crisis makes it essential for the reputation of Parliament, as the paramount instrument of democratic control, that its committee structure becomes a more effective means of scrutiny and review. Each departmental select committee should undertake routine investigations of the kind the Public Accounts Committee has been undertaking since it was founded, but on a larger scale. To gain reassurance, permanent secretaries should be asked once a year as a formal routine to confirm that ministers have not acted unlawfully against domestic or European law; have not given an instruction or direction to an agency or quango which breached a framework document or was otherwise beyond their powers; have not taken a personal part in the awarding of a contract or other legal agreement, and have not been the subject of Public Accounts Committee minutes (as with the Pergau dam). Similarly, the heads of agencies and quangos, when these are reviewed annually, should be asked the corresponding questions on such matters. One would hope the committee would review the performance of an agency or quango at least once a year, and more often if something is wrong with its performance. It should examine any departmental or agency contracts which its officers or the National Audit Office advised as presenting exceptional problems. The National Audit Office, or the Audit Commission where appropriate, could supply staff and other back-up to departmental committees for those activities as it does now to the Public Accounts Committee.

In addition, public bodies produce accounts, and other figures and statistical information, through their permanent secretaries (as accounting officers). If public bodies are to be truly separate, more thought needs to be given to the information they are required to provide on a regular basis. Permanent secretaries, as accounting officers, should be given the formal responsibility of securing accurate information on performance, in addition to their current responsibilities for accounting for resources used.

This bifurcation of the two roles of responsibility to Parliament would require strengthening in three ways. First, it would benefit greatly from the clear adoption of the rule, as in New Zealand, that in relation to agencies and other contracts permanent secretaries' responsibilities cover the meeting of the targets and other objectives set (the outputs); while the broader social purposes (the intended outcomes), which justify those targets and objectives, are entirely a matter for the minister.[50] Second, those in the core responsible under the permanent secretary for contractual relationships with outside bodies would have to show whether the outputs and the efficiency improvements contracted for had been achieved. This responsibility would require the development of accounts to private-sector standards by activity in each framework document. It would then be possible to assess the financial impact of ministerial intervention, as permitted by the framework document.

It is often assumed that deregulation in the public sector will involve the same reporting standards as are implied by law in the private sector.[51] Yet most developed nations expect higher, and in some respects different, standards in the public sector. Not without cost, it would appear to be government policy and that of the PAC.[52] There may be a requirement for further development of administrative law in the UK, as well as more regulation, to provide additional safeguards. Inspection, regulation (where appropriate) and audit functions need to be strengthened (though the cost of extending audit can exceed the benefit). The Audit Commission (or a number of such commissions) would undertake bench-marking and other investigative studies of the quangos, agencies and contracts with private and third-sector bodies as well as overseeing normal financial accounts and reporting. The National Audit Office, as now, could oversee all in the interests of Parliament and form a view on the efficiency of departments, but there are dangers in giving any one auditing body a monopoly power. There could probably be an advantage in developing independent inspectors-general for each department, reporting both to the executive and the legislature on the US model, (they are stated to have achieved huge savings) whose job would be to create or consolidate audit and investigation activity, with considerable powers to investigate tendering procedures, compliance with financial regulations, fraud and abuse of patronage rules.[53]

Therefore, in constitutional terms, a strengthening is required of the accountability of permanent secretaries to Parliament. This view of the role of the permanent secretary as the departmental manager is supported by a Treasury memorandum which sees the permanent secretary as accounting officer as 'solely responsible for overall organisation, management and staffing of the department'.[54] But it sits uneasily with the common comparison of a minister to an executive chairman and a permanent secretary to a chief executive, and even more so with the notion that agency chief executives report direct to ministers. But this dilemma is what confronts politicians: if they want to release substantial resources through greater efficiency, whether for spending elsewhere or to return to the taxpayer, they need to accept they have neither the time nor (usually) the qualifications to act as executive or non-executive chairmen.

The Treasury

Another issue is the role of central departments which do not sponsor agencies themselves but influence them. Traditionally the most important central department has been the Treasury.[55] Its great power over public expenditure has increased over the years because of the exigencies of recurrent and then permanent fiscal crisis, but also, as will be discussed in Chapter 10, because of the decline of other parts of the central government apparatus. Even if most public services became at least self-financing, or only marginally dependent on subsidy and therefore capable of privatization as free-standing entities, the *relative* power of the Treasury would remain great in so far as there remained tax-financed public services. An expert on the 'thickening' of the US hierarchy held out the UK Treasury as an example of how effective a comparatively unlayered department could be.[56]

The influence of the Treasury could decline. The Westminster rules imply that the Treasury initiates all revenue-raising. While expenditure decisions are kept separate from tax decisions, some department is needed to match the two as well as deciding the balance to be struck between borrowing and taxation. But it is not inevitable. In the USA, the Bureau of the Budget, separated from the Treasury, has much less power to realize presidential aspirations to serve macroeconomic and other policies in a budget. Its influence largely depends on that of the president over Congress. Departments and agencies are able to go to the relevant congressional committees and in conjunction with interested industries and other affected parties, determine both taxes and expenditures in the control of the committee. When the president is weak, or not concerned with budgetary policy, deciding taxes and expenditure becomes primarily a matter for resolution between individual departments and agencies on the one hand, and congressional committees on the other. If Britain were to go in the same direction, that too would end the pre-eminence of the Treasury, while stimulating log-rolling and jobbery. However, profound changes in the traditional role of the Treasury were adopted in 1995 without legislation or debate in Parliament. As a consequence the main issue is whether it can continue to safeguard the financial integrity of British government, its departments and public bodies, given as yet no serious diminution in public expenditure and services.

In July 1994 the government confirmed its objectives of the separation of provision from production, the creation of services more responsive to the consumer and injected with more competition and a greater reliance on agencies.[57] This was to be reflected in a clearer separation of the civil service into its two principal roles, which were 'support for ministers on policy matters and the management and provision of public services', a distinction which needs to be developed further and cemented. While not 'wholly distinct', these roles could 'usefully be described separately'.[58] The White Paper promised further devolution of authority to agencies and departments. There was to be deregulation, inasmuch as they would have greater management responsibility. 'Consistent with this, the Government has dismantled many unnecessary centrally determined rules and restrictions.'[59] As an example, responsibility for pay and grading for staff below senior levels was to be delegated to departments. As a result, the role of the centre of the civil service would become one of oversight, ensuring the integrity, quality and political impartiality of the service as well as encouraging best practice.

That White Paper was followed in October 1994 by a review of the functions of the Treasury in the new circumstances.[60] It aimed at a reduction of 30 per cent in Treasury senior management posts, to be achieved by deregulation: 'it is no longer necessary, or in our view sensible, for the Treasury to control the personnel management or the pension entitlements of civil servants in other departments'.[61] While reaffirming the centrality and importance of its role in the control of public expenditure, the review stated: 'we doubt whether to do this it is either necessary or efficient for the Treasury to retain its current panoply of detailed controls over individual departments' gifts, ex gratia payments, projects and so on'. The Treasury's activity was thus to become more strategic and agenda-setting. Its objectives would be the 'promoting of policies and public expenditure priorities which improve the use of resources and the efficiency of markets throughout the economy, within an affordable level of public expenditure'.[62]

The review said that Treasury teams should face most of the important spending departments, and groupings of others, plus a team to deal with issues across departments.[63] The teams were urged not to be short-sighted as in the past, but more prepared 'to advocate or suggest policies which deliver useful savings, improved value for money or a stronger economic performance over the longer term'.[64] There should be 'less emphasis on the blunt instruments of the Treasury's traditional power to veto and more emphasis on the power of persuasion, analysis and argument between strategic partners'.[65] The main elements in the process of containing public expenditure within the government's ceiling would be an annual or biannual paper for each of the Treasury teams facing spending departments, setting out short- and medium-term control objectives, and the recommended strategy for their delivery. They would be integrated into the annual Public Expenditure Survey round. The review also recommended a further review of other Treasury powers of control. At least as important was the suggested relaxation of control over appointments, promotions and salaries as a supplementary method of controlling expenditure, and the consequent recommendation to transfer the Treasury's responsibility for pay and staffing to individual departments or to the Office of Public Services. From now on the function of the centre would be to ensure overall career development, fill the most senior posts, and ensure the independence and integrity of the civil service. In almost every respect these recommendations were adopted.[66]

A still more radical solution would have been to abandon Treasury control over public expenditure and employment entirely, allowing departments to use whatever resources they chose to deliver the annual public expenditure targets which the cabinet or a cabinet committee might set, with a rump of the Treasury public expenditure division acting as its secretariat. However, as with any private holding company, subsidiaries with this much freedom might, through over-optimism, cussedness, or incompetence, not hit their target, and so jeopardize the government's expenditure and taxation targets, inviting fiscal crisis. By the time any significant failure became visible, it would be too late to take effective corrective action. If some departments were allowed to exceed their targets, others would then be encouraged to do so, so that government public expenditure targets would be still more seriously at risk. In addition, ministers might be all the more likely to overspend before an election, or their own retirement, or even if they believed they were about to change posts.

As the custodian of public expenditure, the Treasury needs to satisfy itself that departmental expenditure plans are realistic and likely contingencies have been allowed for. However, its effectiveness in doing so under the new regime by which strategic financial control replaces the excessively detailed bureaucratic control system of the past, presupposes that departments and agencies themselves have effective financial controls.[67] To enable this to happen, departments need both meaningful accounts and an effective control apparatus. While the government has committed itself to the introduction of resource accounting throughout, this has not happened yet.[68] Moreover, to be capable of being an instrument of management and control, separate accounts are needed for each and every activity so that its financial performance may be tracked. A prerequisite for that to be possible requires the systematic identification of such activities throughout government and their separation into distinct accounting units. It was argued in Chapter 8 that the failure to do this systematically has been a serious shortcoming of the Next Steps initiative. Arguably balance sheets need to be constructed for many activities, not simply because private-sector entities do so, but for the better management of assets. Private-sector experience, however, shows that just to construct financial and management accounts does not ensure financial control. A system needs to be set up to enable permanent secretaries to have enough accurate and relevant accounting and other information to have meaningful periodic dialogues with the management of all entities for which they are accountable.

To that end the present financial regime, masterminded by the Treasury, needs transformation to match best private-sector practice. The financial monitoring system has been designed mostly to deal with the daily control of cash, and the planning and achievement of annual expenditure targets. It must now sustain a process of management based on delegated authorities within tight controlled limits, and of frequent discussions of performance, based upon rapidly produced, relevant and analysed financial information. When anything goes wrong, the earlier corrective action can be taken the better. But a process which depends on dialogue only twice a year will not be intensive enough to secure good management expenditure control. No private company would do so. Most take a close look at revenues and costs once a month to be able to initiate management actions quickly to correct deviations of performance from plan.

These changes will require massive training and retraining of a type and on a scale for which the civil service is not prepared. Rapid study is needed of what the curriculum should be and of what facilities are needed: at the least an enterprise on the lines of the Kennedy School of Public Policy at Harvard with a concentration on public-sector management. Sometimes one needs to spend to be able to save.

Even in the leanest conglomerates the centre has enough capacity to inspect, investigate and hold dialogues with subsidiaries so as to reach a view on the health and prospects of the business. It is a foolish business that relies entirely on trust, however competent the management of the subsidiary companies. For the Treasury to relax its old methods of control, without it and departments being equipped to undertake the new methods properly, is a prime example of allowing myth and cost cutting, rather than practical reality, to dictate change. It could be disastrous – politically, managerially and for public expenditure control. Indeed, during a period of transition, while the new systems and apparatus are being developed, more civil servants are needed both in the Treasury and in the departments, to keep the old regime running while the new is being set up. While thereafter it may just be possible to justify cutting back Treasury numbers, if the new system proves particularly successful at securing control within all departments, it is more likely departments will need at least as many, if not more, officials engaged in financial control; so the net effect is unlikely to be a saving in staff numbers, though it should in public expenditure and therefore in taxation.

Ministerial responsibility

There are two main reasons why it has been useful to maintain an interpretation of the doctrine of ministerial responsibility as still applicable. The first is that it pays tribute to the central notion of parliamentary democracy that the people's representatives rule. Provided they are within the law, their supremacy is maintained by their not being bound by their own or other ministers' previous decisions. The second reason is that there are times in any state – emergencies of peace as well as war – when the ability to act quickly is very advantageous and may even be vital.

However, the disadvantages are twofold. If ministers were to use their power whenever they liked, its use could result in unnecessary or insufficiently considered policy change, especially when ministers succeeded one another. Moreover, initiatives which were never given time to work might be continually overtaken. Both these characteristics are not infrequent, especially in the education and training field where policies have been introduced nationally without waiting for the results of pilot projects to be assessed.

In these circumstances the activities of departments and other related bodies cannot possibly be efficient, because they would always be changing their objectives, their organization and their behaviour. Although in some areas of active political concern such as foreign policy, commands will be issued much of the time, in most of government this would be intolerable. Apart from negative as well as positive political consequences, the implications for public expenditure would be severe. In the public as in the private sectors the art of management is to create an environment in which the overall objective (whether profit or not) does not change, and the strategies and targets to achieve can be set for as long ahead as possible. Management energies may then be used to drive towards these targets without distraction, and to respond to changing external factors. The adoption of a more consultative process in policy-making, suggested for other reasons elsewhere in this book, should not only improve the implementation of policies but also, by slowing down the whole timetable and reducing the possibility of repeated new initiatives, create the more certain environment in which good management can flourish.

Appointments policy

At first sight there appears to be a fundamental distinction between public bodies which have a statutory existence, and those which do not and hence are part of the executive. The reality, however, is that even when statutory bodies have well-defined powers to establish real independence, dependence on central government finance may mean ministers can exert similar power over them as over other parts of the executive.

Their most distinguishing feature is that most public bodies and quangos have boards in which powers are vested by legislation. In contrast, where executive agencies have boards it is frequently unclear whether they are executive or advisory, and if advisory then whether to the minister or to the agency chief executive, and they certainly have no statutory existence. The role for non-executives is especially unclear. In the private sector they are, in part, appointed to act as a check on an overmighty chairman or chief executive; they can hardly do this to ministers, although some of them clearly and publicly attempted to prevent the Home Secretary sacking the Prisons Service Agency Chief Executive (soon afterwards, all non-executive members of the NHS board retired and were not replaced).

For executive agencies, the appointment that matters most is that of the chief executive, which is advertised outside and inside the civil service, but made by the departmental minister. Ministerial involvement is regrettable. The independence of a civil servant, who is the head of an agency, is as important as that of any other civil servant and for the same reasons (see Chapter 11). Moreover, the existence of a framework document and the crystallization of authority in the chief executive inevitably prompts a question which never in the past had to be asked of civil servants: are you prepared to carry out the framework document loyally? If that document were only alterable through some public process, preferably under genuine parliamentary scrutiny, it might be sufficient protection for the public interest to permit ministers to make their own appointees to such posts and rely on such documents as a basis for the chief executive to resist ministers, where appropriate, in future. But as such documents are alterable at ministerial will, it is dangerous to allow ministers to make such appointments because the loyalty of such appointees must necessarily be to whatever is in a framework document and to ministers personally. Given the tendency for ministers to deal with some agencies directly without civil service support and possibly with political advice instead, it is all too easy to see a development where agency heads become avowed political appointments. From that it is but a short step towards other senior agency appointments becoming political, most probably grounded on the argument that reinforcements are needed to overcome civil service inertia. American experience suggests that increasing the number of political appointments in any agency does not give an agency a more concerted political direction. Rather the political appointees, coming from no coherent background and of uneven competence, disagree among themselves and demotivate the civil servants by bad management, incoherent policy direction and because promotion opportunities are denied them.

Therefore as long as relations between minister and agencies remain ones of command, appointments within the agency from the top down should be made by the Civil Service Commissioners from the best material available. Moreover, as long as framework documents are changeable without any due process, there must also be a case for appointing non-executive board members with some independent standing as some protection for the relationship between departments and agencies.

At present ministers make most appointments to quango boards, and some of the most important require the approval of the prime minister. Governments have always had a tendency to appoint their friends to such offices. Under the Thatcher and Major administrations, there has been a declining tendency to appoint trade unionists and others from backgrounds favourable to the Opposition parties, and an increasing tendency to appoint people of a business background, using the argument that running a public body requires such executive experience. It has also been argued that positions of great patronage on behalf of the state should be occupied only by people wealthy enough to appreciate the value of money. If such criteria are applied, it would inevitably make it more likely that those appointed will have conservative tendencies. There are still a few appointments – for example, the deputy chairman of the BBC and of urban development corporations – where, informally, the convention is that someone sympathetic to the Opposition is appointed. But even here the government has sometimes preferred to choose its own candidates among presumed Opposition sympathizers, rather than take those offered by the leader of the Opposition. The multiplication of quangos, particularly in health, has led to demands for an independent element in making appointments to public boards. How those appointments are made has important implications for patronage and public-sector ethics and will be discussed further in Chapter 10.

The issue here is how board structure can be used to influence the balance of power between public bodies and their ministers. In some circumstances, boards could strengthen ministers' powers, by allowing every new minister to appoint his own members, or by allowing new appointments when governments changed. But that would have the strongest drawbacks, not only in making appointments seem more overtly political, but in discouraging the non-political in many cases from seeking appointments for which they are well qualified.[69] Much the same effect can be achieved by ensuring that some appointments on any board come up in any year and by the convention that, if a chairman and a minister feel themselves unable to work well together, the chairman resigns without any discredit shortly after an election.

Conversely, continuity of membership provides boards with a measure of independence, which in itself may serve ministers' purpose. Even ministers may agree that a strong, independent board is needed to distance politicians from their identification with difficult choices about resource allocation, and to reflect professional and customer interests. It helps explain why the Arts Council and English Heritage, as well as most art galleries and museums, are set up with strong, independent board members often called trustees. Innumerable technical advisory committees and the many research councils and committees need a similar distance, as do any other bodies from the Law Commission to advisory committees on history wreck sites and on the public lending right.

Powers of appointment give ministers some influence over the kinds of decision that might be made. There seems no reason why all these appointments should be made by ministers and behind closed doors, particularly given current concerns and a not unjustified belief that there is a systematic bias in appointment from the 'establishment'. Many post-colonial governments on the Westminster model created a public service commission which, usually, includes responsibility for appointments of this kind. One possibility would be to introduce such a body in Britain, building on the appointment of a single public appointments commissioner in 1995.

There are also public bodies where ministers need to be distanced from what is intended to be an equitable process. Judicial and quasi-judicial tribunals are of such a kind. Another example is the Central Statistical Office, where professional standards might gain from having some independent professional representation, nominated appropriately. For rather different reasons, the BBC, the Broadcasting Standards Committee, the Boundaries Commission and Independent Television Commission need to be distant from politicians in order to preserve political impartiality and independence. It is not obvious that the government should always appoint them if other suitable arrangements can be found. They need a roughly balancing number of former politicians from the main parties, and parties outside government could therefore choose their own representative. Most of these bodies also need non-politicians, to represent various kinds of client group and consumer.

There should never be so many political appointments to prevent any body pursuing government policy or to exclude the technical or other expertise most boards need. As Archie Kirkwood, MP, told the Nolan Committee:

> if you then found that you were putting people in charge of extremely important decisionmaking bodies which required a degree of leadership that are actually prepared openly to confront the political direction of the government of the day, I think that makes the process of government almost impossible to sustain . . .[70]

In more general terms, as part of the review of public bodies Nolan recommends, there is a need to establish in relation to every public body what skills and backgrounds should be represented on its board, as well as to what extent any of these appointments should be based on independent advice or in some cases independently appointed.

Contracts and quasi-contracts

The next issue is whether relationships reflected in framework documents are to have any authority above that given them by ministers. If they are to allow good resource management and permit efficiency savings, and if ministers and agencies are to have real accountability to Parliament for them, then there must be greater and longer-lasting certainty. The current legal position is that departments and any agencies formed from them come under the executive powers ministers have inherited from the royal prerogative.[71] In creating executive agencies the only change in law needed was to alter some accounting conventions for a small number of agencies.[72]

Accountability would be more protected if there were an enabling statute for executive agencies which established appropriate arrangements for them. There is a case for requiring new agencies to have a statutory basis, to ensure their power and duties are discussed by Parliament, and therefore a case for a generic statute setting down different forms of agency status and framework documents. But to try to set down in statute the powers of agencies and ministers in each case is much more difficult. If it is done in very great detail, it is likely to become inflexible; if done more broadly, it will remain ambiguous.

Nevertheless, if there is to be more predictable power-sharing between ministers and agencies, its basis needs to be written down – most probably not in a statute or as an ordinary legal contract, but as a special statutory instrument, covering the powers and duties of ministers, agencies, their boards and chief executives but also of the permanent secretary and any other officials in relation to them. The enabling statute would set down basic requirements for framework documents and a process for their amendment. The power of amendment might be retained by the minister or require parliamentary approval, preferably only after the minister had given his reasons to the relevant departmental committee.

In many cases the framework document could be simple, amounting to no more than the terms of reference, as, for instance, in the case of the numerous technical and other advisory committees which spend virtually no money. More detailed requirements may be required for tribunals, regulatory or other quasi-judicial bodies, but their main defining feature might be the procedures they are to follow and the circumstances in which decisions are to come to ministers for approval or review, except where they are already laid down in statute. Details defining financial powers, accounting, audit arrangements and scrutiny processes might be expected to be defined for any agency that spends substantial sums of money.

More complicated and innovative would be framework documents which specified clearly the agency's duties for which they were responsible to Parliament through the accounting officer and those which were the direct responsibility of the minister, so following New Zealand practice.

Such a contract should be a public parliamentary document and would need to include the following:

1 That ministers could have the right to give advice or guidance to the agency and might expect that guidance to be followed, provided it was lawful, did not breach the framework document and did not result in the incurring of significant extra cost.
2 That ministers could ask for additional, different or reduced services from the agency, provided they met the net cost of the changes and provided the agency was a suitable body for the task.
3 That ministers could require the agency to reflect public-sector or other ethical standards on such matters as non-discrimination, or to adopt stated administrative procedures, provided it was funded to do so and no distortion of competition arose.
4 That ministers could call for any reports and other information needed to ensure the agency was held to account, provided it was not at disproportionate cost, or that any additional cost was met.
5 That the chief executive of an agency, as its accounting officer, was responsible for providing all accounting and other information for reporting on performance to the departmental permanent secretary. The permanent secretary's own duties would include conducting regular financial and performance reviews appropriate to the size, and type of agency in discharging his duties to Parliament and ministers for the efficiency and probity of the agency.
6 That for purposes of parliamentary scrutiny an agency came under the Public Accounts Committee or another designated committee.

7 That any inspectors empowered by ministers, the permanent secretary or the National Audit Office would have right of access to the agency's activities and its books.
8 That the agency would have the right to be consulted in ministerial and departmental discussions that affected it.
9 That ministers should have a right to make a direction in the national interest which must be published. (This seldom-used provision in nationalized industry statutes was held by the courts to be for national emergencies only.)
10 That ministers should be able to take over command or make other arrangements if the agency could not fulfil its contract, or in a national emergency.

But there might be other options particularly needed for the framework documents of agencies which were a focus of political attention:

11 Specific classes of agency decision or action would have to be notified to ministers for their approval or action.

Under these arrangements a service such as the Planning Inspectorate or the Passport Office might act in a contractually prescribed way which ensured that certain types of decision, or appeal, came to ministers. Regulatory bodies such as the Health and Safety Executive, or the Environmental Protection Agency, might agree circumstances in which ministers would be involved in decisions, without prejudice to their independence. They would need to be ready to take on the implications of new UK and European law and regulation, but the net costs of doing so would have to be met on a basis agreed with ministers. Since most of the costs of the activities of such agencies as interpret or impose regulations are borne by those who have to abide by their decisions, there might be a disproportionality rule to be adjudicated by ministers – under which ministers could be asked whether the benefits of an agency decision outweighed its disbenefits. There might be values affecting the decisions such agencies take – for example, the implied value of human life – which might be reserved to ministers. Such bodies might also be formally required to take part in certain procedures to progress certain kinds of decisions (as the Environmental Protection Agency is with Ofwat and the Department of the Environment in deciding the environmental improvement burden to be borne by water users).

Another example is provided by the Highways Agency, where major investment decisions would be reserved to ministers. Since the early 1970s techniques have been steadily developed for evaluating return from investment in new roads. But there may be environmental and political factors which may override those criteria, and such decisions are for ministers to make and should be explicitly reserved to them. However, when those decisions are made may well also affect agency costs substantially. Taken too early, there may not be enough information for rational decisions; left too late, aborted preparation costs can be very high. The contract with the agency might well lay down the most appropriate point for ministerial decision, and require the costs of decisions taken at a different time to be borne by the minister.

Some agencies may be expected to retain capacity against likely or possible emergencies, at public expense. Another example might be a research establishment which contracted to keep available some percentage of its researchers' time on average for urgent advice to government in some emergency. The purpose behind these contractual stipulations is to recognize that ministerial concerns often differ from commercial ones. But a measure of contractual certainty, combined with incentives to improve performance, is needed, if there are to be real gains in efficiency and savings in public expenditure. An approach which merely reduced the barriers to ministerial intervention could reduce accountability and efficiency below even the standards of the past. That substantial efficiency gains can be reached is demonstrated by the staggering and almost wholly underpredicted efficiency gains of the regulated industries after their privatization. Hence the case for turning so-called quasi-contracts into real, but appropriately conditional, contracts. If this cannot be done, better to stick to the old command relationships within a department without the ambiguities in policy-making and delivery that agency status appears to imply.

Notes

1 Aneurin Bevan, quoted in Day and Klein (1987), p. 76.
2 Harden (1992), pp. 37–41; Lewis (1993), p. 27.
3 As in USA; see DiIulio *et al.* (1993), pp. 24–8.
4 Richards (1989), p. 31.
5 Rose (1987), quoted in Dunleavy and Rhodes (1990), p. 12.
6 Cabinet Office (1994), p. 2, 16; see also Timothy Renton, MP, in TCSC (1991), p. 46.
7 Lewis (1989), p. 225.
8 TCSC (1991), p. 15; Jones and Burnham (1995), p. 162.
9 Greer (1992).
10 Day and Klein (1987); TCSC (1991).
11 Perkin (1989).
12 TCSC (1991), pp. 23, 38; see discussion as it appeared in Scott, Foster (1996).
13 TCSC (1991), pp. 49–50.
14 On the tribulations of an MP trying to ask questions about Next Steps agencies, see Kaufman (1994), p. 20.
15 See Greer (1992), p. 90.
16 TCSC (1991), p. 32.
17 Learmount (1995), p. 93.
18 TCSC (1991), p. 38.
19 TCSC (1991), pp. 49–50.
20 TCSC (1991), p. xxvi.
21 See Drivers Vehicle Licencing Agency (1993), p. 3.
22 As in USA; see Garvey and DiIulio (1994), p. 35.
23 See TCSC (1991), pp. x–xi.
24 Hennessy (1990), p. 608.
25 Heseltine (1980), p. 3.

26 Bagehot (1928), p. 177; see also Sidgwick (1891), p. 423.
27 Hennessy (1990), p. 608.
28 Hennessy (1990), p. 608.
29 Hennessy (1990), p. 609.
30 Ibbs (1988).
31 Hennessy (1990), p. 609.
32 Private information.
33 Scott and Gorringe (1989), p. 8.
34 Gore (1993), p. 75, quoted in Moe (1994), p. 116.
35 Ibbs (1988), p. 25.
36 Fraser (1991), p. 48; TCSC (1991), pp. 37, 48.
37 Butler (1993), p. 404; Cabinet Office (1994), p. 3.
38 Dunleavy (1991), p. 153.
39 Learmount (1995), p. 93.
40 Nolan (1995).
41 Jones (1989), p. 256.
42 Price Waterhouse (1994).
43 Fraser (1991), p. 8.
44 Kemp (1993), p. 16.
45 As there are visible signs in the Scott Report, see Foster (1996).
46 Pliatsky (1992), p. 557.
47 Peters (1993), p. 50.
48 TCSC (1991), p. vii.
49 Boston (1987); Scott et al. (1990), p. 44.
50 Boston (1987); Scott and Gorringe (1989), p. 87.
51 John Watts, MP, TCSC (1991), p. 52.
52 See Major (1994), pp. 1, 6, 8, 17–18; see also Butler (1988), quoted in Richards (1989); Dorrell (1994).
53 Light (1993).
54 As noted by Trosa (1994), p. 26.
55 Brittan (1964); Bridges (1966); Hennessy (1990), pp. 69–78; Drewry and Butcher (1991), pp. 39–41.
56 Light (1995).
57 Cabinet Office (1994).
58 Cabinet Office (1994).
59 Cabinet Office (1994), p. 17.
60 Treasury (1994a), pp. 12–13.
61 Treasury (1994a), pp. 12–13.
62 Treasury (1994a), p. 38.
63 Treasury (1994a), p. 101.
64 Treasury (1994a), p. 105.
65 Treasury (1994a), p. 107.
66 Treasury (1994b).
67 Foster (1971), pp. 171–88.
68 Treasury (1995).
69 Nolan (1995), p. 73.
70 Nolan (1995), p. 73.
71 Hogwood (1993), p. 210; but for New Zealand see Scott et al. (1990).
72 The Government Trading Act (1990) amended its 1973 predecessor.

10

The role of ministers

> To date the public management reform debate has not succeeded in what
> should be its central task: delineating the essential functions of government . . .
> the danger is that an overall judgement about government's core competencies
> may be avoided only incrementally through a residualising process, outsourcing
> being applied piecemeal to different bodies of work.
>
> Dunleavy and Hood[1]

The end of politics is most often described as if politics were to be almost replaced
by the market, and politicians by questionnaires and surveys. We have argued not
that it is undesirable but impossible. There are limits, both absolute and practical, to
privatization and contractorization. Even a Hayekian agenda would not eliminate
all public provision, though much could be devolved to local government. But
even if the market replaced the politicians as providers of goods and services to a
greater extent than seems probable in any developed nation, it should not be the
end of politics. How the state has been hollowed out has created activities which
cannot be left to market disciplines. Moreover, even where activities can be passed
to the market, others, such as inspection, audit and regulation, emerge from the
shadows with a public dimension. Therefore, there would still be ample and
demanding roles for national politicians and a future for politics.

Another reason given for the end of politics is the frequency of politicians' failures; in Vietnam, in devising a common European defence and foreign policy; or, more mundanely, again and again in British economic policy,
or in the declining quality and reduced durability of much UK legislation in
recent years. It would be the end of democracy if these failures were interpreted to mean these political and 'political' tasks would be done better by
administrators or generals. But the experience of the old Soviet Union and its
satellites, like most oligarchies and dictatorships, does not give any comfort that
failures would then be more likely to be avoided.

Ministers have many roles, to the point of overload. Kings used to lead
their armies into battle, until it was accepted others could do it more successfully.
Ministers owe their origins to the realization that monarchs needed counsellors,
who would be more effective had they a greater independence of the monarchy.
Part of the fascination of the political career is that they, more than most, have
escaped Adam Smith's exhortation to specialization through the division

of labour. As techniques of administration develop, some functions can be devolved to others who can do them better, or simply to reduce overload. But management has not been among them because ministers (Chapter 9) have not been and are not suited to be managers. Even when activities are retained within government the notion that ministers can behave towards their departments and other public bodies as if executive or non-executive chairmen directing a holding company is likely to fail: ministers have neither the time nor experience to be part of management; but, as Michael Howard showed in 1995 in connection with the prison service, they have both opportunity and inclination to intervene, so as to undermine attempts at efficiency gains and cost-saving.[2] But there is the key, if unspectacular, ministerial procurement role specifying public services (Chapter 6). They also have other important roles, as quasi-consumers, quasi-clients, quasi-citizens; redressers of grievances; magistrates; sources of appointments; and as planners, leaders and policy-makers.

Politicians as quasi-consumers

If ministers are not to be top management in any real sense, do they have a role as stand-ins for consumers in deciding what is to be provided? There are reasons against this. Market pricing can often replace them by real consumers. Aside from pure public goods and externalities, instead of ministers' rationing scarce public resources for housing, health services and education, those decisions can be left to the market. The price mechanism and the depth of the purse of interested parties could resolve conflicts of interest, as over the use of public land or abuse of the environment. The diversity of provision that would result need not be Hayekian in its neglect of redistribution (though it could be), since that could be done through the tax and benefits systems (Chapter 5).

Where market pricing is not adopted, decisions on what should be provided can be eased for ministers by reliance on market and other consumer research, surveys and such mechanisms as focus groups and panels. In Britain the element of customer choice in the Citizen's Charter recognizes there will then be more public customer satisfaction than if ministers or civil servants decide what citizens want.

In other cases, ignorant or politically biased provision can be avoided by the systematic use of appropriate evaluation procedures, specified in framework documents or otherwise publicly declared. A good example is road investment appraisal. (Other examples in transport would be the techniques developed for the appraisal of road and other safety measures, and for the appraisal of rail and other public transport in congested areas.) Developed from earlier techniques, cost–benefit techniques for highway approval were used regularly from 1974. Based in the early days principally on forecasts of time savings (allowing for congestion) and accident reduction, with more environmental factors entering later, their use had the great advantage that they meant priority could be given to new road construction and to road improvements where these would benefit users (and pedestrians) most, rather than where politicians, pressure groups or political interests suggested. If evaluations were published both of alternative schemes and of ways of implementing them, they would be a considerable check upon the ability of ministers to ride roughshod over them.

Unfortunately, during the 1980s the practice of using them to decide priorities lapsed: as when from the early 1980s, it is alleged, successive ministers of roads swept evaluation procedures aside and with a map of constituencies superimposed on a road map, decided which bypasses would most help win the next election. If a minister wants to override the priority ranking given by such an evaluation technique, he or she can do so. But good government in the public interest requires it is done openly, and that reasons are published for the modification of what was first indicated was in the consumers' interest. Many other areas of government could be helped by systematic use of such existing techniques or the development of new ones.

Roads are an example where politicians act at two removes from the consumer: acting upon expert advice, their job is to ensure that experts take into account consumers' and the wider public interest. The National Health Service is a more complex case. It is being put through a series of contentious hospital closures, increased specialization of facilities, and other reforms which could greatly improve its efficiency. But there is widespread scepticism whether this is possible, as well as dismay in many quarters at what it means for familiar institutions. Such proposals would carry more conviction if it could be shown they had been tested against other options in a relevant evaluation framework, and then monitored to show promised benefits were being delivered. Without published evaluation, it is reasonable to suggest that the actual decisions made depend as much on ministers' capricious exercise of judgement, the influence of one lobby against another or 'political' considerations.

There is a need for evaluation at a more fundamental level. Despite the substantial increase in real resources for the NHS during the 1980s and 1990s, demands for medical care have grown faster, so causing a series of acute rationing problems. They could end if replaced by a market system pricing out those who could not afford treatment, but that solution is not publicly acceptable. In the past the inevitable rationing has been by a mixture of queues and local medical judgements deciding priorities, so as to keep public criticism to a sustainable minimum. But since the onset of fiscal crisis, pressures on resources have made those hidden solutions harder to sustain. Getting by depends on some slack in the system to meet what otherwise would be publicly embarrassing emergencies. Shortage of resources and rising expectations of health care have removed that slack.

As resource shortage makes rationing by experts more problematic, more of the blame tends to be passed to ministers as responsible for the services. So blamed, they in their turn are more likely to jump in and make the rationing decisions. The sheer size of the service, the enormity of the information needed to manage it, and the inexperience of many of its managers, contribute to a scenario where ministers take the blame for what is largely outside their (and anyone else's) control; which then prompts them to intervene with results that are often not fully predictable, plunging both the doctrine of ministerial responsibility and the National Health Service itself into even greater difficulty.

As Chapter 7 indicated, there is a strong case for using general practitioners as expert purchasers, but politicians can perform a service to the consumer scrutinizing those decisions, if necessary with other expert advice. Both central and local politicians can usefully have roles in this complicated market: central politicians to provide financial resources and deal with national purchasing decisions, as with the pharmaceutical companies, and local politicians dealing with the adequacy of the service on the ground.

But, to give the public greater confidence in both, decision-making and evaluation criteria are needed which express government policy and within which lower-level managers can manage. Such an approach, the Qaly, was described in Chapter 8. The other practical option is to leave to local hospitals and doctors to use their own qualitative judgement on how the available resources are used under supervision of local government and rely on local knowledge to achieve an acceptable outcome – with no attempt at national equity. Even then, ministers will find, as they did when local government had more freedom to spend within a block grant than it has now, that they, controlling the purse-strings, will still be blamed by those who ration resources; but at least much of the current muddle would be avoided.

Many other policy issues and decisions which require expert advice – defence, social security, environmental policy and road safety – are not easily understood by ministers, unless tutored, or by citizens, though they can judge the impact on them and their families. But they cannot be left to the market, nor entirely to experts: experts frequently disagree; several kinds of expert may be involved; a given use for public expenditure must be balanced against other possible uses; non-expert issues may be relevant, which may be political or redistributive. The job of the ministers as quasi-consumers is to try to imagine what the citizen would decide about defence or foreign policy, if he were as well informed as the civil service should help the minister to become.[3] The civil service should enable ministers to take decisions in full possession of the relevant facts, and with access to the best advice from inside and outside the civil service on the pitfalls ahead, both political and personal, but above all on the difficulties of implementation. It points out the areas in which they have reasonable discretion given the broad criteria they might be expected to use, so it may be apparent to them and to others if they depart from these criteria towards more 'political' decision-making. There are, however, occasions when ministers take decisions which are less capable of systematic treatment, because speed is necessary or because they prefer to take decisions this way; and when, as a result, it is not easy to use the consumers' interest as the criterion. Whatever the circumstances, the less rigorously the outcome can be tested against well-defined, measurable criteria, the more justice depends on procedural adequacy.[4] In such circumstances procedures need to be devised to reveal why the decisions taken were judged by ministers or local politicians to be in the consumers' interest.

But however much ministers may draw on consumer research or technical expertise to help them ascertain what consumers most want from public money spent on their behalf, there must be *rationing* wherever the market is not cleared by price. While rationing may be left to experts, it is a customary and more appropriate role for politicians. But this role need not belong to central politicians, except for the supreme rationing decision for government, the annual public expenditure round, which determines the level of resources raised by taxation and borrowing. Otherwise the rationing of most public goods and services is more likely to satisfy consumers if it is done locally, as suggested in Chapter 7.

Whatever is left to ministers, rationing and the determination of priorities require factual information on what various consumers want, analyses and costings to discover how requirements may best be met, and as objective advice as possible on the advantages and disadvantages of the main courses of action available. The Citizen's Charter has spread these practices, but its principles still need more complete and systematic adoption in consumers' interest, locally as well as centrally, so reserving to central politicians the decisions that cannot and should not be taken by other means.

Politicians as quasi-clients and citizens

When prices, outputs and quality of goods and services are not wholly determined by the market, they must reflect explicit redistributive judgements, if they are to be rational. One cannot appeal to consumer research or impartial criteria to justify the redistributive elements in such decisions. They are normative.[5] They have to be political. There is limited scope (Chapter 7) for local decisions on redistribution. Therefore, redistributive decisions rightly involve national ministers, except when such decisions are made at European level.

All ministers' policies and decisions can affect the relative income, wealth and other aspects of equity between citizens. Given fiscal crisis and the need to reduce expenditure, the replacement of universal by mean-tested redistribution and the possibility of further targeting and piloting increase the need to distinguish between redistribution in the public interest and that influenced by 'political' considerations. Such transparency ought to be achieved by greater thoroughness in preparation and openness in the presentation of policies. There is also a need to determine impacts on the distribution of income as far as they can be predicted and retrospectively measured. During the 1980s in Britain there has been a growing reluctance in government to measure the impact of policy upon income distribution. This led in 1993–5 to an unprecedented joint action by permanent secretaries to collect the data relevant to assessing the impact of policy changes. Given the importance of those issues, it would seem sensible to revert to earlier practice and require the national central statistical agency to update such information regularly on an independent basis, so that these aspects of redistributive justice are transparent.

The effect of any given redistribution on the client is as susceptible to consumer research as is the provision of public services, whether in cash or in kind. Whether old age pensioners, benefit claimants or children, there will be better-quality service for a given expenditure if what is provided is designed with consumers' interests in mind. All paternalistic decisions by ministers which aim to reflect consumers, citizens or clients, not as they are but as they might be, fall into this category. Nevertheless politicians have to strike a balance between these interests. In a democracy their rationing role is inescapable, but it can be aided, and made more rational and accountable, by the use of relevant information and procedures.

Politicians as redressers of grievances

A kingly function that has descended to ministers is that of redresser of grievances. In many countries ministerial ante-rooms are full of petitioners wanting to present the great man (usually) with an individual or collective grievance. When he passes through, they press their attentions upon him, hoping for notice. Depending on their importance to him, they are seen more or less quickly.

Other countries have different ways of doing much the same thing. In Britain departments have sections that write replies for ministers to respond to grievances. They may come by letter direct to ministers or be forwarded by MPs or by other intermediaries. They may be complaints made by MPs on behalf of constituents or of others they know, including those interests which they are paid to reflect. The role of MPs as intermediaries is bound up with the growth of lobbies working on ministers, but also, and more importantly, with the development of MPs' role as constituency welfare officers. Grievances may take the form of parliamentary questions, or they may sometimes be important enough to be the occasion for a debate.[6]

But there are other ways of achieving the same ends. The nationalized industry consumer councils were transformed when detached from the industries themselves and attached to the new natural monopoly regulators. Complaints soared, mostly because customers saw a greater chance of redress. Ombudsmen have tried to perform similar functions over local and health authorities (though the best role for the local ombudsman needs clarification, as it is not well related to the requirement that local authorities should have internal and external grievance procedures, the last with an independent element). Such developments have been reinforced by the Citizen's Charter movement, but there is further to go.

In effect, a model is developing for redress which is applicable to all public services: a consumer committee structure attached to an official who may be a regulator or an ombudsman. These committees may be local or, as in telecommunications, may represent types of consumer with a common interest. Individuals may be directed to them by MPs or may complain direct to the regulator or committee; the latter normally will redirect their complaints to those who supply the good or service to the consumer. If the answer is slow or unsatisfactory, their staffs will take it up until an answer is received which satisfies them as sufficient. A good reason for having such a committee or committee structure is to have representative consumers on it, whether appointed or elected. The case for attaching it to an official such as a natural monopoly regulator is partly to make the handling of complaints more efficient, but partly also to take over when it becomes a matter of enforcement: when a local authority, quango or agency is slow to do anything.

The growth of some such system covering all public services will not only in itself amount to the development of a kind of administrative law, but it will alter the function of politicians as redressers of grievances. Indeed it could eliminate it, replacing it by more professional, specialized regimes. Nevertheless, there remains a role for MPs and local councillors to help citizens to progress grievances, advise them if their attempts to obtain remedies are rebuffed, and help them towards a faster and cheaper method of redress than the courts. Thus constituency MPs should stay as the first gateway to help sort and forward complaints. Ministers would become a court of appeal for complaints and grievances, when complainants felt the specialized system had let them down and wanted to take the matter further. Whatever the exact role of politicians, it is vital there is a strong disinterested element to ensure that the process of dealing with complaints is impartial, both as to whose complaints are remedied and over the terms upon which remedies are provided. A system in which government-side MPs favour their own or marginal voters and are themselves favoured by ministers has enormous potential for 'political' manipulation and even corruption.

Such systematic development of grievance procedures would also release more time for MPs, in asking parliamentary questions and in debate, to raise national matters for which ministers were directly and personally responsible. Generally, this activity requires a detective instinct, intelligence, persistence and quick-wittedness to be successful. To pursue ministers with questions to unearth impropriety in their handling of affairs is one of the most important activities of Parliament. Unfortunately, few MPs have the tenacity and nose for it. In the recent past, perhaps only one, Tam Dalyell, has been outstandingly good at it, able to strike fear into ministers when they realized he was on their track and to encourage civil servants to persist in deterring ministers from actions that might invite his attention. A healthy Parliament is one that has a sufficient number of Tam Dalyells to keep ministers more or less on the straight and narrow.

Politicians as magistrates

Another ministerial role once more important than now is the judicial, or quasi-judicial, which was often called regulatory and included what is called regulation.[7] Because ministers took many such decisions, civil servants spent much of their time advising them on how to do so or taking such decisions in their name. For example, in 1946 a permanent secretary, Sir F. P. Robinson, wrote a letter to Sir Edward Bridges in which he said:

> There have been as I see it, within our memories, three periods in the Civil Service. The first period was when Government activity was for the most part *regulatory*, giving effect as it were to the national conscience. The chief function of the Civil Servant then was to exercise a balanced and fair-minded judgement, and dole out equality of treatment all round. The next period was the era of the Social Services which brought Civil Services into the daily lives of the citizens . . .[8]

The third period, in his opinion, was that of the Attlee government, where it was much more involved in productive industry.

As late as the 1950s regulatory activity or casework continued as the largest element in the routine work of most departments, and it remains as such in some: for example, the Home Office. Despite its being overshadowed by other activity, successive legislation has added to the decisions that ministers make or have made for them.[9] Ministers advised by civil servants, or civil servants on behalf of ministers, take innumerable kinds of quasi-judicial decisions. Some descend from the ancient royal prerogative of mercy, for example the consideration of pardon, retrial and remission of sentence at the Home Office. Some, for example planning regulations, or the authorization of new roads or power stations, have developed into complicated processes with distinct sets of procedures.[10] Others, such as health and safety regulation, and environmental protection, have themselves been separated from ministerial attention by being hived off into agencies. The term 'regulation' can be used to describe almost any ministerial or official activity which uses the discretion provided by legislation, but is probably best confined to where statutes or traditions in the exercise of the royal prerogative expressly provide for adjudicative ministerial decisions.[11] Many decisions which come to ministers are an outflow from grievance procedures. Just as service-providing agencies need to develop evaluation techniques to help politicians apply their judgement, so the quasi-judicial procedures adopted by regulatory agencies should be designed to aid ministers in their decisions if and when the case files reach them.

The system had many advantages. First, it drew upon common experience. Until the 1950s it was not uncommon for businessmen and professionals, particularly those with political interests, to serve as magistrates. In 1895, 17 per cent of ministers had been JPs. Redlich and Hirst observed that until the last quarter of the nineteenth century most MPs had been magistrates.[12] Many Labour MPs came up through local government as mayors and aldermen in the days when they were automatically magistrates. Other MPs had similar experience in the colonies. Indeed, the experience of sitting in judgement went further: it was part of the professional activity of a wide range of occupations from colonial administrator and military officer, to trade union official, school master and even school prefect. It was a common capability of systems of local and imperial administration. Therefore, the weighing of evidence, oral and written, was a familiar activity when faced by most ministers who found it a large part of what they had to do. But those traditions have now died, and only 4 per cent of ministers in 1992 had previously been JPs.

Second, when it came to complaints about administrative actions, many of the real or alleged abuses originated within the civil service. Ministers might be expected to take a knowledgeable and detached view. They knew enough to reach an informed judgement, but were sufficiently distanced not to engage in a cover-up. The doctrine of ministerial responsibility added an edge to their concern, whetted by the fact that ministers did not run their departments in any managerial or administrative sense, but trusted their senior civil servants to do it for them. In general, as ministers have become more partisan or have been seen to be such, and have intervened more in departmental administration, the use of ministers in such quasi-judicial capacities has been harder to sustain. Even the Home Secretary, who has many such functions with his exercise of the royal prerogative, has recently been accused of being arbitrary or over-hasty in his quasi-judicial decisions, apparently not paying as much attention as he should to the civil service advice put to him. He has been challenged by the judges, to a greater extent and more effectively than in the House of Commons, but less than he would have been if each of the major complaints against him had been the subject of a major debate in the House.

Third, as part of the process of consensus-building in a corporatist state, it pleased ministers to engage in activities which could be regarded as impartial and non-partisan. What is damaging for the reputation of ministers is that many such decisions are no longer seen as attempts to reach an impartial judgement within the law, but as attempts to reflect changes of policy, or seen as 'political' or simply pandering to media management. On occasions examples of regulated decisions, not in themselves matters of political controversy, were the subject of debate in which MPs could develop the merits of a case, frequently influenced by their political predilections, but more by their own knowledge of the arts of weighing evidence, of judgement and of making a good case. A good performance on such an occasion ranked high in the opinion of all quarters of the House, going far to prove the quality of a good minister, and being recognized as the most important way to earn promotion.[13] It also had a positive effect on the morale of the civil service and the respect in which it holds ministers. In the past, a stringent check on ministerial misbehaviour was the knowledge that, if it were important enough, a debate might be called, in which not only the minister in question, but also another minister – even the prime minister – would have to defend action he or she had taken, since the tradition was that one minister opened and another closed the debate. But as Roy Jenkins pointed out, by the time he had returned to Parliament after having been president of the European Commission:

> Except on rare occasions, debate had ceased to be central to the parliamentary process. It had been replaced by the quick exchanges of Prime Minister's question-time and similar responses to statements by major

ministers. There was a variety of contributory causes. One was the personal style of Mrs Thatcher which led her almost never to make a parliamentary speech and never therefore to deploy a sustained rational argument but to concentrate upon the asseveration, sometimes laced with a ringing populist phrase or a passing slur on the opposition, in the answer to a supplementary question. Another is the change of habits in reporting Parliament. Previously the two 9.00 pm to 10.00 pm wind-up speeches of a major debate often dominated the parliamentary coverage. Now their resonance is confined to the relative privacy of Hansard. The sketch writers have long since written their sketches, the gallery reporters know that modern printing technology cannot be upset by anything so demanding as late news, and television naturally finds gobbets better raw material than continuous prose.[14]

Hence the catastrophic decline in the attention the media give to parliamentary debates, precipitous since 1992.[15] In the place of debate has come judicial review, when the judges review whether or not a minister's decision is unlawful; this has increased from 160 cases in 1974 to 2886 in 1993.[16] But a judicial review is an event which sometimes makes a mark in the press but takes place far from Parliament and is not subject to debate.[17] It can be regarded as the setting of one opinion, not always backed by relevant experience or analysis, against another. There must be a risk that over-reliance on judges, and ultimately sometimes on European judges, for such tasks may discredit them without saving Parliament's reputation. Therefore, it may not carry as much conviction or leave such an imprint on public consciousness as a great debate: as for example in 1974, when Tony Crosland, bound by an undertaking made during the election campaign, had to defend his decision to cancel the surcharges which the law had imposed on the Clay Cross councillors for defying the previous government. Even as experienced a parliamentarian and rational debater as Crosland was daunted by the ordeal of preparation and by the knowledge that many of the best debaters as well as the best-informed opinion in the House, even in his own party, were ranged on the other side. Extraordinarily, the 'debate' over the sacking of the head of the Prisons Agency in October 1995 effectively involved only the Home Secretary and the Shadow Spokesman. In the past numerous MPs, not only from one side, would have been testing Michael Howard's defence.

By the mid-1990s many ministers had been long in office, which may have intensified the dislike of some for the hard grind of detailed decision-making. Yet most of these decisions are necessary, and therefore need to be made by civil servants if not by ministers.

There are possibly three ways out of this dilemma. One might be to increase the number of ministers. In 1900 there were around 60 ministers for 50,000 civil servants; in 1979, 107 ministers for some 700,000 civil servants; and in 1995, 113 ministers for around 516,000 civil servants. Other factors suggest a reduction rather than an increase, and any further increase in the number of ministers could reduce the number of other government-side MPs to a minority. Other nations have fewer ministers than Britain has: in 1995 France had 44 to Britain's 113, with no discernible detriment in the quality of government.

A second option would be for ministers to increase the number of their political policy advisers. Many ministers now have one, but rarely more.[18] In contrast, the number of political appointments has increased in the United States and shows no sign of diminishing either under the Clinton–Gore or any previous reforms.[19] But whatever may be the case for political appointments elsewhere, this place would surely be the last for them because of the importance of the tradition of impartiality which integrates politicians and civil servants.

A third way of lifting the overload from ministers is to delegate more decisions to local government. An enormous number of decisions could be transferred in this way given the will to do so (Chapter 7). Decisions to close, discipline or take over local schools, hospitals, welfare centres and so forth would be better taken by elected local authorities on the basis of regular routine, or special, inspection reports with central government coming in on review or appeal.

There is a related problem that may come from disregarding safeguarding procedures. Among the recent events which led to the setting up of the Nolan Committee was the allegation that Dame Angela Rumbold MP, a former minister, had used her position as director of a lobby firm to set up an opportunity for one contender for the site of a station on the approach to the Channel Tunnel to state its case to the Secretary of State for Transport, an opportunity not given to its main rival. This is potentially a dangerous situation. In relation to the countless decisions ministers make, the parties must have reasonably equal access to state their cases. Many informal conversations can drift towards politicians being lobbied over a decision. They learn to know when to say that, to be taken further, a formal approach should be made to them or to another minister or civil servant, when the appropriate civil servants should be present to ensure that ministers have the relevant evidence on the matter, that a fair record is taken to the meeting and that justice is done between parties.[20] In general, when the civil service was the main gatekeeper for ministers, it was able to secure equitable access for all the interest groups judged to have a legitimate interest in a proposed legislative change, other policy issue, or ministerial decision. It meant keeping a control over ministers' diaries which many thought excessive.[21] But it protected them from unfair access and undue influence. It did not stop ministers from making decisions as they pleased (within the law), but it provided procedures which gave all reasonably relevant parties the right to be heard, make representations and ask questions. It obviated the need for more formal legal procedures to ensure fairness, and for more general procedures of administrative law and due process found in other countries. The undermining of this informal system has allowed a 'political' element to enter UK politics, especially worrying as the depth of the purse affects ease of access. It is a mainspring behind the development in recent years of an Americanized lobby system in Britain for which an alternative government is probably insufficiently prepared. Again, we see an instance where equity and the public interest used to be protected not by a grand constitutional provision, but by a convenient administrative procedure.

Where there is a government with a small majority, MPs may use their ability to defeat the government to secure measures or favours they believe may help them politically or personally. As long as politicians see themselves as progressing upwards through the party and through government, party discipline can prevent MPs acting in such a manner. But when politicians see a career in politics primarily in terms of the pursuit of financial rewards during and after their time in Parliament, then they will be tempted to ensure that their opportunities for financial advancement increase. As was argued earlier, the Westminster rules, and other aspects of the system which keep MPs away from particular tax and expenditure decisions, are what currently prevent MPs from acting as US senators and members of Congress to increase their saleability. But ministers are now in a stronger position to take 'political' decisions than they used to be, a position that is strengthening rapidly and could become serious, even irretrievable. (Washington has restricted lobbying by rules which arguably make it very formal: an issue is how far such rules should be taken in Britain.)

There are other mechanisms through which the state may act as decision-maker or regulator. One is the judiciary. In many countries the courts have a role in regulation and administrative law. In Britain, as in the United States, the executive is subject to the judicial review of its action; but this process is largely given to establishing the legality of the action, whether the procedures laid down have been used and whether there has been the appearance of consistency and rationality in decision-making. The courts are still disinclined in Britain to substitute their judgement of facts for that of a minister.[22] Even if the role of the courts were to be extended there would be serious disadvantages because of the expense, duration and cumbrousness of such litigation. Moreover, experience shows that legal process is unsuited to policy analysis.

To provide more flexible arrangements, many countries have separate systems of administrative courts and tribunals to regulate their administrative procedures. Economic regulation as practised in Britain or in the United States has an affinity to the use of such tribunals in its procedures. A strong and well-developed body of administrative law has grown in the United States from within an Anglo-Saxon tradition of law. But European law based on the Code Napoléon and Roman law traditions, given its importance in shaping the administrative behaviour of the European Union, is perhaps a more likely source for this kind of development. One could imagine the Council on Tribunals, at present used mainly to review the procedures of relatively small tribunals, developing into a Conseil d'État, able to review the decisions of any minister.

The likelihood that Europe will become the model is reinforced by the growing power of the Commission, much of whose activity is regulatory. The

Commission proceeds largely by issuing directives and other regulations which then have to be enforced. The spread of this function – so easily justified by the need to secure a level playing field for trade – could replace many regulatory functions conducted by member states' governments. But even if Europe were not to take on more of these functions, the regulatory apparatus of the Commission is likely to lead by example and by processes of appeal to a similar formality, which will make British-style ministerial regulatory decision-making harder to continue. Thus independent, that is non-political, regulation may be supplanting the old, original position within the British constitution, that ministers are the regulators or administrative judges, advised by officials. On balance, however, the democratic advantage of ministers or local politicians taking most such decisions, or civil servants' taking them as ministers' agents, is preferable.

Politicians as sources of appointments

More than in most countries British ministers have made most public appointments. They are among their most important decisions, just as key appointments are in any private-sector organization. As Lord Rayner said, 'the idea that [politicians] can abdicate from a responsibility of ensuring that the right people are in [place] to carry these functions out and to take an interest in their achievements, frankly, I find ludicrous'.[23] The usual method of appointment used to be for the senior civil servants of a department to list people drawn from their own professional acquaintance and possibly from the so-called list of the great and the good in the Cabinet Office. The list was submitted to the departmental minister, who might add some names of his own. But increasingly now headhunters compile the list, with two consequences: names with more relevant experience get onto it, and most, if not all, may be businessmen, since that is the direction in which the headhunters' experience and their own and recent ministerial criteria lead them, reinforcing a general trend from the 1980s of regarding management experience as of paramount importance. In recent times it has become normal to send long or short lists to the whips' office and from there to party headquarters for political vetting. In the most important cases appointments will be approved by the prime minister, who may have his own reservations and suggestions.

Except for the 'political' element, it might continue to be a workable system, if there were not so many appointments: up to 10,000 a year.[24] Given ministers' other preoccupations, their own unfamiliarity with the needs of most of these public bodies and unfamiliarity in some cases with making appointments, all but the most important could be classed among the decisions best left to civil servants, though ratified by ministers. However, as the Nolan Report notes, civil service experience is often also limited. As a result, there is a strong case in many areas for extending the practice within the National Health Service of committees of independent advisers with no operational role, though this raises in turn the question of deciding the criteria for choosing them.[25]

We said earlier how the composition of a board or committee can help preserve a public-sector body's independence, especially if it has its own sources of income, but that in most other circumstances it is a slender defence against interference. We have argued for greater contractual clarity over the areas in which any quango or executive agency has discretion, and those where ministers can override their decisions. Such developments make it both more important and easier that appointments are made of appropriate people, who in their individual capacities and as a team are capable of overseeing any public body and discharging their functions as a board as well.

One consequence of the present arrangement is the extent to which people believed to be government sympathizers are appointed and, closely interwoven in many minds, the extent to which active or recently retired top businessmen are appointed. To many, the second appears a useful cover for the first motive. Managerial, commercial and financial experience nevertheless are important qualities for such board appointments. Yet the fact that it has become almost axiomatic that chairmen of quangos should themselves have been chairmen or chief executives of private companies goes too far. While there are public services where this assumption is reasonable and while many from such a background have been successful quango chairmen, it is rare that it was because they exercised the skills that enabled them to build up or run a successful business. As this book indicated earlier, the private and public sectors are too different for that to hold: relations between ministers and civil servants, public-sector financial controls, and a multiplicity of objectives and constraints mean that private-sector experience does not translate easily and quango chairmen can come from many other backgrounds with as much relevant experience and chance of success (the sackings of Monty Alfred and Derek Lewis, chief executives of the Property Services Agency and the prison service, indicate some of the difficulties).

To oversee the whole process, there is a strong case for a public appointments commission to check that the right qualities are identified when an appointment is made, even if the scrutiny is after the event.[26] Ministers and departments should communicate specifications for individual appointments to the commission with the appointments policy for the whole board, and notify the commission as to the reasons for the appointments made. The brief to the headhunters is crucial. The commission should be able to go through the records of the process, tracing it through to the final selection.

A public appointments commission would not in itself ensure a reasonable political balance. The first difficulty is to define what such a balance is, and it is easier to start by suggesting what it is not. The whips' office and party headquarters may recommend candidates like anyone else; but because their approval has become a major element in making appointments, it has been hard to avoid the suspicion of undue 'political' influence or even corruption. But it would surely be wrong to eliminate ministerial preference. Where a public body is a vehicle for government policy, it is not unreasonable for the chairman and majority of the board to be selected or approved by the minister as likely to be sympathetic to the minister's policies though they should also have other essential qualities, defensible before a public appointments commission. (Having appointments approved by Parliament, as in the USA, has little to recommend it. The Senate has become increasingly partisan in its attitude to appointees.)[27] Where the agency is expected to be more independent, it still would not be unreasonable for the chairman and, say, two other board members to be similarly appointed by the government. A public appointments commission should act not to prevent such political appointments being made, but to ensure that all specifications are drawn up with a sufficient understanding of the qualities required of the post and by the board and that the process is fair, efficient and in accordance with best practice.

The relevant select committee could usefully review a department's appointments annually, taking evidence from it, the public appointments commission and from chairmen. The power of appointment would thus remain a potent political prerogative, in our view, rightly so. However, a shift of public services from central to local government would imply that many more appointments would be made locally, preferably also subject to the oversight of a public appointments commission.

Politicians as planners

Osborne and Gaebler saw the need to plan ahead as a key principle of good government, but in Chapter 3 we noticed that it seemed at variance with the other new public management requirements for greater efficiency and more economical government. So it is. The private sector is not a beacon here. Most Western firms do not plan beyond a few years.

In government, forward planning, contingency planning and R&D are equally vital for a thriving polity and economy. But the short election cycle makes politicians even less likely to plan ahead than industrialists: the growing influence of 'political' considerations will make political horizons even shorter. Thus the civil service necessarily has the greatest interest in securing the future, because of its continuity.

Some forms of political plan-making have fallen largely into disuse since the end of the 1970s. They form one branch of policy-making: *guidance* given by ministers. It has a short- and a long-term function. The only way ministers can influence a statutory body, once set up, is through private advice or public guidance. Private ministerial advice can be influential, especially in combination with financial control, but there are occasions for more formal public guidance in the public interest. Because ministers prefer it, public guidance often appears as instructions to such public bodies, which in law it cannot be. But ministers may reasonably and unreasonably remember reactions to guidance when contracts or appointments are to be reviewed, or budgets renegotiated. They may in this way indicate the factors they are likely to take into account when taking specific decisions, as in planning appeals or Monopolies and Mergers Commission cases.

However, longer-term guidance is more relevant for planning ahead. Ministers often used to produce substantial, long-range documents on issues such as defence, energy, housing and transport policy. Or a task of similar foresight was given to a royal commission or committee of inquiry and a key civil servant role was in servicing such committees. Other countries such as Sweden maintain similar practices. Some such policy papers and reports were criticized as anodyne, and some were; but at their best they had the great advantage of being systematic attempts to set out and confront the main issues of the following ten years or more, to evaluate the scientific and other evidence and to influence private- and public-sector behaviour. At their worst they could be shelved and forgotten. Based on extensive consultation inside and outside government, they might indicate where future legislation would be needed. They were jettisoned by the early Thatcher administration as forms of procrastination hostile to conviction politics. Yet there are, at the time of writing (1996), few policy areas of government where careful investigation and reflection are not now needed as a preliminary, and even as an alternative, to more legislation.

Politicians as leaders

It was said earlier that politicians are needed above all to deal with the very long term and the very short. Therefore leadership is needed if the general public is to face up to painful decisions that often have to be made. The most important decisions are about peace and war, and, underlying them, defence and foreign policy. Since the certainties of the cold war ended, the need for statesmen to take such decisions has become greater. Yet, ministers in most countries have been eager to cash in the so-called 'peace dividend', to squeeze out more money for civil expenditure. This trend may make it even more likely that, as in the 1930s, the world will not be able to stand up effectively to waves of aggression in different regions of the world which may eventually coalesce into wars more threatening to the developed nations.

When crisis approaches, the public has to be persuaded to put aside its immediate concerns and make sacrifices for the longer term – contrast this with the spirit of the 1935 Fulham by-election, when more ordinary leaders took home the message they should give up trying to persuade the public to make preparations to stop Hitler.

The state has the greatest need of political leaders to meet emergencies, whether war or other fundamental political crisis. The ultimate justification of a political education and career reaching the highest positions in the state is as a form of staff college, through which ministers practice their judgement in ever-more difficult decision-making, aided by the best advice, so that they may be ready to recognize and do their best when the future of their people may depend upon them. The abject failure of Britain and other European countries to act in concert quickly on a European foreign and defence policy able to defuse the conflict in Bosnia – so that the United States had to be brought in as the only effective superpower – must rank high among twentieth-century failures in leadership.

Less dramatically, the choices and greater selectivity likely to face politicians in redesigning an affordable welfare state also require a quality of leadership which seems largely lacking. Citizen's charters, research and opinion polling, however useful, also cannot substitute for political leadership which requires politicians to form opinion and not just follow it.

Politicians as policy-makers

Most of those who strove for ministerial office, until perhaps twenty years ago, sought power. But under the influence of Margaret Thatcher's tremendous power, as it grew, there came to be an equal if not greater fascination with policy-making. It would seem to have many causes: the fact that so many recent ministers started as policy advisers or officials at party headquarters; the strong hold academic and ideological controversy has in many sections of the Conservative Party; the effect of the dominant disciplines among MPs being law and history and the concern of the last with *realpolitik*, and the effect on political science and economics of 'political' notions of political economy; as well as ministers' increasing lack of relevant practical experience which means that they can contribute less to questions of implementation and therefore tend to be less interested in them.

The most important outcomes of the activity of policy-making are legislation and guidance. Neither need be the exclusive prerogative of ministers, as they are under the British constitution. In many countries a high proportion of bills come from other members of the legislature, while in the United States the executive has to persuade sufficient members of both houses of Congress to introduce and back a bill. However, the British practice, if combined with strength of party, is the third great safeguard against the corruption of public life, together with the Westminster rules and civil service control over access to ministers. Except where the government's majority is small and crumbling, it does not have to alter legislation to meet the interests of particular legislators which, to judge by American and recent British experience, are more likely to be motivated by 'political' than by public interest considerations. The practice of initiation of legislation by the government means a greater chance of thoroughness and coherence in its preliminary presentation, consultation and implementation. Legislation introduced by the executive is more likely to be single-minded and capable of rational explanation than the largely inexplicable product of legislative compromise.

However, despite this safeguard, the quality of legislation has declined in the 1980s. The most important cause of this was the rise in the volume of legislation characteristic of the Thatcher administration but continuing unabated, reflected not so much in the number of statutes but in their length. The process of making new legislation consistent with old and with European law has become far more difficult and in practice less well done, being one cause of the flood of late amendments (even as late as the report stage) and of the need for yet more amending legislation. In the absence of consistency, the interpretation of the courts has been needed to an extent which even twenty years ago was not the case. One cannot be surprised at this declining quality since much the same number of or fewer civil servants – administrators and lawyers – are coping with much more.

A further cause of new legislation is the sheer number of changes in policy direction that have occurred, as bright ideas have been taken up, even during the passage of a single bill. Such changes in policy direction have been especially numerous in bills on local government, housing, energy privatization and criminal justice. This over-rapid succession of policies has itself been caused partly by too rapid a rotation of ministers, each seeing legislation as their lasting imprint, by the fertility of and more immediate pressure on ministers exerted by political think-tanks, by some pressure groups gaining direct access to ministers and by the tendency towards regarding the civil service role as more one of implementation than of partnership.[28] Because most ministers do not have the experience or time to develop policy in detail to the point of practical implementation, their attempts to exercise control over the process cause delays and prevent civil servants from doing it for them and are another reason for poor, haphazard legislation. Too much legislation, which may have been defensible in the early days of the Thatcher revolution, has had adverse consequences for Parliament. Too many poorly drafted bills, their sense altered by amendments arriving at all stages, has made the intelligent, constructive scrutiny of legislation more difficult than it has always been. Unfairly, it has had the effect of lowering the reputation of civil servants, more than that of ministers, in the eyes of MPs and lawyers.

Yet, not only has legislation been in spate but also proposals for legislation. For instance, according to the President of ACPO and Chief Constable of Hampshire, the police were assailed within two years by five major sets of proposals on police reform and four on criminal justice.[29] Too often national initiatives – especially in education and training – have been rolled out without waiting for an evaluation of the pilot projects which quite sensibly preceded them. Such counter-productive fertility is possible only because of the gradual shrivelling of the integrated Haldane model.*

A current development is that of endless initiatives by ministers to talk up possible policy changes. The novelty of what is proposed has a good chance of securing coverage for the minister in the media. Enough elapsed time between such performances can allow ministers to say rather different things before different audiences without inconsistencies being identified. Confusion is aided by the lapse in Parliament's insistence on its previous rule that all new policy

---

* During the 1960s, a time of considerable preparation for legislation, one of the authors remembers the civil service stating – with hindsight correctly – that if further initiatives were taken there would be counter-productive overload, and succeeding in persuading ministers this was so.

initiatives must first be proclaimed to it rather than to the media. The old rule had the additional advantage of ensuring that proposals were agreed by the government first. Neither is it helpful when the prime minister makes speeches introducing new policy ideas, which he has not cleared even with the departmental minister responsible, as in 1995 over forcing schools to opt out.[30] All these developments make it more probable that white papers are fragmentary and give poor explanations of government policy and that bills are badly drafted and likely to have to be altered. Such serial policy-making can result in extreme and rapid changes in legislation, producing muddle and confusion.

A further related point is the decline in approaches to policy evaluation. In the 1960s abortive attempts were made to review the effectiveness of a department's policies through an overall programme review process. However, the approach was over-elaborate and rapidly fell into disuse. In the 1980s as part of the Financial Management Initiative, good progress was made in establishing a straightforward approach to policy evaluation linked to the greater and more systematic use of statements of objectives and performance indicators. However, these attempts, too, seem to have come to an end under the pressure by ministers to launch new initiatives and the reservations of the Treasury that better evaluation could mean better justification for public expenditure increases. The consequence is that too little is known about the effectiveness of many policy initiatives – especially those whose impact can only be assessed over a long period.

Most countries have developed ways of mitigating the worst effects of over-rapid policy change. In Britain, the practice had been to rely on collective responsibility within government, and on administrative practices which expect ministers to argue through and test whatever innovation they would like to make. Ministers used to go through a process of clearing their own minds, and those of their ministerial colleagues, as to their aims and the advantages and disadvantages of various ways of realizing them. Civil servants would be used as a test-bed, being encouraged to make their individual contributions, and would consult their colleagues in their own and other departments. If the outcome were promising, it would be tested against the judgement of other cabinet ministers who would be advised of the pros and cons by their own civil servants. If the matter were important, agreement by the Cabinet would result in a preliminary green paper in which the government explained its proposals and their rationale, and invited consultation.

The next stage would be a consultative process, often backed by research, in which ministers had to explain and defend what they intended to do to the relevant interest and other pressure groups. If the matter were important, each group would expect a preliminary discussion with ministers, after which they could consult their memberships before they returned to put their considered response. In so doing, ministers' understanding and commitment to their proposals were stretched and deepened. Nothing so impresses the details of his own policy on a minister than having to expound and defend it twenty times to different knowledgeable and critical audiences, culminating in full-dress debates in Parliament on the legislation itself. Such a process can intimidate ministers who lack confidence into inaction. To counter that, ministers need their own advisers as at present and to draw on the advice outside the civil service machine, provided that too is tested with the rest. The alternative of ministers largely listening to cronies, sympathizers and various factions within the party can only lead generally to poor legislation, as it has so often recently.

In recent years such consultations have often been limited, often designed to avoid judicial review and too readily ignored, particularly over the practical issues involved. Consultations would have avoided many recent policy failures. Ministers would have found, not so much that they should have changed their policies – though on occasion they might have done that – as how they might have altered them so that they might be better and more acceptably implemented. Even while some opposed to their policies may not have changed their minds, mutual understanding of issues, even without agreement, makes opposition less strident. People feel less aggrieved if they have been fully and fairly heard after detailed consultation. Opposition to some of the most strongly contested legislation in recent years was greatly intensified because ministers did not go into enough detail explaining what they were about either during consultation or in published papers.

More effective consultation should not simply be a return to the past, because it was in too closed a world. It gave too much weight to producer interests.[31] Independent minds need to be brought in from the universities and elsewhere, not only from political think-tanks. On many matters open invitations to give evidence should be issued. Where matters are technical, committees of inquiry should be set up to sift the technical evidence and reach conclusions on it within tight deadlines without, however, prejudging the main policy options.

Equally important is the breakdown of the old cabinet committee system at which ministers, supported by officials, brokered the main differences between them in the development of policy on its way to legislation. Margaret Thatcher largely replaced this by a system of *ad hoc* committees which gave her more personal power. Over time this system, or lack of it, has become more haphazard in that some cabinet committees survive, but not the official committees to support them. This has placed a greater coordinating role on the Treasury, itself threatened under recent changes. Many matters are now decided by *ad hoc* committees to which invitation depends not on whether one minister has a relevant interest in another's business, but more on prime ministerial whim or a wish to have a sympathetic committee. But policy is also effectively decided by more informal meetings between ministers at which civil servants may not be present.*

---

* Thus a few indignant ministers casually meeting behind the Speakers' chair after a meeting of the National Economic Development Council, where they had been ribbed that they might lose the election, took the decision to abolish it (and inadvertently, as a result, its subordinate economic development committees).

A further cause of inefficiency results from ministers taking decisions not properly recorded or differently reported by different ministers attending the same meeting without officials present. Increasingly, outsiders with a political background come to such meetings, without officials present. There may be no evidence that ministers have faced difficult issues and awkward questions before they have made up their minds, or have even attempted to appreciate and evaluate points of view other than those for which they have some sympathy. But at a more fundamental level, it further threatens the old relationship between ministers and civil servants which relied so much on trust and partnership between them, and on which the integrity and efficiency of public service so much depends.

A particular problem caused by this creative conflict in policy-making concerns Europe. Ministers utter all sorts of views on Europe; but whatever they say in public, it is recognized that they need to approach any meeting with ministers from other EU countries to make decisions, with a single, coherent British point of view. In the next chapter, the importance of reviving the old official Cabinet committees in parallel with those of ministers is argued: it is not accidental that almost the only area in which one survives is Europe. In practice, a committee of civil servants ensures a single policy whenever ministers engage in European policy formulation. But this is usually a coordinating rather than a forward planning activity. Contrast the French, who alone among European governments retain a civil service with the ability to determine well in advance what the French government's views are on any issue and then network through the Commission and other member governments to maximize the chance of its proposals being adopted.

The ministerial role in policy-making is vital and should be decisive but needs to feed upon a richer manure than the product of an introverted political process, which itself is excessively interested in presentation rather than substance, and a sensation-seeking relationship with the media. There is the danger that as ministers rely less on the civil service in the initiation and formulation of legislation, that legislation will become less disinterested and more motivated by 'political' considerations.

Restoring the quality of policy-making, and of the policy documents and legislation which emerge from it, would not only raise the quality of government and the respect felt for it, but also allow Parliament to conduct more substantial debates on all aspects of the process. Such public tests of quality would make it more likely that the policy-making process will take into account facts relevant to it and the opinions of those concerned as consumers, producers or those with other relevant interests. It is an extraordinary criticism of the effectiveness of present methods of testing policy that one so often hears that the committees of that anachronism, the House of Lords, are the places where policies and bills are now best scrutinized. (If nothing else changes, a serious improvement would be to allow ministers, even in the House of Commons, to present and defend their measures before the relevant Lords committees.)

Otherwise, what is increasingly likely to replace open debate is not secret, introverted policy-making by ministers and the bureaucracy, but further development of recent tendencies for ministers to make policies on their own or in coalition with each other or with their own political advisers and sympathetic outside political think-tanks, or, in the worst cases, even to reveal policies to the media first and think later, if at all. (The widespread belief that the publication of all internal documents under a freedom of information act would improve policy-making is a delusion. In the present state of the British press it would only be interested in sensation, not reason. Moreover, it misunderstands the process by which positions are considered speculatively and then examined to successive stages of depth and in consultation with various interests before a final position emerges.) On many such occasions the civil service comes in later, almost being relegated to a position of trying to tidy up something already decided. Because of the symbiosis by which too many politicians and journalists live off each other, too many initiatives are proclaimed which are never adopted, others are adopted which never reach the statute book, and others reach the statute book which have never been properly tested for feasibility. If they are not careful, civil servants may get sucked into a position where, as advisers to ministers, they become more concerned with presentation than policy, which is both a misuse of their training and makes it harder to retain their political independence.

Conclusion

The changes set out in this chapter could make a great difference in the volume of business coming to ministers and in many cases give them better materials for making up their minds. But there will still be ample for them to do, especially given the decisions and other business now rushed, or made for them, on which they need to spend more time in the interests of good government.

Without question the pendulum has swung too far away from analysis, consultation and consensus. It would be ironical, but welcome, if the period of Burkean consolidation and repair the system so much needs were not provided by a Conservative government, but by another.

Notes

1 Dunleavy and Hood (1994).
2 But, also in the past, see Foster (1971), pp. 83–120.
3 See Ranson and Stewart (1994), pp. 91–3.
4 See Wildavsky (1964).
5 Graaff (1957), p. 2.
6 Laski in Turpin (1989), p. 57.
7 Ranson and Stewart (1994), pp. 187–220.
8 Quoted by Hennessy (1990), p. 50; see also p. 123.
9 Johnson (1980), p. 84; see also Lewis (1989); on the USA, see Rivlin (1992), pp. 66–71.

10 See Craig (1988).
11 Jennings (1946), p. 126.
12 Redlich and Hirst (1970), p. 209.
13 Kavanagh (1990); Riddell (1993), p. 272.
14 Jenkins (1991), p. 565; Marr (1995).
15 Marr (1995).
16 Treasury Solicitors Department (1994), p. 3.
17 See Lord Irvine, as reported in *The Times*, 16 October 1995.
18 Fulton (1968), pp. 54, 94–5.
19 Moe (1994), p. 19; Kettl and DiIulio (1995), p. 6.
20 Dalton (1962), p. 21.
21 Crossman (1975), pp. 21–2.
22 Jowell and Oliver (1988).
23 Hennessy (1990), p. 609.
24 Nolan (1995), p. 67.
25 Nolan (1995), p. 75.
26 Nolan (1995), p. 77. A single commissioner was appointed in 1995.
27 Nolan (1995), p. 71; see also Tony Wright MP in Nolan (1995), p. 71.
28 Hutton (1995), p. 289; on the USA see Kettl in Kettl and DiIulio (1995), pp. 42–4.
29 Hoddinott (1994).
30 Also exemplified in Scott, see Foster (1996).
31 Middlemass (1979); Self (1985).

11

What future for politics?

The public do not consider mere passage by a majority in the Commons
sufficient to confer a special moral authority on laws. They want to know
whether their pressure groups have been consulted and have agreed, whether
the proposal was in the party manifesto and whether the measure has evident
public support. The old straightforward parliamentary system of democracy has
been added to and been confused by other concepts of legitimacy and other
methods of obtaining and demonstrating support, the total result of which is to
take away the automatic reverence for the process of law.

J.P. Mackintosh[1]

In earlier chapters of this book, we described how new approaches to management of the state have affected the roles of ministers. In many ways, the
expectation might have been that ministers have less to do. Nationalized industries have been privatized and their regulation transferred to independent regulators. Activities formerly part of central government have been contracted out
and others have, at least formally, been established on an arm's-length basis
with greater authority delegated to their local management. Surveys, and the
Citizen's Charter, franchises and contracts spanning more than one term of
ministerial office have reduced political choice. So have developments in the
European Union. However, some trends have been in the opposite direction,
and others do not appear to have had the effect intended. Activities have been
transferred from local government to centrally appointed and directly funded
central government bodies, and the creation of arm's-length agencies within
central government has, perversely, involved ministers more in their affairs.
And ministers are more directly involved in policy formulation than before.
The very longevity of the Conservative administration, the experience of its
ministers and their changed ways of working with the civil service have meant
that ministers attempt to act far more as policy-makers and managers of their
departments than any previous government.

As we have argued, some of these changes are to be welcomed or regarded
as necessary to stave off fiscal crisis, while we disagree with and make proposals
for change to others. But in the absence of the modifications we propose, the net
effect of the changes since 1979 in the UK has been to give ministers more to do
than ever, and not always constructively. And there are other trends in the
working of the political process which have exacerbated this overload.

What do ministers actually do?

Under the British system and those similar to it, the prime and departmental ministers have always had too much to do. Chapter 10 described the formidable concentration of powers and duties in their hands.[2] Their responsibilities grew with state intervention, but in Britain have continued despite recent attempts to roll back the frontiers of the state. That ministers are overloaded has been widely recognized since the 1970s.[3] The highly active, energetic people drawn to politics have a tendency to overload themselves: Gladstone not only drafted bills, but also wrote theology and classical criticism. How they are overloaded is what matters: are they and other elements in the state acting so as best to increase the chances of good government and, in particular, to lessen the effects of fiscal crisis?

It may seem trivial to describe a typical minister's day, but it is necessary to understand how severe is the problem of ministerial overload. A normal parliamentary day may well start with rising at 5.30 a.m. to make an appearance on a radio or television programme. It will be followed by reading all the newspapers before the first meeting in the department at 8.00 a.m., often with agency chief executives and nationalized industry chairmen. At 9.00 a.m. the ministers may hold a departmental meeting with their political advisers to decide their reactions, mainly to the day's media events: those reactions will be conveyed to their civil servants at hastily convened meetings. If there is no Cabinet meeting, a cabinet committee or parliamentary questions to prepare for, the rest of the morning will be spent in some mixture of receiving deputations, seeing colleagues somewhere in Whitehall and concocting media responses. A few minutes in the car will be spent personalizing a speech to some trade association or reading up a brief before a business lunch. Between lunch and the House of Commons for question-time, a minister will be telephoning to check progress on the initiatives which he started that morning. He will be back in the department in mid-afternoon for another series of deputations, meetings with colleagues and the receipt of telephone calls from the prime minister and others on matters of the moment before going off to a dinner at which he has to give another speech. After that he will go to vote in the House where he will be lobbied by fellow MPs.

During the day the minister's private office will have been trying to slot in meetings to discuss the preparation of white papers, policy decisions to help draft a bill, urgent and less urgent executive decisions, briefing for discussion with colleagues in Cabinet committees and elsewhere, and official letters and directions inside and outside government, often more than a hundred in a single day. Because of other preoccupations, these meetings will be endlessly fixed and refixed. Many will not happen at all, but the issues will appear as items for the minister's consideration in a red box instead. Those boxes will be with him as he goes home in his car towards midnight. When he has read as much as he can, he falls asleep in the early hours, before rising again at 5.30 a.m. Something approaching this round, and at least as demanding, happens every day the House of Commons is sitting. At the weekend there will be all the time spent on constituency business and on red boxes of papers left over from the week, often interrupted by some media concern.

From the standpoint of good government, what makes this situation hard to manage, so that a superabundance of power can result in so much practical powerlessness, is the decline in the relationship of partnership between ministers and civil servants. As ministers try to take more decisions, they find it progressively difficult to take as many or to make them as well. Of course, there are ministers of such energy, capability and decisiveness that they can and do take careful, considered decisions on every matter put to them, even in such circumstances, as well as resist the encroachment of media, speeches and deputations on their time. Given all the pressures, it is remarkable how well most ministers cope, but undoubtedly these pressures are a prime cause of the decline in the quality of policy-making and legislation which is so evident.

How has it changed over the last thirty years? Some changes seem marked. An over-long day has become longer. Thirty years ago ministers' and other formal meetings in the department normally started at 10.00 a.m. Now, in common with the City and industry, such meetings start at 8.00 a.m. and earlier. But involvement with the media, still earlier in the morning, has become common, so that a minister's day has lengthened from about 14 to about 18 hours. Despite exceptions, thirty years ago the broad pattern was that ministers spent the day on Whitehall business until they went down to Parliament in the late afternoon, unless they were up for parliamentary questions or there was another parliamentary occasion they could not miss, when they went earlier. There were more cabinets, because cabinets still tried to discuss issues, and cabinet committees. There was never enough time and there were deputations, openings and speeches, but significantly more time was available to ministers between 10.00 a.m. and 6.00 p.m. for departmental business of the various types set out in Chapter 10. During the evenings there was again an occasional speech outside the House, but in general the evenings were devoted to the business of the House. When ministers were not in the chamber or talking to each other, or, if they were sociable, talking to backbenchers, they were in their rooms reading through their red boxes, which they had a greater chance than now of having done with care before going home for the night.

Since the early 1980s ministers have become increasingly preoccupied by other matters which have now come to take a higher proportion of ministerial time and occasionally even to dominate it: making speeches, party business, receiving deputations, interacting with the media, and interacting with each other.

Speech-making

Ministers have always made speeches but their readiness to do so inside and outside Parliament would seem to have increased greatly since Margaret Thatcher, believing her policies sound, decided at a time of great unpopularity that the answer was to enjoin her ministers to take every opportunity to sell those policies. So ministers can be found from breakfast on, sometimes several times a day, speaking at conferences, seminars, lunches and dinners. While their gift with words makes this a godsend to the organizers of such events, an incoming government might ponder whether it is the best use of ministers' time and energy. The main point is that such speeches will have some sound-bites for the media, but they rarely advance policy-making or consultation on other issues in an ordered, constructive way. The dates, audiences and, to some extent, themes are fixed well in advance, and therefore not in line with the timetable of a consultative process. Seldom are they occasions for detailed persuasion and defence or for authoritative responses from a knowing and critical audience. Cumulatively, they subtract substantially from the time available for the activities described in Chapter 10.

The party

Other occasions for speechifying are the rubber-chicken lunches and dinners which have become more demanding for ministers as they jockey for power within the party. Politicians have always spent time with the party, but the time spent, especially by the ambitious, does seem to have increased. Factions, disputes and recurrent speculation about the leadership in the short and medium term have often made party events more demanding of their time. Factiousness has given constituency parties, particularly their chairmen, more power as MPs woo them to gain backing for their faction while the prime minister and party headquarters urge them instead to persuade MPs to follow the party line. While party activities have an important role in any party, the political opinions of constituency parties tend to differ from those of MPs or the electorate, usually being more extreme. To give them undue weight is itself likely to increase factiousness across a party. The fact that party, lobby and some business circles overlap means that, given the pressures on their time, politicians will find that a high proportion of those they meet outside Whitehall and Westminster, whether businessmen, professionals or others, will be subsets of those groups that are active party members.

Deputations

Third, ministers receive more deputations than they used to, less as part of a formal process of consultation, but more frequently at the instance of a lobby or pressure group. The new Americanized lobby system is responsible for most of this. Ministers' diaries are invaded by backbenchers, mostly their own, more than in the past. When the government has a very small majority, ministers may need to secure the votes of wavering backbenchers, a task made harder by the policy and ideological differences that have divided the Conservative Party. Previous hung parliaments did not have this result. The process draws ministers and their departments too deeply into individual grievances which, it has been argued, would be more effectively handled by other means, at least in their early stages. Moreover, such lobbying of ministers on behalf of constituents can easily pass into lobbying on behalf of other interests. Much of it is a sensible use of ministers' time. If more of it were part of controlled consultation processes, it would do nothing but good. However, a new government may have no conception how much more time it takes than in the 1970s, until its ministers and backbenchers alike are subjected to the same attention. Both would be wise if as far as possible they returned to the old ways and used the civil service first as a filter. While a change of government will alter the relative ease of access of different pressure groups, one may wonder how, in general, a non-Conservative government will react to the Americanized lobby system that has grown up since 1979. To established differences, as in other parties, between right and left, European and anti-European, could be added another between those impervious to lobbies and lobbyists, and therefore to be bypassed by them and those who may be malleable. History suggests some proportion of its backbench MPs will be as eager for the acclaim and the money as any other backbencher has been and will adapt quickly. But for it to be taken to an extent comparable to the recent past would be a bizarre outcome: those with the most resources to lobby will tend to be backed by business, as was argued in Chapter 2. It is surely more than possible that an incoming government might wish to revert to the pre-1979 position to save ministerial and backbencher time for other activities.

The media

The last and largest claimants to more ministerial time are the media, always powerful in politics and of great interest to ministers. For many years most ministers have read not only their own press cuttings but scanned virtually every newspaper. Chances to be interviewed on television and radio have been eagerly sought and the possible media outlets have grown. It is not part of the purpose of this book to examine how ministers' relations with the media have altered. But they have.[4] It is instructive that one of Michael Heseltine's first acts as Deputy Prime Minister was to introduce daily meetings of the Cabinet committee on coordination and presentation of government policy.[5] There were always leaks, but now there are more. There was fierce questioning, but the ferocity and lack of trust have became greater. There used to be more articles on the basis of many sources, which tried to assess the pros and cons of a ministerial decision or policy. Now there are more soundbites. In the past ministers more often made up their minds first, developing their policies further with their officials before they sought out the media. They might consult journalists when making up their minds, especially when the journalists themselves were knowledgeable on the issue and on what positions might be taken by the various interests concerned. If they were wise, an information officer – almost the only class of civil servant to have risen in number in recent years – was present, usually fairly silent, whose main role was to warn ministers how different newspapers would be likely to react to given policy and other developments. Unashamedly the objective was to ensure that the policy would receive the best possible reception in the press, while identifying gaps or failings. But since then the media has largely replaced Parliament as the forum for substantive public discussion of policy issues. Because of the huge demands the media make on the energies of ministers and civil servants, there are great disadvantages to it under any government, but it is bound to be more difficult for a Labour or Liberal Democrat government, for which most of the media has less sympathy – an additional reason for reverting, if possible, to ministers mostly deciding not to go to the media before they are ready.

Some will doubt the practicality of ministers from any party following this policy; but in the recent past Nicholas Ridley and currently Peter Lilley have been economical in the time they have spent with the media. Where there is the will, it can be done. Neither can it be argued that resisting the urge to take every media opportunity results in a worse press for individual ministers or for the government as a whole. Recent experience suggests the reverse. The public gets sick and tired of what are perceived as shallow or over-political arguments, while the media are quick to exploit what they see as weaknesses in ministerial statements and the contradictions between them. Media opportunities not seldom turn into lengthy damage limitation.

Ministers

Last, ministers spend more time talking to each other. Though ministers often met formally, thirty or more years ago they mostly met informally at the House in the evenings. It was a sensible innovation when in 1970 Peter Walker met regularly with all his ministers at the Department of the Environment without officials present, but it has sometimes developed in such a way as to drive a wedge between ministers and civil servants. It has not been unknown for ministers to meet together every day without officials and decide many policy issues first among themselves, making more difficult communication of what they have decided to civil servants. Leaks are partly responsible and have the effect of reducing the discipline of documenting evolving decisions. But almost as important, some ministers, perhaps encouraged by their many years in office, begin to act like permanent secretaries, trying to organize the business of their department in response to the media pressures of the morning in addition to their other occupations. The creation of agencies, which has exposed previously hidden areas of government activity to public and media scrutiny, has widened the range of possible topics for ministerial concern.

The Haldane model

If ministers do not reduce the demands on their time by a combination of the measures discussed in the previous and this chapter, the quality of their policy and law-making and other aspects of their governance will continue to deteriorate. All this is undermining the Haldane basis of relationships between ministers and the civil service. The superiority of the Haldane model of partnership between ministers and civil servants over the Wilsonian model of separation between the two has been urged many times in this book. Four reasons especially should be stressed for exposing and exorcising the ghost of Woodrow Wilson which, unseen, has recently been stalking British corridors of power, trailing in its wake the divisiveness, suspicion and multiplication of codes of conduct that would seem inevitably to go with it:

Overload

A great but double-edged strength of the Haldane concept is that it allows ministers to overcome their overload almost however great it is. As Crossman's private secretary told him when he became minister of housing, several drafts would be put into his in-tray on every issue that came up: Crossman could mark which he preferred or make no indication, in which case 'we will deal with it and you need never see it again'.[6] In so far as ministers do not have the time to answer a letter or write a speech or reach a decision or formulate policy, their civil servants will do it for them.

The problem of helping ministers to make the best use of their time is complicated by differences in their working methods, often unknown to each other and the general public. Some like taking decisions. Others are happiest if most are taken for them, only setting out broad principles. Barbara Castle relished decisions on the widest spread of matters, coming one after another, while Richard Marsh would not accept a choice but required a preferred option to be put up for him to be accepted or rejected. Anthony Crosland preferred to concentrate on one major policy at a time, reading everything relevant to it at a go, while either leaving other matters to pile up or letting civil servants decide them in his name. Some ministers read a lot and some, such as Michael Heseltine, read little, requiring most matters to be explained orally. Some have a very strong sense of agenda and establish exactly what needs to be done before the next meeting, while others never sum up action points and rely entirely on their civil servants to make progress between meetings. A trained civil service adjusts to these and many other differences in style.*

---

* Many ministers are at their best when challenging their advisors, forcing them to produce options and give evidence for their beliefs. During the war Alan Brooke as chief of the Imperial General Staff had to employ 30 staff to deal with Churchill's never-ending stream of questions and ideas, all of which came from his determination to ensure his generals knew what they were doing, why they were doing it and why not something else. Though he was relentless 'inconsistent, blew hot and cold and promoted mutually exclusive policies . . . he differed from other all-powerful leaders in one respect. Napoleon refused to take counsel: his marshals were his servants. Hitler overrode his generals, no battalion, let alone an army group, could be moved without his permission. But Churchill, though he drove Brooke to desperation, gave way to his chiefs of staff provided they were united and stood firm' (Annan, 1995: 46–7). There is a powerful moral for ministers in a democracy here, adapted to peacetime circumstances: Barbara Castle was a first-rate minister because she had something of the same impact.

Such extensive delegation is not possible in a Woodrow Wilson world, but can only be so if civil servants work so closely with ministers that they come to know their minds intimately. One aspect is that they learn to write letters, papers and speeches as ministers would have expressed themselves had they had the time and polish. Thus one of Churchill's private secretaries described how they all picked up his cadences in their drafting.[7] But it goes deeper. Civil servants learn what ideas and information to put up, what solutions may be acceptable, thus economizing on verbal and written communication as Wilsonian methods never can. Moreover, on the assumption that the minister is reasonably consistent, they learn how to simplify the minister's task by drawing attention to analogies: 'In essence decision X is like decision Y we went through a month ago: the same reasoning that led you to prefer solution A then would lead you to A* here.'

But while enormously enlarging the work capacity of ministers if properly done, there are dangers. As demonstrated in the Matrix Churchill affair, some ministers simply may not recall a decision, or the reasoning that led to it, from among a multitude that went through their red boxes. Their civil servants may have known their minds well enough by precedent and analogy to have taken the decision they would have done, a possibility both the general public and lawyers find hard to understand. Even though practically necessary, the position can only be justified as democratic and consistent with ministerial responsibility through a partnership between minister and his closest civil servants. The second danger is that through shortage of time or disinclination some ministers invest a diminishing proportion of their own time in decision-making, to the point where there are not enough meetings on issues and enough recent precedents for civil servants to use. A long time in office and the growth of preoccupations with deputations, speeches and the media increase this risk. A third danger arises from ministers taking more decisions on their own or with each other, so that civil servants are less able to deduce their reasoning. All these factors would seem to have jeopardized the partnership relation in recent years.

To protect the relationship and economize on ministerial time, we have argued for a change which many may judge intrusive: that the civil service resume control of ministers' diaries. One cannot take this to absurd lengths. Most ministers work long hours and always have. They need free time to chat to friends, political cronies, backbench MPs and others. They also need the considerable time most spend in their constituencies. Yet control over their diaries is required during their long working hours: to enhance their efficiency and as protection of their impartiality, and, by extension, through establishing a process less prone to disruption, to enhance the efficiency of their departments.

Information

The key role of the civil service, which distinguishes it from other activities, is that of advice to ministers. To see this activity as analogous to private- or public-sector management, and to organize it accordingly, is a mistake. One reason is the very different kinds of decision that have to be made. Management is about the application in meticulous detail of as much energy, imagination and improvization as it takes to encourage those being managed to fulfil their tasks, within an overall plan which has profit, or its equivalent, as its objective. When all public activities which require such management have been separated out, what is left is a mass of complex activities, judgements and decisions with complicated and shifting objectives, and often no recent or exact precedent. Moreover, the decisions and the processes that led to them have to be recorded for various immediate purposes and for posterity with a clarity and at a length actively discouraged in the private sector.

The information ministers could take into account in virtually anything they do is far greater than they can possibly assimilate. To help, a civil service must be able to gain access to and present relevant knowledge, from whatever source: to check, analyse and test it, with expert input where required. Those who run companies are expected to find out more for themselves, to extract their own information beyond that provided as routine, to trust to their own experience and instincts; but again they have more relevant experience from their careers than ministers from theirs. The role of the generalist is thus to assemble and package the materials relevant to a decision, so that the minister may make it as well-informed and speedily as possible.

> The wonderful thing for me is that I've only got to air an idea and the civil servants, once they have understood it, say 'That's enough, Minister' and go away for a week and work on it – all the detailed work I am used to having to do myself is done for me.[8]

Such a position of power is capable of abuse. History shows that rulers who have relied on a single adviser have usually regretted it. More common in the twentieth century has been a monopoly of advice given by a departmental hierarchy which was too cohesive. One should be suspicious of any suggestion there is only one answer to a problem as in:

> Nearly every problem bears a family resemblance to something which the experienced administrator has handled before. To him it is not some entirely new problem which he is asked to solve at short notice: it is the old wolf in a new-look sheepskin. Something in the shape of the thing strikes him as familiar. His experience tells him where the point of entry will be found; or warns him of the difficulties ahead which others, without his training, cannot see.[9]

Left to initiate policy, the department will usually produce something useful, but rarely of much originality or deep significance. Yet virtually without exception, civil servants, forced to consider other options than the departmental preference, tend to improve them. Not all ministers can be outstandingly constructive, but good ministers are those who have ideas – their own and other people's – and determinedly challenge their civil servants to show why they should not be adopted.

In the past it could be hard for the most determined minister to challenge a 'departmental view', as with the anti-Keynesian Treasury view of the 1920s and 1930s.[10] At times the Foreign Office has been accused of being too single-mindedly arabophile or pro-European, while many other departments acquired fixed views where they believed they knew best. (But the departmental view was not always wrong, as in 1938 in the Foreign Office over appeasement.)[11] More openness is needed in both directions: a greater flow of informed opinion and analysis into departments and of background information out.[12] There should be a greater readiness than sometimes in the past to present non-conforming opinions to ministers and to find time for them to listen directly to opinions other than those filtered through the civil service, while that consultation should extend to include many more consumer and other opinions.

Openness in consultation should be supported by greater openness of information. However, distinctions need to be drawn. To make the advice, as distinct from the evidence civil servants give ministers, available to all is to negate the purpose of that advice. Such advice must be speculative in that it presents options, warns of possible dangers, illustratively takes arguments to an extreme, considers likely causes of objection, and in doing so may well fasten particular positions on to identifiable parties: all set down frankly and cogently. There is abundant evidence to show that the release or leaking of such advice results in selective quotation and misrepresentation, generating heat not light, whether done deliberately or inadvertently. It forces civil servants to water down what they write to the point where their advice becomes ambiguous or opaque and they must rely more on the spoken word, which is less likely to be effective, given the pressure of business. Instead a distinction is needed similar to that which supports the doctrine of legal privilege in the courts: between *evidence*, here mostly meaning factual analysis and information which should be disclosed, and *advice* given, which should not, just as the advice lawyers give clients on the conduct of their case is not disclosed. The value of such disclosure of evidence will be greater the more there are audiences ready to evaluate it: hence, in particular, the importance of better and more continuous scrutiny by a relevant and knowledgeable parliamentary committee.

Experience suggests that the activity of advising ministers requires a permanent elite of high intellectual ability. The tradition that the counsellors of those who rule a nation need to have such a tradition is ancient and persistent, not only in the West and China, but also, most probably, in every culture including tribal ones. While, as earlier chapters have argued, there are many ways in which the operations of the state can be modernized with overall advantage, history shows that the reputation of rulers depends on that of their advisers, requiring an impartial core of advisers of high intelligence and broad knowledge. A government which instead relies on a narrowly drawn band of dependent and like-minded cronies will sooner or later regret it.[13]

There are reasons why a hierarchy is a good means to advise rulers. That hierarchy should contain the young as well as the experienced, so that they may learn the advice given by their seniors and contribute to it. How to advise – how many options to give, when to persist, when to stop, when to insist – requires a judgement, an ability with words and an understanding of character that have to be learnt.[14] That craft is best learnt by practice and therefore through apprenticeship.[15]

However, there are other gains here from traditional methods. More broadly, as Thomas Hobbes put it:

> For experience, being but the memory of the consequences of like actions formerly observed, and counsel but the speech whereby that experience is made known to another, the virtues and defects of counsel are the same with the virtues and defects intellectual; and to the Person of a Commonwealth, his counsellors serve him in the place of memory and mental discourse.[16]

Different advisers have different experiences, ages, temperaments and attitudes. They will vary in their backgrounds and political views. If ministers are to understand how their policies and decisions will affect different citizens, they gain from having people from all parts of the country and with all types of background among their advisers.[17] Educational achievement and London residence constrain this range, but it still provides a broader base than if most advice percolates through political friends and advisers inside and outside government.[18]

One may ask what is it about civil servants' experience that makes it peculiarly valuable. Experience of earlier ministers' decisions is part of an answer; but the value they give also depends on the breadth of their own experience – executive, inspectorial and regulatory as well as advisory – across the public sector as well as in the private sector, as well as their making themselves available to informed opinion on matters with which they are concerned. Knowledge and experience will be all the greater in a unified civil service (where cross-posting between the centre of a department, its outlying agencies and elsewhere is routine) than if civil servants are confined to core activities, so cramping their career development.[19] Something important in the civil service culture would be lost, while 'policy ghettos' would be left at the centre. Civil servants in a wide career structure are the guardians of political education and are better able to arbitrate knowledgeably between interested groups, both those that consume and those that supply services.[20] Without such a structure, central civil servants would need to rely far more on education and training – of a kind not now provided – to understand their client groups than on learning on the job. Reskilling would be required. Major changes would be needed to achieve this.

Regulation and codes of conduct

But there are other reasons for a Haldane approach. The best protection of ministerial probity is that ministers should take all their decisions openly with their civil servants so that they may be advised when a course of action is unlawful or a statement or an answer to a parliamentary question is misleading or likely to be thought against justice by Parliament or the courts or against the Cabinet Office code for ministers. As contracts, executive and other similar agencies have developed in Britain, they have provided more than enough opportunities for patronage to offset other opportunities lost to government through privatization. Osborne and Gaebler (1992) suggest that no one who bids for government contracts should be allowed to contribute to party funds. But this is only part of the problem of corruption and improper influence and is probably impossible to track. That ministers have so many appointments to make gives them enormous influence. The point to note is that while much can be done through audit and other ways to limit malpractice, they require rules, even if not the same as employed in the past. The decline in the Haldane relationship in recent years is one reason for turning to the alternative approach of multiplying regulations to ensure probity, as recommended by Nolan Committee. Experience in the USA shows that one drawback is that such rules need enforcement; that country brought in departmental ethics officers and other arrangements to oversee them and reprove defaulters. But the fundamental reason why such arrangements do not work, as has been apparent in Parliament's reception of the rules governing disclosure of MPs' earnings, is that they merely stimulate ways round them, so leading to yet more rules to plug loopholes, leading to a growing climate of regulation of a kind from which new public management saw the need to escape in the interests of efficiency. There can be no guarantee that these methods will be more effective or cheaper than relying on traditional civil service methods, based on the traditional Haldane relationship: indeed on both counts, rather the reverse.

There has always been a certain amount of low-level fraud in British public life, as well as the occasional scandal. It has generally not involved politicians or senior officials. More interventionist auditing can be adopted to reduce further the likelihood of financial malpractice. Government itself has suggested the extension of the roles of the Audit Commission and of the National Audit Office in this direction.[21] Contractorization and competition make audit easier, provided there are clear specifications.

Enabling democracy

Yet there remains a still more fundamental reason for refreshing and persisting with the Haldane idea. The main contribution of the civil service to democracy is to build on the skills and experience ministers have to help them take the best decisions possible. Ministers have less experience relevant to their office than do heads of firms, for example. Some things do not change. As Bagehot pointed out in the 1860s, because of the curious chemistry of cabinet-making, ministers rarely go to departments to which they can bring most knowledge, do not stay long, leave with their work undone and do not learn from each other's experience.[22] They move up or down or round for reasons little connected with their ability as ministers. (Once prime ministers were readier to listen to the views on ministers' abilities of those who worked for them. One can hear it still at work in Hailsham: 'their quality as administrators usually becomes known, principally to the prime minister, through the civil service grapevine'. Now media relations seem most important for ministerial promotion.)[23] Politicians need not be experts in any role except leadership, for which they require political wisdom, understanding of human nature, imagination, charisma, the ability to speak well and defend positions they have adopted. Otherwise, traditionally they have relied on generalist, but professional, civil servants for expert advice. Bagehot wrote of only having known of one minister without some ability.[24] At any time since, those close to ministers might have said much the same. But that experience needs supplementing by access to other skills and experiences. Thus a former headmaster, for example, may come to feel as comfortable taking a decision on a planning appeal, or the handling of a difficult defence contract, as he would in handling a parent's complaint against a teacher or an unsatisfactory school contractor. The fact that many ministers now have little or no experience outside politics makes this civil service role more, not less, important.

This role of the civil service is of the greatest importance because it allows a nation to retain what was essential to the Athenian notion of democracy: the ideal that any citizen could occupy the offices of state.[25] In a profound sense, it makes democracy possible. Contrast the alternative: that positions of political leadership should be filled by top businessmen because they have run large organizations. We have seen how different they are and what other qualities politicians need. So the Haldane relationship threatened may threaten democracy itself if civil service resources are reduced or distanced to the point where an inexperienced incoming administration does not have the close support it needs to convert its talents into effective government. Moreover, a likely outcome is that a government increasingly relying on outside policy advice, offered by those with the resources to make such policies persuasive, may eventually, as has happened in many nations presumed democratic, find that democracy is replaced by the kind of interest-determined state or plutocracy discussed in Chapter 2.

A tenured hierarchy is traditionally the best way of conveying advice to ministers, so that they make the best use of their powers, partly because some civil servants are older and more experienced than others, but also because it contributes to the political education of civil servants who pass what they know from one generation to another. 'The sort of education which belongs to [politics] . . . is knowledge, as profound as we can make it, of our tradition of political behaviour.'[26] Tenure strengthens the independent judgement of civil servants, and does not allow them to be browbeaten − a minister can always ignore advice he does not want. Hobbes put the essential point as well as it has ever been put (though it does not apply to the more purely executive functions of government when they are well distinguished):

There is also incident to the nature of counsel, that whatsoever it be, he that asketh it, cannot in equity accuse or punish it. For to ask counsel of another, is to permit him to give such counsel as he thinks best. And consequently he that giveth counsel to his sovereign (whether a monarch or an assembly) cannot in equity be punished for it . . . But if one subject giveth counsel to another to anything contrary to the laws, whether that counsel proceedeth from evil intention or from ignorance only, it is punishable by the commonwealth, because ignorance of the law is no good excuse.[27]

Nor does it mean that hierarchies must be tall.[28] Thinning out unnecessary layers is not the same as replacing a hierarchy by an inappropriate management structure.

This does not mean no one should be fired, but unlike industry, where a chief executive expects to hand-pick a team to share his vision in a common, well-defined task, in government such a synchronization of views could be disastrous. It is essential that civil servants continue to be chosen on merit, from a wide diversity of backgrounds and through an independent civil service commission.[29] The appointment of permanent and deputy secretaries is approved by the prime minister, but this ought to be a formality. There would be great attractions in going back to such independence as Sir William Beveridge described at the start of the 1920s, comparing it to a marriage except that:

> The permanent secretary has no voice in choosing the minister and minister none in choosing the permanent secretary. Often the two men never see each other until the day of the wedding. A divorce is as difficult as an Act of Parliament.[30]

Divorce remains nearly impossible.[31] But the convention has grown up that ministers have a right of choice through being able to veto candidates put to them as their permanent secretaries. However well the reality of independent and impartial selection has been preserved, the very longevity of the Conservative government after 1979 inevitably raised suspicions that there was a political element in making such appointments. This suspicion is unjustified – there is no evidence of political sympathy being a criterion – but politicians did change the criteria for appointments away from the traditional ones to a more 'can-do' attitude towards policy-making and other tasks. The suspicion has been reinforced by the Major administration's requiring competition with candidates for each civil service post from outside the service. A particularly unfortunate episode followed from the amalgamation of the two departments of Education and Employment in 1995. The two permanent secretaries remained in tandem for a while in the merged department, before one was chosen who had recently come from outside the civil service. Even a few years ago a permanent secretary after a merger would have been found a place until the next relevant vacancy; but the career civil servant, Sir Timothy Lankester was told that he would then have to compete for it which he declined to do. In many circumstances this might be sensible, but there are two drawbacks. The first is that it increases the power of ministers to the point where there may be the appearance, if not the fact, of political choice. In this case there was a second, inasmuch as Lankester, when permanent secretary to the Overseas Development Administration, had demanded a ministerial instruction, reported to the Public Accounts Committee, as it had to be, to make a much publicized loan to the Malaysian government to construct the Pergau dam, which he saw to be an imprudent and uneconomical use of aid money which the courts later decided to be also unlawful. His view was upheld by the Public Accounts Committee. However innocent the circumstances leading to his departure may have been, it was impossible for many not to draw the moral that, however justified, a permanent secretary who writes such a minute censuring ministerial behaviour will be caught up with in the end. Consideration should be given to adopting or adapting the new New Zealand practice of a contract between ministers and their advisers.[32] It allows ministers to have 'political' or other policy advisers. But during their five-year contract permanent secretaries are to give impartial, dispassionate advice – on what we may call Hobbesian–Haldane lines. That contract is to be renewed by the State Service Commission on behalf of ministers. The Commission may listen to any representation ministers may make on the quality of the advice given, but theirs is the decision, thus ensuring an independent and effective civil service.

Thus civil servants, more especially those in the hierarchy that advise ministers directly, have various duties, above all to give ministers honest and impartial advice, without fear or favour, and whether the advice accords with the minister's view or not.[33] Some duties act as constraints on the submissions to be made. Civil servants must advise on what would be unlawful, what would be unethical in the sense that it is against the conventions which have come to govern the uses of ministerial discretion, in particular what statements or calculations would be dishonest, misleading or otherwise untrue. Beyond them there are duties, the exercise of which by their nature civil servants cannot share with ministers in any given case: which and how many options to bring to ministers' attention; how summarily or in how much detail to give their advice; how much to simplify their advice for instance, by drawing analogies between one situation and another; when to expose differences of opinion within the department where they exist; and how long to persist when a minister seems disposed, inadvertently or deliberately, to ignore or reject their advice. These instrumental duties arise only because decisions frequently have to be made in a rush and compromises made.[34]

But to whom do civil servants owe their duties? Within its compass, this question raises the thorniest issue in political philosophy: what are the limits of political obligation? As head of the civil service, Sir Robert Armstrong answered it in a considered statement:

Civil servants are servants of the Crown. For all practical purposes the Crown in this context . . . is represented by the Government of the day . . . The Civil Service as such has no constitutional personality or responsibility separate from the duly elected government of the day.[35]

Civil servants, then, should serve ministers to the best of their ability and should normally expect to be able to do it unquestioningly; but there is a further question. Is their duty solely to ministers? Or is there a higher duty to which it is subordinate? The overwhelming tendency of the Armstrong memorandum is to imply that there are no circumstances in which civil servants have a duty superior to that to ministers. It is understood that ministers make their decisions on the basis of the advice given them; but suppose they disregard aspects of that advice or even go to the lengths of preferring to decide without advice or only upon the advice of their political colleagues and advisers?[36] Or that in reaching their decisions they behave against natural justice or otherwise unethically or even unlawfully. Is judicial review to be the sole recourse of an aggrieved party, given the restricted circumstances in which it still applies?

Civil servants may fall back on a belief that their duties as professionals require them to give the advice they believe necessary and persist in it as long as they think right. They may find courage in the view that their duty to the government implies a duty to all ministers, transcending that to any one minister. Therefore, when they disagree profoundly with the lawfulness or some other aspect of what the departmental minister intends, they can try to persuade permanent secretaries in other departments to persuade their ministers to raise it with the minister in question or in cabinet: not an easy operation, made more difficult by the decline of the official cabinet committee structure.

The traditional way was to affirm there was a higher duty, not that it was ever expected to be required. As Lord Bancroft, Armstrong's predecessor as head of the civil service, said:

I was trained in the Treasury for good or ill by a man – Sir David Serpell – who still ferociously pursues the public good . . . He showed me how to negotiate, how to draw breath in mid-sentence so as to discourage interruption, how to draft and why the Service belongs neither to politicians nor to officials but to the Crown and to the nation.[37]*

Ferdinand Mount would seem to see the position of the Crown as the way out of the dilemma.[38] Where it can be maintained there is a conflict between one's duty to the Crown and to a minister or ministers, then the first is to be

---

* One of the authors was trained by Sir David Serpell and also by Sir John Moore, later second permanent secretary at the Civil Service Department, who both plainly taught there was a duty to the Crown that took precedence over that to ministers. So hypothetical was it then that the examples used were all about whether, if Britain had been defeated in 1940, a duty to carry on some kind of government would have seemed paramount.

preferred. Whether such a higher duty is owed to the Crown or the people or the nation is perhaps a secondary matter.[39]

But what follows from this? It may be suggested that the civil servant leaks the truth as he sees it, as Clive Ponting did; but neither minister nor civil service nor ultimately the public gains from a situation in which neither trust each other not to leak. The standard and perfectly correct answer is that a civil servant in such a position should go to his permanent secretary, who should examine the facts to see if he agrees or not. If he agrees, he should remonstrate with the minister. If that fails the head of the civil service goes to the prime minister. In most circumstances that should work, but supposing it does not. What then? What is needed is somebody capable of deciding against ministers if that is right. It cannot practically be the Crown, and there are serious drawbacks to it being the law. The answer has to be that it is Parliament which is above ministers.

There is a device, that of the Public Accounts Committee minute which a permanent secretary may send to that committee, giving his opinion that a particular expenditure is unlawful.[40] The then permanent secretary of the Overseas Development Administration took this route to reveal his opinion that overseas aid money had been used improperly to fund the Pergau dam. Many of the unlawful or otherwise improper acts ministers could commit may be handled in this way because so many involve public expenditure. But like so many devices of its kind, it is more effective when it remains a threat than if it often has to be used. With prime ministerial agreement, it has been extended to cover cases where the permanent secretary believes that a ministerial decision self-evidently does not give value for money and must be motivated by some objective other than its legitimate one.[41] The present system still needs reinforcement. There need to be routines that make it mandatory that when serious concerns come up through the civil service, after being fully tested on the way, they are exposed to Parliament. Permanent secretaries can register their opinion that ministers' actions are in the extreme, unlawful, or have disregarded procedures appropriate to that decision, appointment or policy-making. That requires understanding and agreement on what is appropriate.* Rather than the Public Accounts Committee carrying the burden of all such issues, they should be distributed between the relevant departmental select committees (preferably in the form of standing special committees). There should be occasions when permanent secretaries and agency chiefs should be asked formally in front of the appropriate committee whether they have anything to disclose under this head. If only because such behaviour must be assumed to be rare and because of the publicity given such a breach, particularly if it is of something unlawful, one would expect such disclosure to be uncommon.

---

* The practice of the viceroy's council, as recorded by J.S. Mill, its (permanent) secretary, is an interesting precedent. Each member was expected to give an opinion, and reasons were required only when there was disagreement. Usually decisions reflected the majority view, but the viceroy (then governor-general) could set aside a majority opinion if he recorded his reasons. Mill saw the practice as highly satisfactory.

The centre of government

Traditionally the most important department has been the Treasury. The evisceration of the Treasury was treated in Chapter 10 as purely a question of where and how financial control is exercised. A more 'political' explanation picks up on the argument, advanced in Chapter 2, that the 1980s and still more the 1990s have seen a shift of power within the executive from official to politician.

An innovation of the Attlee government was the development of a system of ministerial and official cabinet committees to relieve ministerial overload.[42] A later head of the civil service, judged it to be 'a particular British innovation and . . . very successful at that time in coping with the problem of overload on government'.[43] It was the more necessary because the pressure of business on cabinet made impossible extensive discussions of any but the most important business. Decisions made in cabinet committees were binding on ministers except where altered by cabinet.

Preferring to make most decisions at *ad hoc* meetings with the ministers she believed most relevant, Mrs Thatcher largely emasculated the system in its old form. Except rarely, there now are no longer cabinet papers.* Presentations are generally oral and are meant to record decisions rather than to be a basis for even short discussion (most pre-1979 ministers would have been surprised, even horrified, by such a development). So might an incoming government. Cabinet committees have papers but seldom is there long or repeated discussion. As important was the destruction of the official inter-departmental committees which underpinned ministerial committees. Another Attlee innovation, they had had the task of identifying and settling inter-departmental issues that arise in most legislation and much executive action, to make policy as far as possible coherent and consistent, a practice which contributed to the reputation of British policy-making as among the most coherent and publicly explicable in the world.** These changes were part

---

* Nigel Lawson (1992: 125) has stressed the unimportance of cabinet for decision-making as a change from earlier administration. As evidence one may note how often he refers to decisions taken in cabinet committees, often *ad hoc* or of limited duration, and scarcely ever to decisions taken in cabinet.

**Like so much machinery, its existence may be more important than its use. One of the authors remembers being hauled in front of such a permanent secretary level committee in 1966, working to great effect, beside the Ministry of Transport permanent secretary, Sir Thomas Padmore. It was chaired by Sir Eric (now Lord) Roll, with Sir Douglas Allen (now Lord Croham) and Sir Richard Powell on it, as well as George Pottinger. On being appointed in January 1966, Barbara Castle had rushed to produce a preliminary white paper. It was full of ideas. The official view across Whitehall was both that several of its policies had not been approved by ministers and were, as presented, insufficiently worked up to be weighty enough for a parliamentary paper. So they went through the paper, at times redrafting it so that its content was more tentative. They were right. The policies were all the better for more reflection and consultation. The permanent secretaries could do this because they knew that they would have the support of their ministers if they told them that a white paper or bill was not worthy of the government. This is not an objection to government policy objectives, but to a lack of thoroughness with which they have been thought through, their expression and the need to demonstrate that they can be implemented.

of a process by which power was transferred to the prime minister from Cabinet so she might more easily pursue her 'conviction politics'. As one permanent secretary, Sir Frank Cooper, said in 1986, 'conviction politics is fine for slaughtering sacred cows, but no good for contriving new policies from the offal'.[44] While she remained prime minister, the size and importance of the vacuum created was disguised by her own tireless ability to reach down deep into departmental business and coordinate policy. (Official committees remained to coordinate policy for Europe and for various emergencies. These are also committees the Cabinet Office chairs on *ad hoc* matters crossing departmental boundaries, usually of a technical kind.) Whatever its justification, the destruction of the old coordinating machinery was another cause of increasing policy and legislative failure towards the end of the 1980s, and more especially under her successor.

Into the vacuum the Treasury stepped as the body left with the position and resources at ministerial and still more at official level, capable of performing a policy coordination role. As Nigel Lawson[45] said when chancellor of the exchequer:

> Less well known than the Treasury's interest in monetary policy perhaps, is the fact that the Chancellor has his finger in pretty well every pie in government. This follows partly from his responsibility for government spending and partly from tradition. As a result, he can exert a significant influence on policies which are announced by other ministers and which the public does not associate with the Treasury at all.

Wherever departmental civil servants were engaged in helping ministers formulate policy, so were Treasury civil servants. But as Lawson added:

> This influence is acquired at a price. For it inevitably ensures that both the Treasury as a department and the chancellor as an individual are regarded by most of the rest of the government as the enemy. A chancellor who is doing his job properly has few friends. That is one reason why it is of vital importance to the successful conduct of government that there is an extremely close and special relationship between the chancellor of the day and the prime minister.

The price was higher than Lawson imagined. Under the old inter-departmental committee arrangements the special position of the Treasury was recognized, but alleviated by the greater ability of other departments to press their views on each other. The demise of the old official cabinet committee system meant that issues, for example involving trade, competition or employment policy, were less likely to be concerted across government. Unsupported by similar arrangements enabling other departments to reflect their views authoritatively, the Treasury's prominence above the rest was unstable and bound sooner or later to lead to collision between them, as it did. It involved giving one member of the Cabinet the effective role and power of deputy prime minister without any debate of this development or indeed public recognition of it. Subsequently, under less able or vigorous chancellors, the Treasury became less active and successful in policy coordination, while the irritation remained. Thus, the downsizing of the Treasury – its own decision, matching the similar downsizing it was forcing on other departments – can also be seen as the last stage of a rebellion among other ministers to cut its influence, non-financial as much as financial, and as perhaps the culminating act in the process of transferring power from officials to ministers.[46]

It might be thought that politicians considering their 'political' and other short-term interests might welcome this development, but as well as the difficulties for financial control predicted in Chapter 10, a serious risk is that a consequence will be a further decline in policy coordination and in the efficiency and economy with which business is handled.

The remedy in the first instance is to reconsider the policy of downsizing the senior civil service, or even to bring back some who have left, at least until it is clear that there are enough skilled civil servants at that level to conduct all the old advisory as well as the new managerial and procurement tasks. Otherwise a government after an election in 1996 or 1997 might find itself less able to draw its policy proposals together coherently and to take effective action or to control public expenditure than its predecessors. The second remedy is that the ministerial and official committee systems be restored to a number, regularity and strength where all ministers and departments can express their legitimate concerns in each other's policy-making and other business. There is always a place for ad-hockery but there are severe drawbacks to making it the rule.[5]

To revive the Central Policy Review staff, created by Edward Heath in 1970 and terminated by Margaret Thatcher in 1983, would also assist policy coordination and development across departments but it could not be expected to be effective except as the back-up for a return to a more systematic cabinet committee process. Neither can it be a substitute for such a system in achieving better policy and legislation or in regaining a decent standard of policy coherence across Whitehall.

Changes to Parliament

While the future for ministers is not the same as the future for politicians, they are inextricably connected: the backbencher is father of the minister and both are shaped by the political environment in which they perform. Recently Parliament seems not to satisfy many within it. The conception of it as an escalator, which takes most of the majority through a closed section called ministerial office, towards external profitable advancement, on its own does not amount to a political education.[47] Neither does the narrowness of the careers most MPs have had in recent years before entering Parliament, particularly the high proportion who have started as policy advisers to ministers, research assistants to MPs or staff members in party headquarters.[48] It is perhaps impossible now to return to the situation where becoming an MP is something most do after another career, even though the shortening of many careers in modern times ought to be conducive to political parties concentrating more on candidates in their forties and fifties.

A further possibility would be to reshape the content of an MP's workload to make it more satisfying and useful while still, for the most part, fulltime. How MPs act is conditioned by the rules of the game of which they find themselves a part. A theme of this book is that desirable safeguards are not generally to be found in the laws that make up a constitution, but rather in conventions and working practices, as in traditional workings of the civil service in their interactions with ministers.

We approach the reform of Parliament with some hesitation, but change is needed to redress the balance between ministers and civil servants within the executive and between public interest and 'political' elements in policy- and decision-making.[49] If not unrecoverable, there should be a return to the tradition of debate on important issues. This would have an almost incalculable effect in making ministers ensure that they were able properly to defend their policies and their actions in relation to complaints, grievances and any other alleged misdemeanours. Among the more hidden virtues of such a return is that it would improve the quality of preparation for policy- and decision-making, would re-create a greater sense of teamwork and trust between ministers and civil servants, and help avoid public embarrassment. It should also help raise the discussion of public issues in the media above the soundbite and the merely sensational.

While reviving the great tradition of parliamentary debate would be exhilarating, what is needed first, from the standpoint of the issues in this book, seems plain.[50] It is to build on the 1979 reforms to strengthen the parliamentary committee system.[51] Our arguments support others who have reached a similar conclusion from a different direction.[52] A long history of backbencher attempts to extend and strengthen select committees before 1979 generally foundered on three objections. First, it was suggested that it would take debate from the floor of Parliament, where all members have an equal right to challenge the government. To avoid that accusation, committee activities should enhance the ability of all MPs to make such challenges on the floor of the House of Commons (or similarly in the Lords), not displace it. Second, the House of Commons conducts its business *adversarially*. Some committees – standing committees that consider bills – are adversarial because government and opposition face each other across a room. Others – select committees – are *inquisitorial*, neutral in style and sit in a semicircle. A committee – even the same committee – would conform to past and present usage if it were to be adversarial when it *scrutinized* policy documents and bills and inquisitorial when *reviewing* performance. (Most government activities other than policy-making, however, would gain by a switch from adversarial to inquisitorial attention.) Third, from the earliest times select committees were resisted if they threatened to encroach on the executive functions of government, particularly in the formulation of policy. As a result, they have been expected to *react* to what is put to them by the executive or from other sources, rather than *taking the initiative* on policy, law-making or decisions. In furtherance of this objective, select committees would gain from more structured discussions of white papers and bills, replacing the recent practice of committees producing their own reports on policy which normally have little influence because they are not part of any legislative or other required process. The transformation of US congressional committees into ones that took the initiative on legislation and on tax and expenditure decisions created the iron triangles referred to in Chapter 2. A similar development among UK parliamentary committees would not be desirable.

Scrutiny and performance review, as discussed in Chapter 10, could be done as in the past by a mixture of committees. However, they would be more effective if done by one committee for each department's business, so developing greater knowledge of the department and its related agencies and quangos. Since the mid-1980s the possibility has existed of the little-used mechanism of special standing committees which combine the select committee's power 'to send for persons and papers', that is take evidence, with a standing committee's function of scrutinizing legislation.[53] For it to combine scrutiny and review it would be a further development of what one former head of the prime minister's policy unit, has recommended:

> If the . . . types of committee were amalgamated into one type, established on the lines of the special standing committee, then immediately the scrutiny of legislation would take on a more deliberate and expert character; the use of the guillotine, except in cases of national emergency, would become more obviously scandalous; the committee chairmen and vice-chairmen would take on something of the authority enjoyed by chairmen of congressional committees in the US while not being weighed down by the old American seniority system which regarded longevity rather than merit. The committee would then conduct investigations as well as examine Bills and so be in a position to question the arguments supporting the government's proposal more carefully and authoritatively.
>
> But would not this slow down the whole business and deprive our legislative process of the speed and flexibility on which it prides itself? It would. That is the purpose. Government would have to consider its proposals more carefully before presenting them in the House; and it would have to content itself with a smaller legislative programme.
>
> That would be entirely to the good. Nobody who has contemplated, for example, even a fraction of the incoherent, disreputable, ineffective and constantly-reversed legislation on the financing and structuring of local government over the past thirty years would wish anything different. It is futile to expect modern governments with ambitious ministers to keep to some self-denying ordinance. It is only if Parliament systematically, deliberately and justifiably slows down the process of making laws that we can hope to improve the quality of that legislation.[54]

A development of this kind would also go some way to allaying the concern, much expressed recently, at the lack of accountability of quangos and appointments to them. Contrary to popular comment, there is much information on quangos and their activities in the public domain, but it is subject to little public or parliamentary scrutiny.

But there are dangers. The Westminster rules would stop such committees acquiring power on the American model to dictate tax and expenditure decisions, but their members could have enough influence on the content of legislation and on the review of departmental, quango and agency performance and contracts, to be worth the attention of vested interests. To reduce such possibilities both Houses of Parliament might rule that:

(i)   Select committee members should have no pecuniary interest which affects their impartiality.

(ii) Chairpersons change, perhaps according to the subject matter. The old custom might continue that the speaker's office provided an independent, neutral chairman during a bill, while the government party provides the chairman when government policies are being scrutinized, and the main opposition party provides the chairman when performance is being monitored and otherwise reviewed.

(iii) Chairpersons and members rotate after a few years so as not to build too exclusive a knowledge in a small number of MPs.

(iv) Chairpersons should be paid. Their job, as demanding as that of a junior minister, could command a similar salary. The 1976 committee which considered the procedures for select committees which were largely initiated in 1979, recommended a modest salary. Members' attendance might justify a payment additional to salary for each complete meeting.[55]

Such a development would mean that there should not be the same concentration of ambition on ministerial office since being the chair or member of an important committee would be stretching and rewarding. It would better prepare ministers for many of the tasks of office; it would increase the interest of MPs' careers after as well as before ministerial office and in opposition; and for the same reason, fewer would be subject to the temptations of preparing for a rewarding career after office.

To make membership of the committees stimulating, to enhance their effectiveness and provide an inducement for MPs to resist the strictures of their party managers fearful for party discipline, the committees need proper resourcing. The Public Accounts Committee is supported by the National Audit Office, which carries out reviews and enquiries on its behalf. Select committees require similar support in their *reviewing*, if not comparable in scale, which could be provided either directly, through the NAO, or bought in from other public- or private-sector suppliers. They also need a small permanent staff and a greater ability to buy in temporary advice to help them in their *scrutiny* functions.

There are a succession of stages at which the development of policy into legislation, and its subsequent monitoring would benefit from more rigorous scrutiny and review by parliamentary committee. We have suggested a resumption of the tradition in which two parliamentary papers should precede significant legislation. The first, a green paper, should state the problem which the government believes needs addressing, and indicate the government's preferred solutions in outline. At a hearing of the appropriate departmental select committee, ministers, but not officials, would be questioned on the green paper: the problems prompting ministers to consider legislation, the options they were considering and the process of consultation they would go through before picking a solution. Where there was interest enough, there should be a full-dress debate, in which committee members would expect to explain the nature of their support or reservations to other members. (Committee members might be given the right to be called in such debates that privy councillors have on all occasions.) Influenced by what it had learnt from the committee hearing or from that debate, the government should retire to undergo a considered consultation process (as described in Chapter 10), after which it would publish a white paper explaining and defending the solution it has come up with by comparison with others, backed by as much evidence and analysis as it can provide. The government should make available its own and other evidence, for example from academics, as well as other background facts and figures which had been material to its deliberations. Ministers could decide whether to publish that white paper on its own or whether to publish a bill simultaneously. In either case, it would help discussion and debate if any such white paper contained a full explanatory memorandum covering the entire contents of the proposed bill, worked up at least to the point where it covered a level of detail equivalent to that to be found in instructions it has sent to counsel for drafting purposes. In either case there should be enough time for public and press comment on both, before the committee scrutinized the white paper (and bill, if there is one). To that end, they would conduct a limited number of hearings at which ministers explained how and why they had reached their conclusions, and at which other parties might have an opportunity to state their opinions on the policy and the bill, but concentrating on the practical consequences of what is proposed. Such a scrutiny would be a useful preparation for the second reading debate at which committee members might be prominent in explaining the pros and cons of the bill to other members.

Afterwards the government could continue with the bill as introduced or amend it in the light of the points made. It would then go through the customary bill procedures of both Houses, except that the special standing committee might with advantage use its greater knowledge to act as standing committee on the issue in the Commons. Legislation would benefit from longer scrutiny and less guillotining, but such scrutiny should be easier if the bill is preceded by more detailed explanations of purpose and is itself complete when presented. It would be helpful if it became a rule that no government amendments were considered at the report stage except where it was agreed that they were better drafts of earlier amendments and raised no issues of substance not previously discussed. It might also help if the Treasury solicitor certifies when a bill is deposited that best endeavours have been used to make it consistent with existing domestic and EU legislation.

Major guidance, policy documents and plans, not intended to lead to legislation, could go through part of the same process. Policy documents on such matters as the environment, defence, energy, competition policy or transport should be debated and scrutinized in the relevant committee. Secondary legislation of any importance equally deserves a white paper or explanatory memorandum which should similarly be debated. It is a fine question how many should then come to the floor of either House. White papers preceding minor or secondary legislation and less important guidance could be discussed in the appropriate select committee only. It would follow from these proposals that ministerial statements, now become almost the main occasions in Parliament, would become again a way of dealing, not with policy, but with other matters capable of elucidation through a few questions and answers. Another reversion to the past, likely to ensure matters are appropriately discussed in Parliament, would be to return to the convention that new policies and major decisions are first announced to the House, rather than, with increasing frequency, at a press conference.[56]

Even if there were no revival of the great tradition of parliamentary debate and debates were finally to die, at least some effective checks and balances would have been established on elective dictatorship. Changes in policy, law and regulation would be more extensively and seriously considered. Parliament would have better and more complete material to work on. No other combination of forces would be as likely to improve legislation and executive performance.

Notes

1 J.P. Mackintosh, quoted in Marquand (1988), p. 197.
2 Hennessy (1990, 1995).
3 King (1975).
4 Jones (1955); Marr (1995), pp. 290–302.
5 Hennessy (1995), p. 23.
6 Crossman (1975), p. 22.
7 Colville (1985), pp. 190–1.
8 Crossman (1975), p. 30.
9 Sir Edward Bridges in Fry (1969), p. 59.
10 See Jennings (1946), pp. 135–6.
11 Colville (1985), p. 236.
12 Marquand (1988), pp. 181–2.
13 See Machiavelli in Hood and Jackson (1991), p. 51.
14 Chipperfield (1994).
15 See Sir Robin Butler in TCSC (1993).
16 Hobbes (1914), p. 137.
17 Wilson (1887); Mill (1910), p. 334.

18 Plowden (1994), pp. 145–8; Marr (1995), pp. 234–8.
19 Fulton (1968).
20 Heclo (1974); TCSC (1994), para. 102, Annex 1; see also Marr (1995), pp. 276–7.
21 See, for example, Cabinet Office (1991), p. 40; see also Richards (1989).
22 Bagehot (1928), pp. 157–9; see also Crossman (1975), p. 23.
23 See Hailsham (1978), p. 156.
24 Bagehot (1928), p. 178.
25 Hornblower (1992).
26 Oakeshott (1962), p. 128.
27 Hobbes (1914), p. 135.
28 See Light (1995), p. 13.
29 See Mill (1910), p. 334.
30 Quoted in Thomas (1978), pp. 44–5.
31 Plowden (1994), pp. 92–3.
32 Boston (1992); Wistrich (1992).
33 Cabinet Office (1995).
34 Chipperfield (1994).
35 Armstrong (1985). See the discussions in Hennessy (1990), pp. 344–6; Plowden (1994), pp. 111–15; Hennessy (1995).
36 Plowden (1994), pp. 102–9.
37 Hennessy (1990), p. 346.
38 Mount (1992), pp. 102–4.
39 Chipperfield (1994), p. 5.
40 Plowden (1994), p. 122.
41 As recommended by PAC (1994), para. 52.
42 Hennessy (1990), pp. 311–25; see also Ridley (1991), p. 29; Lawson (1992), pp. 125–6.
43 Lord Hunt in 1988, Hennessy (1990), p. 131.
44 Sir Frank Cooper in 1986, Hennessy (1990), p. 312.
45 Lawson (1992), p. 273.
46 Mount (1992), pp. 134–5.
47 Oakeshott (1962).
48 Riddell (1993).
49 Amery (1947); Laski (1951); Hailsham (1978); Wright (1994).
50 Drewry (1989).
51 Hennessy (1990), pp. 330–7.
52 For example Mount (1992), pp. 185–6; Wright (1994), pp. 47, 103, 116–18; Hutton (1995), pp. 29, 90; Marr (1995), pp. 155–9; see also Eric Caines, Vernon Bogdanor, Fred Ridley, Brian Thompson in TCSC (1992), para. 165; Sir Peter Kemp in TCSC (1992), para. 171.
53 Endorsed by the Second report from the Select Committee on Procedures (1985); see also Mount (1992), p. 186.
54 Mount (1992), pp. 186–7.
55 Drewry (1989), pp. 150–1.
56 Jones (1995) has an account of how this happened, mainly for the convenience of the media; see also Marr (1995), pp. 106–8.

12

Conclusion

Not since the seventeenth century has any one element in the constitution arrogated as much power to itself as ministers have recently. The swelling of elective dictatorship was at first a partnership between ministers and the civil service, in which both together enjoyed a joint supremacy but each moderated each other's power. Margaret Thatcher's sacking of the head of the civil service was remarkable in itself but also symbolized a new era in which the power civil servants had was at ministers' pleasure. At the same time, the effective power of the media has grown, increasing both public awareness of ministers and the risks they face, while detracting further from the stature of Parliament. But the monopoly of power within government which accrued to ministers, as always with monopoly, has led to loss of real power through ministerial overload so that many ministers have found less time for what was needed for effective government. Thus Britain, which during many years of relative economic decline had punched far above its weight in world affairs because of the effectiveness of its governing institutions, tended to lose this comparative advantage.

One manifestation of decline in the status and competence of British government is the increasing activity of judges in government. They review ministers' decisions with growing frequency and find against them more than in the past. Judges have also been called in, as Lord Nolan has, to review politicians' past, and recommend rules for their future behaviour: Nolan would seem to have become an apparently permanent body with a roving and imprecise mandate to sniff out wrong-doing. The voluminous report into alleged maladministration and misdemeanour by another judge, Sir Richard

Scott, was criticized by the press and the opposition as failing to make a case that justified sacking any minister or civil servant. Its more important significance was that it revealed in the greatest possible detail, a world in which accountability of junior ministers to senior ministers, of junior to senior civil servants and of civil servants to ministers had become complicated and varying, while definitive statements of the policies on which they were operating were elusive and ambiguous. Even if it had not been manifest that parliamentary questions had become a game with less to do with truth and much to do with the avoidance of political embarrassment, it revealed that often no sensible basis remained for deciding for what it was reasonable to hold ministers as responsible to Parliament, and therefore what was a sufficient reason for resignation.[1]

Without significant reforms – to processes as much as to structures – it is not, in our view, unrealistic to foresee further deterioration. In Chapters 1 and 2 we described how reactions to fiscal crisis might weaken the public interest ethos which has sustained the quality and integrity of political decision-making in Britain. Future politics could be much more overtly 'political' in the absence of both effective parliamentary scrutiny and the traditional restraining influence of the civil service. But changes to the civil service, while managerially desirable, have weakened its capacity to act in an advisory capacity and weakened the ethos which allowed it to restrain ministerial excess without giving it the skills or the authority to undertake the managerial roles now required. The parliamentary abuses which led to the establishment of Lord Nolan's Committee on Standards in Public Life and the scattered evidence for deteriorating standards within the civil service adduced by the Public Accounts Committee are evidence for changed attitudes and practices, and significant ones. But codes of practice and ethics, reluctantly introduced by the government and the civil service, are hardly sufficient to address the issues concerned. Nolan can only address the symptoms, not what is fundamentally wrong.

These issues are likely to be all the more serious given the proposals by two of the three major political partners in the UK for constitutional reform, such as the introduction of proportional representation, a regional tier of government and the reform of the House of Lords. In the course of writing this book we have become increasingly aware of the garden-weed syndrome: when you pull up one plant, you find its roots connected to every other plant and weed in the flowerbed. We believe reform of one part of the UK system should not be attempted without assessing the consequences for other parts. The conclusion of this book is that steps to redress some of the imbalance caused by the shift in power from civil servants to politicians and the managerial reforms of the last twenty years need to be taken at the same time as or in advance of wider constitutional reform.

We have not attempted to describe reform in comprehensive terms. That could involve matters such as the basis of the franchise, Britain's role in Europe, and the appropriate basis for remunerating MPs, but they are outside the scope of this book. The elements of change we have described, the most important of which are summarized below, are interrelated. Without these changes, there will be a further lowering of the esteem in which politicians are held, probably more low-level fraud and 'political' behaviour and, in consequence, the greater involvement in government of judges and the courts. While a planned development of administrative law is desirable, the regular involvement of the judiciary in political decisions and, effectively, policy-making is unlikely to lead to better government.

The changes in UK government practice, described earlier in Chapters 10 and 11, might have been expected to reduce demands on ministers. In practice, though, the changes have not had the expected impact. Ministers have taken over some of the functions traditionally, and in our view better, performed by civil servants in the management of their departments and in assessing policy choices. Because of other pressures, especially those from the media, they are more overloaded than ever. The combination of a number of these factors, together with a decline in the authority of Parliament, has resulted in the deterioration in policy-making and the quality of legislation.

Earlier in this book we have described desirable changes in the management of the state which would relieve this excessive pressure on ministers. What is required is genuine decentralization, especially to local authorities, contracting out where appropriate and a reassessment of where and how to delegate via agencies and other bodies within central government.

Contracting out and greater delegation to more independent executive bodies have had and will continue to have significant impact on the efficiency, costs and effectiveness of government. But the current arrangements are not satisfactory. There is a plethora of arm's-length bodies of different types with no clear rationale as to what is appropriate for what type of activity, and in some areas arm's-length arrangements have been introduced inappropriately, that is to say, for activities which will always be likely to attract a high degree of political and ministerial interest. What is required is for government to stand back and determine what kind of arrangements are appropriate for different types of activity, including, crucially, what could be decentralized to local authorities, and so rationalize what is currently a muddle.

When coupled with a redefinition of the respective roles of ministers and civil servants as far as both concern policy-making and management of the central government machine, rationalizing the existing structures would go a long way towards relieving ministerial overload and allow ministers to concentrate on their essential central tasks. The corollary would be that ministers would have more time to focus on those things, described in Chapter 10, for which they are most needed – leadership, policy-making and persuasion. There could even be a reduction in the number of ministers.

An additional requirement will be to examine fundamentally the training and personal development of civil servants. This should include the new range of skills civil servants will require in procurement, monitoring and contract management as well as the more traditional policy analysis and evaluation skills which have fallen into disuse. But more fundamentally, given wider changes in society, the changes to the lifetime career concept, the greater and desirable involvement of more outsiders, there is a need for a comprehensive programme of attitude and cultural reinforcement as well as training to reinvigorate civil service values and prepare civil servants more adequately for their roles in the new public management.

The final, interrelated element is reforms to allow Parliament greater scrutiny of the executive. The capacity to scrutinize, to take evidence and to debate in an informed way is important to redress the increased power of ministers resulting from the managerial changes we have described and to improve the quality of policy-making. It will be equally important where power has been devolved to regional assemblies as it should be for the review and scrutiny of the activities and decision-making of the institutions of the European Union.

The changes resulting from new public management have many good features, and a return to the past is certainly not desirable. Nor is it possible. Management capacity has significantly improved, and this should not be lost. Our proposals for reform would go a long way towards eliminating some of the less desirable consequences of the way in which the management of the state has been reformed in the UK. But improving the capacity of the executive to manage itself, important though it is, is insufficient without a parallel enhancement in Parliament's capacity to challenge and scrutinize the executive's actions. Future governments would be wise to consider both legislative and executive elements of change, and build on a combination of the best of the traditions of the past with lessons learnt from the more recent experience of reform in the UK and elsewhere in the world.

Note

1 See Foster (1996).

References

Aaron, H.J. (1992) 'Health care financing', in H.J. Aaron and C.L. Schultze, *Setting Domestic Priorities: What Can Government Do?* Washington: Brookings.

Abel-Smith, B. (1973) 'Social security and taxation', in B. Crick and W.A. Robson, *Taxation Policy*. Harmondsworth: Penguin.

Alt, J. and Chrystal, K. (1983) *Political Economics*. Brighton: Wheatsheaf.

Amery, L.S. (1947) *Thoughts on the Constitution*. Oxford: Oxford University Press.

Annan, N.G. (1995) *Changing Enemies*. London: HarperCollins.

Appleby, P.A. (1946) *Policy and Administration*. University, AL: Alabama University Press.

Armstrong, R. (1985) *The Duties and Responsibilities of Civil Servants in Relation to Ministers. Note by the Head of the Civil Service*. London: Cabinet Office.

Aucoin, P. (1990) 'Administrative reform in public management', *Governance*, 3: 115–37.

Audit Commission (1995) *Making Markets: a Review of the Audits of the Client Role for Contracted Services*. London: HMSO.

Bagehot, W. (1928) *The English Constitution*. London: Oxford University Press. First published in 1867.

Bahl, R. (1984) *Financing State and Local Government in the 1980s*. New York: Oxford University Press.

Baker, K. (1993) *The Turbulent Years*. London: Faber and Faber.

Balogh, T. (1959) 'The apotheosis of the dilettante: the establishment of the mandarin', in H.S. Thomas, *The Establishment: A Symposium*. London: Anthony Blond.

Balen, M. (1992) *Kenneth Clarke*. London: Fourth Estate.

Barker, E. (1946) *Aristotle's Politics*. Oxford: Oxford University Press.

Barker, L. (1992) *Competing for Quality*. Harlow: Longman.

Barzelay, M. (1992) *Breaking Through Bureaucracy*. Berkeley: University of California Press.

Baumol, W.J. (1967) 'Macroeconomics of unbalanced growth', *American Economic Review*, 57(3): 415–26.

Baumol, W.J., Panzar, J.C. and Willig, R.D. (1982) *Contestable Markets and the Theory of Industry Structure*. New York: Harcourt Brace Jovanovich.

Beadle, R. (1993) The prospects for the development of local pay determination in the NHS – evidence from the trusts. Paper to Coopers & Lybrand seminar.

Becker, G.S. (1957) *The Economics of Discrimination*. Chicago: University of Chicago Press.

Becker, G.S. (1983) 'A theory of competition among pressure groups for political influence', *Quarterly Journal of Economics*, 98: 371–400.

Bendick, M. (1989) 'Privatising the delivery of social welfare services: an idea to be taken seriously', in S.B. Kammerman and A.J. Kahn, *Privatisation and the Welfare State*. Princeton, NJ: Princeton University Press.

Benezal, M., Ham, C., Hunter, D., Judge, K. and Robinson, R. (1988) *Health Finance: Assessing the Options*. London: King's Fund Institute.

Benn, T. (1980) 'The case for a constitutional premiership', *Parliamentary Affairs*, 33(1): 7–22.

Bennett, J.T. and Di Lorenzo, T.J. (1989) *Unfair Competition: the Profits of Non-profits*. Lanham, MD: Hamilton Press.

Benton, S *et al.* (1989) *Responses to Robert Skidelsky*. London: Social Market Foundation.

Berg, S.V. and Tschirhart, J. (1988) *Natural Monopoly Regulation: Principles and Practice*. Cambridge: Cambridge University Press.

Beveridge, W. (1942) *Social Insurance and Allied Services*, Cmd. 6404. London: HMSO.

Bewley, T.F. (1981) 'A critique of Tiebout's theory of local public expenditure', *Econometrica*, 49(3): 713–40.

Blais, A. and Dion, S. (1991) *The Budget Maximising Bureaucrat: Appraisal and Evidence*. Pittsburgh, PA: University of Pittsburgh Press.

Bluntschli, J.K. (1898) *The Theory of the State*. Oxford: Clarendon Press. First published in 1852.

Bocherding, T.E., Pommerehne, W.W. and Schneider, F. (1982) 'Comparing the efficiency of private and public production: the evidence from 5 countries', *Journal of Economics*, Supplement 2: 127–56.

Boston, J. (1987) 'Transforming New Zealand's public sector', *Public Administration*, 65(4): 423–42.

Boston, J. (1992) 'Performance of Departmental Chief Executives', *Public Administration*, 70: 405–28.

Boston, J., Martin, J., Pallot, J. and Walsh, P. (1991) *Re-shaping the State: New Zealand's Bureaucratic Revolution*. Auckland: Oxford University Press.

Bramley, G., Le Grand, J. and Low, W. (1992) 'How far is the poll tax a community charge?', in D. King, *Local Government in Theory and Practice*. London: Routledge.

Branson, N. (1974) *Poplarism: 1919–1925*. London: Lawrence and Wishart.

Brennan, G. and Buchanan, J.M. (1980) *The Power to Tax*. Cambridge: Cambridge University Press.

Brennan, G. and Lomsky, L. (1994) *Democracy and Decisions: the Pure Theory of Electoral Preference*. New York: Cambridge University Press.

Bridges, E. (1966) *The Treasury*. London: Allen & Unwin.

Brittan, S. (1964) *The Treasury under the Tories*. Harmondsworth: Penguin.

Brosio, G. (1985) 'Fiscal autonomy of non-central government and the problem of public-spending growth', in F. Forte and A. Peacock, *Public Expenditure and Public Growth*. Oxford: Blackwell.

Bunch, B.S. (1991) 'The effect of constitutional debt limits on state governments' use of public authorities', *Public Choice*, 68: 57–69.

Burke, E. (1845) *Reflections on the Revolution in France*. In *Works*, Vol. 3. London: H.G. Bohn. Originally published in 1790.

Burke, J.P. (1994) 'The ethics of deregulation', in J.J. DiIulio, *Deregulating the Public Service*. Washington: Brookings.

Butler, D. and Stokes, D. (1969) *Political Change in Britain*. London: Macmillan.

Butler, D.G., Adonis, A. and Travers, T. (1994) *Failure in British government*. Oxford: Oxford University Press.

Butler, R. (1988) *Government and Good Management: Are they Compatible?* London: Institute for Personnel Management.

Butler, R. (1993) 'The evolution of the civil service', *Public Administration*, 71(3): 395–406.

Butler, R. (1994) 'Reinventing British government', *Public Administration*, 72(2): 263–70.

Cabinet Office (1989) *The Financing and Accountability of Next Steps Agencies*, Cm. 914. London: HMSO.

Cabinet Office (1991) *Citizen's Charter*, Cm. 1599. London: HMSO.

Cabinet Office (1994) *The Civil Service: Continuity and Change,* Cm. 2627. London: HMSO.

Cabinet Office (1995) *Market Testing Bulletin Special Report*. Glasgow: Business Information Publications.

Cameron, D.R. (1978) 'The expansion of the public sector: a comparative analysis', *American Political Science Review*, 72(4): 1243–61.

Cannan, E. (1927) *History of Local Rates in England*. London: P.S. King. First published in 1898.

Carter, N. (1991) 'Learning to measure performance: the use of indicators in organisations', *Public Administration*, 69(1): 85–100.

Chadwick, E. (1859) 'On different principles of legislation and administration', *Journal of the Royal Statistical Society*, 22: 381–420.

Checkland, S.G. and Checkland, E.O.A. (1974) *The Poor Law Report of 1834*. Harmondsworth: Pelican.

Chester, D.N. (1975) *Nationalisation of British industry: 1945–1951*. London: HMSO.

Chipperfield G (1994) *The Civil Servant's Duty*. Essex Papers in Politics and Government No 95.

Chubb, J.E. and Moe, T.E. (1990) *Politics, Markets and America's Schools*. Washington: Brookings.

Clark, C. (1945) 'Public finance and changes in the value of money', *Economic Journal*, 55(220): 371–89.

Clotfelter, C.T. (1992) *Who Benefits from the Non-profits Sector?* Chicago: University of Chicago Press.

Colville, J. (1985) *The Fringes of Power*, vol. 2. London: Sceptre.

Common, R., Flynn, N. and Meller, E. (1992) *Managing Public Services: Competition and Decentralisation*. Oxford: Butterworth-Heinemann.

Cornford, F.M. (1941) *Plato's Republic*. Oxford: Oxford University Press.

Cornford, J. (1993) 'The case for wholesale constitutional reform', in A. Barrett, C. Ellis and P. Hirst, *Debating the Constitution*. Cambridge: Polity Press.

Cournot, A.A. (1938)*Recherches sur les Principes Mathematiques de la Théorie de Richesses*. First published in 1838. Paris: Rivière.

Craig, P.P. (1988) *Administrative law*. London: Sweet and Maxwell.

Creedy, J. (1993) 'Social security expenditure', in N. Gemmell (ed.), *The Growth of the Public Sector*. Aldershot: Edward Elgar.

Crew, M.A. and Rowley, C.J. (1989) 'Towards a public choice theory of monopoly regulation', in M.A. Crew, *Deregulation and Diversifaction of Utilities*. Boston, MA: Kluwer.

Crosland, C.A.R. (1956) *The Future of Socialism*. London: Jonathan Cape.

Crosland, C.A.R. (1974) *Socialism Today*. London: Jonathan Cape.

Crossman, R.H.S. (1975) *Diaries of a Cabinet Minister*, vol. 1. London: Hamilton, Cape.

Daintith, T. (1989) 'The executive power today', in J. Jowell and D. Oliver, *The Changing Constitution*. Oxford: Clarendon Press.

Dalton, H. (1962) *High Tide and After*. London: Muller.

Davies, H. (1992) *Fighting Leviathan: Building Social Markets that Work*. London: Social Market Foundation.

Day, P. and Klein, R. (1987) *Accountabilities: Five Public Services*. London: Tavistock.

Demsetz, H. (1968) 'Why regulate utilities?', *Journal of Law and Economics*, 11: 55–65.

Department of Trade and Industry (1990) *Competition and Choice: Telecommunications Policy for the 1990s*. London: HMSO.

Dicey, A.V. (1885) *Law of the Constitution*. London: Macmillan.

DiIulio, J.J. (1994) 'What is deregulating the public service?', in J.J. DiIulio, *Deregulating the Public Service*. Washington: Brookings.

DiIulio, J.J., Garvey, G. and Kettl, D.E. (1993) *Improving Government Performance*. Washington: Brookings.

Dorrell, S. (1994) 'The future of the civil services', address to the Council of Civil Service Unions, 22 March.

Dowding, K., John, P. and Biggs, S. (1994) *Population Movements in Response to Taxes and Services*. London School of Economics Public Policy paper no 8.

Downs, A. (1957) *An Economic Theory of Democracy*. London: Harper & Row.

Downs, A. (1967) *Inside Bureaucracy*. Boston: Little, Brown.

Downs, G.W. and Larkey, P.D. (1986) *The Search for Government Efficiency: from Hubris to Helplessness*. Philadelphia: Temple University Press.

Drewry, G. (1989) 'Select committees and backbench power', in J. Jowell and D. Oliver, *The Changing Constitution*. Oxford: Clarendon Press.

Drewry, G. and Butcher, T. (1991) *The Civil Service Today*. Oxford: Blackwell.

Drivers Vehicle Licencing Agency (1993) Framework document. Swansea: DVLA.

Driving Standards Agency (1993) *Annual Report and Accounts: 1992–93*. London: HMSO.

Drucker, P. (1968) *The Age of Discontinuity*. New York: Harper & Row.

Duncan, A and Hobson, D. (1995) *Saturn's Children*. London: Sinclair-Stevenson.

Dunleavy, P. (1991) *Democracy, Bureaucracy and Public Choice*. New York: Harvester Wheatsheaf.

Dunleavy, P. and Hood, C. (1994) 'From old public administration to new public management', *Public Money and Management*, 14(3): 9–16.

Dunleavy, P. and Rhodes, R. (1990) 'Core executive studies in Britain', *Public Administration*, 68(1): 3–28.

Dunsire, A. and Hood, C. (1989) *Cutback Management in Public Bureaucracies*. Cambridge: Cambridge University Press.

Edgeworth, F.Y. (1932) *Mathematical Psychics*. First published in 1881. London: London School of Economics.

Ehrenhalt, A. (1991) *United States of America: Politicians, Power and the Pursuit of Office*. New York: Times Books.

Epstein, P. (1992) 'Get ready: the time for audit performance measurement is finally coming', *Public Administration Review*, 5: 201–5.

Fallon, M. (1993) *Brighter Schools*. London: Social Market Foundation.

Field, F. (1989) in S. Benton *et al.*, *Responses to Robert Skidelsky*. London: Social Market Foundation.

Finkelstein, D. (1994) *Conservatism in Opposition: Republicans in the US*, Memorandum No 9. London: Social Market Foundation.

Fiorina, M. (1977) *Congress, Keystone of the American Establishment*, 1st edn. New Haven, CT: Yale University Press.

Fiorina, M. (1989) *Congress, Keystone of the American Establishment*, 2nd edn. New Haven, CT: Yale University Press.

Flora, P. (1986) *Growth to Limits*. Berlin and New York: Walter de Guyter.

Flynn, N. (1988) 'A consumer oriented culture?', *Public Money and Management*, 8: 27–31.

Foreman, C.H. (1995) 'Reinventing politics? The NPR meets Congress', in D.F. Kettl and J.J. DiIulio, *Inside the Reinvention Machine*. Washington: Brookings.

Foster, C.D. (1971) *Politics, Finance and the Role of Economics*. London: Allen & Unwin.

Foster, C.D. (1992) *Privatisation, Public Ownership and the Regulation of Natural Monopoly*. Oxford: Blackwell.

Foster, C.D. (1994) 'Rival explanations of public ownership', *Public Administration*, 72(4): 489–504.

Foster, C.D. (forthcoming) 'Reflections on the true significance of Scott', *Public Administration*.

Foster, C.D. and Jackman, R.A. (1982) 'Accountability and control of local spending', *Public Money*, 2(2): 11–14.

Foster, C.D., Jackman, R.A. and Perlman M. (1980) *Local Government Finance in a Unitary State*. London: Allen & Unwin.

Fraser, R. (1991) *Making the Most of Next Steps: the Management of Ministers' Departments and their Executive Agencies*. London: HMSO.

Frey, B.S. (1985) 'Are there natural limits to the growth of government?', in F. Forte, and A. Peacock (1985) *Public Expenditure and Public Growth*. Oxford: Blackwell.

Fry, G.F. (1969) *Statesmen in Disguise*. London: Macmillan.

Fulton, J.S. (1968) *The Civil Service, Vol. 1. Report*, Cmnd. 3638. London: HMSO.

Galbraith, J.K. (1958) *The Affluent Society*. London: Hamish Hamilton.

Galbraith, J.K. (1992) *The Culture of Contentment*. London: Sinclair-Stevenson.

Garvey, G.J. (1995) 'False promises : the NPR in historical perspective', in D.F. Kettl and J.J. DiIulio, *Inside the Reinvention Machine*. Washington: Brookings.

Garvey, G.J. and DiIulio, J.J. (1994) 'Sources of public service overregulation', in J.J. DiIulio, *Deregulating the Public Service*. Washington: Brookings.

Gemmell, N. (ed.) (1993a) *The Growth of the Public Sector*. Aldershot: Edward Elgar.

Gemmell, N. (1993b) 'The public sector : definition and measurement issues', in N. Gemmell (ed.), *The Growth of the Public Sector*. Aldershot: Edward Elgar.

Gemmell, N. (1993c) 'Wagner's Law and Musgrave's Hypothesis', in N. Gemmell (ed.), *The Growth of the Public Sector*. Aldershot: Edward Elgar.

Godwin, R.K. (1993) 'Using market based incentives to empower the poor', in H. Ingram and S. Rathgeb Smith, *Public Policy and Democracy*. Washington: Brookings.

Graaff, J. de V. (1957) *Theoretical Welfare Economics*. Cambridge: Cambridge University Press.

Gray, J. (1989) *Limited Government: a Positive Agenda*. London: Institute for Economic Affairs.

Gray, J. (1994) *The Undoing of Conservativism*. London: Social Market Foundation.

Green, C. (1967) *Negative Taxes and the Poverty Problem*. Washington: Brookings.

Green, T.H. (1889) 'Liberal legislation and freedom of contract', in *Works,* vol. 3. London: Longmans, Green.

Greer, P. (1992) 'The Next Steps initiative: an examination of the agency framework documents', *Public Administration*, 70(1): 89–98.

Gregg, P. (1973) *Social and Economic History of Britain*. London: Harrap.

Griffith, J.A.G. (1966) *Central Departments and Local Authorities*. London: Allen & Unwin.

Hailsham, Lord (1978) *The Dilemma of Democracy*. London: Collins.

Haldane, R.B. (1918) *Report of the Machinery of Government Committee: Ministry of Reconstruction*, Cd. 9230. London: HMSO.

Harden, I. (1992) *The Contracting State*. Buckingham: Open University Press.

Harrison, W. (1876) *Elizabethan England*, ed. L. Wilkington. London: Walter Scott.

Hayek, F.A. von (1944) *The Road to Serfdom*. London: Routledge.

Hayek, F.A. von (1960) *The Constitution of Liberty*. Chicago: University of Chicago Press.

Heald, D. (1983) *Public Expenditure*. Oxford: Martin Robertson.

Heald, D. (1990) 'Charging in British government: evidence from the Public Expenditure Survey', *Financial Accountability and Management*, 6(4): 22–64.

Heclo, H. (1974) *Modern Social Policy in Britain and Sweden*. New Haven, CT: Yale University Press.

Hede, A. (1991) 'Trends in the higher civil service of Anglo American systems', *Governance*, 4(4): 489–510.

Heidenheimer, A., Heclo, H. and Adams, C. (1973) *Comparative Public Policy*. London: Gollancz.

Hennessy, P. (1990) *Whitehall*. London: Fontana.

Hennessy, P. (1995) *Hidden Wires*. London: Gollancz.

Heseltine, M. (1980) Ministers and Management in Whitehall. *Management in Government*, 35(2): 61–8.

Hibbs, D.A. (1987) *The Political Economy of Industrial Democracies*. Cambridge, MA: Harvard University Press.

Hirsch, F. (1977) *The Social Limits to Growth*. London: Routledge & Kegan Paul.

Hirschmann, A.O. (1970) *Exit, Voice and Loyalty*. Cambridge, MA: Harvard University Press.

Hobbes, T. (1914) *Leviathan*. London: Everyman. First published in 1651.

Hochman, H.M. and Rodgers, J.D. (1969) 'Pareto optimal redistribution', *American Economic Review*, 59(3): 542–57.

Hogwood, B.W. (1993) 'Restricting central government: the Next Steps initiative in Britain', in K.A. Eliassen and J.C. Kooiman, *Managing Public Organisations*. London: Sage, 207–23.

Hood, C. (1990) 'De-Sir-Humphrey-fying the Westminster model of governance', *Governance*, 3(2): 205–14.

Hood, C. (1991) 'A public management for all services?', *Public Administration*, 69(1): 3–19.

Hoddinott, J.C. (1994) 'Thriving on chaos', paper on policy reform presented at Coopers & Lybrand.

Hood, C. (1994) *Explaining Economic Policy Reversals*. Buckingham: Open University Press.

Hood, C. and Dunsire, A. (1981) *Bureaucratics*. Farnborough: Gower.

Hood, C. and Jackson, M. (1991) *Administrative Argument*. Aldershot: Dartmouth.

Hood, C. and Schuppert, G.F. (1988) *Delivering Public Services*. London: Sage.

Hood, C., Dunsire, A. and Thomson, L. (1988) 'Rolling back the state: Thatcherism, Fraserism and Bureaucracy', *Governance*, 1(3): 243–70.

Hornblower, E. (1992) 'Creation and development of democratic institutions in ancient Greece', in J. Dunn, *Democracy: the Unfinished Journey*. Oxford: Oxford University Press.

Hughes, M.A. (1994) 'Mass transit agencies', in G.J.Garvey and J.J. DiIulio, *Deregulating the Public Service*. Washington: Brookings.

Hutton, W. (1995) *The State We're In*. London: Jonathan Cape.

Ibbs, R. (1988) *Improving Management in Government: the Next Steps: Report to the Prime Minister*. London: HMSO.

Ingram, H. and Schneider, F. (1993) 'Constructing citizenship: the subtle message of policy design', in H. Ingram and S. Rathgeb Smith, *Public Policy and Democracy*. Washington: Brookings.

Institute for Public Policy Research (1991) *The Constitution of the United Kingdom*. London: IPPR.

James, E. (ed.) (1989) *Non-profit Sector in International Perspective*. New York: Oxford University Press.

Jenkins, R. (1991) *A Life at the Centre*. London: Macmillan.

Jenkins, S. (1995) *Accountable to None: the Tory Nationalisation of Britain*. London: Hamish Hamilton.

Jennings, W.I. (1946) *The British Constitution*. Cambridge: Cambridge University Press.

Jennings, W.I. (1959) *The Law and the Constitutions*. First published in 1933. London: University of London Press.

Johnson, N. (1977) *In Search of the Constitution*, 1st edn. Oxford: Pergamon.

Johnson, N. (1980) *In Search of the Constitution*, 2nd edn. Oxford: Pergamon.

Jones, G.W. (1989) 'A revolution in Whitehall? Changes in British central government since 1979', *West European Politics*, 12(3): 238–61.

Jones, G.W. (1991) *Local Government and Social Market*. London: Social Market Foundation.

Jones, G.W. and Burnham, J. (1995) 'The environment agencies', in G. Giddings, *Parliamentary Accountability*. London: Methuen.

Jones, N. (1995) *Soundbites and Spin Doctors*. London: Cassell.

Jorgensen, T.B. (1993) 'Public resource allocation', in K.A. Eliassen and J.C. Kooiman, *Managing Public Organisations*. London: Sage.

Jowell, J. and Oliver, D. (1988) *New Directions in Judicial Review*. London: Stevens.

Jowell, J. and Oliver, D. (1989) *The Changing Constitution*. Oxford: Clarendon Press.

Kanter, R.M. (1983) *The Change Masters*. New York: Simon and Schuster.

Kanter, R.M. and Summers, D.V. (1994) 'Doing well while doing good: dilemmas of performance in non-profit organisations', in D. McKevitt and L. Lawton, *Public Sector Management*. London: Sage.

Kaufman, G. (1994) 'UK: the blank checks of government', *Guardian,* 30 December.

Kaufman, H. (1976) *Are Government Organisations Immortal?* Washington: Brookings.

Kavanagh, D. (1990) *British Politics: Continuities and Change*. Oxford University Press.

Keating, M. and Holmes, M. (1990) 'Australia's budgetary and financial management reforms', *Governance*, 3(2): 168–85.

Kelman, S. (1994) 'Deregulating federal procurement', in J.J. DiIulio, *Deregulating the Public Service*. Washington: Brookings.

Keman, H. (1993) 'Proliferation of the Welfare State', in K.A. Eliassen and J.C. Kooiman, *Managing Public Organisations*. London: Sage, 13–33.

Kemp, P. (1993) *Beyond Next Steps: a Civil Service for the 21st Century.* London: Social Market Foundation.

Kettl, D.F. (1993) *Sharing Power.* Washington: Brookings.

Kettl, D.F. (1994) *Reinventing Government: Appraising the National Performance Review.* Washington: Brookings.

Kettl, D.F. (1995) 'Building lasting reform: enduring questions, missing answers', in D.F. Kettl and J.J. DiIulio, *Inside the Reinvention Machine.* Washington: Brookings.

Kettl, D.F. and DiIulio, J.J. (1995) *Inside the Reinvention Machine.* Washington: Brookings.

King, A. (1975) 'Overload: problems of governing in the 1970s', *Political Studies*, 22(2–3): 284–96.

King, D. (1984) *Fiscal Tiers: the Economics of Multi-level Government.* London: Allen & Unwin.

Kooiman, J.C. and van Vliet, M. (1993) 'Governance and public management', in K.A. Eliassen and J.C. Kooiman, *Managing Public Organisations.* London: Sage.

Krugman, P. (1994) *The Age of Diminished Expectations.* Cambridge, MA: MIT Press.

Landy, M. (1993) 'Public policy and citizenship', in H. Ingram and S. Rathgeb Smith, *Public Policy and Democracy.* Washington: Brookings.

Lane, J.E. (1993) 'Economic organisation theory and public management', in K.A. Eliassen and J.C. Kooiman, *Managing Public Organisations.* London: Sage, 73–84.

Laski, H. (1951) *Reflections on the Constitution.* Manchester: Manchester University Press.

Lawson, N. (1992) *The View from No. 11.* London: Bantam Press.

Le Grand, J. and Bartlett, W. (1993) *Quasi-markets and social policy.* Basingstoke: Macmillan.

Leach, S. (1990) 'Accountability and the post-abolition metropolitan grant system', *Local Government Studies*, 16(3): 13–31.

Learmont, J. (1995) *Review of the prison service in England and Wales and the escape from Parkhurst Prison on 3.1.95*, Cm. 3020. London: HMSO.

Leibenstein, H. (1966) 'Allocative efficiency vs X efficiency', *American Economic Review*, 56: 392–415.

Lewis, N. (1989) 'Regulating non-government bodies', in J. Jowell and D. Oliver, *The Changing Constitution.* Oxford: Clarendon Press.

Lewis, N. (1993) *How to Reinvent British Government.* London: European Policy Forum.

Liberal Democrat Party (1990) *We the People.* London: Liberal Democrat Party.

Light, P.C. (1993) *Monitoring Government: Inspectors General and the Search for Accountability.* Washington: Brookings.

Light, P.C. (1995) *Thickening Government.* Washington: Brookings.

Lim, D. (1993) 'Recent trends in the size and growth of government in developing countries', in N. Gemmell (ed.), *The Growth of the Public Sector.* Aldershot: Edward Elgar.

Lindahl, E. (1967) 'Just taxation – a positive solution', in R. Musgrave and A. Peacock, *Classics in Public Finance.* New York: St Martin's Press. First published 1919.

Loughlin, M., Gelfand, M.D. and Young, K. (1985) *Half a Century of Municipal Decline.* London: Allen & Unwin.

Lowi, T. (1964) 'American business, public policy, case studies and political theory', *World Politics*, 18(4): 677–715.

Lubenow, W.C. (1971) *Politics of Government Growth: Early Victorian Attitudes Towards State Intervention.* Newton Abbott: David and Charles.

Machiavelli, N. (1961) *The Prince*, translated by G. Bull. Harmondsworth: Penguin.
Mackintosh, J.P. (1977) *Government and Politics of Britain*. London: Hutchinson.
Maddison, A. (1991) *Dynamic Forces in Capitalist Development*. Oxford University Press.
Major, J. (1989) *Public Service Management, the Revolution in Progress*. London: Audit Commission.
Major, J. (1994) *The Role and Limits of the State*. London: European Policy Forum.
March, J.G. and Olsen, J.P. (1983) 'Organising political life: What administrative reorganisation tells us about government', *American Political Science Review*, 77(1): 281–96.
Marquand, D. (1988) *The Unprincipled Society*. London: Jonathan Cape.
Marr, A. (1995) *Ruling Britannia*. London: Michael Joseph.
Marshall, A. (1926) *Official Papers*. London: Macmillan.
Mayston, D. (1985) 'Non-profit performance indicators in the public sector', *Financial Accountability and Management*, 1(1).
McLean, I. and Foster, C.D. (1992) 'The political economy of regulation: interests, ideology, voters and the UK Regulation of Railway Act, 1844', *Public Administration*, 70(3): 313–32.
Meltzer, A.H. and Richards, S.F. (1978) 'Why government grows (and grows) in a democracy', *Public Interest*, 52(2): 111–18.
Meltzer, A.H. and Richards, S.F. (1981) 'A rational theory of the size of government', *Journal of Political Economy*, 89(5): 914–27.
Metcalfe, L. and Richards, S. (1987) *Improving Public Management*. London: Sage.
Metcalfe, L. and Richards, S. (1993) 'Evolving public management cultures', in K.A. Eliassen and J.C. Kooiman, *Managing Public Organisations*. London: Sage.
Middlemass, K. (1979) *Politics in an Industrial Society*. London: André Deutsch.
Mill, J.S. (1852) *Principles of Political Economy*. London: J.W. Parker and Son. First published in 1848.
Mill, J.S. (1910) *Utilitarianism, Liberty and Representative Government*. London: Dent. (*Representative Government* was first published in 1861.)
Mills, S. (1986) *The New Machine Men*. Harmondsworth: Penguin.
Milward, H.B. and Provan, K.G. (1993) 'The hollow state: private provision of public services', in H. Ingram and S. Rathgeb Smith, *Public Policy and Democracy*. Washington: Brookings.
Moe, R.C. (1994) 'The re-inventing government exercise. Misinterpreting the problem, misjudging the consequences', *Public Administration Review*, 54(2): 111–19.
Mont, A. de (1993) *Community Contracting*, Memorandum no. 8. London: Social Market Federation.
Mount, F. (1992) *The British Constitution Now*. London: Mandarin.
Mueller, D.C. (1989) *Public choice*, vol. II. Cambridge: Cambridge University Press.
Mueller, D.C. and Murrell, P. (1985) 'Interest groups and the political economy of government size', in F. Forte and A. Peacock, *Public Expenditure and Public Growth*. Oxford: Blackwell.
Mueller, K.J. (1988) 'Federal programmes to expire', *Public Administration Review*, 48(3): 719–25.
Mullard, M. (1993) *The Politics of Public Expenditure*. London: Routledge.
Murnane, R.J. and Levy, F. (1992) 'Education and training', in H.J. Aaron and C.L. Schultze, *Setting Domestic Priorities: What Can Government Do?* Washington: Brookings.
Murray, C. (1990) *The Emerging British Underclass*. London: Institute for Economic Affairs.

Murray, C. (1994) *Underclass: the Crisis Deepens*. London: Institute for Economic Affairs.

Musgrave, R.A. (1959) *The Theory of Public Finance*. New York: McGraw-Hill.

New Zealand Treasury (1987) *Government Management: brief to the incoming government*. Wellington: Government Printer.

Nicholson, M. (1967) *The System*. London: Hodder & Stoughton.

Niskanen, W.A. (1971) *Bureacracy and Representative Government*. Chicago: Aldine-Atherton.

Nolan (1995) *Standards in Public Life: Report*, vol. 1. London: HMSO.

Norton, P. (1982) *The Constitution in Flux*. Oxford: Blackwell.

Nozick, R. (1974) *Anarchy, State and Utopia*. Oxford: Blackwell.

O'Connor (1973) *The Fiscal Crisis of the State*. New York: St Martin's Press.

Oakeshott, M. (1962) *Rationalism in Politics and Other Essays*. London: Methuen.

Oakland, W.H. (1983) 'Income Redistribution in a Federal System', in G.P. Zodrow, *Local Provision of Public Services*. New York: Academic Press.

Oates, W.E. (1972) *Fiscal Federalism*. New York: Harcourt Brace.

OECD (1992) *Historical Statistics 1960–1990*. Paris: OECD.

OECD (1994) *OECD Economic Outlook*, December. Paris: OECD.

Olson, M. (1965) *The Logic of Collective Action*. Cambridge, MA: Harvard University Press.

Olson, M. (1982) *The Rise and Decline of Nations*. New Haven, CT: Yale University Press.

Osborne, D. and Gaebler, T. (1992) *Reinventing Government*. Reading, MA: Addison-Wesley.

Ostrom, V., Tiebout, C.M. and Warren, R. (1961) 'The organisation of government in metropolitan areas', *American Political Science Review*, 55(4): 831–42.

Painter, J. (1991) 'Compulsory competitive tendering in local government', *Public Administration*, 69(2): 191–210.

Paldam, M. (1979) 'Is there an electoral cycle? A comparative study of national accounts', *Scandinavian Journal of Economics*, 81(2): 323–43.

Paldam, M. (1981) 'An essay on the rationality of economic policy: the test case of the electional cycle', *Public Choice*, 37(2): 287–305.

Patten, J. (1995) *Things to Come*. London: Sinclair-Stevenson.

Payne, J.L. (1991) 'Elections and government spending', *Public Choice*, 70: 71–82.

Peacock, A. (1979) 'Public expenditure in post-industrial society', in B. Gustaffson, *Post-industrial Society*. London: Croom Helm.

Peacock, A. and Wiseman, J. (1961) *The Growth of Public Expenditure in the United Kingdom*. London: Oxford University Press.

Peltzmann, S. (1976) 'Towards a more general theory of regulation', *Journal of Law and Economics*, 19(2): 211–40.

Perkin, H. (1989) *The Rise of Professional Society: England since 1880*. London: Routledge & Kegan Paul.

Peters, G. (1993) 'Managing the hollow state', in K.A. Eliassen and J.C. Kooiman, *Managing Public Organisations*. London: Sage, 46–57.

Peters, T. and Austin, N. (1985) *A Passion for Excellence*. London: Fontana Collins.

Peters, T. and Waterman, R.H. (1982) *In Search of Excellence*. London: Harper & Row.

Pliatsky, L. (1980) *Report on Non-departmental Public Bodies*, Cmnd. 7797. London: HMSO.

Pliatsky, L. (1992) 'Quangos and agencies', *Public Administration in London*, 70(6): 555–64.

Plowden, E. (1961) *Control of Public Expenditure HM Treasury*, Cmnd. 1432. London: HMSO.

Plowden, W. (1994) *Ministers and Mandarins*. London: Institute of Public Policy Research.

Pollitt, C. (1990) *Managerialism and the Public Services: the Anglo American Experience*. Oxford: Blackwell.

Pommerehne, W.W. and Schneider, F. (1982) 'Unbalanced growth between public and private sectors: an empirical estimation', in R.H. Haverman (ed.), *Public Finance and Public Employment*. Detroit, MI: Wayne State University Press.

Posner, R.A. (1971) 'Taxation of regulation', *Bell Journal of Economics*, 2(1): 23–50.

Posner, R.A. (1975) 'The social costs of monopoly and regulation', *Journal of Political Economy*, 83(4): 807–27.

Potter, J. (1988) 'Consumerism and the public sector', *Public Administration*, 66(2): 149–63.

Price Waterhouse (1994) *Executive Agencies: Facts and Trends,* Edition 8.

Public Accounts Committee (1994) *17th Report*, session 1993–4. London: HMSO.

Pusey, M. (1991) *Economic Rationalism in Canberra*. Cambridge: Cambridge University Press.

Radcliffe, C. (1952) *The Problem of Power: the Reith Lectures*. London: BBC.

Ranson, S. and Stewart, J. (1994) *Management for the Public Domain*. Basingstoke: Macmillan.

Rasmussen, E. and Zapa, M. (1991) 'Extending the economic theory of regulation to the form of policy', *Public Choice*, 72(2–3): 167–91.

Rathgeb Smith, S. and Ingram H. (1993) 'Public policy and democracy', in H. Ingram and S. Rathgeb Smith, *Public Policy and Democracy*. Washington: Brookings.

Redcliffe-Maud (1969) *Report of the Royal Commission on Local Government in England*, Cmnd. 4040. London: HMSO.

Redlich, J. and Hirst, F.E. (1970) *History of Local Government in England*. London: Macmillan. First published in 1903.

Reeves, A.E. (1992) 'Enhancing local self-government', *Public Administration Review*, 52(4): 401–5.

Reid, G. (1962) *Politics of Financial Control*. London: Hutchinson.

Rhodes, R.A.W. (1994a) 'Reinventing excellence or how best sellers thwart the search for lessons to transform the public sector', *Public Administration*, 72(2): 287–9.

Rhodes, R.A.W. (1994b) 'The hollowing out of the state: the changing nature of public service in Britain', *Political Quarterly*, April–June, 65(2): 138–51.

Richards, S. (1989) 'Managing people in the civil service', *Public Money and Management*, 9(3): 29–33.

Richardson, J.J. (1993) 'Public utilities management', in K.A. Eliassen and J.C. Kooiman, *Managing Public Organisations*. London: Sage.

Riddell, P. (1993) *Honest Opportunism*. London: Hamish Hamilton.

Ridley, N. (1991) *My Style of Government*. London: Hutchinson.

Rivlin, A.M. (1992) *Reviving the American Dream*. Washington: Brookings.

Robbins, L. (1932) *The Nature and Significance of Economic Science*. London: Macmillan.

Robson, W.A. (1948) *The Development of Local Finance*. London: Allen & Unwin.

Rose, R. (1989a) 'Inheritance before choice in public policy'. *Studies in Public Policy No. 180*, University of Strathclyde, Glasgow.

Rose, R. (1989b) 'Charges as contested signals', *Journal of Public Policy*, 9(3) (July to September): 261–88.

Rose, R. (1990) 'Charging for public services', *Public Administration*, 68(3): 297–314.

Rose, R. and Peters, G. (1978) *Can Government go Bankrupt?* New York: Basic Books.

Rowley, C.K. and Tollison, R.D. (1994) 'Peacock and Wiseman on the growth of public expenditure', *Public Choice*, 78: 125–8.

Sander, D., Ward, H. and Marsh, D. (1987) 'Government popularity and the Falklands War: a reassessment', *British Journal of Political Science*, 17(3): 281–313.

Saunders, P. (1993) 'Recent trends in the size and growth of government in OECD countries', in N. Gemmell (ed.), *The Growth of the Public Sector*. Aldershot: Edward Elgar.

Savas, E.S. (1987) *Privatisation: the Key to Better Government*. Chatham, NY: Chatham House.

Scott, G. and Gorringe, P. (1989) 'Reform of the core public sector. The New Zealand experience', *Australian Journal of Public Administration*, 48(1): 81–91.

Scott, G., Bushnell, P. and Sallee, N. (1990) 'Reform of the core public sector: New Zealand experience', *Governance*, 3(2): 138–67.

Sedgemore, B. (1978) *The Secret Constitution*. London: Hodder & Stoughton.

Seldon, A. (1977) *Charge*. London: Temple Smith.

Select Committee on Procedures (1985) *Second report*, session 1984–5. London: HMSO.

Self, P. (1985) *The Political Theory of Modern Government*. Sydney: Allen & Unwin.

Sharkey, W. (1982) *The Theory of Natural Monopoly*. Cambridge University Press.

Sidgwick, H. (1891) *The Elements of Politics*. London: Macmillan.

Skidelsky, R. (1989) *The Social Market Economy*. London: Social Market Foundation.

Smith, S.R. and Lipsky, M. (1993) *Non Profits for Hire: the welfare state in the age of continuity*. Cambridge, MA: Harvard University Press.

Sorensen, R.J. (1993) 'The efficiency of public service provision', in K.A. Eliassen and J.C. Kooiman, *Managing Public Organisations*. London: Sage.

Stewart, J. and Walsh, K. (1992) 'Change in the management of public services', *Public Administration*, 70(4): 499–518.

Stigler, G.J. (1971) 'The theory of economic regulation', *Bell Journal of Economics and Management Science*, 2(1): 137–46.

Stiglitz, J.E. (1983) 'The theory of local public goods twenty five years after Tiebout: a perspective', in G.P. Zodrow, *Local Provision of Public Services*. New York: Academic Press.

Stiglitz, J.E. (1988) *Economics of the Public Sector*. New York: Norton.

Stiglitz, J.E. (1994) *Whither Socialism?* Cambridge MA: MIT Press.

Stockman, D.A. (1986) *The Triumph of Politics*. New York: Avon.

Sullivan, H.J. (1987) 'Privatisation of public service: a growing threat of constitutional rights', *Public Administration Review,* 47: 461–7.

Sundquist, J.L. (1992) *Constitutional Reforms and Effective Government*. Washington: Brookings.

Szymanski, S. and Wilkin, S. (1992) *Cheap Rubbish: Competitive Tendering and Contracting Out in Refuse Collection 1981–88*, Working Paper 137. London: London Business School.

Thatcher, M. (1988) *Statement on Civil Service Management*, 18 February 1988, Column 114. London: Hansard.

Thomas, N. (1989) in H.D. Clarke, M.C. Stewart and G. Zuk, *Economic Decline and Political Change*. Pittsburgh: University of Pittsburgh Press.

Thomas, R. (1978) *The British Philosophy of Administration*. London: Longman.

Thoni, E. (1992) 'Tax and expenditure decentralisation', in D. King, *Local Government in Theory and Practice*. London: Routledge.

Tiebout, C.M. (1956) 'A pure theory of local expenditures', *Journal of Political Economy*, 64(5): 416–24.

Tocqueville, A. de (1946) *Democracy in America*. Oxford University Press.

Treasury (1994a) *Fundamental Review of Running Costs*. London: Her Majesty's Treasury.

Treasury (1994b) *Improving the Treasury* (undated but 15 December). London: Her Majesty's Treasury.

Treasury (1995) *Better accounting for the taxpayers' money. The government's proposals*, CM2929. London: HMSO.

Treasury and Civil Service Committee (TCSC) (1988) *Public Expenditure and Estimates. Seventh Report*, session 1987–8. London: HMSO.

Treasury and Civil Service Committee (TCSC) (1991) *The Next Steps Initiative*, HC496. *Seventh Report*, session 1990–91. London: HMSO.

Treasury and Civil Service Committee (TCSC) (1993) *The role of the civil service: interim report*, HC390. *Sixth Report*, session 1992–93. London: HMSO.

Treasury and Civil Service Committee (TCSC) (1994) *The role of the civil service. Fifth Report*, session 1992–93. London: HMSO.

Treasury Solicitors Department (1994) *Judge Over Your Shoulder: Judicial Review Balancing the Scales*. London: Cabinet Office.

Trosa, S. (1994) *Next Steps, Moving On*. London: Office of Public Services and Science.

Tsarchys, D. (1975) 'Rational decremental budgeting: elements of an expenditure policy for the 1980s', *Policy Sciences*, 4: 49–58.

Tufte, E. (1975) 'Determinants of the outcome of mid term elections', *American Political Science Review*, 69(3): 812–26.

Tufte, E. (1978) *Political Control of the Economy*. Princeton, NJ: Princeton University Press.

Tullock, G. (1959) 'Some problems of majority voting', *Journal of Political Economy*, 67(6): 571–9.

Tullock, G. (1965) *The Politics of Bureacuracy*. Washington: Public Affairs Press.

Tullock, G. (1970) 'A simple algebraic logrolling model', *American Economic Review*, 60(3): 419–28.

Tullock, G. (1976) *The Vote Motive*. London: Institute of Economic Affairs.

Turpin, C. (1989) 'Ministerial responsibility: myth or reality?', in J. Jowell and D. Oliver, *The Changing Constitution*. Oxford: Clarendon Press.

Wagner, R.E. (1989) *To Promote the General Welfare: Market Process Versus Political Transfers*. Berkely, CA: Pacific Research Institute for Public Policy.

Waldegrave, W. (1994) *Recruiting to the Little Platoons*, Memorandum 5. London: Social Market Foundation.

Walker, J.L. (1983) 'The origins and maintenance of interest groups in America', *Americal Political Science Review*, 77(2): 390–406.

Walsh, K. (1991) *Competitive Tendering for Local Authority Services*. London: HMSO.

Webb, S. and Webb, B. (1922) *English Local Government: Statutory Authorities for Special Purposes*. London: Longmans, Green.

Webb, S. and Webb, B. (1963) *Development of English Local Government*. Oxford: Oxford University Press.

Weiss, J.A. (1993) 'Policy design for democracy: a look at public information campaigns', in H. Ingram and S. Rathgeb Smith, *Public Policy and Democracy*. Washington: Brookings.

Widdicombe, D. (1986) *The Conduct of Local Authority Business*, Cmnd. 9797. London: HMSO.

Wildavsky, A. (1964) *The Politics of the Budgetary Process.* Boston: Little, Brown.
Wildavsky, A. (1975) *Budgeting: a Comparative Theory of Budgetary Processes.* Boston: Little Brown.
Wildavsky, A. (1993) 'Budget games are ready for reform', in K.A. Eliassen and J.C. Kooiman, *Managing Public Organisations.* London: Sage, 262–8.
Willetts, D. (1993) *The Age of Entitlement.* London: Social Market Foundation.
Willetts, D. (1994) *Civic Conservatism.* London: Social Market Foundation.
Williamson, O.E. (1975) *Markets and Hierarchies.* New York: Free Press.
Williamson, O.E. (1990) 'The firm as a nexus of treaties', in M. Aoki, B. Gustaffson and O.E. Williamson, *The Firm as a Nexus of Treaties.* London: Sage.
Willman, J. (1994) *Labour and the Public Services.* London: Social Market Foundation.
Wilson, W. (1887) 'The study of administration', *Political Science Quarterly*, 2(2): 198–222. Republished in P. Woll, *Public Administration and Policy.* New York: Harper & Row (1966).
Wistrich, E. (1992) 'Restructuring government New Zealand style', *Public Administration*, 70(1): 119–35.
Wright, T. (1994) *Citizens and Subjects.* London: Routledge.
Yeatman, A. (1987) 'Public management and the Australian state in the 1980s', *Australian Journal of Public Administration*, 46(4): 339–53.
Young, G.M. (1950) *Last Essays.* London: Rupert Hart Davis.
Zifcak, S. (1994) *New Managerialism: Administrative Reform in Whitehall and Canberra.* Buckingham: Open University Press.
Zimmerman, J. (1992) *Contemporary American Federalism: the Growth of National Power.* Leicester: Leicester University Press.

Index